AF588422

The Heaviest Ideas in the Universe: A Philosophy of Heavy Metal

The Heaviest Ideas in the Universe: A Philosophy of Heavy Metal

Edited by

J. Aaron Simmons

and

Benjamin W. McCraw

WILEY

Copyright © 2026 by John Wiley & Sons, Inc. All rights reserved, including rights for text and data mining and training of artificial intelligence technologies or similar technologies.

Published by John Wiley & Sons, Inc., Hoboken, New Jersey.

No part of this publication may be reproduced, stored in a retrieval system, or transmitted in any form or by any means, electronic, mechanical, photocopying, recording, scanning, or otherwise, except as permitted under Section 107 or 108 of the 1976 United States Copyright Act, without either the prior written permission of the Publisher, or authorization through payment of the appropriate per-copy fee to the Copyright Clearance Center, Inc., 222 Rosewood Drive, Danvers, MA 01923, (978) 750-8400, fax (978) 750-4470, or on the web at www.copyright.com. Requests to the Publisher for permission should be addressed to the Permissions Department, John Wiley & Sons, Inc., 111 River Street, Hoboken, NJ 07030, (201) 748-6011, fax (201) 748-6008, or online at http://www.wiley.com/go/permission.

The manufacturer's authorized representative according to the EU General Product Safety Regulation is Wiley-VCH GmbH, Boschstr. 12, 69469 Weinheim, Germany, e-mail: Product_Safety@wiley.com.

Trademarks: Wiley and the Wiley logo are trademarks or registered trademarks of John Wiley & Sons, Inc. and/or its affiliates in the United States and other countries and may not be used without written permission. All other trademarks are the property of their respective owners. John Wiley & Sons, Inc. is not associated with any product or vendor mentioned in this book.

Limit of Liability/Disclaimer of Warranty: While the publisher and the authors have used their best efforts in preparing this work, including a review of the content of the work, neither the publisher nor the authors make any representations or warranties with respect to the accuracy or completeness of the contents of this work and specifically disclaim all warranties, including without limitation any implied warranties of merchantability or fitness for a particular purpose. Certain AI systems have been used in the creation of this work. No warranty may be created or extended by sales representatives, written sales materials or promotional statements for this work. The fact that an organization, website, or product is referred to in this work as a citation and/or potential source of further information does not mean that the publisher and authors endorse the information or services the organization, website, or product may provide or recommendations it may make. This work is sold with the understanding that the publisher is not engaged in rendering professional services. The advice and strategies contained herein may not be suitable for your situation. You should consult with a specialist where appropriate. Further, readers should be aware that websites listed in this work may have changed or disappeared between when this work was written and when it is read. Neither the publisher nor authors shall be liable for any loss of profit or any other commercial damages, including but not limited to special, incidental, consequential, or other damages.

For general information on our other products and services or for technical support, please contact our Customer Care Department within the United States at (800) 762-2974, outside the United States at (317) 572-3993 or fax (317) 572-4002.

Wiley also publishes its books in a variety of electronic formats. Some content that appears in print may not be available in electronic formats. For more information about Wiley products, visit our website at www.wiley.com.

Library of Congress Cataloging-in-Publication Data Applied for:

Paperback ISBN: 978-1-394-33074-4
ePDF: 978-1-394-33076-8

ePub: 978-1-394-33075-1

Cover Design: Wiley
Cover Images: local_doctor/stock.adobe.com, Mikhail/stock.adobe.com, Vastram/stock.adobe.com

Set in 11/13pt STIXTwoText by Straive, Pondicherry, India

Printed and bound by CPI Group (UK) Ltd, Croydon, CR0 4YY

C9781394330744_230626

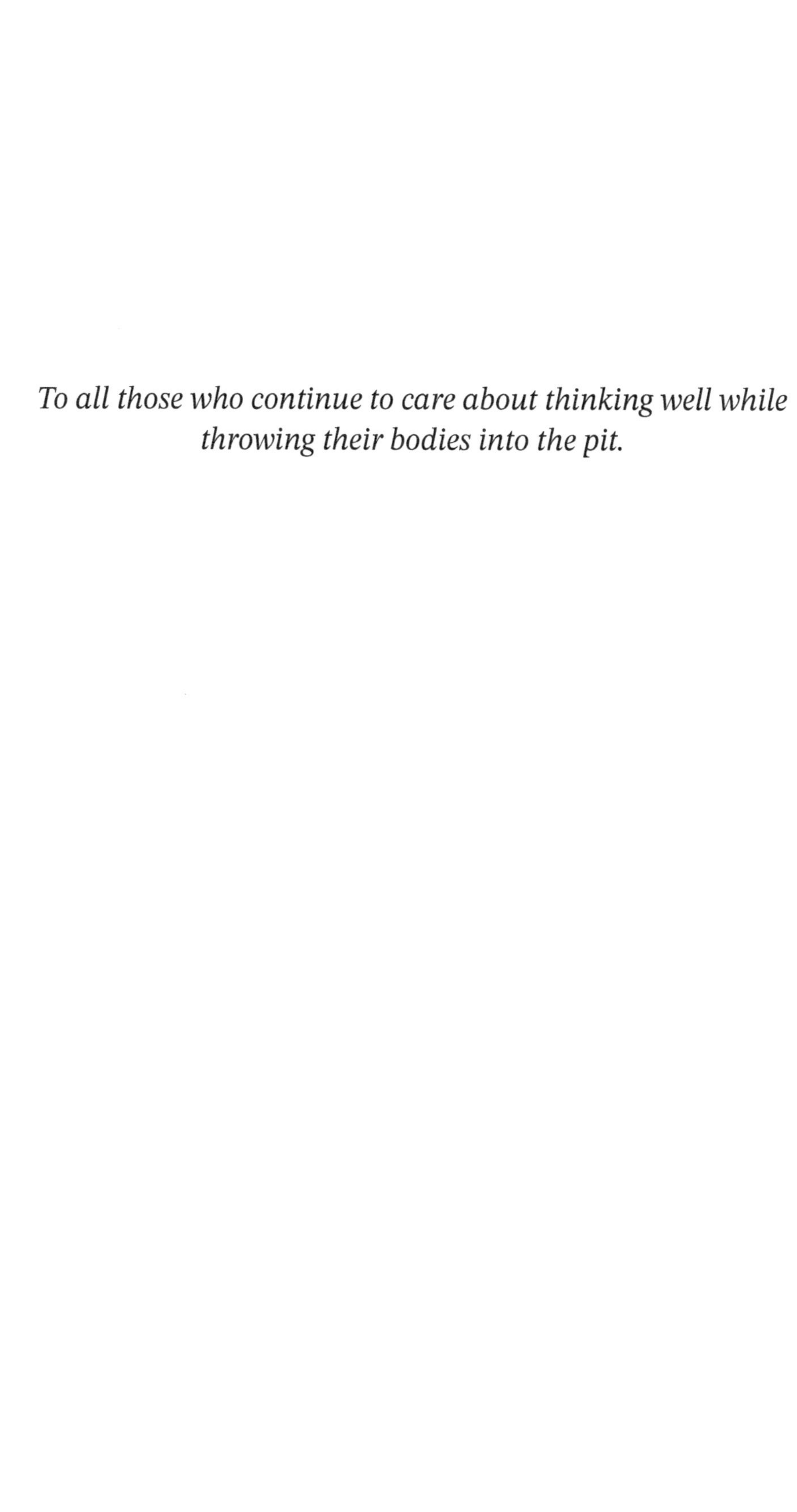

To all those who continue to care about thinking well while throwing their bodies into the pit.

Contents

Contributor Bios

Scott Aikin is an Associate Professor of Philosophy at Vanderbilt University, in Nashville, TN. He specializes in theories of knowledge, American pragmatism, informal logic, and ancient philosophy.

Ley David Elliette Cray (she/they) teaches philosophy at New Mexico State University. Her research and scholarship has focused largely on philosophical considerations of music, performance, comics, stories, religion, gender, and more, with work appearing in *American Philosophical Quarterly*, *Australasian Journal of Philosophy*, *British Journal of Aesthetics*, *Journal of Aesthetics and Art Criticism*, *Journal of the American Philosophical Association*, and elsewhere. Her *Philosophy of Comics: An Introduction* (with Sam Cowling) was published by Bloomsbury in 2022.

Daisy Dixon is a Lecturer in Philosophy at Cardiff University, specializing in philosophy of art. She explores how artworks mold and sustain social hierarchies through the lens of hate speech, and she is currently working on the emerging concept of aesthetic injustice.

James M. Dow is Professor of Philosophy at Hendrix College, Marshall T. Steel Center Chair for the Study of Religion and Philosophy, and Chair of Environmental Studies. Dow has published articles on self-consciousness, expert bodily action, joint action, environmental disobedience, and nature aesthetics and is working on a book—*Expressing Nature's Value*. Dow is an ultra-runner having completed a 100-mile trail run, is obsessed with post-rock music and contemporary art, lives on an Eco-farm Wildland Gardens with Melissa Cowper-Smith, a Canadian mixed media artist, and makes dreamgaze post-punk music with his band THISNESS who recently released an album called "Chimera."

David Hunt is an extreme metal musician who has toured widely around the world and sung on numerous albums with various bands, including spending over 20 years with veteran death metal legends Benediction and, so far, releasing 11 albums with his current main band Anaal Nathrakh. With his music, he has carved an unusually philosophically informed path, frequently drawing on literary and philosophical inspirations in an extended exploration of themes around misanthropy, bitterness, and nihilism. Hunt holds a Ph.D. in philosophy received from the University of Birmingham in 2020 and works in metaethics.

Mikael Janvid is Professor of Theoretical Philosophy at Stockholm University in Sweden. He has published widely in the field of epistemology on topics such as skepticism, understanding, and African epistemology.

Jim Kanaris is Associate Professor of Philosophy of Religion at McGill University, where he teaches courses on theories of religion and continental philosophy of religion under the aegis of a discipline he describes as philosophy of religious studies. He has edited *Polyphonic Thinking and the Divine*, *Reconfigurations of Philosophy of Religion: A Possible Future*, and co-edited *In Deference to the Other: Lonergan and Contemporary Continental Thought*. He is also the author of *Bernard Lonergan's Philosophy of Religion: From Philosophy of God to Philosophy of Religious Studies* and *Toward a Philosophy of Religious Studies: Enecstatic Explorations*.

C. D. Labbas is a philosopher whose usual haunts lie in metaphysics and related areas, here writing under a pseudonym for this foray into something unusual.

Benjamin W. McCraw is Instructor of Philosophy at the University of South Carolina Upstate and Research Associate at the African Centre for Epistemology and Philosophy of Science (ACEPS), University of Johannesburg. He works in epistemology and philosophy of religion. He has published articles in journals including *Social Epistemology, Faith and Philosophy*, *Acta Analytica*, *Journal of Aesthetics & Culture*, *Religious Studies*, and *Philosophia*, and has authored or edited books with Routledge, Palgrave Macmillan, and Wiley-Blackwell.

Jason Miller is Associate Professor of Philosophy at Warren Wilson College. Apart from interests in heavy metal, he writes popular and scholarly articles about the intersection of art and politics, and is the author of *The Politics of Perception and the Aesthetics of Social Change* (Columbia, 2021).

Shelby Moser is an Associate Professor (Lecturer) in the Division of Games and Adjunct Professor in the Department of Philosophy at the University of Utah. She's an analytic philosopher whose work focuses on the ontology of interactivity and rules, the meaningfulness of play in social contexts, and the aesthetics of games. Her favorite subgenres of metal are Black and Doom.

R. T. Mullins (Ph.D., University of St Andrews; Dr. Habil., University of Helsinki) is a Lecturer in Philosophy and Theology at the University of Lucerne, and a docent of dogmatics at the University of Helsinki.

Panos Paris is a Senior Lecturer in Philosophy at Cardiff University. His research is mainly in aesthetics, ethics, and their intersection. Panos is also a Trustee of the British Society of Aesthetics, a Fellow of the Higher Education Academy, a co-founder and former organizer of the Scottish Aesthetics Forum, a co-founder of the Aesthetics & Ethics Research Group, and, most recently, a co-founder and organizer of the Welsh Aesthetics Forum.

Catharine Saint-Croix is Assistant Professor of Philosophy and Stephen R. Setterberg, M.D., Faculty Fellow in Philosophy at the University of Minnesota, Twin Cities. They are also a Research Associate at the African Centre for Epistemology and Philosophy of Science (ACEPS), University of Johannesburg. Their research interests include formal and social epistemology, the epistemology of attention, and feminist philosophy.

J. Aaron Simmons is a Professor of Philosophy at Furman University. The former president of the Søren Kierkegaard Society USA, Simmons has published widely in the areas of philosophy of religion, political philosophy, existentialism, and phenomenology. Simmons is also a professional drummer.

Nick Smith is a Professor of Philosophy at the University of New Hampshire. Formerly a lawyer at a major NYC firm and a clerk for the U.S. Court of Appeals, he specializes in the philosophy of law, politics, and society. Nick is the author of *I Was Wrong: The Meanings of Apologies*, and *Justice through Apologies: Remorse, Reform, and Punishment.* He regularly appears in the media, including *The Wall Street Journal, The New York Times, The Washington Post, The Washington Times, The Boston Herald, The Daily Herald, The Guardian* UK, *NPR*, *BBC*, and others. Nick co-founded and directs the Future Leaders Institute and is the founding director of the UNH Center for Ethics.

Eric Steinhart grew up on a farm in Pennsylvania. He received his B.S. in Computer Science from the Pennsylvania State University and a Ph.D. in Philosophy from SUNY at Stony Brook. He teaches at William Paterson University and is a regular visitor at Dartmouth College. His research has addressed new and emerging religions and spiritualities, spiritual atheism, mysticism, psychedelics, paganism, transhumanism, and mowre. His books include *Contemporary Pagan Philosophy, Atheistic Platonism: A Manifesto, Believing in Dawkins: The New Spiritual Atheism,* and *Your Digital Afterlives: Computational Theories of Life after Death.*

List of Contributors

Scott Aikin
Department of Philosophy
Vanderbilt University
Nashville, TN, USA

Ley David Elliette Cray
Department of Philosophy
New Mexico State University
Las Cruces, NM
USA

Daisy Dixon
School of English,
Communication and Philosophy
Cardiff University
Cardiff, UK

James Dow
Philosophy Department
Hendrix College
Conway, AR
USA

David Hunt
The University of Birmingham
Birmingham
UK

Mikael Janvid
Department of Philosophy
Stockholm University
Stockholm
Sweden

Jim Kanaris
School of Religious Studies
McGill University
Quebec
Canada

C.D. Labbas

Benjamin W. McCraw
Department of History,
Political Science, Philosophy, and
American Studies
University of South Carolina
Upstate
Spartanburg, SC
USA

and

African Centre for Epistemology
and Philosophy of Science
University of Johannesburg
Johannesburg, Gauteng
South Africa

Jason Miller
Public Humanities
Warren Wilson College
Swannanoa, NC
USA

Shelby Moser
Division of Games
University of Utah
Salt Lake City, UT
USA

R.T. Mullins
Faculty of Theology
University of Lucerne
Luzern
Switzerland

Panos Paris
School of English,
Communication and Philosophy
Cardiff University
Cardiff
UK

Catharine Saint-Croix
Twin Cities Department of
Philosophy
University of Minnesota
Minneapolis, MN
USA

and

African Centre for Epistemology
and Philosophy of Science
University of Johannesburg
Johannesburg, Gauteng
South Africa

J. Aaron Simmons
Department of Philosophy
Furman University
Greenville, SC
USA

Nick Smith
Department of Philosophy
University of New Hampshire
Durham, NH
USA

Eric Steinhart
Department of History, Philosophy,
and Liberal Studies
William Paterson University
Wayne
USA

Foreword

Philosophy (**noun**): the study of the fundamental nature of knowledge, reality, and existence, especially when considered as an academic discipline.

Heavy Metal (noun): a type of highly amplified harsh-sounding rock music with a strong beat, characteristically using violent or fantastic imagery.

—*Oxford English Dictionary*

I was first asked about writing this Foreword by a professional philosopher acquaintance of mine, Tom Morris. I met Tom through my surfing buddy Don, a 60-plus year-old fitness maniac who has helped coach Tom with his workout routine. Sitting in Don's humid garage, surrounded by rusting free weights and well-dinged surfboards, there was a vague conversation about a forthcoming academic book centered on heavy metal and philosophy, which was followed by an invitation to contribute a few opening words for it. Without a second's hesitation, I blurted out, "Yes! I'll do it!" Two components of my personality were at play in my automatic agreement: (1) My hideous, virtually Pavlovian, need for approval from anyone even remotely connected with the imposing beast I call "serious writing," which in turn most likely stems from; (2) my decades-long ire at being stereotyped as some sort of musical caveman by a significant portion of the populace the second they learn what I do for a living.

I have spent the entirety of my 30-year career singing in my band, lamb of god, engaged in a ceaseless battle to dispel the clichéd image of heavy metal musicians as beer-swilling, fist-swinging, screeching Cro-Magnon purveyors of senseless noise (even though I have admittedly ticked off a few of those boxes in my well-storied past). I cannot explain precisely how irritating it is for me to hear the comment, "Wow! You're *so well spoken*—not at all what I expected from this interview," from yet another condescending journalist given the thankless task of asking me a few questions for a nonmusic related "respectable" media outlet. Perhaps they expected me to grunt out answers between smashing whiskey bottles over my head? Historically, this negative intellectual stereotype has extended to fans of heavy metal music as well. I'm not exactly sure why this is the case, given the fact that many of my fellow metal musicians and fans I've befriended are among the most intellectually astute people I know—for example, take my friend Paul F. Thompson, who helped guide NASA's Perseverance Rover to Mars in 2021. He's *literally* a rocket scientist. . . but he wears a Slayer shirt to work sometimes. As a person capable of doing incredibly complicated mathematical equations in his head, Paul says that it was the complexity of metal that first drew him to it. In fact, when he first heard Slayer, he heard *math,* interpreting the rhythms within the abrasive sounds as a conscious attempt to find order in chaos.

While I am not an academic of any sort, much less a professional philosopher, that is how I view philosophy: A conscious attempt to find order and meaning within the chaos of life. This is why I was drawn to stoicism over 20 years ago after being recommended Epictetus's *Enchiridion* by a psychotherapist I was seeing during a particularly rough period in my life. Much to my surprise, stoicism has exploded in popularity within the last decade, in no small part due to the gazillion-copy-selling books of my friend Ryan Holiday, a former marketing whiz kid who also happens to be a total metalhead—the dude *loves* Seneca *and* Iron Maiden. While I've read the grumblings of certain academics unhappy with a two thousand year old philosophy taking flight from the Ivory Towers, I think this surge in popularity is a good thing—if one of the goals of studying philosophy is to improve a person's life by guiding one to a deeper understanding of existence (and I hope that to be the case, as I have very little interest in thought exercises for their own sake), why should it remain solely the realm of academics? It certainly can't hurt our fractious society to have more people asking themselves deeper questions.

But considering the end of the definition at the top of this Foreword, the need for rigorous academic consideration is clear to me as well, and this is the purview of trained philosophers. While anyone can board an airplane without a degree, we still need aeronautical engineers to improve upon existing flight technologies and invent new ones. I certainly won't be attempting to design a more reliable, more efficient aileron for commercial jets, but I'm glad someone is. I'm just as grateful for all the philosophers throughout the ages who did some heavy cerebral lifting and left behind such thought-provoking bodies of work for further study.

But why should these deep, technical thinkers bend their minds toward a philosophy of heavy metal, of all things? Once again, I am not a trained philosopher, merely a singer in a heavy metal band, so perhaps I am not the most qualified to answer this question. Nevertheless, I think that as an artist, I have a pretty good idea. Over the years in my band, I have come to realize that the creative act of writing lyrics and then attempting to express the emotion and meaning behind them vocally is my attempt to understand myself, the world around me, and my place within it. In the moment of creation, I am wrestling with the universe, searching for some sort of comprehensible framework within the chaos to hang a sense of meaning upon. I write songs as an inquiry into the nature of reality and as an act of resistance against the bottomless pit of nihilism and existential despair.

That sounds a lot like philosophy to me.

Furthermore, these songs do not exist inside a hermetically sealed vacuum within my own head—once I release a song into the world, it is no longer strictly mine. Fans hear our songs, internalize them, interpret their meaning for themselves, and apply them to and identify them with the particular circumstances of their own life. While this process of internalization is universal to all forms music (for instance, hearing a certain love song that topped the charts during high school can remind a person of their first love, an old gospel hymn may remind someone of a deceased grandparent, etc.), it often takes on a much greater significance within more specialized genres such as heavy metal. Heavy metal is not just "highly amplified harsh-sounding rock music" as per Oxford's definition—it is a vibrant and ever-expanding subculture, one with an extremely dedicated membership, and as such its members often construct a strong sense of identity within and around it. For many fans, heavy metal is a *lifestyle*. People find real meaning within this music and its surrounding community—to my view, anything that can have such a profound effect on human beings is worth a view through the lens of philosophy.

At this point, I think it is worth mentioning that although this is a book of philosophy *for philosophers*, and as such written with a high degree of technicality, all of the authors included in this collection are avid fans of heavy metal themselves, with one author even fronting an extreme metal band. The metal community is well known for gatekeeping, so well-known that Chapter 2 of this book is an examination of the phenomenon. As a member of that community, I myself am protective of it and suspicious of uninformed analysis by outsiders, as historically it has most often resulted in hysterical demonization. It is impossible to write with any sort of authority about something you don't understand, and to truly understand metal and the subculture surrounding it, you have to be immersed within it. It doesn't matter how many three-letter addendums sit behind your name—you can't write about us with any accuracy if you don't understand us, and you can't truly understand us if you are not *of us*.

The authors of this volume are of us. Hails to the metal philosophers.

D. Randall Blythe

Cape Fear, NC 2025

(Singer of lamb of god and author of *Dark Days* and *Just Beyond the Light*)

Introduction

Benjamin W. McCraw[1]
and J. Aaron Simmons[2]
[1]Department of History, Political Science, Philosophy, and American Studies, University of South Carolina, Spartanburg, SC, USA
[2]Department of Philosophy, Furman University, Greenville, SC, USA

Ozzy Osborne died this week (July 22, 2025). The Prince of Darkness has long been an icon in hard rock and heavy metal, but his death signals something a bit more profound because, arguably, Ozzy and Black Sabbath gave birth to heavy metal on Friday, February 13, 1970—at least in the United Kingdom.[1] Thankfully his death does not signal the death of the genre he helped establish, but it does provide the occasion to reflect on the significance of heavy metal as more than just music. It is a cultural phenomenon that has provided the framework for the lived experience of millions of people—including the editors of this volume. More than a style, it is a hermeneutic lens by which the world is made meaningful. For all those teenagers who carved "Ozzy Rules" into their desks at school, and for all the people who can't help but air drum along to "Crazy Train" every time they are stopped at train tracks, Ozzy holds a special significance as something of a midwife for everything that came after him. As with any birth, there were previous influences, causal factors, etc. and, when talking about any contested issue, there's no consensus to be expected here.[2] Philosophy, though, has as longer history. But, even though heavy metal is considerably younger than philosophy—no matter how we want to date its birth—it is old enough to have given rise to significant and numerous academic studies on all sorts of topics.[3] Just as Black Sabbath can be viewed as forming the roots of a tree whose branches now extend to such diverse groups as Opeth, Jinjer, Knocked Loose, and Between the Buried and Me, philosophy has been applied as an intellectual resource for making sense of nearly all areas of human existence and the world in which we find ourselves.

Strikingly, however, with the rise of academic work engaging heavy metal as its subject, there hasn't been much philosophical work doing so. As of this writing, we can find only six serious engagements with heavy metal from a distinctively philosophical perspective.[4] This dearth of scholarly philosophical considerations of heavy metal forms

[1] The US release wasn't until June.

[2] To forestall any unnecessary confusion, we don't mean to say that Black Sabbath birthed the *term* "heavy metal." This term predates them, and there is much to say about its history. See, for instance, Weinstein (2014) on the contested origin, use, and legitimacy of the term.

[3] For a short list of examples, see: Brown et al. (2017), Harris (2007), Phillipov (2012), Purcell (2003), Unger (2016), Wallach et al. (2012), Walser (1993), and Weinstein (1991).

[4] Gracyk (2016), McCraw (2024), Miller (2022), Murphy (forthcoming), Scott (2014), and Xhignesse (2024).

one of the major springboards for this edited collection. Philosophy's content, unlike many academic disciplines, has no intrinsic boundaries, and so finding a topic (like heavy metal) that has been so culturally significant, and has aroused so much academic and popular interest with such minimal serious philosophical reflection is both surprising and also (we think) something to be corrected. So, this collection hopes to stand as something of a midwife for what we hope will become a prominent area of philosophical research in the future. Our aim is not simply to provide some philosophical work in a field that's lacking it but rather to motivate more work so that this field—i.e. the philosophy of metal—might become a topic that philosophers take up more frequently and with more legitimacy. Ozzy, Tony, Geezer, and Bill surely built on what came before them, but they did something new that made possible what couldn't have been imagined before. We are under no delusions that this book will stand alongside the album *Black Sabbath* for its cultural influence, but we do hope that it will do something similar for the philosophical community that *Black Sabbath* did for music: show new ways forward that invigorate generations of people to push into new areas.

So, how best to introduce a collection with such an aim? We don't think it best to attempt a history of the genre: we aren't historians and this collection isn't a history. Similarly, we aren't musicologists, sociologist, or anthropologists, so those tasks are left to others.[5] Accordingly, it might seem natural to follow what tends to be *the* philosophical question, at least in the West: the "*what is X*?" question. *What is heavy metal?* Good question, but we will avoid this approach, even if seemingly very appropriate for philosophers, for a few important reasons. Heavy metal, in its various and exploding subgenres, is too broad and with too many potential counterexamples to analyze in anything short of a full manuscript on its own.[6] We also don't want to assume, or give rise to the assumption, that such a question is the only or the only important question philosophers might bring to bear. That said, some of the chapters in this volume hit on this question in very productive ways relative to narrower subgenres such as death metal and black metal.

[5] And those tasks have been and are being completed. See the references in note 3.

[6] If you doubt this, just go on the internet and claim that any given metal band is or isn't a particular genre. Then just wait for the keyboard warriors to attack.

Instead, in this short introduction, we will lay out some potentially fruitful intersections with philosophy and heavy metal as a prolegomenon to the work continued in the chapters contained herein. We hope it's too obvious to say, but we'll say it anyway: we have absolutely no intention to list *all, most, etc.* of the ways philosophy and heavy metal might helpfully be engaged. But, hell, if someone asks where to start for getting into heavy metal, Black Sabbath is a damn good thing to recommend. Similarly, we hope to recommend a few ways that folks might get interested in the philosophy of metal. When we are willing to consider the "heaviest ideas in the universe" (with a nod to Gojira), we think that we can strengthen our philosophical muscles such that all sorts of other issues might actually become a bit lighter and more manageable. Accordingly, we have intentionally designed this book to be as philosophically rigorous as possible. We have encouraged the contributors to write with a high degree of technicality. We do not want this book to be viewed as simply a philosophy of pop culture sort of volume (even as important and influential as those sorts of books have been in expanding the audience for philosophy to nonspecialists). This book is meant for specialists and we make no apologies about that. When you hope to shape a professional discourse, you must assume the standards of that community and so this book does that within academic philosophy and also metal studies. So, rather than viewing this book as being akin to the pop cover of a metal song—"Taylor Swift sings Metallica," etc.—it should be approached more along the lines of someone appreciating the influence of Bad Brains on lamb of god while also being familiar with Randy Blythe's guest vocal on P.O.D.'s "Drop," as well as with HR's metal health struggles in recent decades.

That said, metalheads, including all of us here, often characterize heavy metal by extremity. Obviously, this won't hold for all heavy metal music or for every single metal band,[7] but we think the lens of extremity can helpfully focus our vision on some places fruitful for a philosophy/heavy metal interchange. So, let us briefly think through a (nonexhaustive) set of ways that the extremity of metal opens up philosophical avenues. With our Plato and Aristotle open on the desk, and the carved "Ozzy Rules" right there next to the books, and with horns raised, we thank all those philosophers and musicians who have made this volume possible. Rest in power, Ozzy.

---

[7] Power metal is the poster child counterexample here.

Extreme Aesthetics

As Unger (2016) examines at length, heavy metal affords distinctive possibilities for extreme aesthetics. Given the author's sociological background, we see more focus on the social aspects of extremity in heavy metal, but we can certainly extend the interest in extreme aesthetics beyond any specific sociological frameworks. Different heavy metal genres, bands, albums, songs, etc. provide different avenues toward more extreme aesthetic concepts and features than we would expect from more traditional philosophical aesthetics.

Heaviness, itself, becomes a clear target for philosophical aesthetics, as Miller (2022) analyzes. But, moving beyond the explicit name of the genre itself, familiar aesthetic tropes offer more fodder for aesthetic reflection. While beauty has long been a central discussion in philosophical aesthetics, ugliness has been less of a focus. And even if ugliness has been a concern, it has come to be the anti-beauty as a negative or undesirable feature. In a sense, ugliness is the problem of evil for aesthetics. But, as with evil as well, ugliness becomes a *goal* and *desideratum* for much of heavy metal—especially extreme metal. We see some aesthetic focus on ugliness (e.g. Kieran 1997; Fenner 2005; Buckman 2017; Paris 2017). But metal's *prizing* of ugliness places it as a unique resource for aesthetics. Similarly, "brutal" is a marker of quality and a sonic goal to which one should strive for certain strains of extreme metal (especially death metal). The valorizing of brutality is clearly set against the more traditional valuing of opposed concepts like refined, compassionate, elegance, and so on. And while brutalism picks out a distinct branch of architecture, extending brutality as an aesthetic approach in its own right has received little philosophical discussion.[8]

And yet even more traditional aesthetic concepts engage with heavy metal and, at times, are transfigured by their metallic usage. A central motivation for the production and consumption of much art is catharsis, as Aristotle inaugurates in his *Poetics*. Heavy metal is no different. But the feelings heavy metal often purges and the sonic means by which this purging itself occurs gives a unique opportunity for heavy metal.[9] There's growing empirical evidence suggesting that listening to angry heavy

[8] Perhaps work by Mbembe (2024) and McCraw (2024) run counter to this neglect.

[9] See, e.g. Henry and Caldwell (2007) for a non-philosophical perspective on heavy metal and catharsis. We submit that a *philosophical* approach to metal-induced catharsis is just as timely.

metal, for instance, doesn't *cause* the listener to *become* angry (when they weren't already). Rather, consuming metal tends to help the listener experience positive emotions. In short, heavy metal "may represent a healthy way of processing anger. . ." (Sharman and Dingle 2015, p. 1). Similarly, the Romantic ideals of nature find resonance in much of the Neo-Pagan influence in much of folk[10] and black metal.[11] Even when heavy metal uses and engages with more traditional aesthetic concepts, it offers a more *extreme* engagement.

Extreme Emotions

The notion of catharsis helps transition to a discussion of how heavy metal can provide for the philosophical reflection on more extreme emotions than we typically see in the scholarship. One of the primary emotions offered in and through heavy metal music is anger. To many, especially those who are not fans of heavy metal, the music just sounds angry. Indeed, Aaron's wife continues to say that she doesn't understand why anyone would want to listen to music where the singer just yells at them the whole time. The anger perceived in heavy metal may serve as a deterrent to some, but it will clearly entice others. For instance, the shouting vocal style of many thrash bands like Slayer and (1980s-era) Metallica sound very angry and, possibly, stem from anger itself. And while anger has a long tradition of philosophical reflection—Seneca's *De Ira* is an obvious example, and we shouldn't forget the role of *thumos* in Plato's *Republic*—anger has often been viewed with a wary eye, if not with outright derision by those who study the role of emotion in virtuous living.[12] But, as with ugliness and brutality, heavy metal prizes things that traditionally have been scorned. It digs into the stuff that others refuse to look at. But, this is perhaps the most philosophical thing it can do. Philosophers take seriously what everyone else takes for granted. Pushing into the margins, the liminal spaces, and even the taboo is often where the best questions begin to emerge. As such, even when anger may, in

[10] Here we're thinking of artists like Cruachan, Skyclad, Heidevolk, Finntroll, Týr, and so on. Also see Manea (2020).

[11] See works from bands like Enslaved, Wolves in the Throne Room, Borknagar, Agalloch, and others. Also see Hagen (2011).

[12] We don't mean to discount those who think of righteous anger as important. See, e.g. Vernezze (2008) and Cogley (2014).

some cases, be socially needed, culturally tolerated, and politically prized, the extremity of the anger presented in heavy metal seems to go beyond what is often accepted in other areas of human life. In heavy metal, even outright hatred may be lauded: misanthropy is not infrequently a *goal*.[13] Indeed, much of heavy metal—especially in the more extreme genres—can be viewed as a kind of aesthetics of hate.[14] Maybe Aaron's wife is on to something?

Another traditional emotion that heavy metal often "extremizes" is sadness. Much of doom metal sounds sad and focuses on very depressive lyrics. And when genres outside of doom include doom influences, the results often intend to make the work more depressive. For instance, death/doom (obviously) integrates elements of both death metal and doom metal to distinctively and characteristically sad results.[15] And, perhaps just as obviously, the subgenre of black metal: depressive suicidal black metal (DSBM).[16]

Much heavy metal also prides itself on being something like horror music in terms of sound, lyric content, and general mood. Black Sabbath's guitarist, Tony Iommi, claims that the band "wanted to create a vibe like you get off horror films" (quoted in Woods 2017). A very quick look at the various subgenres of heavy metal with an eye toward a horror influence would yield a list far too long to include. But, what we find striking is a recent spate of papers on horror *as a feeling, emotion, etc.* rather than simply as a genre of film or literature.[17] With horror comes a

[13] Among artists who have a song explicitly titled "Misanthrope" are Death (*Symbolic* 1995, Roadrunner Records), Ihsahn, the main force behind the central black metal band Emperor (*angL* 2008, Candlelight Records), and Abysmal Torment (*The Misanthrope* 2018, Willowtip Records). Additionally, there are artists named Misanthrope, Misanthropy, Misanthropic, Monument of Misanthropy, and so on. Finally, Misanthropy Records released Burzum's *Hvis lyset tar oss* (while Varg Vikernes was serving his sentence for murder and arson) as well as albums by Arcturus, Fleurety, In the Woods. . ., Katatonia, Madder Mortem, Mayhem, Primordial, and Ved Buens Ende.

[14] The pun on Machine Head's "Aesthetics of Hate" (*The Blackening* 2020, Nuclear Blast) is definitely intended.

[15] See, for instance, seminal albums from Peaceville Records in the 1990s like Katatonia's *For Funerals to Come* (1995, Peaceville Records) and *Brave Murder Day* (1996, Peaceville Records), Paradise Lost's *Lost Paradise* (1991, Peaceville Records) and *Gothic* (1991, Peaceville Records), My Dying Bride's *As the Flower Withers*(1992, Peaceville Records) and *Turn Loose the Swans* (1993, Peaceville Records), and Anathema's *Serenades* (1993, Peaceville Records) and *The Silent Enigma* (1995, Peaceville Records). For other death/doom artists, see Saturnus, Swallow the Sun, Mournful Congregation, Skepticism, Thergothon, Hamferð, and Fires in the Distance.

[16] See, e.g. artists like Shining, Xasthur, Lifelover (ironically enough), Psychonaut 4, and Thy Light.

[17] See, e.g. Gaut (1993), Hick (2022), and Sauchelli (2014). Sauchelli's piece even makes explicit reference to Cannibal Corpse as making "art-horror music" (2014, p. 41).

wide range of emotions with a traditionally negative valence that heavy metal, nevertheless, tends to frame positively: fear, aggression, and so on.

Related to horror is a common negative response to it, typically experienced by those not fans of the genre: disgust. Whether it be the visceral, physical disgust felt because of gory violence or the kind of cosmic disgust distinctively captured by Lovecraft's style of "weird" stories, we find heavy metal trafficking in precisely the same sort of emotions. The explicit, upfront violence of old school death metal, paradigmatically seen (heard? felt?) in the works of Cannibal Corpse exactly parallels the blood splattered films of the Italian giallo masters (Dario Argento, Lucio Fulci,[18] Mario Bava, Ruggero Deodato, etc.), the slasher films of Wes Craven, Clive Barker, and John Carpenter, and the "torture porn" films of the 2000s. But the cerebral, almost transcendental, disgust of Lovecraft's famed Cthulhu mythos and other tales echoes in metal, too.[19] As with enthusiasts of horror, heavy metal artists and fans transform disgust from a negative affect to be avoided into an aesthetic desideratum.

Extreme Values

Finally, some of the kinds of extreme values found in metal might fruitfully intersect with philosophical work. One of the obvious values is transgression.[20] If we go back to Ozzy Osbourne, himself, we see a clear

[18] Fulci is an Italian death metal band who, unsurprisingly, takes their influence from Lucio Fulci's films). Their *Tropical Sun* (2019, Narcotica) is inspired by Fulci's *Zombi 2*, *Exhumed Information* (2021, Narcotica) is influenced by Fulci's *Voices from Beyond*, and *Duck Face Killings* (2024, 20 Buck Spin) comes from Fulci's *The New York Ripper*.

[19] Bands like The Great Old Ones and Sulphur Aeon are exclusively and explicitly themed on Lovecraft. For overtly songs Lovecraftian songs, see (hear): The Black Dahlia Murder's "Thy Horror Cosmic" (*Unhallowed* 2003, Metal Blade Records), Black Sabbath's "Behind the Wall of Sleep" (*Black Sabbath* 1970, Warner Brothers Records Inc), Cradle of Filth's "Cthulhu Dawn" (*Midian* 2000, Music For Nations), Electric Wizard's "Dunwich" (*Witchcult Today* 2007, Rise Above Records), GWAR's "Horror of Yig" (*Scumdogs of the Universe* 1990, Pit Records), Metallica's "The Thing that Should Not Be" (*Master of Puppets* 1986, Elektra Records), Morbid Angel's "Angel of Disease" (*Abominations of Desolation* 1991, Earache), Nile's "4th Arra of Dagon" (*Those Whom the Gods Detest* 2009, Nuclear Blast) and "Von Unaussprechlichen Kulten (*Annihilation of the Wicked* 2005, Relapse), Revocation's "Madness Opus" (*Deathless* 2014, Metal Blade), Rigor Mortis' "Re-Animator" (*Rigor Mortis* 1988, Capitol), Septicflesh's "Lovecraft's Death" (*Communion* 2008, Season of Mist), and Sleep's "From Beyond" (*Holy Mountain* 1993, Earache). The breadth of the time periods and genres contained in this short list is striking and speaks to the intense influence Lovecraft exerts on heavy metal across the genre. See also Sederholm (2016).

[20] See McCraw (2024, pp. 6–7) for more on transgression and its role in death metal. Kirner-Ludwig and Wohlfarth (2018) argue that the core features of extreme metal stem from its transgressive function and aim(s).

expression of the desire to transgress popular music and culture—and *violently* so:

> When I was a kid, I was hungry. I had my ass hanging out of my pants. I hated the fucking world. When I heard the silly fucking words, "If you go to San Francisco, be sure to wear a flower in your hair" I wanted to fucking strangle John Phillips [of the Mamas & the Papas]. I was sitting in the industrial town of Birmingham, England. My father was dying of asbestos from industrial pollution and I was an angry young punk.
>
> (quoted in Wiederhorn and Turman 2014, p. 30)

A transgressive aim helps to explain and underscore much of the sounds, lyrics, and images central to heavy metal. The extreme sounds of thrash, death, and black metal obviously transgress the polished melodicism of much popular music. Harsh vocals, in particular, are easy to see as set against the clean, beautiful vocals prized by many other musical genres. The extreme, often violent and gory lyrics in metal transgress both traditional nonmetal genres but also transgress by offending mainstream moral sensibilities. Metal is, in this way, almost anti-pop, and necessarily so. But, we also suggest that the extreme value of transgression also touches upon some other central extreme values.

As mentioned above with death metal, violence is a hallmark of much heavy metal. It may be the fantastical, dragon-slaying violence of power metal. Or it could be the realistic or caricatured violence of death metal. The misanthropic, sometimes self-directed, dark violence of black metal is also easy to see in much of the subgenre. The sounds themselves can be violent: the wall of sound, amplification, and downtuned sonics of much heavy metal have a physical, sometimes violent, effect on the listener. And we shouldn't forget about the playful violence of the mosh pit.[21]

Transgression also helpfully engages with other extreme values that hold for much of heavy metal: resistance and rebellion.[22] Resistance may take its most obvious form in *political* resistance, seen in heavy metal bands across subgenres, times, and places, but resistance *as such* has

---

[21] That harm occurs in the pit doesn't mean that moshing, across the board, *intends* violence on those in them. Of course, there are those who may so intend it—so called crowd killers—but they tend to face harsh criticism for such actions. And, being in a thing like a mosh pit, it's easy to have others in them enforce anti-crown-killing norms via the pit itself. . .

[22] See, e.g. Scott (2016) and Hjelm et al. (2011).

no particular target. It's just against *something*. Heavy metal resists the mainstream. Heavy metal can also, and often most interestingly, resist *itself*.[23] The long-standing association of heavy metal with Satanism and immoralism, plausibly, stems from metal's desire to transgress and resist the *religious* sentiments of mainstream culture. Obviously, some artists may take their Satanism seriously and theologically,[24] but it's also pretty clear that not all artists who prize their Satanism think of their commitments in theistic or even religious terms.[25]

But the commitment to Satanism became a shibboleth for certain members of the original black metal scene. One must be "true" (trve) to that scene, its music, and its culture by being "kvlt". This leads to another important extreme value in heavy metal: authenticity.[26] Even in the relatively nonextreme subgenre of power metal, authenticity is a significant marker for membership and seriousness as well as an honorific. Manowar's (in)famous rallying cry "death to false metal" could hold for their extreme cousins.[27] Being authentically *metal*, then, becomes a (sub) culture for many fans rather than simply a genre that one tends to enjoy hearing.[28] Heavy metal, accordingly, becomes a way of being, living, or identifying oneself that takes it beyond simply a matter of one's sonic preferences (at least for *some* fans). The way that the desire for authenticity, especially among like-minded people in one's community, transitions to a culture accent another way that heavy metal offers an extreme value: identify-conferring enculturation.

One final extreme value is worth mentioning. Many heavy metal artists and songs explicitly accept nihilism or absurdity. To take as a single example, White Ward explicitly cite Camus' absurdism as the general theme,

---

[23] For example, see Reyes' (2013) analysis of black metal as aiming to out-extreme death metal.

[24] We're looking at you, Deathspell Omega.

[25] For instance, consider these comments from Manheim of the core black metal band Mayhem:

> Everything that was extreme, [was] good, everything that could upset a Christian was good. Behind it was rebellion. . .the emerging of the black metal genre. . .it's not based on Satanism and rituals and religion. On the contrary, it was more in opposition to people in power and people who don't believe that you are a free man who should be able to have free will. Of course we used Christianity as an enemy in the expression, but if you lived in Norway you would understand why.
>
> (quoted in Patterson 2013, p. 131)

[26] See Bayer (2017).

[27] And it inspires parody even in the metal genre: see Tragedy's *Death to False Disco Metal* (2013, self-released) and Nanowar of Steel's *Dislike to False Metal* (2023, Napalm Records).

[28] See, e.g. Kahn-Harris (2007), Spracklen et al. (2011), Allett (2011), Weinstein (1991), and Purcell (2003).

and Aephanemer's "Sisphysus' Bliss" (*Memento Mori* 2016, self-released) and Witchcryer's "Sisyphus, Holy Roller" (*When Their Gods Come For You* 2021, Ripple Music) explicitly deal with Camus' famed "Myth of Sisyphus." As with Camus, these metallic absurdities might be optimistic, but other uses of nihilism in heavy metal are more pessimistic.[29] Nihilism and absurdity have significant, long-standing footholds in philosophy, and so this extreme value, like the others discussed, provides a natural point of intersection with heavy metal.[30]

Chapter Summaries

Having laid out some of the main philosophical issues and questions at stake in a philosophy of metal, we will now turn to the specific arguments of the individual chapters.

In *Part One: None So Vile: On Ethics*, Nick Smith, Catharine Saint-Croix, Scott Aikin, and David Hunt all offer chapters that consider the various questions that attend the moral dimensions of metal creativity and culture.

Nick Smith's chapter, "Conflicted: Moshing, Meaning, and the Dialectics of a Problematic Community," is a sustained engagement with the phenomenon of the "mosh pit." As the main title of his essay straightforwardly indicates, the pit is not something that allows for easy moral judgment. It is a place of violence and problematic social norms and yet it is also a place where true community and inclusion are possible. Smith goes as far as to suggest that the mosh pit can even be a site of ethical action. After thinking through this deep and essential tension,

---

[29] For example, Anaal Nathrakh's "You Can't Save Me, So Stop Fucking Trying" (*Vanitas* 2012, Candlelight Records) quotes from philosopher of religion William Lane Craig's (2008)

> *Reasonable Faith: Christian Truth and Apologetics*:
> The entire universe marches irreversibly towards its grave.
> So not only is the life of each individual person doomed;
> The entire human race is doomed.
> The universe is plunging toward inevitable extinction
> Death is written throughout its structure.There is no escape. There is no hope.
> However, they omit the key clause at the beginning of Craig's discussion of an absurd universe:
> "For *if there is no God*, then man's life becomes absurd".
>
> (2008, p. 71, emphases added)

[30] Consistent with metal's resisting itself, consider that Living Sacrifice's "Nietzsche's Madness" (*The Infinite Order*, Solid State Records, 2010), is effectively a reflection on, and then rejection of, nihilism.

Smith concludes that part of the attraction of the pit is that it is risky and edgy. Steps must be taken, however, to facilitate the promise of pit culture without allowing the violence and immortality so often found there to override the benefits.

One of the things that might frequently be heard in the context of the pit culture described by Smith is the charge that someone is a "poser" if they don't carry themselves in the "right" way. Looking directly at this phenomenon more broadly in metal, Catharine Saint-Croix's "'What a Poser!' Snobbery, Identity, and Gatekeeping" is a nuanced account of the difference between different ideas of philosophical snobbery. Through a sustained consideration of the imagined encounter of a metal-newbie at a record store wearing an Insane Clown Posse shirt while trying to buy a Slayer album, Saint-Croix illustrates the moral dynamics that attend our distaste for snobbery. Going on to discuss the idea of gatekeeping as a moral challenge and the charge of being a poser as a kind of reinforcement of dominant power structures and social narratives, Saint-Croix concludes by taking up the case study of transphobic feminism as itself a form of "gender snobbery."

Moving from the embodied activities of moshing and determining who gets to be part of the in-group to the idea of fighting mystical beats on snow-covered mountains, Scott Aikin's "We Sing Songs about Swords and Wizards from Space: Fantasy Metal and the Aspiration of Re-enchantment" provides a careful account of why metal needs to be fantastic in very particular ways. Unpacking what he terms "transcendental anxiety," Aikin notes that our lives are defined by a kind of disenchantment anchored in the paradox that we take ourselves to be free, good, and meaningful and yet find ourselves in a world that seems determined, awful, and meaningless. How can we bear the weight of this frustration? Aikin contends that metal offers an important resource in the way that it invites imaginative escape without avoiding the realities that characterize our existence. The fantasy of metal music is a form of value affirmation. It allows us to tell a different story of who we are and why it matters. In this way, Aikin argues that metal offers a moral opportunity and a very important kind of lived hope becomes possible in light of such imaginative construction.

David Hunt concludes this first Part by considering the arguments that might be offered for why metal music is fundamentally immoral and, as such, deserves to be censored as a result. In his "A View from Nihil: Heavy Metal, Censorship and The End of Morality," Hunt considers the charges that metal predisposes people to act in immoral ways and that it normalizes such immoral behavior more broadly. Terming those who want to ban metal music, "metalbadists," Hunt responds to these charges of "metalbadism" by offering a substantive defense of metal music as not able to "make" people do things in ways that give credence to metalbadism. Concluding by turning to the work on moral error theory by Richard Joyce, Hunt contends that metal music might indeed present aspects that would give us moral pause, but none that warrant the censorship advocated by the moral/metalbadists.

Part Two, Preachers of Death: On Philosophy of Religion features three chapters from C.D. Labbas, Eric Steinhart, and Ryan Mullins. Focusing primarily on issues of concern to philosophy of religion, these chapters illustrate not only the possibilities for metal as a resource for philosophy of religion, but also the range of views available within such debates.

C.D. Labbas's "The Idea of the Unholy" is a remarkable experiment that flips Rudolph Otto's notion of religion on its head. Famously Otto's *The Idea of the Holy* claims that there is a definitionally *sui generis* dimension of religion, which he terms the numinous or "holy." Labbas interrogates this idea and claims that metal actually operates according to a similar, but inverted, logic, whereby the idea that operates so deeply within these experiences of the numinous is the "unholy." After laying out the stakes and borders of this notion, Labbas then turns to the normative question of the value of such experiences of the unholy. Suggesting that metal might help to shape our moral, religious, and aesthetic sensibilities, Labbas concludes by provocatively positioning metal as a kind of existential archive.

Almost building on the possibilities offered by Labbass, Eric Steinhart's "Black Metal is Religious Music" looks at the various possible arguments that could be offered for considering black metal as religious. After considering a variety of options, Steinhart claims that the "predator defiance" model (along with what he terms the "religious function" and "music of creation" arguments) offers the most plausible account of why black metal is rightly understood as religious. Steinhart's chapter invites a reconsideration not only of black metal but also of the very category of "religion" itself as a kind of lived practice within culturally discrete spaces of meaning-making.

In the last chapter of Part Two, Ryan Mullins approaches things from a slightly different way by suggesting that his personal experiences as a metal fan have led him to particular places regarding his understanding of what it means to be a Christian and also a metalhead. "Christianity and Metal:

Reflections from a Former Scene Kid" is something of a metal autobiography from Mullins. It details the way that metal shaped his own identity and his relationship to his Christian faith. Although Mullins concludes that there is a lot in metal that leaves him cold regarding the possibilities of moral value, he nonetheless notes that metal, itself, invites a deep awareness of the need for something more, something excessive, something beyond nihilism.

Moving from ethics and religion to a direct consideration of aesthetics, *Part Three: The Science of Noise: On Aesthetics* looks at the various issues anchored in the performance, music, and culture of heavy metal and features chapters from Ley Crey, Daisy Dixon and Panos Paris, Jim Kanaris, Jay Miller, and James Dow.

Starting things off, Ley Cray's "The Role of Performance Persona in Black Metal Aesthetics" argues that the corpse-paint, fictitious names, and even biographical backstories are not mere accidental aspects of black metal, but are central to the aesthetics of the genre as such. The idea here is that part of what black metal offers to its fans is something beyond a naïve correlation to normal existence. In a way parallel to Aikin's account of fantasy metal, black metal requires a distance from one's ordinary existence such that deeper dimensions of freedom and expression are possible.

Building on Cray's account, Daisy Dixon and Panos Paris's "Freedom—Nature—Satan: On the Beauty of Black Metal" extend the idea that black metal flirts with what Labbas termed the "idea of the unholy." Arguing that the thematics of freedom and nature and Satan in black metal are all a kind of beautiful expression of a particular ethics in black metal. An ethics that radically frees us from the potential bondage of external authorities and moral straightjackets. By reframing the moral dimension, they open spaces for a renewed engagement with black metal (in all its horrific presentations) as plausibly considered beautiful.

Shifting gears a bit from the focus on black metal, Jim Kanaris offers a sweeping trip through more traditional heavy metal in his "'The Light in the Window is a Crack in the Sky': Enecstatic Considerations of Metal." Developing a different aspect of the individualism mentioned by Dixon and Paris, Kanaris claims that heavy metal facilitates a kind of self-making whereby the individual stands out from the crowd in particular ways. This "enecstatic" depth is one that Kanaris highlights through a very personal trip through his own musical experiences and the way that not only his taste, but also his identity, was shaped as a result.

Whatever the genre of metal, one of the hallmarks of metal concerts is headbanging. In a chapter titled, "Headbanging as Kinaesthetic

Judgment," Jay Miller provides a profound analysis of headbanging as a kind of embodied response to musical expression. In what he terms an "aesthetic response to the heaviness of heavy metal," we express our moral being. Accordingly, headbanging is about far more than just swinging around long hair and giving yourself a headache. It is a mode of living whereby we are called by the music to a kind of knowing. This expanded conception of headbanging is, Miler contends, something that calls us to rethink what it means to experience music as "heavy" in the first place.

All of the chapters up to this point have to one degree or another made reference to the "heaviness" of heavy metal. But what exactly does such an idea indicate? In a chapter titled, "Heavy Timbres: What Makes Heavy Music *Heavy*?" James Dow attempts to offer one possible answer to this persisting question. Taking his impetus from the influential essay, "What Makes Heavy Metal Heavy?" by Jay Miller, Dow objects to Miller's idea of "Heaviness Mysterianism" such that the qualities of heaviness are indescribable to some degree. In contrast, Dow contends that heaviness can be positively described by focusing on the timbre of particular pieces of music. After a careful engagement with the arguments offered by Miller, Dow concludes with his positive vision for how to rethink what it means for music to be heavy.

Finally, *Part Four: Violent Sleep of Reason: On Epistemology* features chapters by Mikael Janvid, Benjamin McCraw, and Shelby Moser.

Mikael Janvid starts things off by looking at the role of trust in the epistemology of testimony in his chapter: "Anti-Social Black Metal Epistemology: Forming Beliefs without Trust in an Evil Environment." After laying the groundwork by stipulating the main contours of social epistemology regarding the role of trust in testimony, Janvid turns to second-wave black metal (especially the band Gorgoroth) in order to illustrate the potential ways that black metal might offer a kind of freedom for epistemically conscientious agents looking to escape the frameworks of power and authority that too often are untrustworthy from the outset.

Benjamin W. McCraw's contribution to this volume is one that illustrates the ways that epistemic discourse is morally laden. In his "Talk Shit, Get Kissed: Death Metal, Misogyny, and Epistemic Resistance," McCraw looks at the truly horrifyingly misogynistic lyrics and imagery on display within much of death metal in order to suggest that things might not be as simple as it might initially seem. Drawing on the work of Kate Manne, McCraw contends that her precise definition of misogyny allows for a more rigorous critique of those aspects in death metal that are well worthy of moral opposition. However, McCraw also shows that there are some threads in death metal that are actually quite feminist in tone and impact. In some shocking turns of events, McCraw concludes that death metal might, itself, offer profound resources for challenging other aspects of death metal.

In the final chapter of the volume, Shelby Moser returns us to the question of the phenomenon of "heaviness" in her "The Heaviness of Play in Heavy Metal." Just as James Dow suggested that we could develop a positive account of the heaviness of heavy metal by looking at the timbre of the musical offerings, Moser suggests that such a positive account can be found by considering the role of "play" in metal music. Suggesting that a serious philosophical consideration of play can help better to understand the "normative attitudes and behaviors" of metal culture, Moser argues that the value of play is often overlooked in heavy metal. Seeking to correct this lack of attention, Moser locates play as central to the "*gestalt* of heaviness" that one finds on offer in the various musical styles that form heavy metal as a broad category of music and culture.

Whether you are a professional philosopher or a metalhead who is interested in what professional philosophers might say about heavy metal, we hope that you will throw up your horns, join us in the pit, and think deeply about the heaviest ideas in the universe.

Oh, and one final word before we move on: SLAYER!!!

References

Allett, N. (2011). The extreme metal connoisseur. *Popular Music History* 6: 166–181.

Bayer, G. (2017). Being Lemmy Kilmister: performativity and metal. *Rock Music Studies* 4 (3): 221–233.

Brown, A.R., Spracklen, K., Harris, K.K., and Niall, S. (ed.) (2017). *Global Metal Music and Culture: Current Directions in Metal Music Studies*. London: Routledge.

Buckman, C. (2017). A Kantian analytic of the ugly. *International Philosophical Quarterly* 57 (4): 365–380.

Cogley, Z. (2014). A study of virtuous and vicious anger. In: *Virtues and their vices* (ed. C.A. Boyd and K. Timpe), 199–224. Oxford: Oxford University Press.

Craig, W.L. (2008). *Reasonable Faith: Christian Truth and Apologetics*. Crossway Books.

Fenner, D.E.W. (2005). Why was there so much ugly art in the twentieth century? *The Journal of Aesthetic Education* 39 (2): 13–26.

Gaut, B. (1993). The paradox of horror. *British Journal of Aesthetics* 33 (4): 333–345.

Gracyk, T. (2016). Heavy metal: genre? style? subculture? *Philosophy Compass* 11 (12): 775–785.

Hagen, R. (2011). Musical style, ideology, and mythology in Norwegian Black Metal. In: *Metal Rules the Globe: Heavy Metal Music around the World* (ed. J. Wallach, H.M. Berger, and P.D. Green), 180–199. Durham, NC: Duke University Press.

Henry, P. and Caldwell, M. (2007). Headbanging as resistance or refuge: a cathartic account. *Consumption Markets & Culture* 10 (2): 159–174.

Hick, D.H. (2022). Horror and its affects. *The Journal of Aesthetics and Art Criticism* 80: 140–150.

Hjelm, T., Kahn-Harris, K., and LeVine, M. (2011). Heavy metal as controversy and counterculture. *Popular Music History* 6: 5–18.

Kahn-Harris, K. (2007). *Extreme Metal: Music and Culture on the Edge*. NY: Berg.

Kieran, M. (1997). Aesthetic value: beauty, ugliness and incoherence. *Philosophy* 72 (281): 383–399.

Kirner-Ludwig, M. and Wohlfarth, F. (2018). METALinguistics: face-threatening taboos, conceptual offensiveness and discursive transgression in extreme metal. *Metal Music Studies* 4 (3): 403–432.

Manea, I.-M. (2020). Aesthetic heathenism: pagan revival in extreme metal music. *[Inter]sections* 23: 59–76.

Mbembe, A. (2024). *Brutalism*. Durham, NC: Duke University Press.

McCraw, B.W. (2024). Brutal truth: modern(ist) aesthetics and death metal. *Journal of Aesthetics & Culture* 16 (1): 1–13.

Miller, J. (2022). What makes heavy metal 'heavy'? *The Journal of Aesthetics and Art Criticism* 80 (1): 70–82.

Murphy, S.T. (forthcoming). Why delight in screamed vocals? Emotional hardcore and the case against beautifying pain. *The British Journal of Aesthetics*.

Paris, P. (2017). The deformity-related conception of ugliness. *British Journal of Aesthetics* 57 (2): 139–160.

Patterson, D. (2013). *Black Metal: Evolution of the Cult*. Port Townsend, WA: Feral House.

Phillipov, M. (2012). *Death Metal and Music Criticism: Analysis at the Limits*. Lanham, MD: Lexington Books.

Purcell, N.J. (2003). *Death Metal Music: The Passion and Politics of a Subculture*. Jefferson, NC: McFarland & Company, Inc.

Reyes, I. (2013). Blacker than death: recollecting the "black turn" in metal aesthetics. *Journal of Popular Music Studies* 25 (2): 240–257.

Sauchelli, A. (2014). Horror and mood. *American Philosophical Quarterly* 51 (1): 39–50.

Scott, N. (2014). Season in the abyss: heavy metal as liturgy. *Diskus (Frankfurt Am Main, Germany)* 16 (1): 12–29.

Scott, N. (2016). Heavy metal as resistance. In: *Heavy Metal Studies and Popular Culture* (ed. G. Riches, D. Snell, B. Bardine, and B. Gardenour Walter), 19–35. London: Palgrave Macmillan.

Sederholm, C.H. (2016). H. P. Lovecraft, heavy metal, and cosmicism. *Rock Music Studies* 3 (3): 266–280.

Sharman, L. and Dingle, G.A. (2015). Extreme metal music and anger processing. *Frontiers in Human Neuroscience* 9 (272): 1–11.

Spracklen, K., Brown, A.R., and Kahn-Harris, K. (2011). Metal studies? Cultural research in the heavy metal scene. *Journal for Cultural Research* 15 (3): 209–212.

Unger, M.P. (2016). *Sound, symbol, sociality: the aesthetic experience of extreme metal music.* London: Palgrave Macmillan.

Vernezze, P.J. (2008). Moderation or the middle way: two approaches to anger. *Philosophy East and West* 58 (1): 2–16.

Wallach, J., Berger, H.M., and Greene, P.D. (ed.) (2012). *Metal Rules the Globe: Heavy Metal Music around the World.* Raleigh, NC: Duke University Press.

Walser, R. (1993). *Running with the Devil: Power, Gender, and Madness in Heavy Metal Music.* Middletown, CT: Wesleyan University Press.

Weinstein, D. (1991). *Heavy Metal: The Music and Its Culture.* Da Capo Press.

Weinstein, D. (2014). Just so stories: how heavy metal got its name—a cautionary tale. *Rock Music Studies* 1 (1): 36–51.

Wiederhorn, J. and Turman, K. (2014). *Louder Than Hell: The Definitive Oral History of Metal.* New York: It Books.

Woods, R. (2017, February 4). Black Sabbath: “We hated being a heavy metal band”. *BBC News.* `https://www.bbc.com/news/uk-england-birmingham-38768573` (accessed 8 August 2025).

Xhignesse, M.-A. (2024). The heaviest metal. *Philosophia* 52: 681–697.

Part I

None So Vile: On Ethics

Chapter 1
Conflicted: Moshing, Meaning, and the Dialectics of a Problematic Community

Nick Smith
Department of Philosophy, University of New Hampshire, Durham, NH, USA

Born in 1972, I grew up with moshing in an uncritical way as it migrated from Southern California to D.C., New York, Boston, and into middle America.[1] I remember sleeping over at my grandparent's after trick-or-treating in 1981 and enjoying the usual Saturday night television lineup: Lawrence Welk, Barbara Mandrell, The Love Boat, and Fantasy Island. Something unusual punctuated prime time: Fear performing "Beef Bologna" on Saturday Night Live (SNL). As a

[1] For excellent histories, see Blush (2001) and Azerrad (2001).

child, this looked fun and silly—but also a little scary. Were those people really fighting or were they acting? Was it a Halloween joke, like the other SNL skits? Did I just hear the F-word? When the broadcast cut abruptly, I wondered if the studio had lost control and if there was a riot. Or was that a staged disruption and part of the show, like how fake commercials are comedy segments on SNL?

I experienced moshing first-hand when a few friends erupted hearing Anthrax's "Caught in a Mosh" from a boom box in a farmhouse kitchen circa 1987, banging into appliances and collapsing into a "pig pile."[2] Parents sent us to the barn for the rest of the evening. One of my friends at the grocery store where I worked showed up with a Stormtroopers of Death (S.O.D.) shirt. The crew got to talking about Star Wars versus Nazi stormtroopers, and how S.O.D. were referring to the latter. One of the more sophisticated cashiers chastised the kid in the shirt along the lines of: "They say 'Speak English or Die'. They're racist and that shirt is gross." Deploying edgelord tactics common today, the S.O.D. fan pointed to his shirt: "It's a JOKE. Don't you see the anarchist symbol? Anarchists hate Nazis." I was confused, like after Fear on SNL. Metal was interesting and alternative, but also kind of wrong. I wanted to be a little "edgy," but the wrongness overflowed with ambiguity. Metal and moshing were *questionable*. What is this? Why do I like it? Should I not identify with this stuff? If I wear a death metal shirt, am I wearing it ironically—and is that an ambiguity I want to cultivate? Is this interesting and important, or juvenile and insensitive? The questions evolved through college and continue into my adulthood. I've written and presented on various kinds of metal, asking "why hardcore goes soft" through commercialization and why the "splinter in your ear" probably does not do much to transform the world.[3] I've been knocked unconscious (GWAR, very slippery), had my watch bitten off when trying to help someone up (Slayer), witnessed my friend get a tooth knocked out (Melvins), and accompanied my own teenagers into the heart of some active situations where they've suffered some injuries. I've broken up fights, helped strugglers get out of pits, and administered medical aid to various people. Why do I place myself and my family in these situations?

---

[2] Anthrax, "Caught in a Mosh," *Among the Living*, Island Records, 1987.

[3] See Smith (2005) and Smith (2002).

I confess to a conflicted relationship with metal, and with moshing in particular.[4] Some of my happiest, most life-affirming moments have been in metal pits. This is embarrassing to admit in an academic context, especially as an over-50 white male philosophy professor who enjoys a very fortunate life filled with many good things. But metal pits scratch a very satisfying itch. Why does such a juvenile, alcohol and testosterone soaked, violence-glorifying scene offer such appeal? Is my enjoyment something I should avoid or outgrow, like laughing at an inappropriate joke or attending an N.F.L. game while players suffer from C.T.E.? Are there ways to preserve the best in moshing and minimize the worst without killing the spirit? In this chapter, I will make three arguments. First, moshing presents considerable negative aspects that range from literal violence and death to the sorts of absolute commodification of the semblance of alternative life that reinforces the status quo, as Adorno warned. Second, moshing can be a highly meaningful and—despite *prima facie* appearances—ethical activity. Third, measures can be taken at various levels—by individuals, by community leaders, by bands, by venues, and by legislators—to steer moshing culture toward its better angels.

I should note that this paper sometimes conflates metal and punk. Some readers will prefer cleaner boundaries between the genres and will assert that metal and punk pits differ significantly. Some will assert that metal pits tend to be more problematic than punk pits, with metal generally trending more far right. I find these complex and interesting issues—see, for example, Jello Biafra's comments below on Nazi punks—that would benefit from further studies, including how these dynamics have evolved since the 1970s. I hope readers will keep these important nuances in mind.[5]

McMoshing, WWF Aesthetics, and the Commodified Semblance of Resistance

First, the obvious: Moshing is dangerous, and the danger is inherent to the appeal. Various studies document the rates of moshing injuries, finding head injuries the most common and crowd surfing an especially

[4] This papers sometimes conflates metal and punk. Some will prefer cleaner boundaries between the genres, and will assert the metal pits differ significantly from punk pits.
[5] Thanks to A. Seth Young for this fruitful line of inquiry.

dangerous activity.[6] According to one study, between 7 and 20 per 10,000 moshers require transportation to a hospital. Studying moshing injury rates presents obvious difficulties, including the fact that not all attendees enter the pit for all or even a portion of the show. Most attendees avoid the pit at most shows, so the rate of injury for "full-time" moshers would likely be much higher. Many suffering injuries will not seek medical help, in part because moshers expect "battle wounds" and seeking medical care can seem contrary to the ethos and even emasculating. Deaths and catastrophic injuries in mosh pits are more likely to be reported. Well-publicized deaths have occurred at shows from Smashing Pumpkins (two deaths, one in 1996 and another in 2007), Lamb of God, Limp Bizkit, Pearl Jam (9 dead), and the Travis Scott Astroworld "mass casualty event" (10 dead). Large gatherings of excited people present inherent risks, and even mild concerts can end in death. When teen heartthrob David Cassidy announced at a 1974 concert that he planned to retire, the ensuing mob crushed a 14-year-old girl to death. So while this is not an issue specific to hardcore shows, this genre explicitly invites and celebrates violence.

Some metal artists see themselves as responsible for these harms and have discouraged or banned moshing at their shows. The Smashing Pumpkins' Billy Corgan announced at a 1996 show that they "publicly take a stand against moshing!"[7] Slipknot's Chris Fehn stated that "especially in America, moshing has turned into a form of bullying. . . . The big guy stands in the middle and just trucks any small kid that comes near him." "They don't mosh properly anymore," Fehn explains, "It sucks because that's not what it's about. Those guys need to be kicked out" (Childers 2014). At the Drive In's Cedric Bixler-Zavalar chastised a 2006 audience: "All the guys, if you wanna go beat the shit out of each other please don't do it at our show . . . when we write songs we don't intend so that you guys can get out your male aggression. I like to dance" (Jonze 2012). Ian Mackaye would often lecture against moshing from the Fugazi soapbox, and Reddit boards are filled with lore of people getting kicked out of pits for being too hardcore. In an evolving artistic genre dedicated to pushing boundaries, metaphysical and definitional questions arise about the nature of moshing: what is moshing, what doesn't count as "proper" moshing, what are

[6] For discussions of injury rates, see Milsten et al. (2017), Janchar et al. (2000), and Pogrebin (1996).
[7] See discussion in (MTV.com 1996).

the constitutive norms and limits, who decides, and who controls the pen when defining the limit between dance moves and assault?[8]

Many fans will, frankly, mock these concerns from the dance police as un-metal wankery. Like the people who complain about the N.F.L. becoming "too soft" for protecting players from brain damage, you can hear the Viovod anthem directed at anyone who tries to lecture on moshing safety: [Expletive] off and Die. Some bands will do everything in their power to make pits as violent as possible, for example cajoling large festival crowds into Braveheart-looking "walls of death" where hundreds or thousands of mostly young men sprint into each other from opposite directions on the band's command. Photos and videos of these events capture the Berserkers at Ren Faire vibes.[9] For many bands and audiences, a raging pit signifies an intense and effective performance that whips the crowd into a frenzy. The term "praisepit" typically refers to especially enthusiastic group religious worship, but it can also recognize the relation between moshing and appreciation: the liveliness of the pit is a kind of metal ovation. Middle fingers to the band provide another common form of performatively defiant ironic appreciation.

Which brings us to Travis Scott. Building on the historical overlaps between moshing, hip hop, and rap, Scott cultivated the "raging" aesthetic of his brand to great success.[10] As described by Mark Elibert in the 2025 Netflix documentary, "Hip Hop has always been going against the system. . . . [Scott] was positioning himself to be that person to be like 'yeah. . .fuck the system'."[11] Encouraging moshing, crowd surfing, stage diving, and climbing on venue structures, Scott often incited the crowd by exhorting "We want rage!" and "Rage with me!" (Williams 2021). As a child, Scott dreamed of becoming a professional wrestler, and he wanted his shows to "feel like it was the WWF" (Green 2015). Prominent critic Trent Clark explains that "Travis Scott's whole aesthetic is about rebellion. . . . The shows have a lot of raging." According to Clark, "with the death of punk rock, hip-hop has indeed adopted and patterned the new generation of mosh pits. . . It's not uncommon to see a lot of crowding and raging or complete wild behavior at a Travis Scott show" (Williams 2021).

[8] Genuine thanks to Sean Murphy for pointing out these important questions that deserve their own paper.

[9] For photos, see Grundke (2017).

[10] For a discussion of the migration of mosh pits to hip-hop, see Caramanica (2021).

[11] For a discussion of the origins of Scott's rager reputation and analysis of the events leading to Astroworld's mass casualty event, see Bamiro and Poulter (2025).

Rebellion as a profitable brand has been a well-worn theme in Adorno and other critical theorists. But while formalist rebellion in the style of Jackson Pollack or Arnold Schoenberg might induce a wave of pearl-clutching, Scott's attempts to extract profit from disaffection itself literally annihilates the alienated. Scott was arrested in 2015 at Lalapalooza and again in 2017 at the Walmart Arkansas Music Pavilion for inciting riots at performances (Coscarelli 2021). A 2017 concert in Manhattan left Kyle Green paralyzed when he was pushed off an overcrowded third-story balcony while Scott exhorted his fans to jump (Dillon 2021). Publicity along the lines of "People get carted out of my show" was well worth a few thousand dollars in disorderly conduct fines, 12 minutes of police detention, and a year of court supervision. These legendary "ragers"—note that a "rager" can also refer to a binge drinking party without any moshing—increased Scott's crossover appeal with the hardcore community, and he occupied the center of popular culture as he dated and fathered two children with Kylie Jenner of Kardashian fame. The Astroworld album launch included collaborations with Nike, Nerf, Hot Wheels, Reese's, Dior, and the Houston Astros and Houston Rockets. McDonald's offered the Travis Scott Happy Meal—apparently without crediting Happy Flowers' 1989 "Unhappy Meal" noise punk classic. Scott's "Sicko Mode" on the Astroworld album became a Billboard Number One single. His virtual concert within the Fortnite video game had 28 million viewers, a remarkable moment in the evolution of rage.

This contextualizes the 10 deaths at the 2021 Astroworld Festival. Advertising emphasized storming security barricades, riotous moshing, and tightly packed aggressive pits (Sharp 2021). The documentary *Look Mom I Can Fly* shows Scott's security team warning the Astroworld event staff: "You will see a lot of crowd-surfers in general, but also you see a lot of kids that are just trying to get out and get to safety because they can't breathe, because it's so compact. . .You won't know how bad it can be with our crowd until we turn on" (Coscarelli 2021). Concert producers Live Nation sold 50,000 tickets for a venue designed for 35,000 and lost control of entry points, allowing thousands more unticketed fans to pour in by overpowering guards and easily collapsing perimeter fencing. Promotional videos glorified gate-crashing. Via Twitter, Scott encouraged "sneaking in." The postmortem videos and analysis show 50,000 people—some raging while others scream for help with compressed lungs. People call 911 from the crowd, climb onto the stage to plead for help because "people are dying," and chant to end the show. Drake joins Scott on the stage to preen and further incite the crowd. Aware of mounting dangers and seeing people crushed and unconscious, Scott instructs the crowd to "give a middle finger to the sky" if they are ok. The show goes on, and the *New York Times* reported that Scott continued in part because of the contractual condition that he would be paid 4.5 million only if he finished the show.[12] A nine-year-old boy watching from his father's shoulder is crushed to death. The show ends 15 minutes early. Ten died from compression asphyxia and related injuries.

Twenty years ago, I wrote on the blatant contradictions of noise metal as it became a mainstream critique of the mainstream. We can rehearse Adorno's greatest hits applied to Scott's latest commercialization of raging against the social order. "Even when the public does, exceptionally, rebel against the pleasure industry," Adorno writes, "all it can muster is that feeble resistance which that very industry has inculcated in it. . ." (Adorno and Horkheimer 1972, p. 145). Moshing in general and Scott's version of raging in particular exist in an ideological semblance of resistance. As Adorno puts it, "all are free to dance and enjoy themselves, just as they have been free, since the historical neutralisation of religion, to join any of the innumerable sects. But freedom to choose an ideology—since ideology always reflects economic coercion—everywhere proves to be freedom to choose what is always the same" (Adorno and Horkheimer 1972, p. 145). The "pseudo individuality" Adorno described pervades metal culture, moshing, and rager scripts. In some instances, the obviousness of the contradiction gives rise to a second-order critique: "This is not a Fugazi T-Shirt." Adorno coined the "absolute commodity" as the art object that parades its contradictions as the priceless yet just very expensive thing of bourgeois revolutionaries. Sometimes metal's second-order self-awareness takes an openly ironic stance. Sometimes this becomes ebullient satire, as when GWAR cosplays with Jerry Springer, Joan Rivers, and Fox News. But the culture industry easily absorbs the critical and self-reflective significance of any art, and we seem to have entered a phase where metal and its forms of expression via dance exist primarily as violent and extreme commodities reinforcing the status quo. In 2025, that status quo seems especially unsettling.

Metal and moshing have long struggled with questionable attitudes toward race and gender.[13] Nazis and skinheads have been hanging around moshing since the early days, and reviewing posters and promotional

[12] For a discussion of the settlements, see Goodman (2024).
[13] See Spracklen (2020).

materials from the 1980s demonstrates how even anti-authoritarian bands like SSD would stylize their "SS" with the very obvious Schutzstaffel runes of Germanic mysticism. Sometimes described as a shock value nihilistic spit in the mainstream face, metal played with fire. Fascist iconography in hardcore music attracted second-wave white power skinheads. Aggression and Iron Cross aesthetics provided a tent big enough for both Straight Edge and Hate Edge. When both the left and right attack the mainstream, they sometimes converge. Policing boundaries became an explicit theme. When the Dead Kennedys released "Nazi Punks [expletive] Off," Jello Biafra recognized how moshing appealed to the far right. He explained in a 2012 interview:

> I wrote that song in 1981, and at the time, it was aimed at people who were really violent on the dance floor; they didn't call it mosh pits yet. It began to attract people showing up just to see if they could get in fights in the pit or jump off stage and punch people in the back of the head and run away. I noticed some of the really bad thugs were clearly not teenagers, they looked quite a bit older, which makes me wonder if they were really undercover cops. People started asking me "Are you down with this? Things are changing, the audience is younger, hard core is coming up and it's a more extreme form of punk," and I liked that kind of music, but I thought if we're gonna play this music, we need to distance ourselves from that side of the scene. The initial premise of the song was "You violent people at shows are acting like a bunch of Nazis," and that was as far as it went. Then the real ideological Nazis began coming out of the closet. They attacked Dead Kennedys shows after that. One time, a more hardcore version of (Britain's) National Front showed up in tandem with the road crew of a band, and that connection always creeped me out. Punk is such an extreme form of music, the most extreme form of rock and roll ever invented, and it's always attracted different kinds of extremes.
>
> (Brown 2012)

In other words, extreme music attracts extremists. The lyrics of this anti-fascist anthem try to explain the difference between anti-authoritarian critical theorist punks and violent authoritarian cultist punks:

Punk ain't no religious cult
Punk means thinkin' for yourself
You ain't hardcore, 'cause you spike your hair

When a jock still lives inside your head...
If you've come to fight, get outta here
You ain't no better than the bouncers
We ain't tryin' to be police
When you ape the cops, it ain't anarchy...
Ten guys jump one, what a man
You fight each other, the police state wins
Stab your backs when you trash our halls
Trash a bank if you've got real balls...
You still think swastikas look cool
The real Nazis run your schools
They're coaches, businessmen and cops
In a real fourth Reich, you'll be the first to go...
You'll be the first to go, you'll be the first to go
You'll be the first to go, unless you think[14]

As much as I embrace the "thinkin' for yourself" ethos and the long-held reputation of punk and metal as generally anti-authoritarian, Biafra's need to draw this distinction speaks to how blurred the lines had become. If Biafra recognized this danger in 1981—and again in 2012 when white power musician Wade Michael Page murdered six people in a Wisconsin Sikh temple—we should wonder about the company we keep in the metal pits of 2025. I attended multiple Pantera shows in the 1990s, thinking the fan base was dodgy but the shows were worth it. By 2016, Phil Anselmo was giving the Sieg Heil, screaming "white power," and getting shows canceled in Germany and Austria.[15] Suspicion of these artists is justified, though I am fairly certain that certain hardcore artists—for example Hüsker Dü's Bob Mould—will age gracefully.

We sometimes speak of something "glorifying violence," but we do not need to ally with Tipper Gore to appreciate that in many senses moshing does, in fact, glorify violence. Fascism also glorifies violence according to all major accounts.[16] Many metal lyrics scream and growl the praises of all manner of death, cruelty, decapitation, disembowelment,

[14] Dead Kennedys, "Nazi Punks [expletive] Off," *In God We Trust, Inc*, Alternative Tentacles, 1981.

[15] See the *Rolling Stone* interview for a discussion of the events, Anselmo's apology, and his views on race (Grow 2016).

[16] See, for example, the centrality of violence to fascism in accounts provide by Paxton (2005) and Stanley (2020).

cannibalism, and malevolence.[17] This is so obvious that the cliché rises to satire, pushing into fascist and other taboo themes to test the boundaries of offensiveness. Stormtroopers of Death's Scott Ian thought literal readings of their Nazi references were "ridiculous": "Some people thought we were racist, and those people are stupid." Bandmate Dan Lilker corroborated: "The lyrics were never intended to be serious, just to piss people off" (Bodenner 2016). Anselmo claimed his white power episode referred to being drunk on white wine.[18] We saw a similar rhetorical strategy from Elon Musk's raised arm salute at the presidential inauguration and his subsequent Nazi-themed puns chastising anyone who took offense. "I can't believe he trolled so hard," Musk's supporters crowed, and if you take it literally, then you're an idiot. Aesthetic negation is a readily conscripted mercenary's weapon, and the far right and the far left both rage against the middle with whatever is at hand. Sometimes they find themselves unwitting allies collapsing the establishment.

Embodied Solidarity and the Tragic Sublime

This brings us to another Nazi-adjacent troll: Nietzsche. As with moshing, I have conflicted opinions about Nietzsche. Other than perhaps Diogenes, Nietzsche seems like the most metal philosopher. The beyond good and evil ethos, the obsession with religion, the provocative style and adversarial tone, and his "barely sane" vibes make it hard to imagine metal existing without Nietzsche. Nietzsche provided many metal-worthy passages, and you could randomly choose any Nietzsche text and probably generate viable lyrics. For example: "The great epochs of our life come when we gain the courage to rechristen our evil as what is best in us" (Nietzsche 1974, p. 168). For a more literal Pantera will to power mood: "In this state one enriches everything out of one's own fullness: whatever one sees, whatever wills is seen swelled, taut, strong, overloaded with strength. A man

[17] Sean Murphy reminds us that "emotional hardcore" tends toward very different content: "looking at emotional hardcore thematically, we see that the lyrics engage with themes like self-disappointment, anxiety, abandonment, love, loss, longing, existential emptiness, sadness, nihilism, and a slew of other emotional and existential maladies. A heavy sound for some heavy feelings." See Murphy (2025) and Murphy (2024a,b).

[18] "Anselmo's initial reaction to the uproar was to make light of it, saying 'white power' was an inside joke because he'd been drinking white wine backstage. 'No apologies from me', he said at the time. But that changed within a couple of days" (Grow 2016).

in this state transforms things until they mirror his power—until they are reflections of his perfection" (Nietzsche 1968, p. 268). Early German existentialism sounds like a caricature of Bro-Metal manosphere, but as with Nietzsche, things are more complicated.

The *Birth of Tragedy* captures especially well how metal and moshing can provide the sort of aesthetic experience that transforms nihilism into life affirmation. Nietzsche writes, for example:

> Here, when the danger to his will is greatest, *art* approaches as a saving sorceress, expert at healing. She alone knows how to turn these nauseous thoughts about the horror or absurdity of existence into notions with which one can live: these are the *sublime* as the artistic taming of the horrible, and the *comic* as the artistic discharge of the nausea of absurdity.
> (Nietzsche 1967, p. 18)

In this light, metal artists have alchemical abilities of turning the darkest existential threats into joyous release. Judging by the look of it, mosh pits tend to attract those wrestling with the call of the void. Many refer to metal and moshing as cathartic, but Nietzsche better captures the ethos. Gather dreadnaughts to dance and imbibe various stimulants and intoxicants, and we have a setting fitting of young Nietzsche's idea of a profoundly good time:

> If we add to this terror the blissful ecstasy that wells up from the innermost depths of man, indeed of nature, at this collapse of the *principium individuationis*, we steal a glimpse into the nature of *Dionysian*, which is brought home to us most intimately by the analogy of intoxication. . . .
> (Nietzsche 1967, p. 18)

After a flurry of metalogical word salad such as "narcotic draught," "hymns of all primitive men," "Germanic Middle Ages singing and dancing crowds," "emotions awake," "complete self-forgetfulness," "St. Vitus's dancers," "Bacchic courses," "Babylon and the orgiastic Sacae," "folk-diseases," "poor wretches," "cadaverous looking and ghastly," and "glowing life of the Dionysian revelers rushes past them," Nietzsche continues:

> Transform Beethoven's "Hymn to Joy" into a painting; let your imagination conceive the multitudes bowing to the dust, awestruck—you will approach the Dionysian. Now the slave is a free man; now all the

> rigid, hostile barriers that necessity, caprice, or "impudent convention" have fixed between man and man are broken. Now, with the gospel of universal harmony, each one feels himself not only united, reconciled, and fused with his neighbor, but as one with him, as if the veil of maya had been torn aside and were now merely fluttering in tatters before the mysterious primordial unity.
>
> (Nietzsche 1967, p. 20)

This is classic Nietzsche working both sides waxing poetic about a state of ecstatic transcendence where people from all walks of life simultaneously dissolve their individuality and also exercise their will. Music plus pro-social intoxicants drive the selfing/unselfing cultic scene, viscerally seducing us into embodied life. We experience this together in a pit, literally colliding wills while genuflecting on the unifying power of the band. As Boris puts it, a communion of "amplifier worship" arises with the "multitudes bowing to the dust, awestruck" (Nietzsche 1967, p. 20). The experience approximates a sense of both self-expression and community, both will and the negation of will. Religious themes within musical form and content reinforce the existential heaviness, invoking premodern rituals and meaning systems. "Now the slave is a free man" when he moshes and momentarily exists untethered by various boundaries and hierarchies, and feels unity in this abyss with fellow dancers. Think here of Sunn O))), droning "heady metal" in their druid robes before entranced crowds. But it is, of course, an illusion. The lights come on, we don't actually pray to metal gods, and we have not overthrown anything. We go back to work in the morning, we buy some merchandise as we exit the play-cult exhilarated by a mild and temporary collective illusion. It is also on the verge of funny, often more Spınal Tap than political rally. If anyone takes it too seriously—for example by actually fighting, being too intoxicated, or stalking the band—they get kicked out of our heavy metal play date.

But, for a brief time, we can experience something like a superabundant ideal of life. Like Giacometti's account of the existential thrill of being hit by a car making him feel like he was, finally, "living," moshing can provide an intensity distinct from other art.[19] Adorno spoke of certain modernist works being like a punch in the nose to habits of cognition of modernity, but for us the experience of Schoenberg does not carry the same impact. For many of us, moshing offers a proximation of a respite

[19] See Lord (1985), Chapter 10.

from excessive instrumental rationality in moments of intense aesthetic engagement. When the grind and banality of existence sap energy, metal seduces us to life and raises spirits. The heavy metal play date strikes me as a funny idea, but for Nietzsche play—becoming again a child rather than a camel or lion—stands as perhaps the highest achievement for adults.

But unlike listening to metal at my desk to summon the will to grade papers or doing my taxes, moshing offers an in-the-flesh community.[20] If travel is life intensified, moshing distills a lot of humanity. The self-expression and the selflessness intertwine, with as much life-affirming thrill from helping someone up as from going hard. Moshers are not actual brothers in arms and aren't even Fight Club wannabees, but they are inviting each other to aesthetic physical contact outside of sport. That is rare, interesting, and a potentially meaningful form of camaraderie in this collective art game we call moshing. As Nietzsche would put it, we are "a living thing that seeks above all to discharge its strength" (Nietzsche 1966, p. 13). There are a few other relatively safe and legal places where adults can publicly "discharge" in such a frenzied manner. Many forms of dance provide similar opportunities across many subcultures, from vestiges of premodern rituals to people describing their "transcendent" experiences at repeated Phish and Grateful Dead shows.

All things considered, moshing creates a vital outlet for aesthetic engagement, especially for certain demographics of the disaffected suffering from acute cases of grappling with the "terror and horror" of the tragic view of existence in a "botched civilization."[21] The cultic aspects reenchant the world, providing a kind of pop-up tribe receiving musical communion. Part extreme sport, part therapy, part gallows humor, part solidarity, it makes sense that metal and moshing provide deep meaning for many. One commentator explains: "Metal is the aural representation of my spiritual need to transgress traditional boundaries, not just of music, but of general social expectation. Deeply rooted in me is a desire to search for the liminal space where the divine can still be found outside of where authority says it should be" (Coker 2025). Perhaps this takes metal too seriously, but many readers will appreciate this point. When I

[20] Can someone mosh alone? That presents a definitional question avoided in this paper, but I imagine many readers have enjoyed moments of enthusiastic solo dancing to metal.
[21] "Botched civilization" is Ezra Pound's phrase in his poem "Hugh Selwyn Mauberly." Pound was imprisoned for treason as a fascist supporter.

mention both that moshing provides some of the happiest moments and that this fact is embarrassing, Nietzsche again captures the tension:

> Perhaps such readers will find it offensive that an aesthetic problem should be taken so seriously—assuming they are unable to consider art more than a pleasant sideline, a readily dispensable tinkling of bells that accompanies the 'seriousness of life,' just as if nobody knew what was involved in such a contrast with the 'seriousness of life.'" Let such 'serious' readers learn something from the fact that I am convinced that art represents the highest task and the truly metaphysical activity of this life.
> (Nietzsche 1967, p. 20)

Although we're hardly Wagnerian self-creators, the pit does cultivate such "metaphysical activity." It also provides plain old physical activity, which *Rolling Stone* documented in an article title "Why Moshing is Good for You" (McCaffrey 2017). Perhaps this is nostalgia for my own youth or desperation for activities more meaningful than screen rotting, but as a parent, I hope my children continue to have these opportunities for such existentially rich play. Are there ways to encourage the best parts of moshing while discouraging the worst, and do so without destroying it? I think so, to some extent.

Pit Elders, Shepherds, and Counselors: Regulated Rage?

Offering "Best Practices," "Pit Praxis," or an etiquette guide for moshing sounds like another SNL skit. Telling people how to "mosh properly" evokes "if it's too loud, you're too old," a saying apparently popularized by Ted Nugent (Sullivan 2007). I once took my 15-year-old to a show, and he got whacked in the mouth by a guy who suddenly started throwing high elbows. Seeing the shock on my son's face and unsure if he lost a tooth (he didn't), I told the guy, "elbows down" and pointed at the shell-shocked kid. He seemed apologetic and even sheepish, and I immediately regretted saying anything. I brought an inexperienced young person into that situation, and I scolded an adult trying to have a good time exorcising their demons. Perhaps he wasn't moshing particularly *well* according to my vague and implicit set of standards, but too many rules can ruin the game—especially when the game is about certain kinds of freedom and self-expression. As Nietzsche puts it in his resistance to always subordinating aesthetics to ethics, there are good reasons that the "fight against purpose in art is always a fight against the moralizing tendency in art, against its subordination to morality" (Nietzsche 1990, p. 90).

But, as discussed, there are real dangers. People die. People also die skiing, skateboarding, and in other sports that serve a similar existential purpose in embodied risk-taking. Higher risk often correlates with higher potential rewards. Skiers wear helmets. Mountains designate trails by degree of difficulty. It is difficult to imagine protective headgear in the pit, but something like labeling "double back diamond" shows might have a place. We can approach minimizing the bad and optimizing the good in moshing at different levels: by individuals, by community leaders, by bands, by venues, and by legislators.

At the individual level, it helps if people understand what they are getting into. An inexperienced and heavily intoxicated young person stumbling into a large, aggressive pit endangers everyone. Like a novice skier thinking they can handle an advanced trail and exposing others to risk as they lose control, people interested in moshing should be self-aware of their abilities. Thoughtful observation of the situation before diving in is generally a good strategy. Novices should avoid the most dangerous situations, such as large, raging crowds with limited exit paths or festival "walls of death."

For those who would appreciate more explicit guidance on this nuanced and dynamic social situation, the Shreveport law firm Morris and Dewett provides solid advice. A southern personal injury firm dedicating a page to "Mosh Pits: Rules, Etiquette, and Everything You Need to Know about Rage Culture" might seem odd, but it attests to attorneys' awareness of potentially lucrative cases arising from moshing-related damages. Morris and Dewett explain that "mosh pits can be seen relatively regularly at rap shows leaning into rage culture and less ragey electronic dance music (EDM) festivals. Pits can even break out in surprising places, like among Swifties" (Morris and Dewett 2025). They offer a summary of "the music world's mosh pit rules to keep the experience safe and fun" with this preface:

> Mosh pits can seem chaotic and dangerous on the surface, but they generally operate with an underlying set of unspoken rules and expectations that promote safety and fun for everyone involved. At the heart of moshing is a sense of camaraderie, respect, and surprising control.

> Proper mosh etiquette keeps everyone safe from unnecessary harm. That's not to say that mosh pit participants never leave with a blackened eye or broken bones. Accidents inevitably occur when large adults play rough and throw their bodies into a pulsating crowd. However, the intention behind a good mosher does not involve harming others. The idea of community over chaos rules the mosh pit, and many veterans of hardcore music shows share stories like warriors returned from battle. At the core, a sense of wild abandon is at play. Few other events allow adults to let animalistic instincts (mostly) take over to the point of catharsis. However, a sense of community and control is at the heart of a good mosh pit. If someone falls, moshers should help them back up so they don't get injured. This communal element is one of the most important aspects of mosh pit culture that breed fun and camaraderie. Avid moshers often describe it as a feeling of "brotherhood." Sometimes, a "bad apple" or a newbie unfamiliar with mosh pit culture can jump into a pit and start swinging fists, clearly seeking to cause harm. Generally, the pit has its way of handling these misfits, but not always before damage is done. And even in a pit of the most well-meaning and experienced moshers, serious accidents can happen.
>
> (Morris and Dewett 2025)

They follow with sections on "Helping Fallen Participants," "Respecting Personal Space," "Recognizing Exit and Entrance Points," "Creating a Positive Atmosphere" ("A smile or a well-timed head nod can let fellow moshers know you appreciate their adherence to the pit's unspoken rules"), "Keeping Anger in Check," "Allowing Exits for Others," "Safety Precautions," "Inclusivity in the Mosh Pit," and more advice on "Enjoying Mosh Pits Responsibly." They also offer some legal advice: "If you fall and suffer a blow to the head, you should speak with a blunt force trauma lawyer regarding your options. For mosh pit accidents at typical concert venues, a premises liability lawyer can answer your questions and evaluate your claim." "If you or a loved one finds themselves a victim of a mosh pit injury," they conclude, "Morris & Dewett Injury Lawyers may be able to help" (Morris and Dewett 2025). If we should have adults—and lawyers—in the room, Morris and Dewett seem like reasonable counselors.

In addition to concert attendees individually arriving prepared, experienced crowd members can be extra vigilant, modeling the "help each other out" ethic and scanning for potential dangers. If you know from experience how these situations evolve, you become a Pit Elder. Pay attention to people falling and then help them. If someone spills a drink, help with that so it does not result in a slip and fall injury. If you see tension mounting between dancers that might take a turn for the worse, dance between them. At a recent show, we saw an overzealous teenager annoying an older guy with clenched fists who seemed ready to fight. A simple solution was to befriend the young guy, dance with him, and de-escalate by steering him in another direction. We did not need to scold anyone, and this small intervention added to the fun. The vocalist of the band—an elder in the New England hardcore scene—saw this transpire, and thanked me after the show. That recognition felt genuinely meaningful for me, like blessings of the metal community. If you see something out of line, alert security and keep an eye on it. Alert others, especially those who seem to be attentive and experienced. If someone looks hurt, help get them out and get them medical attention. Sometimes people injured in pits are very intoxicated and may resist help or medical intervention. Make the handoff to professionals.

Some of the most serious injuries and deaths result from asphyxiation and crowd crush. Many of us have felt versions of this when we dance hard, start breathing heavy, and are so tightly packed that we can barely restore breath. Be alert for early warning signs, especially when people struggle to remove themselves and access less dense areas. Hold space for them or forge a path of exit if you can. Working through a crowd can be both physically and socially difficult, so an experienced "snowplow" clearing the way can be a significant and even life-saving help for people struggling to remove themselves. Areas near the stage can be especially dangerous in this regard as people pile up and compress between a barrier stage and an active pit. If you see someone struggling, it can help to "box out" people near them. Address these issues early to prevent an Astroworld situation where the pileups are hundreds deep. Sometimes security is excellent, and checking in with them as a friendly face can help. Security is often understaffed and underpaid. Sometimes security is incompetent. I believe I have a duty to do what I can in the rare situations where help is needed. If you feel that a show has become too dangerous, several bands have suggested that holding your arms over your head in an "X"—a widely recognized signal to stop and provide assistance—can be the clearest way to communicate to the band in that environment (DiVita 2021). If Pit Elders become too intoxicated, they become more of a liability than an asset on these fronts.

Audience members can only do so much, and bands, venues, and lawmakers set the structural conditions for these situations. Part of the safety challenge results from moshing transcending musical genres. Most people know what to expect at a Napalm Death show, and the crowd has a high ratio of "elders" who know how to comport themselves and who can recognize and diffuse potential dangers. This might not be the case when masses of people find themselves in a raging crowd at a large Travis Scott or even Taylor Swift show, which can become like dropping tens of thousands of novice skiers on a double black diamond. As we saw at Astroworld, some navigated this with children on their shoulders. We do not need to parse comparative blame of concertgoers, parents, and promoters to appreciate that the artists and venues play a significant role.

Artists and venues literally set the stage. Band members monitor and orchestrate crowds. As experts in the ecosystems of their pit, they are uniquely qualified to identify and call out problems. As revered authorities, they hold a unique power to influence the behavior of their fans. If band members explicitly address an issue in the crowd, they have the microphone and the credibility. Metal theatrics calibrate the energy in a venue, slowing down or speeding up pit tempo with song selections, props, breaks, and various other levers they push and pull to create high-energy shows. If needed, the band can stop playing, turn on the lights, and drain the room. Bands can also make clear that certain views are not welcome at their shows, including racism, misogyny, and transphobia.

If, however, the band cultivates a "raging" and "out of control" identity, lifting the veil and addressing safety issues can break the fourth wall. Unmasking the "more hardcore than thou" image can undermine a band's credibility, which can in turn have commercial consequences. "Old guard" metal bands can be less concerned about damaging their long-established *bona fides* and should have more expertise preventing, recognizing, and addressing dangers. Artists greener to the scene will have less experience, a more vulnerable image, and less financial security to face the consequences of stopping a show. Astroworld combined many of these dangers: promotional materials promising gate-crashing rager chaos, oversold tickets, 50,000 concertgoers unfamiliar with the dangers of such an environment, a young artist on stage riling up the crowd as he is paid to do, a cameo from Drake adding more fuel while screaming concertgoers are pleading *en masse* to stop the event, and the show continuing for 37 minutes after it had been declared a mass-casualty event. Before Scott even went on stage, the festival's manager of security texted a colleague: "There's panic in people's eyes. . .This could get worse quickly" (Brown 2023). He followed up: "I would pull the plug but that's just me. . . . I know they'll try to fight through it but I would want it on the record that I didn't advise this to continue. Someone's going to end up dead." Subsequent investigations raised questions about what and when Scott knew about the situation, and why he continued to perform. He claimed he was doing his job and awaiting instructions. "Normally if it was something drastic," he told the Houston Police Department, "someone would have to come hit the button or pull the plug." Sound engineers and other event staff on site claimed that Scott and his event producers knew of the mounting deaths, continued performing, and had expected and encouraged such "mayhem" (Brown 2023). Ten people died. No criminal indictments resulted.

If artists, promoters, and venues stand to profit from such dangerous events without facing criminal liability and if insurance covers civil exposures, it begins to resemble another Houston-based disaster: the Deepwater Horizon explosion killing 11 and causing immense environmental damages. In both situations, warning alarms were sounded, the show went on, people died, no one went to prison, and insurance covered losses. When incentive structures prioritize profits over lives, governmental regulators can increase safety standards, compliance, and civil and criminal penalties for violations of crowd management laws. This can include stricter occupancy and crowd density limits, staffing and staff training requirements, unreserved and open seating restrictions, banning stage diving and crowd surfing, and concert-specific safety approvals.[22] Video surveillance of crowds and mosh pits to identify offenders and enforce restrictions has predictably gained support, so concert attendees should be aware that they are on camera—a panoptical reality spreading throughout private and public life (Milsten et al. 2017). Such laws, however, have proven difficult to establish and vary considerably by jurisdiction (Milsten et al. 2017). Crowd-surge, hooligan, and white-supremacist violence in international soccer stadiums present similar challenges in fanatical event management, and the United States could learn from the international crowd management community.

The regulatory path faces many obstacles in the United States. Of course, monied interests who own venues and profit from concerts generally support limiting their civil and criminal liabilities for concert injuries and deaths. Culturally more "freedom-loving" and less paternalistic than comparator nations, the moshing demographic in the United States seems unlikely to lobby for political action for safer

[22] See safety discussions in Milsten et al. (2017).

shows. Artists surely do not want to be held personally liable for injuries and deaths at their shows, and in one case the difference between United States and European attitudes played out rather dramatically. In 2010, Lamb of God's Randy Blythe "threw" teenager Daniel Nosek off a stage in Prague. Reading the testimony and viewing the video, Blythe's actions looked rather typical of metal shows. Fans often rush the stage, and it is common to see energetic dancers try to climb up onto the stage to almost immediately jump off—classic "stage diving." Band members often give them a "push," sometimes in good fun that looks more like a pat on the back as they rile up the crowd and sometimes more firmly with annoyance because someone has overstayed their welcome or is getting in the way. In the heat of performances with frenetic body contact all around, there are many context-specific nuances that can blur the line between assault and performance. The artist, the venue, the crowd, the region, and other factors all impact the mood and norms. The situation also speaks to the need of metal artists to protect themselves after Pantera's Dimebag Darrell was shot to death mid-performance in 2004 by an obsessed fan who rushed the stage. When Blythe pushed Nosek, the young fan hit his head and subsequently died. The Czech police charged Blythe with manslaughter. With Blythe having returned to Richmond, Czech authorities unsuccessfully sought cooperation from the United States. Upon returning to the Czech Republic in 2012, he was arrested and tried. The United States metal community rallied in support of Blythe's innocence, generating a petition with 27,500 signatures and public statements from Dave Brockie of GWAR and others.[23] Within the United States, it seemed unthinkable that pushing someone off a stage could land a famous artist in a former Nazi and Iron Curtain prison. Ultimately acquitted, Blythe committed to becoming "a spokesperson for safer shows." The lesson for the community, however, remains unclear. Even with 10 dead at Astroworld and Travis Scott and Live Nation executives allowing the show to go on while watching dead or dying bodies passed overhead in the most macabre crowd surfing, no one received criminal penalties. "Caveat Emptor" could make a good libertarian metal band name, and the "assume the risk" mentality runs deep. This cocktail of radical individualism plus financial disincentives makes significant state intervention into concert safety unlikely.

[23] See discussion in Michaels (2023).

Especially in the United States, moneyed interests design these laws to protect moneyed interests.

In conclusion, moshing is problematic, and much of its meaning is a function of its problematicness. I recently attended a Deftones show at TD Garden with mostly reserved seating—reserved both in the sense of a pre-purchased spot to occupy and reserved as quiet and mostly keeping to oneself. From the bleachers, I envied the moshing general admissions crowd on the floor. But those tickets were going for over $300, a considerable premium to upgrade my metal experience to first class. Like Satanic Panic, the nearly ungovernable thrill of metal and moshing only increases its desirability—and its commercial value. Travis Scott's 2024 follow-up tour to Astroworld became the second highest grossing rap tour of all time, suggesting that Scott and Live Nation executives suffered little in the court of public opinion for the 10 deaths (Frankenberg 2024). The confidential settlement agreements with the families of the dead—sums covered by event insurance rather than from the pockets of culpable executives—now seem like worthy investments to commodify the chaos of Scott's brand. We can wonder if GG Allin could have been a commercial success in the general social and political context of 2025, perhaps opening at Astroworld with a Live Nation budget. What would we pay to see that, in person or from a distance on pay-per-view?

The norms and regulations guiding moshing vary by genre and region, and especially in the United States, it is unlikely that governmental or other collective action will do much.[24] So we're probably on our own, with some counsel from lawyers who will continue to sue promoters until market forces make shows safer. Most of the mosh pit injury litigation, however, ends in confidential settlement agreements paid by insurers. This does little to make shows safer when insurance premiums are less than the profits to be gained.[25] So the next time you or your loved ones attend a show, you should not expect the artist, the promoter, the venue, or the government to ensure your safety. This leaves us mostly as individuals convening to consider the force of Slayer's categorical imperative and social contract of grace in the pit: "That's what you're here to do, help each other out. This is a song called *War Ensemble. . . .*"[26]

---

[24] For a collection of essays on global metal culture, see Wallach et al. (2011) and Varas-Díaz et al. (2023).

[25] See discussion of tort liability in mosh pits in Kim (2023).

[26] This appears in the introduction to the live version of "War Ensemble," Slayer, *Decade of Aggression*, American Records, 1991. It can be heard at https://youtu.be/-zy-80RQUis.

References

Adorno, T.W. and Horkheimer, M. (1972). *Dialectic of Enlightenment*. Translated by John Cumming. New York: Continuum.

Azerrad, M. (2001). *Our Band Could Be Your Life: Scenes from the American Indie Underground 1981–1991*. Boston: Back Bay Books.

Bamiro, Y. and Poulter, H., directors (2025). *Trainwreck: The Astroworld Tragedy*. Netflix.

Blush, S. (2001). *American Hardcore: A Tribal History*. Port Townsend, WA: Feral House.

Bodenner, Chris. 2016. Track of the Day: 'Speak English or Die'. *The Atlantic* (8 February).

Brown, August. 2023. Houston Police Release Long-Awaited 1200-Page Report on Travis Scott Astroworld Disaster. *Los Angeles Times* (28 July).

Brown, August. 2012. Jello Biafra on 'Nazi Punks' and Hate Speech. *Los Angeles Times* (9 August).

Caramanica, Jon. 2021. How the Mosh Pit and 'Raging' Came to Hip-Hop. *The New York Times* (9 November).

Childers, Chad. 2014. Slipknot's Chris Fehn: Moshing Shouldn't Turn into Bullying. *Loudwire* (10 December).

Coker, Sam. 2025. Metal Music: A Hunger for Transgressive Spiritual Spaces. *Open Spaces* `https://www.openhorizons.org/metal-music-a-hunger-for-transgressive-spiritual-spaces.html` (accessed 11 April).

Coscarelli, Joe. 2021. Before the Astroworld Tragedy, Travis Scott's 'Raging' Made Him a Star. *The New York Times* (8 November).

Dillon, Nancy. 2021. Man Paralyzed at 2017 Travis Scott Show 'Devastated' for Astroworld Victims. *Rolling Stone* (6 November).

DiVita, Joe. 2021. Lamb of God's Randy Blythe Shares Tips to Effectively Signal a Problem at a Show. *Loudwire* (15 November).

MTV News 1996. Fan Crushed at Smashing Pumpkins Show. *MTV News* (19 May).

Frankenberg, Erik. 2024. Travis Scott''s Circus Maximus Set New Record for Highest Selling Tour by a Solo Rapper. *Billboard* (November 2024).

Goodman, David. 2024. 'Someone's Going to End Up Dead': Settlements over Fatal Astroworld Concert. *The New York Times* (8 May).

Green, Mark Anthony. 2015. How to Rage with Travis Scott. *GQ* (3 August).

Grow, Kory. 2016. Phil Anselmo Opens up about Racism, Pantera''s Legacy, Childhood Abuse. *Rolling Stone* (22 December).

Grundke, Vincent. 2017. These Are the Most Epic 'Wall of Death' Photos from Germany's Wacken Festival. *Vice* (12 August).

Janchar, T., Samaddar, C., and Milzman, D. (2000). The mosh-pit experience: emergency medical care for concert injuries. *American Journal of Emergency Medicine* 18: 62–63.

Jonze, Tim. 2012. Why I Don"t Need a Faceful of Sweaty Armpit to Appreciate a Gig. *The Guardian* (20 July).

Kim, Miles. 2023. Tort Liability in the Mosh Pit. *The Columbia Journal of Law & the Arts* (27 September).

Lord, J. (1985). *Giacometti: A Biography*. New York: Farrar, Straus and Giroux.

McCaffrey, Shannon. 2017. Why Moshing Is Good for You. *Rolling Stone* (21 April).

Michaels, Sean. 2023. Lamb of God Frontman Breaks Silence after Being Acquitted of Manslaughter. *The Guardian* (8 March).

Milsten, A.M., Tennyson, J., and Weisberg, S. (2017). Retrospective analysis of mosh-pit-related injuries. *Prehospital and Disaster Medicine* 32 (6): 636–641.

Morris, T. and Dewett, J. (2025). Mosh pits: everything you need to know about rage culture. `https://www.morrisdewett.com/mosh-pit-rules-and-guide/` (accessed 11 April 2025).

Murphy, S. (2024a). Why delight in screamed vocals? Emotional hardcore and the case against beautifying pain. *The British Journal of Aesthetics* 64 (4): 625–646.

Murphy, Sean. 2024b. Sean T. Murphy (Southern Utah University) Why Delight in Screamed Vocals? Emotional Hardcore and the Case Against Beautifying Pain. *New Work in Philosophy* (30 June 2025).

Nietzsche, F. (1966). *Beyond Good and Evil*. Translated by Walter Kaufmann. New York: Vintage.

Nietzsche, F. (1967). *The Birth of Tragedy*. Translated by Walter Kaufmann. New York: Vintage.

Nietzsche, F. (1968). *The Will to Power*. Translated by Walter Kaufmann and R.J. Hollingdale. New York: Vintage.

Nietzsche, F. (1974). *The Gay Science*. Translated by Walter Kaufmann. New York: Random House.

Nietzsche, F. (1990). *The Twilight of the Idols*. Translated by R.J. Hollingdale and Walter Kaufmann. New York: Penguin.

Paxton, R. (2005). *The Anatomy of Fascism*. New York: Vintage.

Pogrebin, Robin. 1996. Hard-Core Threat to Health: Moshing at Rock Concerts. *New York Times* (9 May).

Sharp, Rachel. 2021. Astroworld Under Fire as Promotional Video Showing Chaos at Past Gigs Remains Online after Eight Killed. *The Independent* (8 November).

Smith, N. (2002). Why hardcore goes soft: Adorno, Japanese noise, and the extirpation of dissonance. *Cultural Logic* 4 (3).

Smith, N. (2005). The splinter in your ear: noise as the semblance of critique. *Culture, Theory & Critique* 46 (1): 43–59.

Spracklen, K. (2020). *Metal Music and the Reimagining of Masculinity, Race, and Nation*, 2020. Bingley, UK: Emerald Publishing.

Stanley, J. (2020). *How Fascism Works*. New York: Vintage, 2020.

Wallach, J., Berger, H.M., and Greene, P.D. (ed.) (2011). *Metal Rules the Globe: Heavy Metal Music Around the World.* Durham, NC: Duke University Press.

Varas-Díaz, N., Wallach, J., Clinton, E., and Araújo, D.N. (2023). *Defiant Sounds: Heavy Metal Music in the Global South.* Lanham, MD: Lexington Books.

Williams, Austin. 2021. 'We Want Rage': 2015 Video Shows Travis Scott Hyping Crowd at Lollapalooza. *Fox News* (8 November).

Sullivan, Caroline. 2007. Is Music Too Loud, or Are You Too Old?*The Guardian* (June 5).

Chapter 2

"Poser!" Snobbery, Identity, and Gatekeeping

Catharine Saint-Croix[1,2]

[1]Department of Philosophy, University of Minnesota Twin Cities, Minneapolis, MN, USA

[2]African Centre for Epistemology and Philosophy of Science, University of Johannesburg, Johannesburg, Gauteng, South Africa

Introduction

> **ICP.** Aaron is working behind the counter at Acute Cacophony Records when Petra, a young woman wearing an Insane Clown Posse (ICP) shirt, steps up to the counter to ask where the Slayer records are. Aaron looks up from his phone, sees her shirt, and says "Can you even name any of their songs?" Petra panics and her mind blanks. After half a second, Aaron points to his colleague re-stocking the bins and sighs, "Go ask him. He's on poser duty."[1]

Aaron is a metal snob.[2] But, as I'll argue below, nothing about this encounter is snobbish according to existing philosophical accounts of snobbery. That's for two central reasons. First, philosophers have largely focused on aesthetic judgments. But, Aaron's judgment isn't about the aesthetic quality of ICP, Slayer, or anything else. His judgment is about the social group *metalheads* and what they ought to be like. Second, relatedly, philosophers have not focused on the social function of snobbery. Accusations of poserhood, however, put this function right out front: Gatekeeping.[3] In this chapter, I argue that snobbery—at least in the cases like **ICP** where it seems morally objectionable—is best understood through its motivational profile. Snobs are those who empower themselves to engage in unwarranted, identity-protective gatekeeping and thereby discourage or block individuals from exploring the lives they reasonably wish to explore. This perspective provides grounds for expanding the extension of snobbery beyond the bounds of aesthetic judgment and plucks at a thread that unifies several existing accounts of snobbery. To begin, I explain existing accounts and demonstrate that cases like **ICP** do not fit them. In the next section, I explore the relationships between gatekeeping and accusations of poserhood. This explanation provides grounds for the conception of "gatekeeping snobbery," which I develop in the section that follows. I then argue that the motivation underlying gatekeeping snobbery not only picks out a common thread binding several of

---

[1] I adopt the spelling "poser" rather than "poseur" because I take it to better capture the understanding of the term as used by the subcultures at the center of this paper. See Cook (2025) "Only Posers Spell it 'Poseur'" for further discussion.

[2] Aaron is also a jerk and bad at his job.

[3] Ironically, as Patridge (2018) points out, accusations of snobbery have been used for the same function.

the accounts previously discussed but also helps to explain why we find snobbery off-putting, even to the point of moral culpability. In closing, I reply to an overgeneration worry and trace out consequences of the view. Notably, I show that many cases of transphobic "feminism" turn out to be instances of gender snobbery.

Philosophical Snobbery

Even though the snobbery in **ICP** occurs within the context of an aesthetic domain (metal music), this case fails to exhibit key features of aesthetic snobbery, as it is discussed within philosophy. The literature has identified four forms of snobbery: social contagion snobbery (Kieran 2010), attitudinal snobbery (Patridge 2018), contextual snobbery (Patridge 2018), and straight-up classist snobbery (Johnson King 2023).[4] In this section, I review these accounts and argue that **ICP** fits none of them.

Kieran (2010) argues that snobbery is a property of aesthetic judgments, arising from their causal origins. *Social Contagion Snobbery*[5] occurs when aesthetically irrelevant social features play a causal role in forming one's judgement of some aesthetic object's value. Both the formation of the judgment and its realization are fundamentally driven by the desire to feel or appear superior in relation to some individual or group. The snob's error is that their primary reason for appreciating the work is not the work itself, but the social prospects of appreciating the work. True appreciators are distinguished from snobs by the fact that they care about their experience with a work for itself. In contrast, snobs appreciate or pronounce on some aesthetic object because as doing so enables them to appear socially superior.

Kieran's account aims to reconcile the fact that a snob's claims can be true with the observation that we often feel as though snobbery somehow undermines their judgment. The reason for this feeling, Kieran argues, is that the snob's judgments are based on the wrong kinds of reasons. Snobs make aesthetic claims for social reasons, and therefore, we should not trust those judgments (even though they may turn out to be true!). Kieran

[4] Though, as Patridge (2023, p. 5) points out, we might also draw these together into two forms.

[5] Patridge (2018) dubs Kieran's (2010) account "social contagion snobbery" to distinguish it from her own.

is surely right that the pronouncements of snobs are dubious, and any account of snobbery ought to try to accommodate this fact. But, Kieran's account prevents those whose aesthetic acumen is authentically earned from being snobs.

In a case like ICP, this matters because the causal story of Aaron's aesthetic judgments of metal music may be completely free of desires for social superiority. People can become snobs about a form of art even when they came to appreciate it genuinely. Moreover, unlike opera or classical music, a refined palate for metal music is not widely regarded as demonstrating general social superiority. The same goes for other "alt" genres. This is because there is neither historical nor modern upper-crust association for these art forms (sometimes, as in the case of punk, they *cultivate* explicitly low-class associations). So, metal is not an apt target for Kieran's snob. Thus, the aesthetic judgments in the background of **ICP** likely have the wrong causal structure for social contagion snobbery.

ICP also evades Kieran's definition because the target is wrong. Social contagion snobbery focuses on judgments about particular aesthetic objects as such. But, no such judgment is central to **ICP**: Aaron is not appreciating an aesthetic object. He judges that because Petra is wearing an ICP shirt, she probably isn't a "real" metalhead, but this is entirely compatible with Aaron actually *liking* ICP. Even the judgments behind Aaron's views about "real" metalheads need not be aesthetic judgments. He might, for example, think that "real" metalheads would know better than to wear an ICP shirt to the metal store, since ICP are rappers. Or, he might think that ICP are the sort of group usually loved by edgy kids who will grow out of their edginess in a month or two. These are not aesthetic judgments. Instead, they are judgments about the behavior and preferences of people in particular social groups. I return to this point in the next section.

But not all snobs are social contagion snobs. Patridge (2018) offers two further accounts of snobbery: *attitudinal snobbery* and *contextual snobbery*. The *attitudinal snob* behaves in ways that demonstrate their self-superiority. This self-superiority is rooted in the view that the snob's aesthetic judgments are more refined than others and that this refinement makes them "more socially valuable, or more socially worthy, or just a better sort of person than their perceived appreciative inferiors" (245). Attitudinal snobbery involves the view that superior capacity for aesthetic judgment renders one more socially worthy—just a better sort of person.

Aaron, however, need not believe this in order to act the way he does. He does not need to think that his appreciative skills are better than Petra's. Aaron just needs to think that Petra (1) doesn't have the sort of knowledge that a "real metalhead" would, and (2) that she isn't authentically interested in metal. He might make no judgment at all about her appreciative capacities or might think something like, "If she'd just bother to listen, she'd see that Black Sabbath is the best metal band." Moreover, Aaron needn't take himself to be a better sort of person. Were Petra the shift manager for a food shelf, a surgeon coming off of a 12-hour shift, or a grade school teacher on her way home from a long day, he might think she's a "better sort of person." He just needs to not want to associate with people who aren't metalheads. Whether he regards metalheads as "better people" is a different question, and not one that bears on whether his behavior toward Petra is snobby. Despite shaming Petra and calling her a poser, Aaron does not appear to be an attitudinal snob.

Patridge also identifies *contextual snobbery*, which "involves a failure to see that the nuances of a social context can affect the sorts of appreciative judgments that are appropriate to make in that context" (2018, p. 249). More specifically, contextual snobs deploy their (perhaps merely apparently) more sophisticated appreciative capacities "in ways that one ought not, where part of the explanation for this involves features of the social context and background presumptions about the socio-hierarchical ranking of the appreciative skills in question" (Patridge 2018, p. 249). The thought here concerns the background social knowledge we share: Displaying sophisticated judgments about "high-class" aesthetic objects can be a way of demonstrating social superiority. Given that, if you know that I don't have access to education about or experience with those objects, ostentatiously displaying your knowledge of them is a sure-fire way to demonstrate social superiority relative to me. Thus, it is inappropriate to do so in polite social contexts.

To see the sort of case Patridge has in mind, imagine that you're hanging out with friends from the neighborhood you grew up in for the first time in a decade or so. The conversation turns to putting on a movie, and classic suggestions are flying around the room: *Clueless! Mean Girls! 10 Things I Hate About You!* And, before you can stop yourself, you hear yourself saying, "but, we should really watch something from the Criterion Collection, don't you think?" Feeling the air go out of the room, you freeze. Everyone looks at you with a mix of embarrassment at their unsophisticated taste and cringe for you—this is contextual snobbery.

ICP does not exhibit this form of snobbery because there is no such failure on Aaron's part. He is not failing to calibrate his expressions to the social demands of the context. Quite to the contrary, he is setting and meeting them.

Finally, Johnson King (2023) argues that the paradigmatic form of snobbery is what she calls *straight-up classist snobbery*, which occurs when an individual's aesthetic judgments are inappropriately influenced by their low-class associations with the aesthetic object in question. This is evident in people's use of class-loaded concepts like "tacky," "trashy," or "chavvy." Aaron also eludes straight-up classist snobbery. This is because his views about what real metalheads are like have nothing to do with class-influenced valuations.

So, Aaron's case does not fit the mold of any of these species of snobbery. Aaron's judgments about metal music and Petra aren't caused by a desire for superiority (he genuinely likes the music for its own sake), he doesn't think he's a better person than Petra (though he does think he's a metalhead and she's a poser), he doesn't misunderstand the social appropriateness of his actions (he very clearly intends to shame Petra, and his co-worker is in on it), and he doesn't believe that liking ICP is low-class (he just thinks no one who's *really* a metalhead would *also* like ICP or be wearing an ICP shirt at the shop).

Though I'll argue that contextual snobbery is not exactly a form of snobbery below, I think each of these accounts gets at something important. In fact, I think they all point to different aspects of the same, underlying motivational flaw that is characteristic of snobby behavior more generally: unwarranted identity-protective gatekeeping. The sort of gatekeeping that Aaron does is just the most direct outgrowth of this. To see this, we turn now to gatekeeping itself.

Gatekeeping

Gatekeepers decide who merits passage. In social contexts, gatekeeping is a matter of determining who is (or is not) allowed into a social group. Some social groups, such as *honor roll student*, have designated gatekeepers (e.g. the administrator or computer program checking that you do, in fact, have the requisite GPA). But, many social groups do not have such designees. This is because social group membership is seldom so formally articulated—the honor roll is the exception, not the rule.

Social Blueprints and Group Membership

Instead, social group membership is usually assigned on the basis of the extent to which we cohere with the *social blueprint* associated with that group. Social blueprints are broadly shared "clusters of beliefs, concepts, attitudes, and so forth that give rise to [. . .] concrete practices" (Dembroff and Saint-Croix 2019, p. 547). For example, the social blueprint surrounding metal music consists of beliefs about the traits of a piece of music in virtue of which it ought to be called "metal" (versus, say, rock, hardcore, punk, etc.), the broadly held attitudes about metal music (e.g. metal is "hard," maybe scary), conceptions of what people who like metal music are like (e.g. they listen to a lot of metal music, they wear a lot of black, are often men who have long hair, etc.), and so on. Being perceived as possessing enough of these traits (usually over a sufficient duration) results in being assigned membership in the group.[6]

Such assignments determine how individuals are treated by those around them: Those assigned social group membership are treated as members of the group. In the case of *honor roll student*, this is obvious. Honor roll students are given a special designation on their diplomas, their names are printed in various newsletters, and perhaps the school sends them specially prepared college application materials. They are treated differently in virtue of being recognized as honor roll students. The same goes for fuzzier cases, too. If you are assigned the social group *climber*, people are more likely to chat with you about climbing, invite you along to go climbing, or get you climbing-themed gifts around the holidays.

This difference in treatment also extends to the way people think about you and your dispositions: Your assignment to a particular social group in virtue of fitting the social blueprint enough of the time means that the default assumption will be that you also fit other, untested aspects of the blueprint. Continuing with the *climber* case, if you are assigned the social group *climber*, people will assume that you are generally athletic, that you'll probably take them up on an invitation to go hiking, that you can do a pull-up, that you know who Alex Honnold is, and so on.

[6] Note that being "assigned" group membership should be understood as a matter of social perception, rather than a matter of social ontology. As will become apparent, being assigned a social group is not the same as being a member of that group.

Importantly, these social group assignments can be wrong. This might happen because the social blueprint for a group does not match the actual conditions for group membership or because the perception that an individual coheres with that blueprint is mistaken. As an example of the former, someone who identifies as a woman, but has a masculine presentation (never wears make-up, doesn't wear clothing that emphasizes the shape of their body, doesn't adopt feminine vocal presentation or mannerisms, and so on) might not be assigned the social group *woman*. In this case, that would be because the social blueprint associated with *woman* doesn't match the actual group membership conditions for *woman*.[7] An example of the latter would be a clerical error in the honor roll case that caused your GPA to look higher than it really is.

Posers and Gatekeepers

Against this background, we can offer definitions of *poser* and *gatekeeper*. A *poser* is one who inauthentically behaves in ways that cohere with the social blueprint associated with a particular social group for the sake of being perceived as a member of that group. Within "alt" subcultures—metal, punk, hip-hop, skate culture, etc.—the term *poser* is used derogatorily, with the lack of authenticity being called out as a disqualifying characterological failure. This is the sort of behavior described in hardcore band MDC's *Poseur Punk*:

> There you go, scruffy and mean
> All tattooed and pierced for the scene
> Smoking that cigarette to capture your pose
> All the groovy looks for the clothes you chose
> Everything is about making you look good
> As if other people and objects really could
> Hey, Mr. Peabrain, it's what's inside
> Not what's on the outside that is so contrived
> Why don't you just try to be real?
> That vanity is making you a heel
> Find what you want and then do it right
> A little tip, it won't happen overnight (*MDC* 2004)[8]

[7] There is much to be said about the nature (or existence) of such conditions. I do not aim to enter into that discussion here, except to say that adherence to customs of femininity is likely either insufficient or irrelevant to them.

[8] MDC, *Poseur Punk*, Magnus Dominus Corpus, Beer City Records, 2004.

The poser adopts the mannerisms (scruffy and mean), behaviors (smoking), and fashions (tattoos, piercings, clothing styles, etc) of the punk scene, but does so for the sake of vanity. In doing so, the poser adheres to externally perceptible aspects of the *punk* social blueprint in order to be perceived as a punk, but lacks the beliefs and authentic affection for the music, politics, and culture—"it's what's inside, not what's on the outside," "find what you want and then do it right"—that really matter.[9]

Someone who calls another person out as a poser is acting as a *gatekeeper*. The primary characteristic of gatekeepers is that they are vigilant against inappropriate inclusion in their group. As such, they care deeply about what makes for a "real" member of their group and watch out for posers and others who inauthentically portray themselves as group members. One behaves as a gatekeeper, then, not only when they are actively keeping someone out of a particular group, but also when they are assessing someone's appropriateness and when they are ruminating or opining on what is required for proper membership in the group. Gatekeepers might call out or otherwise shame those they have identified as inappropriately included (or attempting to become inappropriately included), but they need not. Instead, they may simply treat them as if they were not group members. This might manifest in snubbing behavior (refusing to talk to them at a show) or merely in thought (making assumptions about their preferences).

Gatekeepers can also be wrong. Gatekeepers often operate by looking for subtle failures in a poser's attempts to cohere with the relevant social blueprint. In **ICP**, Aaron sees Petra's shirt and takes it as evidence that she doesn't actually understand the social blueprint for metalheads. He then tests her by asking her to name Slayer songs and, because he's bullied her into silence, concludes that his hunch was right. But, Aaron is wrong about Petra—she isn't inauthentic, she's just intimidated and new to the scene.

Despite Aaron's poor behavior and the term's broader pejorative connotation, gatekeeping is not always a bad thing. As Dormandy and Grimley (2024) point out, scientific gatekeeping concerns determining what research counts as "science," and it is important that pseudoscientific research that does not meet the epistemic standards of scientific practice is kept out of scientific journals. In this case, gatekeeping is valuable

[9] These motivations—vanity, fitting in, and so forth—are not the broad social superiority set out by Kieran (2010), Patridge (2018), and Johnson King (2023). We return to this point in the next section.

because of the many important social roles played by work labeled as "scientific." For example, scientists may be called upon to offer expert scientific testimony in legal settings, and our schools teach science rather than pseudoscience. "Transracial" identity is another case in which gatekeeping is often warranted, given the social meanings attached to ancestry (Botts 2018; Sealey 2018).

With this in mind, let's return to *Poseur Punk*. The central concern is clear: The poser is adopting the look without adopting the attitude. The song's speaker views some aspect of the internal attitudes associated with punk—such as personal freedom or anarchist/leftist political orientation—as required for being a real punk and they view the poser's vanity as antithetical to being a real punk. By calling out the song's target, they are acting as a gatekeeper. But are they a snob?

Gatekeeping Snobbery

To answer this, let me begin by explicating the concept of snobbery at hand. Gatekeeping snobbery is behavior characteristically motivated by unwarranted, identity-protective gatekeeping and is often carried out under the guise of authoritative judgment. A gatekeeping snob is one who is disposed to behave this way.

Identity-protective gatekeeping occurs when someone who is or takes themselves to be a member of a particular social group engages in gatekeeping for the purpose of asserting or protecting *their membership itself* or the *value of their membership.*

It is worth observing that publicly engaging in gatekeeping is a means of fulfilling that purpose: Insofar as social group membership is concerned, the opinions of members of the group itself often carry significant weight. Thus, acting as if one has the authority to do so is a way of asserting one's group membership.

Protecting Value

The "value" one protects through identity-protective gatekeeping depends on both the social blueprint associated with that group and an individual's dispositions toward it. Consider, for example, the social group *classical musician*. The social blueprint for this group includes upper-, middle-, or high-class backgrounds, social "refinement", artistic talent, dedication, and intelligence, among other things. For an individual who values these associations, being seen as a classical musician is, of course, valuable. For someone who prefers *not* to be associated with, say, a high-class background (such as the titular figure of *Poseur Punk*), however, such associations are unwelcome.

This individualization of value matters because it is this value—rather than general social values or hierarchy—that determines the motivations and actions against which we will evaluate the question of snobbery.

Identity-protective gatekeeping focused on the value of group membership protects that value *for the individual*. So, someone who values being a classical musician *because* (or in part because) of its high-class associations might gatekeep quite differently from someone who values it for the artistic associations. The former might look at Joshua Bell's subway busking experiments as unbecoming of a classical musician, while the latter might adore them (Macdonald 2022). Thus, if both of these musicians encountered a classical busker, the former might dismiss them as "not a real classical musician, because classical musicians don't make their money busking," while the latter might have no such gatekeeping reaction. This difference arises because, for the former, including street musicians among *classical musicians*, destabilizes the *high-class* element of the social blueprint, which they value.

Applying the View

Consider the *Poseur Punk* case. Quite plausibly, this is an instance of identity-protective gatekeeping: The song's speaker argues that the poser punk isn't *really* a punk because what *matters* is "what's inside." Insofar as the speaker worries that letting people who don't care about the attitudes and politics of punk be real punks devalues the culture and identity for them, this is a case of identity-protective gatekeeping.

Whether it's a case of snobbery, however, will depend on whether this identity-protective gatekeeping is warranted. The kind of warrant in question here is moral. Though I will not offer a particular first-order moral theory, the role of moral judgment is evident in the analysis of different instances of gatekeeping. Consider the example of transracial identity again. As Sealey (2018) argues, this may be a case of warranted gatekeeping because of the important cultural role that ancestry plays in the social blueprint for race and the moral value of maintaining that role. In the case of science, as we saw above, gatekeeping is warranted because of the social role that the demarcation of science plays—failing to do so risks causing harm to people.

By contrast, turning to **ICP**, part of what makes Aaron's behavior repugnant is the likely consequences. Suppose that this encounter deflates Petra (as it's intended to), and she loses interest in metal music and getting into the scene. Aaron's behavior thereby undercuts her exploration of a budding interest, which is a harm to her. This, I take it, is a fact for which Aaron is morally culpable. His gatekeeping of Petra serves no morally valuable purpose, whereas Petra's exploration did. And, this is how **ICP** differs—at least arguably—from the *Poseur Punk* case.

In the *Poseur Punk* case, we may surmise that what is valuable about punk identity for the speaker is having and being able to identify others who share the liberal, anarchistic, free-expression-focused political and social orientation that goes with much of the punk scene. Supposing that this is morally valuable, that value is threatened by dilution. Insofar as it this is correct, the sort of gatekeeping that MDC does with *Poseur Punk* may be warranted because it protects that valuable component of the social blueprint for punk. Importantly, it is also an *invitation* to the subject of the song to join in this culture. Where Aaron's behavior pushes Petra out, MDC's does not.

This discussion makes some important features of gatekeeping snobbery evident. First, whether a particular thought, action, or individual is snobby will turn on the moral facts of the case. Those facts might, as in **ICP**, concern the consequences of a behavior or they might, as in the case of *Poseur Punk*, depend on the moral value the social blueprint. Second, the severity of an instance of snobbery will depend, in part, on the severity of the moral fault involved. This is why it is particularly important not to lose sight of cases like those on which Johnson King (2023) focuses: Snobbery rooted in classism is important not only because it is common but also because it reinforces a classist social structure, which is a pernicious and pervasive source of wronging. By contrast, someone proclaiming that "Slipknot is for posers" while hanging out among their equally snobby friends is clearly a metal snob, but not a particularly egregious one. Policing the boundaries of "metal" is not, in and of itself, particularly morally significant and, since no one like Petra is around, the consequences of this action are minimal. Third, it will sometimes be difficult to discern whether a particular action is snobbery. If you read the lyrics of *Poseur Punk* and concluded instead that MDC is a bunch of snobs, you likely wouldn't be alone. For example, you might find the social identity of punk far less valuable than I have suggested it is, in which case the defense I've offered of MDC will fall flat. This is a reasonable disagreement, and one that is difficult to settle. It follows that the question of whether *Poseur Punk* is an instance of gatekeeping snobbery will be difficult to settle, too. I take this his difficulty to be a positive feature of my account because disagreement over whether someone was being a snob is a common feature of discourse on the matter. Finally, discerning whether someone's behavior is gatekeeping can also be difficult because discerning their intention—whether to draw you in or keep you out—can be difficult. We return to this point later.

Gatekeeping Snobbery in Context

I have defined Gatekeeping Snobbery as a distinctive form of snobbery. In this section, I explore the extent to which the same motivational profile underlies other forms of snobbery discussed in the literature.

Common Motivation

To begin, there are many ways the identity-protective motivational profile might manifest. For example, one might deploy their aesthetic judgments in ways intended to illuminate their own refinement relative to those around them. This is a way of asserting membership in the social groups associated with those judgments. Such behavior is essential to Patridge's (2018) affect-focused attitudinal snobbery. Patridge's conception is narrower because she focuses on cases rooted in the view that one's superior capacity for judgment renders them "a better sort." Nevertheless, the behavior serves the same purpose: asserting one's higher-class status.

Another manifestation might be allowing the social blueprint for a particular group to guide the way you form or express judgments. Suppose, for example, you arrive at Vessel—a white-walled coffee shop with Phothos and Monstera nestled in gold-accented white pots—and step up to the marble service counter to order your espresso. Suppose further that, upon sipping, you judge that the astringent, citrusy pucker you experience is "excellent" because you are sure that this is what members of the intelligentsia like you now judge to be excellent, despite the fact that you dislike the taste. This is identity-protective gatekeeping because it is action taken out of concern for the appropriate behaviors of group members (in this case, oneself as a member of the intelligentsia), and it is unwarranted because it is deceptive (if outwardly expressed) and inauthentic. But, it is also exactly the status-seeking avowal of aesthetic judgment that Kieran (2010) identifies as snobbery. So, while Kieran's conception of snobbery is focused on the etiology of one's judgments, that etiology has much in common with the characteristic motivational profile of gatekeeping snobbery.

Johnson King (2023), too, is concerned with etiology, but in a subtler way: Her focus is the distorting infiltration of status-relevant influence through concepts like "tacky" or "chavvy." These concepts, she argues, either embed the devaluing of things associated with lower-class people or are used by those behaving as snobs to articulate the same. Deployment of these concepts drips with distancing superiority, even if the judgment isn't itself formed out of the desire for superiority. As Johnson King writes, straight-up classist snobs, "get aesthetic evaluations wrong *because* they under-value that which they associate with being lower-class" (2023, p. 204). This is identity-protective gatekeeping because it serves to assert that one is *not* a member of the lower-class and it is unwarranted because it reinforces classist attitudes and stereotypes.

Thus, there is reason to think that these forms of snobbery—straight-up classist, attitudinal, and social contagion—are distinctive manifestations of the motivational profile that I have argued underlies gatekeeping snobbery.

What About Contextual Snobbery?

Snobs should be distinguished from what we might call *uncouth appreciators*. These are people who have genuine and genuinely formed appreciative attitudes, but are awkward, overly effusive, or otherwise inappropriate in expressing them. The uncouth appreciator is not interested in what makes someone a proper group member. They often offer their judgments as a way to invite others into the group that they love, without any motivation of keeping out the riff raff. But, there's a problem: The uncouth appreciator's expressions are easily misread.

This is because, generally speaking, human beings are deeply sensitive to being ostracized. So, the uncouth appreciator's effusive expression of an aesthetic judgment can, all at once, raise the salience of social groups attached to such aesthetic judgments, demonstrate the speaker's knowledge and experience (thereby suggesting group membership), and highlight the audience's lack thereof. Because we do not have direct access to others' motivations, wariness of being excluded or ostracized raises the specter that the speaker's motivation isn't just appreciation, but rather gatekeeping. Thus, in absence of reason to think otherwise, we (or at least the socially anxious mindreaders among us) can receive the uncouth appreciator as a snob, rather than a mere enthusiast. This dynamic, I think, underlies the kinds of cases Patridge (2018) has in mind when she defines *contextual snobbery*.[10]

The experience of being on the other end of contextual snobbery is indistinguishable from that of being the target of snobbery as I've suggested it should be understood. Nevertheless, I think we should distinguish the oblivious uncouth appreciator from the snob. This is for two reasons. First, insofar as snobbery is a vice of character, the motivational profile matters. And these two behaviors have very different motivational profiles; they pick out quite different character flaws. Second, and relatedly, because they pick out different character flaws, they have very different remedies. The uncouth appreciator might be mortified to realize that they were coming off as classist or otherwise snobbish, and the remedy is for them to become better attuned to the social nuances of their situation so as to avoid causing similar offense in the future. By contrast, the snob, as I've described them, is unlikely to be moved in this.

Overgeneration and Gender Snobbery

Before closing, I want to briefly address a looming objection: overgeneration. I've argued that gatekeeping snobbery is an important, underappreciated form of snobbery. I've also argued that the underlying motivational profile associated with it is a common thread uniting gatekeeping snobbery, straight-up classist snobbery, social contagion snobbery, and attitudinal snobbery. But one might worry that this motivational profile picks out too broad a class of cases to offer a useful understanding of snobbery.

Here are two ways this might go. First, gatekeeping snobbery extends well beyond the boundaries of aesthetic judgment. As defined, nothing constrains gatekeeping snobbery to the aesthetic realm. Even our central case, **ICP**, isn't really about an aesthetic judgment; instead, it is about the social blueprint concerning a particular group of aesthetic appreciators. And, I do not contest this point at all. The existing literature on snobbery

[10] However, this dynamic is broader than what Patridge identifies because it doesn't require a preexisting context in which the expression of such judgments is unwarranted. For them, a change in core values is necessary.

has focused on aesthetic snobbery, and for good reason: Nonaesthetic motivations are not only common but also obviously inappropriate in the context of aesthetic judgment, as Kieran (2010) emphasizes. But, snobbery arises anywhere wherever the desire to defend one's place in the social world arises. There are Ivy League snobs and public school snobs, car snobs and public transit snobs, co-op snobs and Target snobs, analytic philosophy snobs and continental philosophy snobs, and so on. Snobbery is everywhere, and it useful to pull on the common threads between these. Nevertheless, that common thread is merely a thread: While the motivational profile underlying gatekeeping snobbery is shared with the other forms of snobbery I've discussed, it is important that these other forms illuminate the particularities of aesthetic snobbery.

The second version of the overgeneration worry is more pressing. Identity-protective gatekeeping is common. Consider, for example, the modern dialogue around transgender recognition. On January 20, 2025, the President Trump signed an executive order entitled "Defending Women from Gender Ideology Extremism and Restoring Biological Truth to the Federal Government" (Trump 2025), which stipulates definitions for sex and gender terms in a way that intends to foreclose the legitimacy of transgender identity, at least according to the federal government. This executive order is the highest-profile outgrowth of a long-standing anti-transgender movement that, as the title of the order suggests, is often understood in terms of "protecting women." This order and the surrounding movement are many things, but—according to the present account—they are also an instance of snobbery. But this, the worry goes, is obviously false: There's no such thing as gender snobbery, and so we can see that the account overgenerates instances of snobbery.

This, however, is a bullet I am willing to bite. Absent an ability to establish warrant for the gatekeeping of trans* people from the categories with which they identify, what is left is akin to calling trans* people posers. Though there are many other, more urgent layers to such anti-trans* behavior, there is nevertheless a common thread binding the identity-protective accusation that trans women are "fake" and the accusation that someone like Petra is a poser. That thread is gatekeeping snobbery—gender snobbery indeed exists. Such snobbery even exists within queer communities. For example, where we police whether someone is "too femme" to be nonbinary, we may be engaging in gender snobbery. The point is this: Though we focus on paradigmatic cases—aesthetic, class-based—snobbery is a common feature of human interaction across many dimensions of our social lives.

Conclusion

I have argued that gatekeeping snobbery is an important, overlooked form of snobbery. It is important not only because it captures clear cases of snobbery that evade other accounts but also because the motivational profile underlying gatekeeping snobbery is a common thread binding several forms of aesthetic snobbery identified in the literature. Moreover, focusing on this common thread helps to broaden our understanding of snobbery beyond the aesthetic and to identify the ways in which it is not merely a failure of judgment, but a flaw in character.

References

Botts, T.F. (2018). In black and white: a hermeneutic argument against "transracialism". *Res Philosophica* 95 (2): 303–329. https://doi.org/10.11612/resphil.1626.

Cook, R. T. (2025). Only Posers Spell it "Poseur'. Unpublished manuscript.

Dembroff, R. and Saint-Croix, C. (2019). 'Yep, I'm gay': understanding agential identity. *Ergo: An Open Access Journal of Philosophy* 6: 571–599. https://doi.org/10.3998/ergo.12405314.0006.020.

Dormandy, K. and Grimley, B. (2024). Gatekeeping in science: lessons from the case of psychology and neuro-linguistic programming. *Social Epistemology* 38 (3): 392–412. https://doi.org/10.1080/02691728.2024.2326828.

Johnson King, Z.A. (2023). On snobbery. *The British Journal of Aesthetics* 63 (2): 199–215. https://doi.org/10.1093/aesthj/ayac050.

Kieran, M. (2010). The vice of snobbery: aesthetic knowledge, justification and virtue in art appreciation. *The Philosophical Quarterly* 60 (239): 243–263.

Macdonald, K. (2022). The Time when Joshua Bell went Busking in the Subway, and No-one Noticed. *Classic fm*.

Patridge, S. (2018). Snobbery in appreciative contexts. *The British Journal of Aesthetics* 58 (3): 241–253. https://doi.org/10.1093/aesthj/ayy024.

Patridge, S. (2023). Aesthetic snobbery. *Philosophy Compass 18* (9): e12,940. https://doi.org/10.1111/phc3.12940.

Sealey, K. (2018). Transracialism and white allyship. *Philosophy Today* 62 (1): 21–29. https://doi.org/10.5840/philtoday201829197.

Trump, D. (2025), Defending Women from Gender Ideology Extremism and Restoring Biological Truth to the Federal Government. Executive Order, 20 January 2025.

Chapter 3

We Write Songs About Swords and Wizards from Space: Fantasy Metal and the Aspiration of Re-enchantment

Scott Aikin

Department of Philosophy, Vanderbilt University, Nashville, TN, USA

1

Modern life is dreary. We can start from the fact of alienation, nearly universal, from our own time. We spend our hours at work, and leisure too often feels like it's in the service of making us more efficient at work when we return. Any Monday email will attest to the hope that the weekend rejuvenated us enough to attend to the pointless stupidity of whatever we are up to 9–5. Everything exciting is a product, and even our own alienation has been sold back to us. What else would explain the existence of Hot Topic and Cheesecake Factory? But this alienation is not merely a factor of our economic system and our respective roles in it. Rather, it's something baked into our understanding of ourselves as both animal and rational beings. We must look upon ourselves with conflicted understanding. Modernity only amplifies this phenomenon of the doom of our understanding. A few examples will suffice.

It feels as though we have free will, that we can control what we believe, what we value, and how we chart our courses through life. It's a cornerstone to conventional thought that people are responsible—that they did what they did freely, so could have done otherwise and can answer as to why they did what they did. But a few moments of reflection show that this all is an illusion. We have considerably less control over our minds as we'd like to think. Try as you like, you can't now help but think of an overweight dog wearing a cowboy hat. Moreover, you can't believe that Socrates was the first President of the United States, nor can you, just by wanting to, make yourself find something disgusting (perhaps worms wriggling on rotten meat) as appetizing. The person you are is the product of years of conditioning and an animal body with particular needs, and you can't undo that with just a wish. But here's the irony: a good deal of that conditioning is encouragement to think of yourself as freely participating in your life in that very basic animal body. Surely, it's horrible to realize that you, as a physical animal, are determined by physical laws and the material conditions that make your animality possible. But, again, given that conditioning, we are perfectly capable of seeing the truth of our being determined things, but yet we return to believe in our freedom. That's why we are alienated, and this is the doom of our understanding.[1]

This, for lack of a better term, is a form of *transcendental anxiety*. That's a heavy philosophical term for the deep conflictedness that comes from thinking of ourselves from inside as free and rational and from outside as things that function according to causes. Here's how

---

[1] For an overview of how the illusion of freedom persists even when it is clear we are determined, see Caruso (2012). This view of determinism (and the ineliminable illusion of freedom) is old, and it was the ancient Stoics who theorized paths for maintaining consistency in light of the tension. See Aikin and Stephens (2023) for an account of Stoic approaches.

they double up: given that we are rational and can understand human behavior as having causes, we invariably do that. So, we make predictions about how people will act, we think of education and culture as a causal environment that yields behavioral results, and we worry about the influences of friends. That's all a causal approach to our lives, but from the outside. The conflict is that from the inside, it all feels free and spontaneous, and according to reasons and purposes. But from the outside, it's all causes and brute. This conflicted understanding, again, manifests itself in a number of ways. The free will issue is already on the table, but now consider a few more. Our knowledge is supposed to be the product of our rationality, our responsiveness to what evidence and reason point to. But, animals that we are, our ideas of what counts as evidence are products of our particular times, and we gather our evidence in ways that depend on the world merely causing us to have thoughts. We rely on our sensations to produce beliefs (so, we are empiricists), and we make deductions on the basis of patterns we intuitively see as good (so, we are rationalists). But for as much as this feels like evidence and logic, these are merely causes that come along with being the kind of creatures we are, with the particular sensory and cognitive systems we have. Nothing true is guaranteed to come about from hominids and how they happen to picture the world. At best, it's a detailed story produced by a complex society of primates. Knowledge, the crown of our rationality, now looks like an ape's delusion.[2]

Value, too, from this perspective, slips away. Again, the illusion pulls us in—it's just obvious that friendship, loyalty, and honesty are all valuable. But it takes only a second of reflection to begin to explain them away. Are they not reducible to pleasures or to some merely stable social arrangement? For the sake of those other goods, only contingently related to them, are they valuable. And so, we act as though friendship is valuable in its own right, but we must do so because acting as though it is merely for the other goods makes those other goods harder to get. (You don't get the goods that friendship yields if you are motivated to pursue the friendship for those other goods. . . you get them only if you proceed as though you are in it just for the friendship.) Same thing for love—it's

[2] This is a broadly skeptical argument, one that shows that knowledge, from a causal perspective, seems impossible. For a full account of this view, see Hookway (1990), where a form of 'soft skepticism' is proposed—we can keep our beliefs, but we will always be conflicted about their support and their origin.

really for the sake of the stable pleasures we get from it, but if you think of it that way, you destroy it. In that regard, it is an illusion that must be maintained, ironically, for us to get the illusion's goods. But that's why the lie is so deep, and why we return to it again and again. Lovers must, as it were, pull the wool over their own (and each other's) eyes for their love to maintain its value.[3]

Modern life is dreary because we are rational creatures who must live in the illusions that our reason has both created and undermined. We live a lie, one that we have told ourselves. And we cannot have done otherwise. Modernity, with the depiction of us as *homo economicus* and with further clarity on our animal origins, has only made this more explicit, and so more galling. We carry the tools of doom for what's valuable and rational within our own intelligence.

Religion's appeal, here from the perspective of the bottom of the existential well, is real. A God, one to suffuse the world with meaning, to make us more than talkative dust, to make it all make sense, has a significant and undeniable pull. But, of course, hold on to your wallet when someone tells you that story. And most of us know it's all terribly implausible to begin with.[4] The state, alternately, with its promise of patriotic service and clarity with our place and social role, is a similar draw. But it does not take long to see how these stories are those that turn those who believe it into instruments of domination. Sports fandom, family life, professional development, self-help, and radical social critique, too, have similar patterns. All false promises of meaning, ones that we see through upon inhabiting those roles for a very short time, or inspecting those lives even cursorily from the outside. Our reason both animates and murders meaning. Weltschmerz and existential anxiety are only obverses of the coins for faith and hope.[5]

---

[3] This line of argument is one deployed by Cicero (2012) in reply to Epicurus and the Epicureans about value–in essence, if pleasure is the only true good, then one has denuded the social world and our connections of the value they have to provide us with the pleasures they promise. Love, if it is only about the pleasure, doesn't provide pleasure. In essence, hedonism turns out to undercut the pursuit of pleasure.

[4] The atheistic hypothesis seems the most reasonable, given the problem of evil and the incoherence of God's purported perfection. See Aikin and Talisse (2011) for a rundown of the case for atheism.

[5] This return of the doom, as a result of reflection, is a feature of what I have elsewhere termed the "Owl of Minerva Problem" (2020), which is that our reflective capacities offer improvement of our lives but also occasion new pathologies of reason. For another version of the problem of the world being scraped of value, see McDowell's (1994) approach.

2

What I've called transcendental anxiety, or the doom, the repetition of valuing and reasoning in light of those values, only to undercut them in that reasoning, is a pattern that seems hopeless. But we return to those values (and the illusion returns), so we are brought back to think we know many things, that we have a purpose, and that we've devised a path to freedom. In light of that return, it is worth focusing on how we may do so with self-consciousness. That is, once we've seen the demythologizing force of reason, how might our values be stated so that we acknowledge the coming devastating critique?

One temptation in answer to this question is to see the cycle of critique and long for a path of certainty of value. A path that identifies perfection and undeniable clarity, so that reason's reflection only amplifies those values and that meaning, instead of undercutting it. This was Plato's (and many, many others') vision—to leave the cave of illusions, to see the world and truth as it is, and have it so that the prospects of returning to the world of illusion no longer holds any charm. We live in the light, in truth, and with undeniable and real goods. That's the idealist's vision, and it's a powerful one, for sure. But we have good reason to think this path, too, is an illusion, borne more of wishful thinking and out-of-proportion self-confidence in being able to see through illusions. Perhaps something more modest is achievable. Here's one thought: there are methods of re-enchantment that wear their critical status on their sleeves—they acknowledge that they are illusions, that they could not possibly live up to our sustained critical reflection. Yet they capture us, nevertheless.

The fantasy genre of literature is one such method of re-enchantment. World-building, telling stories of deeds and stakes, remembered and related. There are ages with transforming magic, weapons of power, responsibilities conferred, and binding oaths. Monsters are to be confronted, adversaries are to be defeated. Heck, there may even be some lazy storytelling with "chosen ones," but things make sense. And the heroes, in making their stands, vindicate the values they defend; come to know deep truths, and do so as free beings. But it's all explicit that, as make-believe, it can't be real. Regardless, we animate a world with these values knowing that they would never pass inspection as depictions of our world. The illusion, as fantasy, animates—even as we acknowledge it as not real. That's something worth working out.

3

Fantasy metal, songs about swords and wizards from space, is a genre of both heavy metal and fantasy literature. The metal part of this, I believe, is ancillary to the fantasy part, but it plays a supporting role. I will return to this shortly. For now, let's consider the fact that Led Zeppelin had songs about the Misty Mountains and various other references to Tolkien's world, Black Sabbath's "The Wizard" not only features a harmonica (in heavy metal!?!) but paints a picture of magic's power of grounding meaning and producing joy, and the video of Ronnie James Dio's "Holy Diver" is straight out of a D&D campaign. In every one of these instances, among many, many other cases, a world of magic and mystery is invoked, one with giants, evil, heroes, and most of all, meaning. Contemporary fantasy metal covers the same ground. The Sword's songs of the world of George Martin's *Game of Thrones* invoke the religion of The Seven, manning the wall in the North preserving humanity's hopes, and promises of vengeance are exemplary. As are Khemmis's imaginings of being progeny of ill-starred Cadmus and epic retellings of nights of injury and hopelessness. As are Howling Giant's integration of druids and wizards into a space Odyssey of abandoning Earth and being held hostage by forces beyond imagination.

Fantasy is *serious play*. It is explicitly so on both fronts. It is explicitly *play* because the stories are of adventure, with trolls and magic rings—kid stuff, on its face. But this simplicity allows for clear and *serious* stake-setting—a return to a lost homeland, the fate of an age, preventing the rule of a bad king, and saving the family farm. And just as the bards of those imagined lands retell those stories for audiences with rapt attention, our rockers relate them to us.

But why must it be metal? The answer is that it doesn't have to be metal. Traditional folk musics have plenty of fantasy built in, to start. And there are alternative forms the music can take on in this. But what makes metal special is the thundering doom of the bass, the deeply distorted guitar, and the relentless drums. My wife, who is not a fan of metal, once quipped that most metal songs she hears "sound like the part of the musical where the bad guy or the dark hero gets his solo," and she wasn't wrong. Imagining the crushing doom of evil's triumph, articulating the motivations (in resentment, boredom, or even in the transcendental anxiety we've reviewed), impels us to return to our values. We still feel the doom as doom. And when we are asked, "So what if Sauron conquers Middle Earth?" "So what if the mothership of Earthlings, depicted in Howling Giant's *Black Hole Space Wizard* album series, blinks out in a cosmic whimper?" "So what if the 'Hidden Masters' of The Sword's invocation return to eradicate or enslave humankind?" The answer is that it'd be a shame to see what is fragile and striving to be destroyed. And so, against that background of doom, we witness seeds of blooming hope. And the weight of a particularly disgusting bass riff highlights that.

It's all make-believe, driven with a wistful glance at Tolkien's or Scott Bakker's volumes detailing other lands and times, the roll of a D-20, and maybe smoke from a bong. It's nostalgia for a life we never lived, a life where the stakes are clear and things matter. And in the midst of the guitar solo, we imagine the shard of a fabled crystal is found and returned. Or, as the bass line gets even deeper and more crushing, the reality and finality of the end looms. Doom awaits us all. And it's still meaningful. Yet, it is here that our dissociation from our lives is both at its height and in highest contrast. We can see the epic sacrifices and profound tragedies in the fantasy tales, in times that never were and between people who are not real, but we have a challenge seeing our own lives of quiet toil as having meaning. Or a tradeoff for someone working two jobs and juggling a family and hoping to produce a little art in Middle Tennessee as profound. Doom comes for us there, too. But so does the striving.

4

I've argued that the world, ourselves, and our values have been disenchanted. Or at least, we've become disenchanted with them. It's a feature, not a bug, of being human. That's the doom, and we are it. Modern life, with its multiple sources of alienation and information, amplifies that disenchantment. That's the doom we now so efficiently bring to ourselves. The aspiration of re-enchantment is real, but there is strong evidence that the same sources of disenchantment will undercut those programs, too. Religion, statism, self-help, and even being a cynical complainer all have false promises of meaning. And we already knew that. Fantasy literature is a literal re-enchantment (since there are wizards and magic, you know), but it makes no promise of not being false. In fact, it is explicitly so—as though to double down on it by explicitly announcing itself as *fantasy fiction*.

But a new problem emerges. Isn't such a program mere *escapism*? One builds a fake world to slip away into? Yes, it's cool to visit the gnomes and elves, demons, and space wizards. But does such a visit make a difference? Does it change our alienation, or is this merely a concession to it? That playing like we are magic heroes or listening to their stories is as good as we can do. Just as I opened this essay by complaining that we trade so much of our time for employment and even our rest time is conceived as preparation for returning to our 9–5, so might one complain of my line of argument here about fantasy. Yes, a D&D session in the basement, or a great afternoon with a book about elves, or a face-melting experience of doomy shredding might re-energize us, but it's still just one more past time. It's all yet another way our alienation can be repackaged and sold to us as an alternative. Shouldn't we have the same transcendental anxiety about the things that even promise a little respite from transcendental anxiety? Isn't being into this stuff, even taking it ironically, still bad faith, distraction, and maybe even titillation at something that we really shouldn't enjoy? Anyone who has reveled in the sound of an ancient evil invoked in songs about Chthulu or unspoken elder gods should shudder at this—you take pleasure in imagining what it would be like to be something terrible. It's bad to feel good about bad things. Maybe it's just harmless fun, but maybe also we are made worse by it.

The problem, as I see it, is that this objection is correct, but only to a degree. Fantasy literature and fantasy metal *is* escapism. It may yield a commentary on the world as it is, it may highlight a value we miss in ourselves or have forgotten, or it can just give us moments of guilty pleasure. But these are all temporary, and they do not change the background conditions of our incapacity to be at home with ourselves and the world we've made. And we have no alternative, really. Doom comes for us all, and other metal genres have explored that. Black metal artists may rage against it all, hoping for a demon to come and tear it all asunder. Or for us all to become moss on an old rock. Death metal is a cynical jerk of the wheel into the abyss. And all the Satanic stuff? Ugh. But fantasy genres remind us of what's tragic about our transcendental anxiety, and it highlights why our relationship with value and our humanity is worth maintaining. Despite the fact that it is all fleeting to our reflection. Doom comes for us all because we (and our capacity to debunk our values) are our own doom. But we are also the source of the values that spring anew. Howling Giant's song of the mothership on *Black Hole Space Wizard I*, striving to find a new Earth after having to leave the one we've ruined, closes with the refrain, "It's not the end. . . This. Is. Not. The. End." For sure, it's all make-believe, but also for sure, that's how to face the doom.

References

Aikin, S. (2020). The owl of Minerva problem. *Southwest Philosophy Review* 36 (1): 13–22.

Aikin, S. and Stephens, W.O. (2023). *Epictetus's Encheiridion: A New Translation and Guide to Stoic Ethics*. Bloomsbury.

Aikin, S. and Talisse, R. (2011). *Reasonable Atheism*. Prometheus Books.

Caruso, G. (2012). *Free Will and Consciousness: A Determinist Account of the Illusion of Free Will*. Lexington Books.

Cicero, M.T. (2012). *On Moral Ends*. Trans. Raphael Woolf. Cambridge University Press.

McDowell, J. (1994). *Mind and World*. Harvard University Press.

Hookway, C. (1990). *Skepticism*. Routledge.

Chapter 4
A View from Nihil: Heavy Metal, Censorship, and the End of Morality

David Hunt
The University of Birmingham, Birmingham, UK

Metal music, especially in respect of its lyrical content and artwork, has over the decades been the focus of a great deal of mainstream anxiety, moral panic, and attempts to ban artists or their albums. From facing censorship, bans, or prosecution to being banned from an entire country, there has been no shortage of controversy and, in some people's opinions, malign influence around metal music.[1,2] Few episodes in the history of the genre, however, can compare in either

[1] Examples which can easily be found on the internet include Dismember's song "Skin Her Alive" from their album "Like an Everflowing Stream" which faced obscenity charges and calls for a ban in the United Kingdom and Cannibal Corpse's debut "Eaten Back to Life" which was subject to bans in countries including Germany and Russia.

[2] In 1992, under pressure from the Catholic Church, Iron Maiden were barred by the Chilean government from performing in the country (https://www.latercera.com/noticia/la-trastienda-de-la-frustrada-visita-de-iron-maiden-a-chile-en-1992/ (in Spanish)).

notoriety or extremity to the real-world actions involved in the Black Metal scene of the early 1990s. On a personal level, as a young listener, I was fascinated by an article in the UK magazine *Kerrang!* which shone light on the burgeoning Norwegian Black Metal scene, and the events which grew out of that scene were widely discussed and have since passed into metal legend, for good or ill.[3,4]

In this chapter, I want to defend music, at least in one specific way, against the charge that it is somehow responsible for the negative actions which those who might seek to restrict or ban certain types of music accuse it of being. For obvious reasons, I will focus on heavy metal music and extreme metal music in particular. My aim is not to present a definitive argument that metal cannot be in any way part of the explanatory story we would want to tell about certain types of action—that would be interesting, certainly, but beyond the scope of a single chapter such as this.

Rather, I want to somewhat more modestly look at one strand of what I take to be a number of different thoughts, arguments, or stances tangled up in calls to restrict or ban metal music. And I want to argue that tugging on that one strand leads to the conclusion that metal music cannot *make* agents act in destructive or otherwise deeply undesirable ways. That being done, as a by-product I want to suggest that we can focus more clearly on other aspects of the tangle and reply to those who would seek to ban certain types of music "OK, well it can't be because of *that,* so what are we really talking about?" I will even note a couple of candidates for what we might really be talking about along the way, though it will be beyond the limited scope of this piece to follow those candidates down their respective rabbit holes.

The effects which music can have on its listeners are of course profound and varied, with entire fields of study considering such topics in philosophy, psychology, and beyond.[5] Equally, many things may be wrapped up or implicit in calls for censorship of metal music—aesthetic judgments, claims about the music's effect on agents' psychologies, cultural assumptions, and so on. There are various ways in which some of these perspectives may be philosophically understood—for example, by reference to speech acts and arguing that music has effects which may

[3] *Kerrang!* issue 436, 27th March 1993.

[4] See, e.g. *Lords of Chaos* by Michael Moynihan and Didrik Søderlund, Feral House, 1998.

[5] For an overview of the philosophy of music, see Kania (2024). For a psychological perspective with suggested further reading, see DeAngelis (2020).

be understood as analogous to perlocutionary speech acts, i.e. that metal music inspires or functions to create beliefs or similar attitudes in its listeners.[6]

Without digressing wholesale into the philosophy of free speech, I can see at least three relevant levels on which the claims which are implicit in calls for banning metal music could operate: that heavy metal somehow *makes* agents act in certain ways, as I will discuss here; that heavy metal somehow *persuades* or *predisposes* agents to act in certain ways, i.e. by reordering or adding to an agent's set of desires (or similar attitudes); or that heavy metal *normalizes* certain forms of behavior and therefore, so to speak, implies permission for certain actions which would not otherwise be thought permissible. Another avenue to explore might be whether music can create delusions or states of self-deception in its listeners.[7]

I do not propose in the space of this single chapter to argue decisively for these categories or to settle all debate over the panoply of potential readings or intentions behind calls for the censorship of metal music. Rather, I will focus on the first of the above claims which I believe is implicit in at least some calls for censorship—whether this is realized by those who make such calls or not—that heavy metal somehow *makes* agents act in destructive ways in which they would not otherwise act. If something interesting can be said in response to that implicit claim, then this chapter will serve as at least one step toward disambiguation and so throw the spotlight more clearly on what else might be the case.

I should also say here near the outset that in most of what follows I will exclude overtly politically exhortative music.[8] Partly this is because music with such an explicit political intent throws up a number of additional issues peculiar to that part of the musical map which I would argue do not apply to music based around other motivations—including music which may seek to hold up an artistically tendentious mirror to society

[6] For a seminal text on speech acts, see Austin (1962), pp. 94ff. For a list of references to the application of speech act categories such as perlocution to other domains—in this case primarily pornography—see Howard (2024, §3.3).

[7] My initial response to the latter suggestion would be that surely it would be the delusion itself or some psychological issue peculiar to the agent concerned which were "to blame" rather than music. But it could nonetheless be fruitful to examine this idea further. For more on delusions and states of self-deception, see, e.g. Bortolotti and Mameli (2012).

[8] Examples might include the white supremacist heavy metal band Centurion, or so-called National Socialist Black Metal.

but which does not genuinely exhort listeners to act in any particular way.[9] However, I will return to political music toward the end of the chapter and will have a little more to say about it in light of the argument I have made in the meantime.

I will otherwise cast the net quite widely and take "metal music" to encompass parts or all of heavy metal, broadly and intuitively defined as anything from Extinction Dismemberment and Mayhem to Motörhead and Black Sabbath. In doing so, I will hope to ensure that an opponent could not accuse me of considering only an innocuous part of the musical map and ignoring the "real problem," whatever that might mean.

For economy I will use "banning" as a shorthand for general calls for the restriction or censorship of metal music, whether they actually involve banning albums, artists, or genres or not, similarly to how metaethicists use "*x* is morally wrong" as a token moral judgment, their arguments about which often generalize to other similar judgments. Also for brevity's sake, I will call the position that heavy metal is somehow bad because it makes agents do harmful which things they would not otherwise do and so should be banned "metalbadism," and those who would wish to ban or censor metal music "metalbadists."[10] The strategy here, then, is to look at what would need to be the case for metalbadists to be correct that music can make an agent act in ways in which they would not otherwise act, and to suggest that it cannot, in fact, be the case.

Essentially this whole set of issues boils down to what we might mean by "make." A number of potential meanings can be ruled out immediately. First, I do not think it plausible to interpret metalbadism as involving a claim that metal music entirely overrides agents' capacity for practical reason and thus *make* agents do anything in so direct a sense. Many hundreds of thousands of people listen regularly to metal, including very extreme metal, and are not thereby reduced to marauding musical zombies (surely we would have noticed such creatures stumbling around!).

---

[9] Examples here might include Antichrist Superstar-era Marilyn Manson, the well-known Faith No More song "Be Aggressive" or even my own band Anaal Nathrakh.

[10] I do not necessarily take metalbadism to be a robustly or systematically defended position (though the Parents Music Resource Center in their well-publicized campaign against Dee Snyder et al. in the 1980s may be thought to have come close). However, this is not a straw man argument—by focusing on the notional "metalbadist" and drawing analogies to a metaethical framework I believe that we can clarify and potentially push back against real-world attempts to censor or eliminate heavy metal music.

The same would be true for a more subtle relative of this view, according to which music might not override, but can nonetheless influence or similarly affect agents' capacity for practical reason. Music might make someone significantly more likely to act in a certain way which they would not otherwise, while stopping short of removing their ability to choose their own actions. Again, while perhaps more credible and interesting to examine than a claim that music makes agents into something akin to zombies, I do not think this is sufficiently plausible to form a satisfying basis for metalbadism. Perhaps a more developed form of metalbadism than I have space here to articulate could make headway on this front, but for present purposes simply consider that we would hardly consider it a valid defense if when on trial for murder a metal fan said, "Yes your honour I did kill him, but you cannot hold me responsible – you see, I had been listening to Slayer!"

Were such a defense offered, we would be left asking far more salient questions about the agent themselves than about the oeuvres of the Thrash legends. After all, I have heard many hours of Slayer's music, and while I may be a little odd, I have never committed murder. I would imagine that most people reading this would be in a roughly similar position. I do not therefore take seriously the proposition that whatever music's possible effects on agents' rationality may be, it overpowers rational agency in such a way that music itself can be held responsible for their actions—certainly not to the extent that someone might behave in a way entirely contrary to their everyday character when incredibly drunk, high on drugs or subject to, in the legal sense, temporary insanity. So if we are to make sense of the metalbadist's claim, we must be dealing with more or less practically rational agents.[11]

That being the case, I will address the "make" part of metalbadism as a claim that metal music provides largely rational agents with (or gives them, or grounds) authoritative practical reasons—that is, authoritative reasons to act in a certain way. On this view, music does not *make* agents act in the sense of forcing them against their will, but rather it somehow makes it the case that the agents in question have reasons to act destructively, and those reasons are authoritative for them. Being practically

[11] I will look more closely at what practical rationality consists in shortly, but at this stage, an intuitive definition of "able to consider their salient practical reasons with some minimal level of clarity and broadly correct reasoning, and to relate their actions appropriately to those reasons" will suffice.

rational, they then act on what they take to be their authoritative practical reasons.

The next question, then, is what might ground the kinds of practical reasons required such that music is "on the hook" for agents' destructive actions, and not some other factor of the agent or their circumstances? For example, if a specific agent antecedently desires to kill someone else, and then does so after listening to Cannibal Corpse, I think we would be quite comfortable in deeming this a case of correlation without causation—the agent, or perhaps more precisely the agent's desires are where we would rightly put the blame. Music, even music which some might accuse of being excessively violent, would not be responsible in any particularly meaningful sense.

One commonly understood source of practical reasons is an agent's desires and beliefs. While it may or may not be a view which David Hume actually held himself, this is often termed a Humean Theory of Reasons: "If there is a reason for someone to do something, then she must have some desire that would be served by her doing it."[12] However in the present context, this does not support metalbadism—if an agent's reasons for burning down a church or killing someone are grounded in that agent's desires, then it is that agent's desires, or the agent themselves, which are responsible for the agent's actions, rather than music.

It could of course be argued that music might affect or alter an agent's desires, but that is one of those rabbit holes I mentioned earlier—on the one hand, while doubtless incredibly interesting, and potentially fruitful for our notional metalbadist, it would be exceedingly complex to investigate the interplay between agents' antecedent desires and their musical or more widely cultural environment. But more importantly here, on the other hand, it would be beside the point. In this limited piece, I am, as I said above, looking at whether music *in and of itself* can make agents act in destructive ways and so be held responsible for those actions, not whether it can alter agents' desires.

What we are therefore seeking on the metalbadist's behalf is a convincing argument that music provides practically rational agents with authoritative *desire-independent* practical reasons and can thus be deemed responsible for those agents' actions rather than simply an aspect of their environment. Put another way, what the metalbadist needs, and

[12] See Finlay and Schroeder (2017).

what we are therefore looking for in order to give metalbadism the fairest crack of the whip we can, is a convincing argument that music can give agents reasons to do things which they would not otherwise desire to do.

This is where things get significantly tricky for metalbadism. I say this because we have good cause to doubt the authority or even intelligibility of desire-independent practical reasons. This is a much-discussed position in metaethics and is put forward by (at least some) defenders of moral error theory, sometimes called moral nihilism—the view that ultimately there is nothing, nor can there ever be anything, which is morally permitted, required, or forbidden. In a metaethical context, this is a seismic and potentially deeply alarming claim, entailing as it does that not only is there no moral reason to refrain from shop lifting or to keep your promises, but that there is nothing morally wrong with rape, that we have no moral grounds on which to criticize the Nazis or cannibalism, and conversely that there is nothing morally good about acting to prevent children—even one's own children—dying of starvation.[13]

In the more limited context of this chapter, the principal issue for metalbadism is that many of the arguments which moral error theorists adduce against moral obligations also tell against desire-independent practical reasons in general.

What, then, is the problem with authoritative, desire-independent practical reasons according to moral error theorists, and how to does that play out in our context of metalbadism? In order to explain this, I will turn to probably the foremost moral error theorist, Richard Joyce.[14]

Joyce argues that morality rests on putative desire-independent reasons such that if an action is deemed morally wrong, this means that agents ought not to perform that action, regardless of their desires or aims.[15] This is intuitively plausible to most people when it comes to

[13] The starting point for the majority of modern debates around moral error theory is Mackie (1977). For more recent discussions, see, e.g. Olson (2014) and Streumer (2017).

[14] While acknowledging other formulations and defenses of moral error theory, I focus on Joyce's view as developed in (2001) partly because it has been widely discussed and was for example described by the prominent metaethicist Russ Shafter-Landau as "surely the most elegantly written, comprehensive and well-argued defense of a moral error theory yet to appear" (see 2005, p. 108). However, more importantly, I focus on Joyce because the way he constructs his arguments for a moral error theory is neatly compatible with the argument I want to make here.

[15] See Joyce (2001), p. 134: "In short, when we say that a person *morally* ought to act in a certain manner, we imply something about what she would have reason to do regardless of her desires and interests, regardless of whether she cares about her victim, and regardless of whether she can be sure of avoiding any penalties."

morality—we would typically accept that the widely agreed upon moral injunction against murdering others for fun applies to agents regardless of whether a particular agent had desires and beliefs compatible with a spot of jolly murdering. "Oh, but I really wanted to kill him!" is no better a defense in the moral case than listening to Slayer was in the legal case we imagined a few paragraphs ago.

This conception of the objective, agent-independent nature of moral normativity which underlies error theorists' arguments is of course open to debate, and highly regarded opponents have argued at length that morality should not be understood in this way—suggesting for example that moral discourse should instead be thought of as a mode of expressing conative attitudes such as desires rather than as a field of discourse involving objective moral facts and desire-independent reasons.[16] However, as I discussed above, in the context of this chapter, we are dealing with a characterization of metalbadism which does indeed require the existence of authoritative, desire-independent practical reasons. And in Joyce's words, "there is no sense to be made of such reasons" (2001, p. 77).

One way of looking at Joyce's argument for this claim is as proceeding from a question which may be familiar to heavy metal fans—"so what?" If, when confronted by a practical reason, an agent can sensibly reply "so what, what has that got to do with me?" then that reason cannot be thought to be authoritative for that agent. It may be a practical reason in some sense, but it is not a reason *for them* to act or refrain from acting in any particular way.

An example might be the rules of a game—it is constitutive of playing a sport that one generally attempts to obey the rules of the game, thus if you want to play tennis you have a reason to act in accordance with the rules of tennis. Whereas if you do not wish to play tennis, you have no particular reason to use a tennis racket to hit a ball such that it lands between certain lines on the floor, and so on. Accordingly, if someone tells you that it is wrong to hit the ball into the car park and go to the pub instead, as someone who is not interested in playing tennis you can entirely sensibly reply "so what, what has that got to do with me?" Even if there is a reason not to do so in some sense, it is not a reason *for you*.

In order for the kind of desire-independent reasons which both morality (as Joyce understands it) and metalbadism depend to be authoritative for an agent, they must not be susceptible to this "so what?" response.

[16] For possibly the most widely influential account of this kind, see Blackburn (1998).

Rather, the reasons in question must be reasons *for* the agents concerned. And any proffered reason cannot be a reason *for you* if you can sensibly reply "so what, what has that got to do with me?"

Having established this, Joyce's strategy in arguing for a moral error theory then becomes one of trying to find a kind of desire-independent practical reason which is truly authoritative for agents regardless of their desires or aims and which can therefore forestall this "so what?" response. If he can do so, then morality is potentially vindicated—we will have an account of desire-independent reasons which can be authoritative for agents regardless of their desires or aims and so we can build up a picture of moral normativity from there. But if even the very best account of putative practical reasons cannot give us a way to make sense of practical reasons *which are authoritative for agents regardless of their desires or aims*, then we must conclude that a moral error theory is true.

The analogy for metalbadism is that if the kinds of practical reasons which music might provide agents with can sensibly be responded to with "so what, what does that mean to me?" then they cannot be said to be authoritative reasons for that agent to act destructively regardless of their desires or aims and so music cannot be held to be responsible in this limited sense for that agent's actions. Rather, the responsibility would fall on the agent or perhaps on their desires, depending on how one wanted to flesh out the story—not on music itself.

Recall that I mentioned above that my strategy here is to consider what might need to be the case in order for metalbadism to be true. I then argued that metalbadism depended on the existence of authoritative desire-independent practical reasons. This means that, like Joyce, we are seeking ways to avoid the "so what?" response and thus locate the kind of authoritative, desire-independent reason on which metalbadism depends. If we can do so, then metalbadism may be vindicated and so the charge that metal music makes agents do bad things, at least in the limited sense under discussion here, and so should be banned, stands. If we cannot, however, then metalbadism fails and we can conclude that metal music cannot, in fact, be held responsible for agents' destructive actions in the relevant sense.

Turning back to Joyce then, he suggests (2001, pp. 49–51) that the best chance of forestalling "so what?" responses might be offered by grounding an agent's practical reasons in the requirements of practical rationality itself, which he calls "the framework that tells us what our reasons for acting are" (2001, p. 49). The thought here is that requirements of practical rationality can forestall "so what?" responses, and so constitute reasons which are authoritative for all agents because the very act of asking the question "but what does that mean to me?" in response to a suggested reason for action commits one to practical rationality. Thus to ask a question like "I know that's a requirement of practical rationality, but what has it got to do with me?" makes no sense. This is because asking that question in itself demonstrates that one is "in the business" of considering and potentially accepting reasons, of taking them to be authoritative, and so on. Therefore, no practically rational agent can sensibly accept that they have a reason to ϕ which is a requirement of practical rationality, but then reply "but what has that got to do with me?" Practical rationality, Joyce argues, thus offers hope of grounding the kind of universally authoritative reasons which morality requires.

In fact, this basis in practical rationality seems to be the *only* promising candidate for successfully forestalling "so what?" responses, since the authority of normative reasons is always likely to be questionable unless the very act of questioning commits one to the principles on which the theory of normative reasons under consideration is founded. In other words, if moral reasons turn out not to be requirements of practical rationality, it is hard to see how they could ever escape the "so what?" problem and have legitimate authority for all moral agents.

Joyce's task thus becomes one of analyzing practical rationality to see if we can use it to make sense of the kinds of authoritative desire-independent reasons it promises to ground. If we can, then it may be possible to forge an appropriate link between the kinds of reasons on which morality depends and requirements of practical rationality and so to rescue morality from error. By analogy, the same will be the case for metalbadism. But if we cannot make sense of the required kinds of reasons, a moral error theory beckons in the moral case, and metalbadism fails in our current case.

The question which therefore arises is, "what does being practically rational consist in?" Joyce's answer is that one is practically rational to the extent that one is guided by one's subjective reasons (2001, p. 54). Essentially, Joyce persuasively argues that practical rationality consists in being guided by one's subjective reasons, which he defines as what one takes one's objective reasons to be, given that one may not be aware of all of the relevant facts or capable of deliberating on one's practical reasons with perfect clarity. To flesh that out a little, as I touched upon above we can broadly follow Hume and say that an agent's objective reasons are those which, all things considered, that agent believes will conduce to the satisfaction of their desires. However, Hume's account leaves no room for the rational appraisal of an agent's (competing) reasons. Thus, Hume famously concludes that "Tis not contrary to reason to prefer the destruction of the whole world to the scratching of my finger" (*A Treatise on Human Nature* [1739], 2.3.3.6, SBN 415–416).

Joyce finds Hume's view helpful but argues that we can go beyond Hume and in fact can rationally appraise an agent's reasons. In order to do so, Joyce builds on Hume's view and, following Michael Smith (primarily 1994 and 1995), further divides an agent's reasons into objective reasons, subjective reasons, and irrational reasons.

On Joyce's view, an agent's objective reasons are those which would conduce to the satisfaction of their desires, but which an agent may or may not be in a position to fully appreciate. For example, if a comet is going to crash into my house during the middle of the night, on some level we might say that I had a reason, assuming that I do not want to be killed by a comet, to leave the house for the evening. However, if I know nothing about the comet, given my limited epistemic position, it would not be rational for me to do so.

Next, an agent's subjective reasons are those which not only does the agent believe will conduce to their desires, but which have survived a process of deliberation (or at least would do so). To put this in another way, they are the reasons an agent takes on reflection to be their objective reasons, given their epistemically restricted viewpoint. Let's say that I have thought about my various desires and appetites, for example to sleep for a week or to go out and get drunk at a heavy metal concert, and have decided upon a goal or end of getting enough sleep because it makes my life more bearable to be well rested. I have thus adopted going to bed at a reasonable time every night as a goal and so have privileged my desire to sleep over my other desires. This desire, coupled with my belief, which I take to be justified, that going out and listening to heavy metal all night will frustrate my desire to be well rested, constitutes a reason to avoid doing so and get an early night instead. Since I have no way of knowing about the comet heading toward my house that evening, I take this to be an objective reason.

Finally, my desire to pursue those more hedonistic activities is what Joyce calls an irrational desire. That is because although I may satisfy *a* current desire by going out to raise some hell, I would also be frustrating an end which I have adopted after due consideration, i.e. to get enough sleep each night. Therefore, while my desire to drink and listen to loud music, coupled with a belief that going to a concert will satisfy this desire, constitutes a reason for me in one sense, it is not a reason which would survive deliberation. In fact, acting upon it would frustrate the ends and desires which I have thought long and hard about. Thus, Joyce would call it an irrational reason, albeit one which it would be fortunate for me if I acted upon it, given that I might be out of the house when the comet hits.

Heavily paraphrasing and condensing Joyce's argument, then, we arrive at a point where the requirements of practical rationality have been defined—being practically rational consists in being responsive to one's subjective reasons. Since those subjective reasons *do* depend on an agent's desires for their authority, practical rationality has not yielded a way to make sense of desire-independent practical reasons being authoritative for a given agent.

Going back a couple of steps to see how this matters in context, remember that Joyce was attempting to find the account of practical reasons which offered the best chance at forestalling "so what?" responses and so yielding authoritative desire-independent practical reasons. The idea was that the requirements of practical rationality was the strongest—indeed perhaps the only—candidate since one cannot respond to an apparent practical reason by saying "So what? What has that got to do with me?" without thereby committing oneself to practical rationality itself. However, since even the best candidate cannot give us a way to make sense of the authority of desire-independent practical reasons, we must conclude that there is no sense to be made of such reasons. That being the case, and since moral normativity depends on the existence of such reasons, we must accept that an error theory of morality is true—it is not the case that any agent is ever under a moral obligation.

There is much more to say about the finer details of Joyce's arguments, and about what might follow from the truth of a moral error theory, whether it be Joyce's or another variation. In particular, we might wonder what on earth we are to do about it if the error theorists are right![17] However, in the case under consideration here, this is superfluous. The analogy to metalbadism should hopefully be quite clear. In considering what

---

[17] Among other literature, this post-error-theory "what now?" question was the primary focus of my own Ph.D. thesis, "How to be a child, and bid lions and dragons farewell: The consequences of moral error theory," available online at https://www.academia.edu/56586340/How_to_be_a_child_and_bid_lions_and_dragons_farewell_The_consequences_of_moral_error_theory_PhD_Thesis_.

would need to be the case for metalbadism, i.e. the claim that metal music makes people do bad things which they would not otherwise do and so should be banned, to be true I argued that metal music would need to provide practically rational agents with authoritative desire-independent practical reasons. Following Joyce, we can say that there is no sense to be made of such reasons, and so metalbadism cannot be true, and therefore, the metalbadist's claim can be dismissed. Music is thus, at least in this specific way, vindicated.

As I noted near the outset, none of this is to say that there might not be other ways of interpreting calls for metal music to be banned. Many other claims and perspectives could be wrapped up in those calls, and in this piece, I wanted only to tease out one strand. However, hopefully this has helped to clarify things somewhat and show that we can validly reply to such calls "OK, so you can't be arguing that metal music *makes* people do bad things, so what are you really arguing?"

In order to answer that question I think we would need to look more closely at the reasons why disaffected, often young people might come to have desires which are compatible with excessively destructive actions and psychological features which at the same time make them attracted to certain forms of music.[18] I mentioned earlier that I would return to explicitly politically exhortative music, and would point to this as a specific example of this wider cultural-psychological point—the mechanism by which politically exhortative music appears to operate, at least according to one expert on the matter, is to act as a gateway through which disaffected youths who are attracted by (among other things) rebellious music are then intentionally drawn in further by politically manipulative cultural factors.[19] At best, then, one might argue that music is part of the mechanism, but it is very clear that music is by no means the whole of the mechanism, and arguably only plays the role it does because music is a near-universally resonant medium of expression.

---

[18] I say *excessively* destructive since having some degree of destructive desires is arguably a standard facet of human psychology, at least at some stages of development. In fact it seems likely that having music which recognizes this fact is part of the cathartic effect which some music can have. However, it would again be outside the present scope to pursue this theme here.

[19] Arno Michaelis is an ex-white supremacist heavy metal singer who subsequently went on to write "My Life After Hate" (2012) and is now a speaker and interventionist involved with a number of anti-hate organizations. An illuminating film in which he sets out the way in which recruitment into neo-Nazism operated, including the role played by white supremacist music, is available at https://www.youtube.com/watch?v=d-g3Z8IWsdU.

In any event, when trying to set out what those who would restrict or ban certain types of music are really talking about, it should be clear that the resulting picture would need to take in far wider aspects of culture and psychology than it is possible to encompass here. And I would suggest that any blame would need to fall far outside of a simplistic attempt to hold music itself responsible, whatever the complexities and nuances of the interaction between an agent's musical consumption and the culture which they both create and are embedded within. But this I leave this to others, should they wish to take it up. That's where the real fun starts.

References

Austin, J.L. (1962). *How To Do Things With Words*. Oxford: Clarendon Press.

Blackburn, S. (1998). *Ruling Passions*. Oxford: Oxford University Press.

Bortolotti, L. and Mameli, M. (2012). Self-deception, delusion and the boundaries of folk-psychology. *Humana. Mente Journal of Philosophical Studies* 20: 203–221.

DeAngelis, T. (2020). Music's power over our brains. *Monitor on Psychology* 51 (8): 24.

Finlay, S. and Schroeder, M. (2017). Reasons for action: internal vs. external. In: *The Stanford Encyclopedia of Philosophy (Fall 2017)* (ed. E.N. Zalta and U. Nodelman). Metaphysics Research Lab, Stanford University.

Howard, J.W. (2024). Freedom of speech. In: *The Stanford Encyclopedia of Philosophy (Spring)* (ed. E.N. Zalta and U. Nodelman). Metaphysics Research Lab, Stanford University.

Joyce, R. (2001). *The Myth of Morality*. Cambridge: Cambridge University Press.

Kania, A. (2024). The philosophy of music. In: *The Stanford Encyclopedia of Philosophy (Spring)* (ed. E.N. Zalta and U. Nodelman). Metaphysics Research Lab, Stanford University.

Mackie, J. (1977). *Ethics*. London: Penguin Books.

Michaelis, A. (2012). *My Life After Hate*. Milwaukee: Authentic Presence Publications.

Olson, J. (2014). *Moral Error Theory – History, Critique, Defence*. Oxford: Oxford University Press.

Shafter-Landau, R. (2005). Error theory and the possibility of normative ethics. *Philosophical Issues* 15: 107–120.

Smith, M. (1994). *The Moral Problem*. Wiley-Blackwell.

Smith, M. (1995). Internal reasons. *Philosophy and Phenomenological Research* 55: 109.

Streumer, B. (2017). *Unbelievable Errors: An Error Theory about All Normative Judgements*. Oxford: Oxford University Press.

Part II

Preachers of Death: On Philosophy of Religion

Chapter 5
Christianity and Metal: Reflections from a Former Scene Kid

R.T. Mullins

Faculty of Theology, University of Lucerne, Luzern, Switzerland

Every intellectual movement needs a soundtrack to capture the sentiment and imagination of a generation. Italian Communists had ska. American Straight-edge had punk and hardcore. For me, the soundtrack of my intellectual awakening was metal. Aesthetics and cultural movements go hand-in-hand. Your ethical or political movement needs a good soundtrack. Yet, there is rarely a systematic philosophy or worldview in the aesthetics and music by themselves. The music will contain inchoate ideas, but that is what invites you into deeper reflection. In this chapter, I will offer my own reflections on my journey through Christianity and metal. Engagement with metal helped foster my ability to assess arguments and worldviews, understand the relationship between emotions and truth, and taught me why one should not base their ethics on fashion trends.

Worldview Assessment

The first edition of James Sire's book, *The Universe Next: A Basic Worldview Catalogue* came out in 1976, and is currently in its sixth edition. This book introduced the basic idea of a worldview to American evangelical audiences and captured the popular imagination of that community in many ways. The idea behind a worldview in itself is not entirely remarkable. A worldview is a system of beliefs about ultimate reality, ethics, and other big philosophical questions about the meaning of life. Sire's book helped many American Christians start thinking about how to identify other worldviews like naturalism, nihilism, existentialism, postmodernism, pantheism, New Age, and deism. This book, and many others, helped create a culture of American Christians who saw worldviews hiding behind every corner. These worldviews were rivals to Christian theism that needed to be identified and rejected.

I was born in 1983. By the time I started listening to music that I actually had an interest in, there was a particular cultural landscape that had developed. There was a skepticism about "secular" music and an emphasis on finding "Christian" alternatives to that music. Various evangelistic and apologetic ministries popped up that specialized in such things. These ministries would identify lists of musical artists that one should stay away from and then present lists of safe Christian musical artists who sounded just like their secular counterparts. I would be at a Christian conference for teenagers, and someone would say, "If you like Slayer, you should listen to Living Sacrifice instead." It just so happens that Living Sacrifice is pretty great, but this whole approach to music strikes me as odd.

It is difficult for me to adequately explain the oddity because it was so long ago, but I think the oddness is something like this. First, there was a general sense in various apologetics and evangelistic ministries that alternative worldviews are not really there to be understood and appreciated. They are only there to be identified and rejected. One must always be on guard against them. Second, there was a general sense that every artist had a clear worldview that one could identify in their work. It was the job of a good Christian parent to identify that worldview and see if it is safe for their child to listen to the music. Third, I don't remember much discussion on the idea that one could consider other worldviews in an effort to make up one's own mind. That kind of discussion seemed to come later in the early 2000s after various Christians were fed-up with the way that music was being viewed in American Christian subcultures.

I don't want to be entirely negative about this. I did start to learn the value of developing my own worldview throughout this. I did start to learn to identify other worldviews. As I will discuss soon, I quickly learned how to identify inconsistency in other people's beliefs and arguments. Identifying inconsistency is key for any good philosopher. Thus, as my musical tastes developed, so did my philosophical proclivities.

You Can't Listen to That

Like most people, my musical tastes have changed over the years. When I was a child, I listened to whatever music my parents played for me. I have vague memories of listening to Michael Jackson and singing along. I have clear memories of hearing Tina Turner and getting sick in the car. To this day, I still associate Tina Turner with getting car sick. I had a bizarre Beach Boys phase that took me years to explain. Starting when I was 7, all of my family members kept buying me Beach Boys cassette tapes as birthday presents. This lasted for a few years. I didn't understand why everyone kept buying me Beach Boys stuff. I would listen to them regularly, but I wasn't exactly feeling those good vibrations. That was because I thought it was my only listening option. It wasn't until I was in my late 30s that an older cousin informed me that my mom had told our relatives that I loved the Beach Boys and that their music would be the perfect gift for me. Apparently, everyone thought I was a massive fan. Based on what, I do not know. I do remember going through an MC Hammer phase and that was based on a genuine interest from me. After all, Hammer is too legit to quit. That most revered MC also taught me that I have to pray just to make it today.

I first started getting into heavier music in Jr. High. Grunge and alternative were my gateway drug. I would listen to Silverchair, Bush, and Nirvana. My mother did not approve of my departure from top 40 radio and started demanding to examine the lyrics of the music that I was listening to. She was certain that there had to be a clear message contained within the lyrics. In retrospect, I take a kind of sick pleasure in imagining my mom reading the lyrics of any Bush song and trying to discern their true meaning. Those lyrics are nothing but profound sounding nonsense designed to make the singer look deep and attractive to young women. But remember my American Christian cultural context—there has to be a worldview hidden behind the lyrics. So my mother persisted in scrutinizing every word in the CD's liner notes. I'm certain that she was unable to figure out the true meaning of it all, but she did eventually land on something objectionable. My mom would disapprove because the lyrics were "too depressing." We certainly don't want anyone encountering depressing lyrics in a song. That could be a disaster for young Christian minds. So I was told that I could not listen to such music. It just did not present a safe worldview.

By Freshman year of High School, I had discovered Nü Metal bands like Korn, Limp Bizkit, Deftones, and Slipknot. I was still not really satisfied with these bands because something was missing. Then, I discovered the hardcore scene with bands like Zao, Living Sacrifice, Norma Jean, and so many others. I started listening to metal bands like The Black Dahlia Murder, As I Lay Dying, and many other bands with death in their names. I even played guitar in a band called To Die Alone.

Simply listening to this music did not foster a sense of philosophical inquiry within me. Instead, it was the reactions from teachers, parents, and other concerned citizens that helped spark my philosophical curiosities. For example, I remember my Bible teacher doing a lesson on music appreciation and worldview assessment. We all had to bring to class one song that we enjoyed. We would listen to the song with our classmates and then try to dissect the meaning of the song. My English teacher tried a similar homework assignment where we had to examine the meaning behind three different songs from musical artists that we were listening to. This exercise quickly alerted me to the fact that there is not a clear worldview hidden behind every lyric. Some of the punk and metal songs that I tried to examine made absolutely no sense. My teacher said that was a sign of nihilism. At the time, I thought it was indicative of a more basic phenomenon—most people do not have a well-developed worldview. I still agree with that assessment, but now I think there is another phenomenon going on as well. Most people don't know how to write lyrics with a coherent meaning. Also, the flow of the lyrics needs to fit the rhythm of the song. What is being sung needs to sound good with what is happening with the music. That does not always allow for philosophical precision in the meaning of the lyrics, nor is philosophical precision even of interest when most people sit down to write lyrics. Regardless, this so-called worldview engagement started to spark in me some critical questions. Is there really a meaning in everything? Is there really any consistency in what the adults are telling me?

Again, such philosophical curiosities grew in response to reactions from others. My first real interest in philosophy came from my love of identifying inconsistencies in others and responding to people's objections.

Over the years, I have encountered various objections to listening to such "dark" music. I remember once sitting in a car with a classical violinist. I was listening to the new Black Dahlia Murder album *Unhallowed*. The violinist asked me, "When Jesus comes back, do you really think that will be the music playing as the skies part ways?" I immediately said, "Why not?! What better way to usher in the apocalypse."

Then, of course, there were the obvious objections to listening to metal. Here is a common list of objections that I have encountered more times than I care to remember:

- They sound like demons with all that screaming. You can't listen to demonic music.
- You can't listen to anything that focuses so much on death and destruction.
- It is so violent.
- It worships the devil.

Allow me to address these objections one by one. Consider my mom's objection that the lyrics were too depressing. The suggestion is that Christians should never listen to any artistic content that is depressing. Being an overly sarcastic teenager, I would often retort, "I guess I should never read the book of Lamentations." The book of Lamentations is written from the perspective of the prophet Jeremiah who has just witnessed the destruction of his city. He is watching his nation fall into captivity at the hands of his enemies. The poetry of Lamentations is understandably dark. Are we never to engage with dark artistic expressions as Christians? That surely has to be unbiblical. After all, the book of Ecclesiastes famously starts out by declaring that life is meaningless, just a chasing after the wind. If that is acceptable, but some depressing metal lyrics are not, then I should like to know what the justification is for this dichotomy.

Depending on one's theological beliefs, the justification will be hard to make. To see this, consider Make Them Suffer's song "Erase Me."[1] The lyrics say, "Why would you save me? I'm not worth saving. You're suffocating. So just erase me. Annihilate me. Assassinate me. I'm not worth saving. So just erase me." Surely a Calvinist would agree with this

[1] Make Them Suffer, "Erase Me," How to Survive a Funeral, Rise Records 2020.

sentiment. In fact, on most Augustinian and Calvinistic views, humans are not worth saving at all. Reflecting on the fact that humans are worthless, yet God freely chooses to save us, is meant to stir the heart to worship God. The old Isaac Watts hymn "Alas and Did My Saviour Bleed!" contains the line, "Would he devote that sacred head for such a worm as I?" If this hymn is acceptable to sing in a church service, then I should very much like to know what is so objectionable about the lyrics of "Erase Me." Both "Erase Me" and Calvinist theology have the same lowly view of man, and both see this as the occasion for certain emotional expressions of awe and wonderment.

Perhaps the lesson to be learned here is that certain emotions are appropriate to express at different moments, depending on the context. The author of Ecclesiastes tells us that there is a time for a wide range of emotions, and the author expresses some pretty grim emotions at times. In Chapter 3, the preacher says,

> For everything there is a season, and a time for every matter under heaven: a time to be born, and a time to die; a time to plant, and a time to pluck up what is planted; a time to kill, and a time to heal; a time to break down, and a time to build up; a time to weep, and a time to laugh; a time to mourn, and a time to dance; a time to cast away stones, and a time to gather stones together; a time to embrace, and a time to refrain from embracing; a time to seek, and a time to lose; a time to keep, and a time to cast away; a time to tear, and a time to sew; a time to keep silence, and a time to speak; a time to love, and a time to hate; a time for war, and a time for peace.
>
> (Ecclesiastes 3:1–8)

If anything seems to be biblical, it is that there are certain emotions that are fitting to the various circumstances of life that befall humans. This is a theme that I shall return to later. For now, I want to carry on dealing with objections.

What about listening to demons? As a Christian, I would certainly not endorse taking life advice from demons. I gather that they are not the most reliable bunch. However, I have never encountered a demon, if any exist. I honestly have no idea what a demon sounds like. I always found it odd when people would tell me that metal music sounded demonic. I would often ask, "Have you heard a demon before? Do they really sound like this?" Look, as a professional theologian, I have read the

Bible through many times. I don't recall any description of what a demon sounds like. So this objection makes no sense.

What about the next set of objections? These objections say that you cannot listen to anything that focuses so much on death, destruction, and violence. Well, this excludes vast portions of the Bible from being acceptable for Christian consumption. The Old Testament alone contains stories of violent rape, dismemberment, the glorification of war, fire raining from heaven, and the destruction of civilizations. There is even a story of an incredibly fat king who gets stabbed to death while sitting on the toilet! (Judges 3) If this is appropriate for Christian consumption, then I am struggling to see why I cannot listen to the latest Bleed From Within album.

What about devil worship? I'm not a big fan of devil worship, but it is unclear to me how many bands actually worship the devil. Sure, there are various black metal bands from Norway that claim to worship the devil, but it is difficult to know what is for show and what is for real. Consider the sordid history of the band Mayhem. Some of them talked a big game about worshipping the devil, but only a few of them actually went and burned churches. One of the founding members was killed by the singer partly because he didn't actually worship the devil! Also, recall that my parents endorsed my Beach Boys phase. Apparently, it is acceptable for the Beach Boys to hang out with Charles Manson, but it is unacceptable for me to listen to any black metal.

As I see it, most of the bands are talking about the devil for show. Alice Cooper concurs. He recognized that everyone needs a bit of spooky fun every now and then. There is no need to actually worship the devil, but there is a great value to playing make believe. As a Christian, he would know.

Most bands have a surface level fascination with themes of death, destruction, demons, and war because it makes them look tough as nails. But if you push them to endorse those things in a very real way, you will quickly see that rough exterior fade away. For example, the Russian band, Slaughter to Prevail, has many songs about war and violence. One of their biggest hits is a song called "Demolisher."[2] Yet, when Russia invaded Ukraine in 2022, Slaughter to Prevail immediately released a video saying that they condemn all acts of war and unnecessary violence.

---

[2] Slaughter to Prevail, "Demolisher," Kostolom, Sumerian Records 2019.

They immediately condemned the invasion of Ukraine and had to leave Russia because of their public dissent to the war. They openly acknowledged that while their songs and music videos often contain themes of war and violence, they pointed out that there is a difference between artistic expression and actual violence. The artistic expression is sensationalized in order to offer a cathartic release of anger.

This is a striking difference from some of the songs one encounters in the Bible. Immediately following the crossing of the Red Sea, Aaron's sister Miriam writes a song praising God for throwing the Egyptians into the sea (Exodus 15:21). This is not a sensationalized bit of make believe. This is someone genuinely relishing in the destruction of her enemies. This leads me to ask a broader question about the appropriateness of emotions. When are certain emotions acceptable and when are they not?

Emotions and Truth

There was something rotten in the state of Indiana and its Christian subculture's approach to music, emotions, and truth that I encountered growing up. Emotions and truth were often seen to be in conflict, and yet I was constantly being told to show various emotions at different moments. "Don't chase those feelings. Chase the truth of Christ." "Don't listen to that music. It is depressing." "Sing louder in church because you need to show God that you are thankful." How does any of this fit together?

Perhaps some definitions are in order. To start, allow me to define truth. I take truth to be some kind of correspondence with reality. A declarative sentence is true if it accurately describes the way the world is. For example, "the naked cat is sitting on my lap" is true if and only if there is a naked cat sitting on my lap. Do you honestly expect me to have a normal fluffy cat? Of course not! I have a cat that looks like a mythical creature born of nightmares.

Emotions have an interesting relationship to truth and values (Deonna and Teroni 2012, pp. 40–50). I take an emotion to be a felt evaluation of a situation. Emotions have a cognitive and an affective component to them. Emotions are cognitive in that they represent the world as being a certain way. In particular, emotions represent one's circumstance as having certain values or disvalues. Your emotions are affective in the sense that there is something that it is like to have that particular evaluation.

When you have an evaluation of a situation, it feels a particular way. For instance, when some people see my dark-skinned cat in his naked glory, they find themselves in awe. They evaluate my cat, who is named Constantine, to be awesome. This felt evaluation is true if Constantine does in fact have the property of *being awesome*. This emotion is false if Constantine is not actually awesome. In case you are wondering, Constantine is in fact awesome, and his awesomeness gives rise to certain appropriate emotions like awe, wonder, and amazement.

This relationship between truth and emotions should not be foreign to the Christian worldview. Jesus understood it well. In Matthew 11:17, Jesus chides a stubborn audience by saying, "You played the flute, but no one was dancing. You sang a sad song, but no one was crying." Allow me to explain a bit of what is going on here because it should help you see the relationship between truth and emotions.

In Matthew 11:1–19, we find John the Baptist in prison. John has heard of the ministry of Jesus and decides to send his disciples to inquire about a few details. In particular, John and his disciples wish to know if Jesus is the one who is to come (i.e. the messiah). If Jesus is not the one to come, they ask if they should look for someone else. Jesus does not seem terribly impressed by this question. He tells John's disciples that the blind have received their sight, the lame have been made to walk, the dead have been raised, and the poor have good news preached to them. One can almost feel the discomfort of John's disciples as they hear this reply from Jesus. They ask, "Jesus, are you the one who is promised to come?" And they get a reply that basically says, "Well, I have raised the dead. What do you think?"

As John's disciples leave, Jesus starts speaking to a crowd about John the Baptist. Once again, one can see that Jesus is not entirely pleased with the question from John. Jesus says, "What did you go out into the wilderness to see? A reed shaken by the wind?" (Matthew 11:8) To say that this is dripping with sarcasm would be an understatement. Jesus goes on to point out that John is really looking for a prophet and that John is in fact a great prophet.

Jesus then turns his frustration away from John and toward an unbelieving Hebrew people. He asks who he should compare this present generation to. The question is rhetorical since Jesus immediately provides an answer. Jesus says that the current generation is like a group of children whose playmate calls out, "We played the flute for you, and you did not dance; we sang a dirge, and you did not mourn" (v. 17). Jesus goes on to explain that this current generation has misidentified John. John came to prophesy, but the people have accused him of being possessed by a demon. Then Jesus says that the Son of Man has come, and the people have called Jesus a glutton, a drunkard, and friend of sinners. In other words, Jesus' audience just does not seem to be grasping who Jesus actually is.

Why do I reflect on this passage from Matthew? The child's song that Jesus quotes is rather intriguing and quite possibly illuminating for my purposes. What is the point of this song that Jesus quotes? What would this reference say to Jesus' audience? What is the big deal about someone playing the flute and no one dancing? What is wrong with someone singing a sad song and no one crying?

The song seems to presuppose *emotional truth*. An emotion is true if it represents the world as being the way the world is, and if it motivates a fitting response. An emotion is false if it fails to accurately represent the values in the world, and if it motivates an inappropriate response (see Roberts 2013, pp. 91–92). The song that Jesus is quoting seems to be presupposing this. There is something wrong with the child who hears the flute, but does not dance. The flute should provoke the child to dance because it is a delightful tune. There is also something wrong with the child who hears the sad song, but does not cry. Why? Because the child must have a really hard heart if he does not cry at such a sad song. There is something wrong with the child's emotional response to the sad song.

What purpose does this song play in Jesus' sermon to this crowd? Jesus is saying that, in a similar way, there is something wrong with the way that this generation has responded to John and Jesus. The child who hears the sad song but does not cry is somewhat daft. The person who hears John the Baptist speak and claims that John is possessed by a demon is also daft. John came to tell people of their sins, and the need for repentance. John is demanding a certain kind of emotional response—contrition, repentance, conviction, guilt, and so on. Yet, John is not getting that response from as many people as Jesus thinks should be responding. The emotional response to John just is not appropriate to what the situation demands.

The child who hears the flute, but does not dance is somewhat thick. The child is not responding with the sort of delight that is appropriate to the song. In a similar way, the crowd is not responding to Jesus with the sort of delight that is appropriate to Jesus' coming. Jesus is healing sickness, removing sins, and raising the dead. That is good news that demands a dance of celebration! Yet, that is not the response that Jesus perceives his audience to have. His audience is just as thick as the child who does not dance to the happy tune of the flute. Jesus' statement seems to affirm that one's emotions can be true or false depending on how they correspond to objective reality.[3]

Setting the Mood

There is something so deeply important about the ability and opportunity to express the wide range of human emotions. Though we often talk about emotions leading us into irrational behavior, emotions are so marvelously rational. They can fit a situation so well, and they can track the values in a situation in the most satisfying way. Yet, we often struggle to fully process our emotions. Our lives are a buzzing, baffling confusion, so it is difficult to take everything in. Poison the Well says, "emotions catch up with me, I am too fast for them."[4] As someone who has struggled with flattened emotional affect, I understand this well. I sometimes try to run away from emotions in order to deal with the never-ending tragedy of life, but it is deeply unhealthy to suppress one's emotions. There is a deep human need to get our emotions out in appropriate ways.

We try to find many different ways to express these emotions. If you need to cry, you might watch a sad movie, or listen to a sad song. If you need to get the party started, you put on your dance playlist. There is something so therapeutic about getting our emotions out while listening to music.

Music can add or subtract value to a situation, and the corresponding emotion can track this. Imagine a scenario where you are on a romantic date at a fine Italian restaurant. The music that is playing in the background can add to the ambience, but if the music is loud Polka that ruins the moment. We need music to fit the situation.

I suffer from dysthymia, which is form of chronic low mood. One of the things that is so frustrating about dysthymia is that a bout of low mood can occur when things in my life are going perfectly fine. The low mood does not fit the situation, which makes me feel even worse. When

[3] Within the philosophy of emotions, there are many different standards of correctness by which an emotion may be judged. I have focused on truth and fittingness to the situation, but there are other standards related to the intensity of the emotion, and the fitting of the emotion with one's own background commitments and considered judgments. For more on this see Deonna and Teroni (2012) and Pearson (2018).

[4] "Mid Air Love Message," *The Opposite of December...A Season of Separation*, Trustkill Records 1999.

I am feeling depressed, I need to connect with that depression in a way that helps me reflect and move on. The Devil Wears Prada reflects on this in their song "Chemical."

> Waking up to no meaning
> I stare at the ceiling
> Count the imperfections that
> Surround my being
> Can tell how I'm feeling
> And it hurts more when you ask
> There's a hole in my
> head and heart
> But I'm a long way from the start[5]

As I reflect on moments of depression, sometimes "I want to scream, but it won't help." But you know what helps me get out of bed. Acknowledging that the way I feel is only chemical.

> Back when I couldn't move, was frozen
> I told myself it's all good
> It's only chemical.

One of the ways to deal with my dysthymia is realizing that the way I am feeling is a chemical reaction in my brain that does not reflect my current circumstances. That can help me start to evaluate the way my situation actually is.

What about when you need to get the party started? Sometimes you just have to take a line from Every Time I Die and say "I've been bitten by the party animal."[6] But you need to find a good party that will go into the wee hours of the morning. Every Time I Die's "Turtles All the Way Down" has some great advice here. They say, "I'll come to your party if it goes until 4 question marks at least. 3 or less and it's not worth my time at all."[7]

Once you have found a good party that goes all night long, you need some music to lighten the mood. Black metal is not the way to go. You

---

[5] The Devil Wears Prada, "Chemical," The Act, Solid State Records 2019.
[6] Every Time I Die, "We're Wolf," *The Big Dirty*, Ferret Records 2007.
[7] Every Time I Die, "Turtles All the Way Down," *New Junk Aesthetic*, Epitaph Records 2009.

might need some German techno deathcore to get you into the dancing mood. Electric Callboy understands this well in their song, "We've Got the Moves."

> Summer mood, hot sand under my feet
> Cold beer, cheap wine
> Yeah, that's all that we need
> We got the moves, we got the moves
> And everybody's like
> "Oh, fuck yeah, let's do it again!"
> We got the moves, we got the moves
> And everybody's like
> "Yesterday we drank too much, let's do
> it again!"
> We got the groove, we got the groove
> So everybody, put your hands straight up!
> Tonight is the night![8]

Yet our need for emotional expression goes deeper than occasional bouts of depression and getting ready to party. We empathetic creatures so desperately want to be understood. We crave it. We want the world to understand us, to get us (see Morton 2017). When Haste the Day plays their song "Substance," all the kids at the show are screaming, "I want you to know what I am going through!"[9]

Music is often a great way for us to emotionally put ourselves out there, and try to connect to others. We will sometimes find a song that so perfectly captures what we are going through that we feel like we have met a soulmate.

All of this makes sense to me, given my theistic beliefs about a maximally empathetic God (see Zagzebski 2013). According to Francis McConnell, humans "want to feel that their suffering means something at the center of the universe. It means that they crave at least to be understood through the understanding which comes out of sympathetic sharing of distress" (McConnell 1924, p. 290). For McConnell, God's moral perfection demands that God empathize with our pain and suffering. McConnell writes,

---

[8] Electric Callboy, "We Got the Moves," Tekkno, Century Media Records 2022.

[9] Haste the Day, "Substance," Burning Bridges, Solid State Records 2004.

> The Cross is, first of all, God's supreme satisfaction of his own conscience, the preservation of his own self-respect. God has sent men forth into a terrible universe without consulting them, and has thrust into their hands the awful boon of freedom. He is thus under enormous moral obligation. He need not have created men, but having created them he cannot discharge his moral bonds to them and to himself short of Calvary. There is no responsibility in the universe so heavy as that of Creatorship. If the Biblical teaching, that the earthly pain of man is in part at least a consequent of moral evil, has within it a grain of truth it is hard to see how a moral Creator could have peace of conscience without sharing the pain made necessary by the moral imperfections flowing from an unsolicited gift of freedom.
>
> (McConnell 1906, pp. 109–110)

Morality or a Fashion Statement

Speaking of morality, I want to offer some lessons I have learned about morality from heavy metal. After being in the hardcore music scene for several years, I quickly learned a valuable lesson: You should never base your morality on fashion trends. This is an important point in general, but my experiences in the music scene gave me vivid examples of what happens when your morality is nothing more than a fashion statement. While I appreciate the fact that at times one must prioritize fashion over function, morality is meant to be based on practical reasoning. If some alleged moral demand is not practical, then it is not a genuine moral demand.

During my late teens and early 20s, veganism and straight-edge were quite popular. As you probably know, when something is popular, various people will try to outdo one another by going more extreme. I saw this far too often in the hardcore music scene. For example, I had many friends flirt with veganism because it was cool. However, there were several problems with this. First, their motivations to become vegan were often not grounded in reasons related to animal cruelty. Instead, their motivations were to look cool and get laid. Second, we are talking about teenagers with limited incomes and very limited culinary skills. Many of my vegan friends had a diet that consisted of Taco Bell tortilla shells filled with beans and rice. This naturally led to an extreme weight loss and a chronic fatigue with the inevitable result that my friends' veganism would last for only a few months. This fashionable moral trend was simply not practical.

One of the most outstanding examples of this came from a band in my local music scene. The name of the band completely escapes me at this point. I am sure that it was some unnecessarily long band name. Long band names smashed into one word, separated by straight-edge X's were quite popular at the time. It was probably XtheXbeautyXofXdyingXslowlyX or something of the sort. What I can remember is this. Their musical career lasted less than a year. When they first started playing shows, they had a lot of energy and would preach against animal cruelty from the stage. Their merch table would have pamphlets from PETA, but as they grew more extreme, they soon started distributing leaflets from The Animal Liberation Front and other groups on the US terrorist watch list. In an effort to be more edgy, and more cool, their diet became more restrictive. I remember seeing their last show. As they took the stage, their bodies were completely emaciated. They could barely hold their instruments, and it looked like they might pass out before finishing their set. What may have started out as a genuine interest in protecting the value of animals eventually became an impractical display of self-flagellation.

Allow me to offer one more example of this. At one point in my early 20s, I moved to Atlanta for university. I auditioned for several bands, and I was invited to join two. I ended up declining both. I declined one because I found myself with little time given my studies. I declined the other because I found their views outrageous. They were a straight-edge band that called themselves something like Creation's End.

The ethos of straight-edge is often associated with no drugs or alcohol. It was a rejection of the excesses, decadence, and moral degeneracy of the hippies, and a reaction to the rampant drug use of the early punk era. The basic moral principle behind the straight-edge movement is sometimes expressed as "Don't rely on anything that could be a crutch."

I had encountered many different straight-edge kids back home in Indiana, but none as extreme as this band that I auditioned for in Atlanta. When I asked them about what all counted as a "crutch," we began to have a rather illuminating philosophical discussion. The band believed that humanity is the problem that plagues creation and that humanity needs to naturally die out. Further, humans must have some sort of tough resilience in the face of our natural condition. One must not rely on anything that could count as a crutch. My Christian faith was one point of contention because faith could be seen as a crutch used to help one through times of hardship. Another point of contention was my asthma medication. I was relying on my daily asthma pills to breathe, and that also counted as a crutch. This form of straight-edge was not merely against illegal drugs, but extended to medically prescribed drugs as well. I found this to be a bit much and kindly declined their offer to join the band. If I wanted to die from lack of asthma medication, I would have joined the band Suffocate Faster.

Let me be clear about something. I am not here offering an argument against being vegan straight-edge. I am simply pointing out the reality of what happens when morality is not based on sound reasons, but instead based on fashion trends. When the zealotry of idealistic youth grabs hold of some seeming moral truth, they can push it to the most impractical of extremes. If morality is meant to be practical reasoning, this is certainly not the way to go. I learned a lesson here about basic moral reasoning. If an ethical theory tells you to do something that is obviously wrong or absurd, then there is obviously something wrong with that ethical theory.

I don't want to give the wrong impression here. There are moral examples to be found in heavy metal. Many of which should be quite amenable to the reflective Christian. Allow me to mention two.

Being a good Midwestern boy, I would be remiss if I did not mention a Hoosier hardcore band. Burn It Down has a classic song called "Kill Your Idols" that contains sentiments that Christians can agree to.

> What are you made of?
> Who's your creator?
> Who comforts you,
> When you sleep?
>
> What animates you?
> Who do you pray to?
> Are you the master?
> The master of all that you see?
> We'll see what they're made of
>
> You dance around the fire
> Of such transient desires
> You bow your head
> To a decaying ground
> Your TV, your sensuality
> Your magazine cuts me
> Like a million bodies washed out to sea
> What do you live for?

I see you worship yourself
And everything that they taught you to be

Kill their idols
Kill their idols
Kill their idols
We'll kill their idols[10]

Given the biblical teachings against idolatry, I see no reason why a Christian should object to the message of this song. Of course, the lyrics are sung with tough-guy hardcore vocals, and I heard from a cousin's next-door neighbor's friend that this is what demons sound like, so maybe this is somewhat dubious.

Here is my second moral example: Thy Art is Murder, "Holy War." It offers reflections on the evil of holy war. Surely a Christian can stand behind the rejection of using religion to justify war. Check out these lyrics.

Die for Christ, die for Allah, die for Jerusalem, die for Torah
Father and son marching in rhythm
Firing bullets through the skulls of the children
Holy war, mortars and martyrs
Holy war, unholy followers
Holy war, brainwashed with death
Holy war, unholy mess
I reject the laws of the misguided
False prophets imprison nations fuelling self-annihilation
I reject pocket lined political demons
Who arm the ignorant for election season
Empires buried in sand
A history of the failures in man
Armies of guardians, servants of bibles
Reciting verses as they stand before rifles
Millions of lives erased
Hatred marked as madness
Violence in leaves of scripture
A world aflame with malice
We will all die for nothing

[10] Burn It Down, "Kill Their Idols," Eat, *Sleep, Mate, Defend*, Escape Artist Records 1998.

There is silence in the house of God
There is only the cry of hell
There is silence in the house of God
There is only the cry of hell
Holy war, mortars and martyrs
Holy war, unholy followers
Holy war, brainwashed with death
Holy war, unholy mess
Die for Christ, die for Allah, die for Jerusalem, die for Torah
Father and son marching in rhythm
Firing bullets through the skulls of the children
Holy war, holy war
We will all die for nothing
We will all die for nothing[11]

The moral outrage of using religion to justify a godless war is an important lesson that any preacher should be able to stand behind. Of course, this is not a moral lesson that I learned from heavy metal. Thankfully, I did not need a metal song to learn that religious wars are evil. But this song offers a vivid, artistic expression of the moral outrage one ought to have in the face of religious war. Something about this emotional expression in the song seems so rational, so fitting to me. I see no need for a concerned Christian parent to deem this song unsafe. Instead, I should think that a Christian could say "Amen!"

Appreciating Rival Worldviews

I want to return to the theme of considering alternative worldviews. Earlier, I talked about how rival worldviews were originally presented to me as things to identify and reject. It was not until later in my teenage years that I encountered discussions on studying rival worldviews in order to make up my own mind. As I have grown as a philosopher, I now see the value in coming to appreciate differing views on all manner of subject matters. My main research agenda is studying different conceptions of God and the God–world relationship so that I can make up my own mind about the nature and existence of God. I want to give you just a little

[11] Thy Art is Murder, "Holy War," Holy War, Nuclear Blast 2015.

sample of how considering rival views can help facilitate one's reflections on questions about the nature of ultimate reality and the meaning of life.

I want to start with Zao's "The Funeral of God" album. When this thing came out in 2004, I remember thinking that Zao had jumped the shark. God is a necessarily existent being, so it is metaphysically impossible for God to cease to exist. That was my immediate reaction, but thankfully I gave the album a chance, though the album is certainly not my favorite from Zao. This ain't no "Liberate Te Ex Inferis," but I digress. "The Funeral of God" invites the listener into a particular worldview. Say that God created everything, but then became so fed up with humanity that He simply walked away. What would that look like? In "The Last Song From Zion," God tells humanity that He is going to answer the prayers of their "black hearts. . .Man's will be done."[12] God is going to step away from creation, and let mankind use their free will as they see fit. As the story of the album unfolds, humanity descends into war and self-destruction. Humans start to "Praise the War Machine," chanting "666. The number of man brought upon by man." In "Truly, Truly, This is the End," after witnessing the devastation that mankind has brought upon itself, humanity starts to tell stories of a king who once walked the sky before he was dethroned by the tribe of Judas. Humanity starts to regret what has happened, and waits for God's return. Yet the album ends on this note of unanswered waiting. In the final track, "Psalm of the City of the Dead," the lyrics read,

> As we wait here for a sign we are greeted by the end of time,
> These streets aren't paved with gold,
> You are my everything,
> My soul is growing cold.[13]

There is no real sense in the album that God will return. As a theologian and philosopher, listening to this music forces me to confront important questions. Is God really like that? Is God the kind of being who could give up on His creation? What kind of moral responsibility does the creator of the universe actually have toward His creatures? Christianity proclaims that God has made various promises to humans, promises to

---

[12] Zao, "The Last Song From Zion," *The Funeral of God*, Ferret Records 2004.
[13] Zao, "Psalm of the City of the Dead," *The Funeral of God*, Ferret Records 2004.

raise them from the dead, judge the wicked, and heal the righteous and meek. Will God make good on those promises at the eschaton?

Next, consider a completely different view of reality in which there is no God, but only this ever-expanding universe. As one contemplates the vastness of the universe, it is natural to wonder if far off galaxies contain life. For some, this might create a sense of excitement and wonder. It certainly excited many theists during the scientific revolution (Cf. Lovejoy 1966). Yet, I am often curious how much excitement this should illicit. Remember what we know about the universe based on our own experience and current science. Current cosmological predictions have the universe ending in heat death in which biological life will no longer be possible. Our own lived experience does tell us of great beauty, but it also speaks of terrifying destruction.

> To see this, consider The Acacia Strain's song "Names."
>
> Who would've crossed oceans
> Now have seen outstanding waters
> Wondering what we could've done differently
> Galaxies burnt out and frozen forever
> Extermination
> Life never known
> Interdimensional agony
> You will have never known it was even there
> All places, all things have souls
> All souls can be devoured[14]

Think about this for a moment. Imagine being an explorer who encounters fallen kingdoms; long lost civilizations that humanity has never heard of before. Now extend that imagination to the entire universe. Worlds coming into existence and ceasing to be; worlds that I never even knew were there. That moment in the song is haunting. It is the cold reality of living in a vast universe. There are so many galaxies that I know nothing of that have long been destroyed. Places of great value that have come and gone without my recognition. It invites serious questions. Is that my fate too? Is that all of our fates? Living in a vast universe where things of value cease to be. As Conducting From the Grave's song

[14] The Acacia Strain, "Names," It Comes in Waves, Closed Casket Activities 2019.

"Eternally Gutted," says, "In this world, empires rise and fall, ages come and go. The only thing that's certain, everything will someday die."[15]

Feeling the full force of the inevitability of death is not something that one can embrace all at once. It comes in waves. It always comes in waves. I find something terrifyingly lonely about these thoughts. That sense of loneliness, perhaps even a sense of panic, stirs me to assess different worldviews, sentiments, and philosophical propositions. It makes me appreciate the empathetic God of the Christian scriptures. If this God exists, then certain truths follow. Though no one else may see my value, God does. If God does not exist, my value will be washed away with the coming destruction of the cosmos. To be clear, I am not making the point that life is utterly meaningless in a godless universe, nor am I saying that there are no objective values in a godless universe.[16] My claim is that all concrete values eventually cease to be in a godless universe that ends in the total destruction of life. Whereas in a Christian universe, not all who wander are lost. The God of the Bible is a God who has promised to preserve valuable things for all eternity.

All of this leads me to ask: What kind of universe are we living in? Are we living in a Godly universe in which nothing is truly lost because all will be restored at the great unveiling? Or is it a godless world where everything of value will end with the heat death of the universe? It's either this or the apocalypse.

References

Deonna, J.A. and Teroni, F. (2012). *The Emotions: A Philosophical Introduction*. New York: Routledge.

Kraay, K.J. (ed.) (2018). *Does God Matter? Essays on the Axiological Consequences of Theism*. New York: Routledge.

Lovejoy, A.O. (1966). *The Great Chain of Being: A Study of the History of an Idea*. Cambridge: Harvard University Press.

Mawson, T.J. (2019). *Monotheism and the Meaning of Life*. Cambridge: Cambridge University Press.

McConnell, F.J. (1924). *Is God Limited?* London: Williams and Norgate.

---

[15] Conducting From the Grave, "Eternally Gutted," When Legends Become Dust, Sumerian Records 2009.

[16] For more on the current debates over God and the meaning of life, see Kraay (2018) and Mawson (2019).

McConnell, F.J. (1906). *The Divine Immanence*. New York: The Methodist Book Concern.

Morton, A. (2017). Empathy and imagination. In: *The Routledge Handbook of Philosophy of Empathy* (ed. H.L. Maibom), 180–189. London: Routledge.

Pearson, O. (2018). *Rationality, Time, and Self*. Cham: Springer International Publishing.

Roberts, R.C. (2013). *Emotions in the Moral Life*. Cambridge: Cambridge University Press.

Zagzebski, L. (2013). *Omnisubjectivity: A Defense of a Divine Attribute*. Milwaukee: Marquette University Press.

Chapter 6
The Idea of the Unholy
C.D. Labbas

The numinous only unfolds its full content by slow degrees. . . . But where any whole is as yet incompletely presented, its earlier and partial constituent moments or elements, aroused in isolation, have naturally something bizarre, unintelligible, and even grotesque about them. This is especially true of that religious moment which would appear to have been in every case the first to be aroused in the human mind, viz. daemonic dread. Considered alone and *per se*, it necessarily and naturally looks more like the opposite of religion than religion itself. If it is singled out from the elements which form its context, it appears rather to resemble a dreadful form of auto-suggestion, a sort of psychological nightmare of the tribal mind. . . . One can understand how it is that not a few inquirers could seriously imagine that "religion" began with devil-worship, and that at bottom the devil is more ancient than God.

Rudolf Otto, *The Idea of the Holy* (1917), p. 136

We're not here to entertain you —
We're gonna make you scream!
When you wake in Hell tonite,
You'll think it was a dream.

Venom, "Burn this Place (to the Ground)"
From the album *Possessed* (1985, Neat Records)

Introduction: Thrills and Ills

"Why do you like that stuff? What could you possibly get out of it?"

I expect most passionate fans of heavy metal have encountered some variant of this question. Too often, the question reflects a kind of class bias more than any genuine puzzlement; metal is widely stigmatized as mere noise or illiterate chest beating, so the would-be respectable citizen voicing this question is really asking, "Why do you like that stuff which we all know is obviously garbage?" But the question *might* reflect a genuine puzzlement.

Let me relate a true story.

I've been a fan of metal since my early teens. In college, a good friend of mine was taking a course introducing musical theory, and she—who had never really paid attention to the stuff I listened to—was curious to hear it now, given her recent education. I, of course, was pleased to have the opportunity to share. I selected a modest number of diverse tracks for her; we sat and listened carefully as we went through each one. After each, she made some comments—the substance of which is completely lost to memory—relating what she had learned in the class to the pieces she had just heard. She seemed to be having fun applying that knowledge and left my dorm room with the same upbeat attitude.

She then—as she told me later—strolled back to her own dorm room, entered, felt suddenly ill, ran to the bathroom, and vomited.

Now there are two things that we might find curious here. First, assuming that the vomiting was indeed an effect of listening to this music, how could music that she enjoyed in the moment also have this slightly delayed effect of shock and nausea? How was it both fascinating to her in the moment yet apt to cause such discomfort only minutes later? Second, why did hearing of this give me a terrible sense of *delight*? This person was (and remains) a dear friend; I certainly did not wish her harm. But knowing this music that thrilled me so much caused her such physiological distress felt like some kind of *vindication* of my love of the music. In some way, what makes the experience so potentially upsetting also makes it rewarding.

The puzzle here is reminiscent of that often posed by those thinking about the appeal of art forms more widely recognized as having artistic value—tragic theater, say, or melancholy movies. And it is even more reminiscent of the question posed about a cultural production more closely related to metal, namely, horror movies. Why do people go through the trouble of making themselves feel horrified, or depressed, or shocked?

There is a sizable literature on this question, but my own focus is on a more narrowly circumscribed phenomenon: certain strains of heavy metal that are not merely sad or horrifying but which seem simultaneously both to celebrate what is sad and horrifying and to work against one's taking any sort of unalloyed joy in that celebration. Such pieces show up in more than one subgenre of metal, though they show up most frequently in black metal and to a lesser extent in death metal.

In this paper, I aim to sharpen the puzzle over the appeal of such music, propose and defend an explanatory hypothesis, and then consider a normative question about its value in light of that hypothesis. My hypothesis, in brief, is that these strains of metal are valued by fans and creators because of their ability to trigger what the theologian Rudolf Otto deemed *numinous* experiences in his classic study *The Idea of the Holy* (Otto 1917).[1] Numinous experiences are (to a rough approximation) ones in which the subject seems to apprehend something wholly alien, of great power, both dreadful and fascinating, in an experience that enlivens the subject even while making her feel as if she is herself unreal in the face of this entity. My hypothesis is not, however, that afficionados are seeking the holy. Instead, they conceive of the experience as an apprehension of the *unholy*, and it is the combination of the attractive features of the experience and this way of understanding it that governs the development and appreciation of these forms of art.

My first two tasks are to zero in on the relevant phenomenon and set out the hypothesis more carefully. I then turn to an overview of numinous experience as introduced by Otto, in which I show how it can be fit into a diabolic framework, and argue that my hypothesis makes unsurprising a range of facts about these kinds of metal. Finally, I raise a normative question: supposing my account of the appeal of this music is correct, what could be the value of it? Is there anything to be gained by subjecting oneself to such sonic attacks and undergoing experiences that present themselves as apprehensions of the unholy?

[1] As I recur to this text throughout, quoted material without attribution is to be understood as referring to Otto (1917).

The Target Phenomenon

Above I spoke of certain works of extreme metal that seem both to celebrate what is terrible and to work against taking real joy in such, noting that this is especially common in some black metal. But you may well wonder what this category includes. To help zero in on the phenomenon, I have assembled a somewhat random list of 31 samples (see the Appendix) that represent material from the first half of the 1980s until the first half of the 2020s. The selections differ from each other in various ways, but all, I think, exhibit to some degree the phenomenon in question. Let me just discuss a few to help fix ideas.

The earliest item on the list (1984) is the legendary "Triumph of Death" by the Swiss band Hellhammer. This nearly 10-minute track alternates between passages in which a shrieking guitar combines with percussion in a way that evokes crashing and stumbling, overlain with unhinged, screaming vocals, and passages in which things achieve a degree of order and a modest pace—just enough to give one a sense of forward motion. These latter passages encourage the listener to enjoy it as a more standard piece of music, perhaps nodding her head with the rhythm; but these are in every case interrupted with a return of the first kind of passage, so that the bits of trundling forward serve to emphasize the failure to make progress.

Moving ahead to 1997, consider the instrumental "I Filled with Woes the Passing Wind," by the band Judas Iscariot on their album *Of Great Eternity*. This piece lacks not only vocals but all percussion as well, relying solely on guitar riffs to generate a sense of rhythm. The song fades in with a melancholy pattern, repeated in a hypnotic and somewhat mechanical fashion, eventually breaking to a more sweeping chord, fringed with lighter notes that give the whole affair a delicate character despite its weight. The result is reminiscent of a funeral dirge, though instead of coming to a resolution, the opening riff resumes and fades out, giving a sense of an endless cycle—as befits the album title.

Let's move forward another decade and consider "Vulgar Asceticism" from Leviathan's album *Massive Conspiracy Against All Life* (2008). This nine-minute song fades in with a somewhat industrial sounding pulse underneath a trebly guitar; once fully in view, there appears a lurching riff that gives the impression of someone repeatedly lifting or straining to pull something along. Before this pattern closes, one hears a noise rising up behind the music—a sound that might be an electronic buzz, or a scream—which rises and then falls in pitch just as the major riff falls apart, at which point the song shifts to what feels like a march, one increasingly made irregular by moments at which the percussion fails to make the next step at the right time. In the last three minutes the march falls away to a more upbeat, energetic, and even celebratory tone, during which the trebly edges grow more pronounced until the bass drops away entirely and nothing remains for almost a full minute other than a snarl of wailing riffs, only slowly fading away, as if a multitude of sharp objects were held aloft in a tumult of air and then settled like feathers to the ground.

Coming closer to the present day (2017), consider "The Nazarene Bastard Crowned" from the debut album by Celestial Bodies, *Spit Forth from Chaos*. This two-minute blast of chaos might be thought of as a combination of free jazz, amplified guitar, and distorted electronic noise. The piece bristles with sharp noises and a feeling of hysteria, and it is not hard to sympathize with someone who says it is not music at all. Consider these comments from a review of *Spit Forth from Chaos* published in *Metal Temple*:

> Simply put, this is black metal mixed with noise . . . a heavy emphasis on noise. Each song sounds like a cacophony of random sounds, static, and screams. . . . As far as black metal goes, you couldn't ask for a better vocal performance but unfortunately it is wasted because this isn't actual music, in the traditional sense anyway. Simply put, I fail to understand how anyone could put this into their car, roll the windows down, and enjoy these "tunes" on a cool winter night. I also can't understand why anyone would listen to this when working out or doing anything really. . . . Actually, I wouldn't even call it atmospheric; that would imply the songs are built upon sonic landscapes that use their depth to conjure images and emotions into me when I close my eyes. When I close my eyes and listen to this, I can only picture paraplegics falling down never ending flights of stairs.[2]

I wouldn't play this in the car for background while driving around, either. It's not the sort of thing that makes sense as a backdrop for other activities; it rather insists that you attend to it exclusively. Nonetheless,

[2] Review by Justin Wittenmeier, August 6, 2017, found at metal-temple.com/review/celestial-bodies-spit-forth-from-chaos/, retrieved March 2025.

doing so can be exhilarating—even while the music sounds like "paraplegics falling down never ending flights of stairs."

It may be that the resources already present in the literature on the appeal of tragedy or horror can explain this exhilaration. But when it comes to *music*, there is, I believe, a further aspect that makes the puzzle more pressing. While one may say that a movie or painting "speaks" to one, it is quite different when the artwork is itself actual speech—directly calling on us, perhaps making us feel a need to respond in kind. Think of the common practice of call-and-response found in churches, political rallies, sports events, or anything else designed to have a big impact on the listening audience. The ease with which we fall into such activity is one manifestation of the way speech affects us in a particularly personal way: we can ignore what we see, but it is much harder to ignore a voice that addresses us.

Music is well recognized as having peculiar emotional power, and its connection with speech may help explain this. It surely helps explain what inspired Arthur Schopenhauer to assign such a special role to music in his general metaphysical system. Consider this remark from the first volume of *The World as Will and Representation*:

> [M]usic is by no means like the other arts, namely a copy of the Ideas, but a *copy of the will itself,* the objectivity of which are the Ideas. For this reason the effect of music is so very much more powerful and penetrating than is that of the other arts, for these others speak only of the shadow, but music of the essence.
>
> (Schopenhauer 1969, p. 257)

You can rest easy: I'm not going to defend Schopenhauer's metaphysics. But I think the idea that music expresses an agent's *will* captures something important: to hear something as music may be to hear sounds as if they were deliberately produced by an agent. A person can demand our attention by speaking forcefully to us, and the power of music to affect us deeply likely depends on a similar mechanism. This power of affecting us more intimately makes the puzzle here sharper. The appeal of a frightening movie is *prima facie* puzzling. The appeal of music that emulates a voice that delivers terrible messages to us is significantly more puzzling—especially when it is so demanding as to make it hard to treat it as a backdrop, as is the case with a great deal of the extreme metal at issue.

A Somewhat Perverse Hypothesis

Why, then, would one want to subject oneself to a sonic assault that demands attention, feels especially intimate, and seems to rub one's face in some horror?

My hypothesis takes as its cue a familiar complaint lodged by detractors of heavy metal, namely, that it is *satanic*. The worry that popular music is in league with the devil predates metal, of course, but it seemed to reach a crescendo in the 1980s and the "Satanic Panic." It's not obvious just how that charge of Satanism was to be understood.[3] Were we supposed to believe that the artists and fans who thrilled to such music were self-consciously devoted to evil? The charge is not credible. Even limiting ourselves to the strains of extreme metal that are my topic, its popularity is too extensive to suppose its popularity is due to the reach of such individuals. And speaking as a fan who has known many other fans whom I know to be decent, fair-minded people, there must be some distinct explanation of why it appeals to *us*.

Still, the charge of Satanism is obviously not made up out of whole cloth. While there are only teasing suggestions of the satanic in the foundational 70s, in the early 80s, there emerged bands that adopted it as an explicit stance in lyrics and imagery (in obvious symbiosis with the Satanic Panic). Venom is the clearest example of such in-your-face celebration of the demonic, declaring themselves to be "In League with Satan" on their debut *Welcome to Hell* (1981, Neat Records). Undoubtedly, this was driven by a desire to cause outrage (and hence publicity) and many others followed suit—Slayer, Destruction, Mercyful Fate, Possessed, and Bathory, to name some of the most prominent. What is striking, however, is that the devilish themes proved durable, far outliving their utility as devices for prompting outrage. It is now *more than forty years* after these themes blossomed in the early 80s, yet there now exist countless bands who have adopted this same posture. Evidently, something about the theme is attractive beyond its ability to stir controversy. But what?

---

[3] In fairness, I should note that there is one reading that seems plainly implied, but it presupposes the actual existence of Satan. This is the charge that the music is the result of his influence on the relevant individuals. Call this the "externalist" reading if you like. If you take the existence of Satan seriously, though, you would be on firmer ground identifying other things as satanic in this sense, e.g. authoritarian governments.

My hypothesis, again, is that this music can trigger numinous experiences understood as apprehensions of the unholy. Numinous experiences are attractive, and the satanic theme persists because of its role in shaping access to those experiences. When married to certain musical forms, it provides a technique for inducing them. That technique might be only intermittently successful; it might be limited in its effect to those steeped in the practice; and the results might often be just fleeting echoes of the powerful exemplars. But such irregular reinforcement is enough to explain the value placed on the music and the satanic themes.

There are three important claims on which my hypothesis rests. One is that the character of numinous experience is such as to *allow* it to be conceived of as an apprehension of the unholy. Since numinous experiences are said by Otto to be the foundation of religious conviction, my hypothesis may seem simply perverse. But the position is not as strange as it may seem. Otto himself noted this possibility in the passage cited at the start of this chapter. And a look at just how he characterizes numinous experience will make it clear how someone viewing it as an approach to the diabolic could find its features not just to allow but even to *confirm* his understanding.

The second claim on which my hypothesis rests is that these strains of extreme metal have features appropriate to inducing such experiences. One might agree that it is possible to apprehend numinous experiences as apprehensions of the unholy but doubt that there is any serious connection between the music and these experiences. I will be arguing that there is such a serious connection, showing that many features of the music and surrounding culture are predictable on the hypothesis that artists have in fact enjoyed such experiences and aim to replicate them with their work.

The third claim is simple: it is that numinous experiences in general are attractive in that subjects who have had them value them and crave more. This is something Otto called the "element of fascination." For the person who undergoes it, he writes, the numinous is

> not merely something to be wondered at but something that entrances him; and beside that in it which bewilders and confounds, he feels a something that captivates and transports him with a strange ravishment, rising often enough to the pitch of dizzy intoxication. (31)

Otto does not tell us *why* this kind of experience fascinates, though as a matter of observed fact he seems correct. For now, though, I will take this claim for granted, returning to it in the final section when I ask whether we *should* find it fascinating when understood in the perverse fashion I propose.

The Mysterium Tremendum and The Unholy Numinous

Otto's most basic contention is that the kind of experience he deems "numinous" is key to our idea of the holy, but he does not take the concept of the holy—as now understood—to be coextensive with the numinous:

> We generally take 'holy' as meaning 'completely good'; it is the absolute moral attribute, denoting the consummation of moral goodness. . . . It is true that all this moral significance is contained in the word 'holy', but it includes in addition—as even we cannot but feel—a clear overplus of meaning, and this it is now our task to isolate. Nor is this merely a later or acquired meaning; rather, 'holy', or at least the equivalent words in Latin and Greek, in Semitic and other ancient languages, denoted first and foremost only this overplus: if the ethical element was present at all, at any rate it was not original and never constituted the whole meaning of the word. (5)

In light of this, he wants a term to stand for the holy "*minus* its moral factor" and "numinous" is to play this role (6). He characterizes this experience by offering as an initial statement that "we are dealing with something for which there is only one appropriate expression," namely, *mysterium tremendum* (12). He then uses this phrase as a frame on which to hang more detailed characteristics, starting with *tremendum*.

In *tremendum,* he distinguishes three elements. The first is introduced as "awefulness" or a kind of dread, something that elicits a shudder or tremor of a certain sort. Strikingly, he describes this in relation to the "wrath of God" when he says that this "numinous tremor" corresponds to something that has been puzzling to theologians:

> [I]t is patent from many passages of the Old Testament that this 'wrath' has no concern whatever with moral qualities. There is something very baffling in the way in which it 'is kindled' and manifested. It is, as has been well said, 'like a hidden force of nature', like stored-up electricity,

> discharging itself upon anyone who comes too near. It is 'incalculable' and 'arbitrary'. Anyone who is accustomed to think of deity only by its rational attributes must see in this 'wrath' mere caprice and wilful passion. (18)

The second element Otto discerns in numinous experience is described as "overpoweringness" or "majesty" (19). He is careful to distinguish this from what we ordinarily experience when we find ourselves at the mercy of something else with greater power. In numinous experience, he says, the subject not only recognizes the power of the object but also sees himself in a diminished fashion: the subject feels "one's own submergence, of being but 'dust and ashes' and nothingness" (20). To appeal to a contemporary analytic idiom: the experience presents not just a claim about causal relations (the object has great power) but a claim about the metaphysical status of the relata: the subject is presented to herself as a being of lesser status—not real, or perhaps nothing in herself. What the subject appears to perceive is something supreme not only in power but in metaphysical status.

The third element distinguished under the heading of *tremendum* is that of "energy" or "urgency." Otto links this to talk of "vitality, passion, emotional temper, will, force, movement, excitement, activity, impetus" (23). More usefully, he characterizes this element as standing in opposition to a philosopher's God of "mere rational speculation" (23). The point may be put by saying that the experience not only has representational content but *imperatival* content as well. Unlike a mere "philosopher's God" which one might contemplate without feeling urged to do anything, the object of numinous experience is presented as commanding one to act.

The final element in Otto's characterization is hung on the term *mysterium*. The object of the experience is presented as something we cannot understand—where this is not just a result of our cognitive limitations but is due to some deep metaphysical divide:

> The truly 'mysterious' object is beyond our apprehension and comprehension, not only because our knowledge has certain irremovable limits, but because in it we come upon something inherently 'wholly other', whose kind and character are incommensurable with our own. (28)

This metaphysical talk is itself hard to understand. More helpful, perhaps, is his earlier comment that the wholly other character of the thing experienced is such as to induce stupor: "*Stupor* is plainly a different thing from *tremor*; it signifies blank wonder, an astonishment that strikes us dumb, amazement absolute" (26). To be stupefied is quite different from being in a state of not understanding something; one could be in that latter state while still being possessed of one's wits. Rather, being stupefied is a matter of being rendered incapable by the thing in question. It's not that we are just dumb; we are *struck* dumb.

We have, then, four main elements in numinous experience.[4] For convenience, I propose to call them *Dreadfulness*, *Supremacy*, *Urgency*, and *Otherness*. How might experiences with these features be conceived of as encounters with something unholy?

Dreadfulness

Otto uses depictions of the "wrath of God" to characterize this element, emphasizing the way this wrath can be arbitrary, unbound by a moral compass. Of course, an immoral agent may act in this way, but perhaps one would expect an encounter with the devil to be more predictable: perhaps he would reward the wicked and punish the virtuous? Such a devil would be akin to the supernatural mafia—a power to which one pays tribute but not something anyone would worship. A devil worshipper, however, would imagine something not so discriminating: such a supreme devil would rain plague and mayhem on the just and the unjust. He would be arbitrary, unpredictable—impossible to appease because of his lack of coherent policy. No method of "worship" could serve as propitiation; the only option is a kind of surrender to the chaos. And this is just what Dreadfulness presents.

Supremacy

Supremacy is manifested when the subject sees herself "submerged" in the object of the experience, as having a lesser ontological status in some way. This may be an unnerving event, but could still be seen as a good thing if that in which one is submerged is seen as something of

---

[4] As mentioned above, Otto also talks about "the element of fascination." But he distinguishes this from the other features, saying that they concern the content (*tremendum*) and form (*mysterium*) of the experience (31). I read him as saying that fascination is solely a feature of the subject's reaction, not something that helps characterize the object of the experience.

unsurpassable positive value. But if that thing is seen as unholy, it is hard to imagine something more horrifying: to see oneself as a mere puppet of mad and evil forces.[5] There is, further, the fact that the idea of submergence itself could be seen as a kind of deep violation: seeing oneself as nothing may be a kind of draining away of one's worth and dignity. Indeed, it might be a paradigmatic *horrendous evil*—to echo Marilyn Adams—perhaps akin to "psychophysical torture whose ultimate goal is the *disintegration of personality*" (Adams 1989, 300, emphasis added).

Urgency

If one encounters God in a numinous experience, it is unsurprising that the experience would include an imperative. But, of course, the Devil may issue commands as well. In fact, the idea of receiving murderous imperatives from a demonic entity is well-established in common lore, as is the idea of someone mistaking such for guidance from God. Given this, it is especially easy to see a gestalt shift from seeing Urgency as part of an experience of the holy to seeing it as an experience of the unholy.

Otherness

Given traditional concepts of the divine, an encounter with God seems bound to present him as wholly other. But what of the diabolical? One tempted to worship the devil will see the evil figure as having the same exalted metaphysical status: differing from us in the same way God is supposed to differ. More telling, perhaps, is Otto's suggestion that we think of stupor as the reaction to the wholly other. If one is not merely incapable of understanding but is *struck* dumb by the agent manifest in the experience, that agent is in fact inflicting what looks like a harm. To put it another way: a holy agent would not *want* you to be struck dumb, to leave you in a stupor, but an evil one may delight in leaving you incapacitated.

[5] The horror of being such a puppet is well illustrated by the extraordinary piece of nonfiction by horror writer Thomas Ligotti, *The Conspiracy against the Human Race* (2010), in which this idea—that we are puppets of a chaotic nature—is woven into his overview of the power and aesthetics of horror.

Extreme Metal and The Unholy Numinous

The numinous may, then, readily be apprehended as the unholy numinous. But why think that these strains of metal are guided by the aim for such experience? The fact that explicit satanic symbolism and lyrics is found in much of this music supports the idea that the experience would be conceived of in this negative fashion. What I want to focus on, though, is the way features of the music and culture clearly connect with the goal of triggering numinous experience in the first place.

To this end, I want to consider three things:

- Sonic features of the music and vocals
- Media presentation and lyrics
- Fan assessment

Sonic Features of the Music and Vocals

Let me draw to your attention a remark Otto makes relating numinous experience explicitly to sound (Appendix 3: "Original Numinous Sounds"). He fastens on an example from the *Kena Upanishad* which reads (as per Otto's rendering on 191–192):

> This is the way It (sc. Brahman) is to be illustrated:
> When lightnings have been loosened:
> aaah!
> When that has made the eyes to be closed —
> aaah! —

According to Otto, this tells us that Brahman is "that in whose presence we must exclaim 'aaah!'" and adds:

> [o]ne cannot "illustrate' the numinous character of this 'aaah' by any better analogy than that of the lightning here given. The unexpectedness and suddenness of the lightning-flash, its dreadful weirdness, its overpoweringness and dazzling splendour, the fright and the delight of it, give it an almost numinous impressiveness, and indeed often do produce an actual numinous impression on the mind." (192)

Perhaps the most effective way of conveying to outsiders the character of heavy metal is to liken it to being in a powerful storm, complete with thunder, lightning, rain, and wind.[6] Exemplars of the kind of metal I'm discussing vary in their sonic features, but the overwhelming majority make the analogy with a storm quite apt: great volume, multiple sounds mixed in a cacophony, a sense of instability and danger, and so on.[7] Thunder and lightning thus work both to evoke the Dreadfulness element of the numinous and the experience of heavy metal.

One may object: Otto also points to the importance of *silence.* In the section entitled "Means by which the Numinous is expressed in Art" (Chapter 9), he notes that the most direct methods for this are "in a noteworthy way *negative*, viz. *darkness* and *silence*" (68). He returns to the theme of silence a bit later in discussing explicitly religious music:

> Even the most consummate Mass-music can only give utterance to the holiest, most numinous moment in the Mass—the moment of transubstantiation—by sinking into stillness: no mere momentary pause, but an absolute cessation of sound long enough for us to 'hear the silence' itself. (70)

If silence is so apt, how could the high-volume cacophony of metal also be apt? There is an important commonality between silence and a wall of noise: in both, the listener must strain to discern any object or pattern. This is exactly what is predicted by Otherness: the numinous object is alien, hard to make out, and this effect can be achieved either through silence or by a great buzzing confusion of noise.

That the element of Otherness is at work in extreme metal is confirmed as well by the effects of such. Just consider a caricature of the fan right after attending a powerful performance: there he sits with glazed eyes, half-conscious, unable to speak—that is, in a *stupor.*

---

[6] Otto only mentions lightning in this passage, of course. My point is not that he somehow managed to fix on the exact natural phenomenon that is well-suited for describing the experience of heavy metal. My point is only that there is a significant resemblance. A silent flash of lightning at a distance can still convey the sense of a great storm elsewhere. And the fact that Otto praises the lightning metaphor *in the context of discussing a kind of inarticulate vocalization* ("aaah!") just serves to make it more likely that he would recognize the storm of metal as akin to a numinous experience.

[7] I say the overwhelming majority are like this, but some are relatively quiet: what should we make of those? Consider one of the samples on my list: Xasthur's "Masquerade of Incisions" (2009). The amplification is not intense, but the production induces a significant amount of fuzz and static that plays a similar role. Just now (March 18, 2025), to check my memory of the song, I listened to the song as posted on YouTube (at www.youtube.com/watch?v=saKsOh7IIfM) and the first comment on the video was "I've always admired how the suffocating sound spreads like a haze." Despite being quiet, the song imposes a *suffocating* feel—another way for dreadfulness to make itself manifest.

One immediately distinctive feature of extreme metal is the use of distorted vocals: from high-pitched shrieks to low-pitched growls and guttural sounds, these are often the first thing outsiders note about such music—and find off-putting. The element of Dreadfulness is evoked by such vocals: the wild unleashing of capricious energy. This alone would not predict distortion, however; it would only predict volume, chaos, or the like. But couple this with Otherness and the distortion is entirely fitting. Indeed, others have noted the link between these vocals and negative (aka apophatic) theology. The wholly other nature of the numinous object calls for something that resists interpretation. Niall Scott cites Edia Connole (2014) as saying that "apophasis . . . is a powerful, widely, and significantly present, but little recognized feature of black metal" and adds his own comment that "This commitment to unknowing and unsaying is not just evident in the lyrical content of black metal, but also in its performance—in the unintelligible screaming vocalizations and in its gestures and utterances of a transgressive refusal" (Scott 2018, p. 189).

Perhaps most striking, however, is the fact that the distorted vocals are predictable as reflecting the element of Urgency: if we're after an experience in which the subject feels commanded with great emphasis to do something, what better way to proceed than to have someone screaming at you? Of course, it may be unclear what it is they are screaming for you to do, but that is common to experiences of the holy as well.

Media Presentation and Lyrics

One finds in much extreme metal a practice of cloaking the material in the guise of something hard to penetrate. Infamously, band logos are often designed in such a way as to make them difficult to read. Another quite striking manifestation of otherness can be found in the case of *Les Légions Noires*, an insular group of black metal musicians in France in the early 1990s. Several pieces from this group made use of an invented language ("Gloatre") apparently created by the artist who calls himself "Vordb. Na R.iidr." The character of Gloatre can be gleaned from this sample of titles used from demos for the band Brenoritvrezorke in 1995:

- Vaszagraèbe Éakr Uatrè Brenoritvrezorkre
- Vèrmyaprèb

- Nèvgzèrya
- Èrvoelbtre[8]

The language here is not merely alien but seems designed to be hard to vocalize, just as the items in a wall of noise may be hard to discern.

One common media trope in black metal is the use of stark black-and-white artwork. For influential exemplars, consider the covers of three classic Darkthrone albums: *A Blaze in the Northern Sky* (1992), *Under a Funeral Moon* (1993), and *Transilvanian Hunger* (1994, each with Peaceville Records). The impression one gets from these, often enough, is of catching a brief glimpse of a scene normally in darkness—something briefly illuminated by a flash of lightning, perhaps.

But what of the lyrics? It must be conceded that the care with which these artists compose the lyrics can vary enormously. Some artists evidently put a great deal of labor into their lyrics, however, and these can be revealing. One band known for this care is Deathspell Omega. Consider these lyrics taken from "Odium Nostrum" on their album *Si Monumentum, Circumspice* (2004, Norma Evangelium Diaboli):

Odium
Oh Merciless Hatred;
Spare nothing, spare no one
Oppressive heat, intense flavour
From the pupil of the one-eyed mongrel to the distant depths of the macrocosm
We are all waiting for the releasing hour

Praise the God of our salvation;
Hosts on high, His power proclaim

Odium
Oh Merciless Hatred;
Burn the Me in me,
And thus every cell of humanity.
May the essence of impurity redeem my soul
Unleashed hatred be my salvation and thy ghoul

[8] For these titles and more, see the entry for Brenoritvrezorke in the metal-archives database: www.metal-archives.com/bands/Brenoritvrezorkre/144971 (accessed 20 March 2025).

What is of interest here is not the appearance of the devil but the echoes of numinous experience. In the above lyrics, the object of veneration is not presented as some sort of ally with whom one might find common cause; rather, Odium spares no one, not even the speaker, who asks him to "burn the Me in me"—invoking the Supremacy element: feeling oneself unreal, drained. For another example, consider these lines from "Holy Poison" by Funeral Mist (2003, Norma Evangelium Diaboli):

> Holy poison, holy doom
> Reborn for infection in the womb of wombs
> A spiral of Chaos, God against God
> Now set me free in the plan of life
> The plan of God, holy doom
> A legion of spasms in the limbs of the bearer
> God against life against God against all
> Holy poison, holy doom...

The object here is called "God," but this God is against himself, is against life, against all. Again, the object of veneration is not an ally but something that condemns the worshipper to its holy poison, some kind of doom. Here we have Supremacy as well as Dreadfulness and Urgency.

There is at least one case I've come across where the accompanying packaging seems an uncannily good fit for my hypothesis. The band known as (sic) "Death. Void. Terror" includes on the back cover of their debut *To the Great Monolith* (2018, Iron Bonehead Productions) some text that includes this:

> The purest expression is derived from the seed planted by exposure to the Great Monolith. Such exposure requires relentless concentration of the practitioner to withstand its force, while simultaneously being able to remain disengaged from any immediate surroundings. This form of detached concentration is ideally achieved through the unconscious state, meaning that the immediate senses must be abandoned in favor of surrendering one's expressive abilities to direction by the Void. It is in this context that pure expression can be sought and that conventional boundaries of contemporary composition and humanist genre predefinitions can be transcended. Only then can a manifestation of the Great Monolith be witnessed.

All the elements of the numinous are to be found here: Dreadfulness in the great force of the monolith, Supremacy in the appeal to surrender, Urgency in the appeal to directions from the void, and Otherness in the claim that "conventional boundaries" of expression are inadequate.

Fan Assessment

If my hypothesis is correct, one should find in fans' assessment praise for elements of the sort just described. These vary in reflectiveness and care just as lyrics do, but it is not hard to find reviews that fit this prediction. The most salient recurring theme is delight in describing the way the music beats the listener into submission. Here is part of a review of the album *Epidemic of Violence* by Demolition Hammer (1992, Century Media):

> The solos in this track are blistering and malignant, piercing your skull just like the spikes in an iron maiden. The next four tracks provide a noxious combination of death and thrash metal, blistering solos causing necrosis in your ear canals, brutal riffs that'll leave black and discharging pustules in your lungs and spine-shattering bass-lines. . .[9]

Or this review of the album *Hellfire* by 1349 (2005, Candlelight Records):

> The first time I heard this I instinctively turned the music off with a frown. The feeling of sticking my head into a nest of electric wasps was almost nauseating. A few weeks later I came back, feverishly drawn to this horribly fast grinding firestorm. And now, years later this album is permanently placed on my top ten list ever. A masterpiece.[10]

From a review of the album *Malignant Worthlessness* by the band Pissgrave (2025, Profound Lore Records):

> Lurching forward, each song lumbers into life in a way that somehow drags like a hammer on the floor while casting a storm of rusted

[9] Review posted October 17, 2023, on www.metal-archives.com by Enserric_the_Thrasher.
[10] Review posted September 5, 2010, on www.metal-archives.com by Bogfind.

> blades through the air like a swarm of locusts. The bludgeoning rhythmic onslaught and claustrophobic guitars work tremendously together in creating a savage listening experience that to most will inflict pain, but a freakish few will enjoy these delightfully depraved pieces of fetid butchery.[11]

One more example: this is from a review of the album *Satan Alpha Omega* by Deiphago (2012, Hells Headbangers Records):

> Where most extreme metal bands encapsulate their infamy into familiar rhythmic environs, this is extremely, ergonomically unsafe and highly stress inducing. It's like having your spine removed and cast into a giant hamster wheel with ravenous daemons doing laps inside, the nerve endings still attached to the rest of your being. And yet, it's internally consistent. There is a method to this madness. . . . Primordial, ugly and repulsive, it will rape your ears, then leave [you] bleeding on your doorstop without so much as a goodbye or apology. It's not an album you experience to 'enjoy' . . . but to 'destroy'. Not in any way 'great', but grating with as much beatific hostility the trio can muster with the 20+ years of history behind it. If this sounds in any way attractive to that misanthropic imp that awaits restlessly within your psyche, seeking to punish you at any given moment, then suffer it well.[12]

The reviewer here is quite aware of the paradoxical character of his or her attraction to the music. It is especially impressive that they describe the band as exhibiting "beatific hostility"—exactly what my hypothesis predicts.

Before bringing this section to a close, I want to draw attention to one of the oddities found in extreme metal that may seem to run counter to my hypothesis. Surprising though it may seem, a Swedish band known as Reverorum ib. Malacht, which employ many of the sounds and techniques I have been describing, explicitly bill themselves as purveyors of "Roman Catholic black metal." They see themselves as Christians, not devil worshippers. How should we understand this? Consider what Karl

[11] Review posted February 21, 2025, on www.metal-archives.com by Nattskog7.

[12] Review posted August 14, 2012, on www.metal-archives.com by autothrall.

Emil Lundin, one of the founders and central figures of the band, has said about black metal in general:

> Upon its foundations, black metal made a temple. This temple was a feeble but laudable attempt at reaching God in a spiritually impoverished, stagnant culture. Its altar and incense that of the audial and visual. As firstborns they crawled, with random attempts at learning how to eat. To everything its time. We are born, and we breastfeed. But eventually the human will need solid food. The youth-culture that spawned the religious rudimenta of black metal can no longer nourish.
> (Lund and Rosenthal 2017)

He sees the initial drive of black metal as a desire for God, in effect, though it fails to get there. Strikingly, when describing the music of his own band, he writes:

> Malacht is dark. It sounds alien and it is dirty as fuck. No. We rarely have audible riffing, nor do we care if we do. But we portray the depths of human despair and darkness. Not because it is good, but because herein lies the key to redemption. Face the world for what it is. Therein lies the fruit of salvation. Here is our worship. At the foot of the cross. Our good is dying. This is the banality of evil. Allahu akbar [God is most great].
> (Lund and Rosenthal 2017)

The difference between what Reverorum ib. Malacht does and the other explicitly anti-theist bands do lies not in the methods or in the basic experiences they aim to produce but in whether they see something *beyond* that dreadful experience. For Lundin, the portrayal of despair and darkness is a prelude to something holy. For the others, it is the whole story.

The Voice from The Whirlwind

Suppose my hypothesis is correct: much of this metal is driven by the desire to trigger the unholy numinous. What shall we think of the value of this music and the cultural structure supporting it? My hypothesis may explain why people are drawn to this music, but explanation is not, of course, justification.

If theism is correct, then perhaps it could be justified in the way Lundin does in his explanation of the music of Reverorum ib. Malacht:

as a critical prelude to encountering the holy. If there really is an all-powerful evil force, it could be justified by saying it is simply an insight into reality, and we should in fact bow down before it. But neither of these is true. And with apologies to my theist friends, I find these claims simply unbelievable. How could a card-carrying atheist and materialist like myself find this of value?

I mentioned earlier that in his discussion of the element of fascination, Otto doesn't offer an explanation of why the numinous is fascinating. He does, though, make a remark very relevant here:

> It may well be possible, it is even probable, that in the first stage of its development the religious consciousness started with only one of its poles—the 'daunting' aspect of the numen—and so at first took shape only as 'daemonic dread'. But if this did not point to something beyond itself, if it were not but one 'moment' of a completer experience, pressing up gradually into consciousness, then no transition would be possible to the feelings of positive self-surrender to the numen. The only type of worship that could result from this 'dread' alone would be that of . . . expiation and propitiation, the averting or the appeasement of the 'wrath' of the numen. It can never explain how it is that 'the numinous' is the object of search and desire and yearning, and that too for its own sake and not only for the sake of the aid and backing that men expect from it in the natural sphere. It can never explain how this takes place, not only in the forms of 'rational' religious worship, but in those queer 'sacramental' observances and rituals and procedures of communion in which the human being seeks to get the numen into his possession. (32)

In other words, Otto holds that it is only because of the underlying role of the actual divine in these experiences that it can effect fascination over the long run. If not for that role, the result would be not veneration but deal-making. But he is simply mistaken about this. Consider the reviews of metal sampled above that emphasize fascination along the lines of the element of Supremacy. It may be a kind of masochistic impulse, but there is no question that the desire to become one with one's oppressor is a real thing and is at work here.

So, what else explains the attraction? The answer, I think, is straightforward: the numinous presents itself as revealing an important truth, and we care about the truth. Neither the holy nor the unholy numinous draws us as a function of nothing more than sensory stimulation. The extreme metal I've described may thrill with its sonic features, but those can be oppressive, unpleasant—and, to recall my opening anecdote, even vomit inducing. Its appeal is the same: it appears to reveal an important truth.

The apparent truth is that an evil agent, all-powerful and supreme, governs the world. But let me be careful: it is not an evil agent that pursues a definite code of inflicting harm on the good and rewarding the wicked. The *Dreadfulness* of the unholy numinous presents the world as determined by a *capricious* evil agent, unpredictable and beyond propitiation.

There is no such agent. The way the unholy numinous presents the world is simply not true. But here is something that *is* true: the world displays the kind of randomness, misery, and injustice that could easily have resulted from a chaotic agent of evil. The value of the unholy numinous is its ability to *help us face this fact*. We must do so without superstition—without falling into a foolish belief in the Devil or an even more foolish belief in God[13]—but there is value in recognizing the extraordinary pervasiveness of evil and suffering in this world, an intrinsic value of simply recognizing the horror that goes beyond whatever salutary effects the experience may bring in its train. It may be that we could recognize the horror without subjecting ourselves to such a harrowing experience. But it is *fitting* to appreciate it in such a way: part of what the horror of the world calls for is recognizing it while feeling it as a dreadful truth.

There is, finally, one further reason this method of facing the horror is of value. The persistence of religious belief is, I think, plausibly due to a hard-wired inclination to anthropomorphize the world at some level (see Guthrie 1993). Whenever we want to assess the value of the world as a whole, this may lead us inexorably to seeing the world as if it were the working of a single agent. If this is inevitable, it may be that the *only* way to keep clearly in view the horror of the world is to see it as the product of a supreme and capricious devil of the sort I've delineated. Extreme metal provides a kind of mechanism for reminding ourselves of this truth and *feeling* it, given our limited psychological means. To put the point bluntly: if

[13] I'm thinking here of the "evil god challenge" posed by Stephen Law (2010). Law's basic point is that the theodicies that have been proposed for explaining why a good God would allow this actual evil can be generally matched by reverse theodicies for explaining why an evil God would allow this actual goodness, where those reverse theodicies seem just as persuasive as the original. I think he understates the case: the reverse theodicies are more persuasive. It is easier to understand why a perfectly malicious being would want to leave you some hope for thinking that a good God exists, but it's not so easy to understand why a perfectly good being would want to leave you wondering if perhaps it's an evil God that exists.

we are doomed to see faces in the clouds, to see the world as the expression of some personal agent, the *closest* we can get to the truth is to see that agent as the devil—chaotic, unkind, overpowering, inexhaustible, and mad.

Appendix

Representative samples ordered by date of release

- Hellhammer, "Triumph of Death" from *Apocalyptic Raids* (1984, Noise Records)
- Venom, "Possessed" from *Possessed* (1985, Neat Records)
- Bathory, "Chariots of Fire" from *Under the Sign of the Black Mark* (1987, Black Mark Productions)
- Beherit, "Witchcraft" from *The Oath of Black Blood* (1991, Turbo Music)
- Burzum, "Det Som En Gang Var" from *Hvis Lyset Tar Oss* (1994, Misanthropy Records)
- Darkthrone, "Skald av Satans Sol" from *Transylvanian Hunger* (1994, Peaceville Records)
- Emperor, "Into the Infinity of Thoughts" from *In the Nightside Eclipse* (1994, Candlelight Records)
- Morbid Angel, "Hatework" from *Domination* (1995, Earache Records)
- Mütiilation, "Born Under the Master's Spell" from *Vampires of Black Imperial Blood* (1995, Drakkar Productions)
- Abruptum, "Vi Sonus Veris Nigrae Malitiae" from *Vi Sonus Veris Nigrae Malitiae* (1996, Full Moon Productions)
- Belketre, "Voarmtre Zuèrkl Vuorhdrévarvtre" from *Ambre Zuèrkl Vuorhdrévarvtre* (1996, Self-Released)
- Judas Iscariot, ". . .I Filled with Woes the Passing Wind. . ." from *Of Great Eternity* (1997, Elegy Records)
- Weakling, "Desasters in the Sun" (sic) from *Dead as Dreams* (1999, Self-Released)
- Funeral Mist, "Holy Poison" from *Devilry* (2003, Norma Evangelium Diaboli)
- Haemoth, "Stigma Diabolikum" from *Kontamination* (2005, Southern Lord Recordings)
- Marduk, "Cold Mouth Prayer" from *Rom 5:12* (2007, Blooddawn Productions)

- Mayhem, “Anti” from *Ordo ad Chao* (2007, Season of Mist)
- Leviathan, “Vulgar Asceticism” from *Massive Conspiracy Against All Life* (2008, Moribund Records)
- Xasthur, “Masquerade of Incisions” from *All Reflections Drained* (2009, Hydra Head Productions)
- Deathspell Omega, “Malconfort” from *Paracletus* (2010, Norma Evangelium Diaboli)
- Black Cilice, “Blood to Murder” from *A Corpse, A Temple* (2011, Discipline Productions)
- Deiphago, “Human Race Absolute End” from *Satan Alpha Omega* (2012, Hells Headbangers Records)
- Teitanblood, “Anteinferno” from *Death* (2014, Norma Evangelium Diaboli)
- Tetragrammacide, “Extra-Terroristical Chaosophic Intelligence” from *Typhonian Wormholes: Indecipherable Anti-Structural Formulae* (2015, Iron Bonehead Productions)
- Spektr, “From the Terrifying to the Fascinating” from *The Art to Disappear* (2016, Agonia Records)
- Celestial Bodies, “The Nazarene Bastard Crowned” from *Spit Forth From Chaos* (2017, I, Voidhanger Records)
- Havohej, “Seven Jinn” from *Table of Uncreation* (2019, Hells Headbangers Records)
- Ecchymosis, “Aesthetic Devotion Towards Coprocraniotomy” from *Ritualistic Intercourse within Abject Surrealism* (2020, New Standard Elite)
- Reverorum ib. Malacht, “Bönehuset” from *Vad är inte sju huvud?* (2020, Rubeus Obex)
- Unsalvation, “Incarnation of the Light Bringer” from *Decimation by Revelation* (2021, Bestial Burst)
- Mons Veneris, “Bleeding His Holiness” single (2023, Self-Released)

References

Adams, M.M.C. (1989). Horrendous evils and the goodness of God. *Proceedings of the Aristotelian Society* 63: 297–323.

Connole, E. 2014. Interview on black metal theory. `queenmobs.com/2014/11/interview-on-black-metal-theory-dominik-irtenkauf-interviews-edia-connole` (accessed 29 May 2017).

Guthrie, S.E. (1993). *Faces in the Clouds: A New Theory of Religion*. Oxford University Press.

Law, S. (2010). The evil-god challenge. *Religious Studies* 46: 355–373.

Ligotti, T. (2010). *The Conspiracy Against the Human Race*. New York: Hippocampus Press.

Lund, K.E. and Rosenthal, J. 2017. Interview with Lund by Rosenthal from August 15, 2017. Posted at www.invisibleoranges.com/reverorum-ib-malacht-interview/ (accessed 24 March 2025).

Otto, Rudolf. 1917. *The Idea of the Holy*. Originally published as *Das Heilige* in Wrocław, Poland, by Trewendt and Granier. Translated into English by John W. Harvey and published by Oxford University Press in 1923. Passages quoted are taken from the 1950 reprint by Oxford University Press.

Schopenhauer, A. (1969). *The World as Will and Representation*. Translated from the original German publication from 1818 by E. F. J. Payne. Dover Publications.

Scott, N. (2018). Black metal's apophatic curse. *Théologiques* 26 (1): 185–206.

Chapter 7
Black Metal Is Religious Music

Eric Steinhart
Department of History, Philosophy, and Liberal Studies, William Paterson University, Wayne, USA

Black Metal Is Sacred Music

Religious themes have long been central in black metal music.[1] Black metal has long been inspired by the ancient Pagan religions of Egypt, Greece, and Rome (Fletcher and Umurhan 2019). It takes religious ideas from Gnosticism, Satanism, and Norse-Germanic Paganism, and from Tolkien and Lovecraft (Norman 2013; Kuusela 2015; Sederholm 2016). Indeed, black metal is often portrayed as *religious music* (Moberg 2012; Granholm 2013; Scott 2014; Bivins 2017; Cluness 2022; Messick

[1] Here, I use the term "black metal" broadly, to include black metal itself, but also some adjacent music in genres like death metal, drone, and doom. These genres overlap. Here, I entirely exclude fascist metal.

et al. 2023; etc.). But what does religion mean here? And what makes black metal *music* religious?

Probably the easiest argument for the religiosity of black metal is functional: (1) Black metal performs some religious function. (2) Music that performs that religious function is religious music. (3) Therefore, black metal is religious music. Here's an obvious way to provide this argument with some content: Black metal *praises* or *glorifies* some religiously significant figures. For example, much first- and second-wave black metal glorifies Satan or Odin, and they are religiously significant figures. Likewise, Christian metal glorifies God. But music that praises or glorifies some religiously significant figure is religious music.[2] Therefore, black metal is religious music. This argument works pretty well for some black metal. But it fails to account for the religiosity *of the music*.

After all, just as black masses imitate Catholic masses, so you could sing hymns to Satan that sound like church music.[3] Music that glorifies Satan might well sound dark, but it need not be metal. Much of the music that glorifies Norse Pagan deities has its own dark folk style which is not metal at all.[4] And lots of Pagan music sounds like Renaissance or folk music.[5] In general, musics which praise or glorify religiously significant figures perform their religious function through their *lyrics*. The lyrics can be set to all sorts of musics. Religious lyrics don't make religious *music*. Moreover, in black metal, the lyrics are almost always unintelligible or even nonexistent. To account for the religiosity of black metal music, some other version of this argument is needed.

---

[2] Praise is one religious function of music. Another common religious function is to induce religious altered states. For instance, Sufi Qawwali music is devotional trance music. Snaza (2016) argues that certain black metal albums, such as Blut aus Nord's *MoRT* (Blut Aus Nord, 2006), obliterate the ego. This ego-annihilation is a kind of religious altered state. However, I have not seen this theme developed in discussions of the religiosity of metal music.

[3] There are many nonmetal hymns to Satan. These include the "Hymn to Satan" by Edythe DeVinney Eyde, aka Tigrina (Los Angeles: A Darkling Publication, 1941). It is not metal at all. Or consider Peter Gundry's "Lucifer's Hymn" (*The Shadow's Bride*, Peter Gundry, 2016), as well as his "Goëtia" (*Goëtia*, Peter Gundry, 2018) and "Malleus Malificarum" (*The Elixir of Life*, Peter Gundry, 2014). Gundry's work is good old classical music. David MLLR's "Zed Aliz Zed (Lucifer Gnosis Mantra)" (*Zed Aliz Zed*, 2,159,292 Records DK, 2018) sounds like drony Tibetan music. Myers Music's "Ave Baphomet" (Myers Music, 2024) sounds like Gregorian chant. Cult of Belial's "Powerful Black Flame Chant" is just chanting (online at https://www.youtube.com/watch?v=Hb4Sb4gKFJo, accessed 23 May 2025). Anton LaVey's *The Satanic Mass* just sounds like church music (*The Satanic Mass*, Murgenstrumm, 1968).

[4] Consider the dark folk music by the Norse Pagan bands Heilung, Vigundr, Danheim, and so on.

[5] Consider Pagan music by Trobar de Morte, or Faun's "Walpurgisnacht" (Luna, Polydor, 2014).

Religions typically involve gods, and many researchers have begun to link gods with the biology of *predation*. Thus, Atran says God concepts emerge from an "*evolutionary program for avoiding and tracking predators and prey*" (2002, p. 78, his italics). Likewise, Trout says "animal predators were the *first gods*" (2011, p. 192, his italics). This point about gods generalizes into the *predation regulation theory* of religion (the PRT), which defines religion like this: *a religion is a socio-culturally elaborated system of primarily symbolic strategies for regulating predator-prey relations.* Many writers have suggested something like the PRT (Burkert 1983, 1996; Atran 2002, ch. 3; Guthrie 2002; Trout 2011, ch. 7; Martin 2013; Wiebe 2013). Here, I will use the PRT to argue for the religiosity of black metal music: (1) Black metal music is *predator defiance music.* (2) Predator defiance music is religious music. (3) Therefore, black metal is religious music.

But there is another venerable argument that black metal music is religious: (1) Black metal is the *music of creation.* (2) The music of creation is religious music. (3) Therefore, black metal is religious music. The music of creation first appears in the ancient Pagan cosmologies of Pythagoras and Plato. The Platonic Demiurge organizes the universe according to musical principles (Leask 2016; Pelosi 2017). The Platonic music of creation is further developed by Philo and Plutarch (Demulder 2020; Levy 2020; Petrucci 2020). Plotinus also affirms the music of creation (*Enneads* [E], 5.8.1, 5.9.11, 6.3.15.20-23). Augustine and Bonaventure interpret the Platonic music of creation in Christian terms (Gersh 2009; Casarella 2016). The music of creation occurs in Tolkien (Davis 1982; Houghton 1995). The music of creation also appears in Lovecraft. Since Paganism, Tolkien, and Lovecraft all influenced black metal, it's reasonable to think of the religiosity of black metal *music* in terms of the Platonic music of creation.

I will combine the religious function argument and the music of creation argument to show that black metal music is religious music. Since metal music is heavily inspired by mythology, it's fair to combine these two arguments into a *philosophical myth*. And, since the foremost philosophical mythmaker was Plato, I'll combine them into a kind of Platonic myth. According to my Platonic myth, predator defiance music plays an essential role in the creation (or emanation) of all the beings among beings. This predator defiance music is black metal music. Consequently, black metal music is religious.

Black Metal Is Predator Defiance Music

Black metal music encodes auditory threat signals (McIver 2013, p. 36; Thompson and Olsen 2018, p. 129; Ollivier et al. 2019, p. 3; Herbst and Mynett 2023, pp. 20–21; Olsen et al. 2023, p. 21134). The auditory threat signals in black metal signify the presence of an animal (or animals) that is aroused, aggressive, dangerous, large, heavy, and close. They signify violent attacks by hungry predators or violent defensive reactions of prey. The sonic features which encode these threat signals include low frequencies; loudness; distortion; dissonance; dark or distressing chords, keys, and modes; vocal alarm calls and distress signals (screams, shrieks, growls, etc.). The visual imagery associated with black metal also encodes threat signals (Watier 2022). Fans and nonfans of metal music respond equally and immediately to these threat signals (Ollivier et al. 2019). Since this threat signal is immediately apparent, I will refer to it as the *extrinsic signal*.

Three arguments aim to show that black metal encodes at least one other signal besides its extrinsic threat signal. The first argument is the *cognitive difficulty argument:* (1) Black metal contains an obvious extrinsic threat signal. Because of their direct biological salience, our brains have evolved to process biological threat signals rapidly and fluently. (2) If black metal contains only this extrinsic signal, then it is cognitively easy to process. However, black metal is cognitively extremely difficult to process (Hannan 2018; Swallow and Herbst 2022; Xhignesse 2024). (3) Therefore, black metal does not contain only its extrinsic signal, but contains at least one additional signal.

The second argument is the *appropriate reactions argument*: (1) Nonfans hear the extrinsic signal. They have hard-wired biologically appropriate negative reactions to that signal. They report negative emotions like "tension, fear, and anger" (Thompson and Olsen 2018, p. 129; Ollivier et al. 2019, p. 1). Along with "negative experiences such as confusion, disgust, and irritation" (Thompson et al. 2019, p. 229). (2) Fans also hear the extrinsic signal. And if fans hear *only* the extrinsic signal, then they will react negatively as well. (3) However, fans do not react negatively to metal music; on the contrary, they react positively. Fans listening to metal report "feelings of positive energy and power (Thompson and Olsen 2018, p. 129). Fans report experiencing *power* and *joy*, as well as *peace*, *wonder*, *nostalgia*, and *transcendence* (Ollivier et al. 2019, p. 2; Thompson et al. 2019, p. 226).

Fans "reported using their music to enhance their happiness, to immerse themselves in feelings of love, and agreed that their music enhanced their well-being" (Sharman and Dingle 2015, p. 9). (4) Therefore, fans do not hear only the negative extrinsic threat signal. They hear at least one additional signal which causes them to react positively.

The third argument is the *systematizing argument*: (1) People who have *systematizing personalities* tend to love metal music (Greenberg et al. 2015). Likewise Schmaltz et al. (2021) showed that metal music fans have personalities with a high *need for cognition*. (2) If systematizers and people with a high need for cognition love works of art in some genre, then works in that genre contain highly complex, intricate, and subtle patterns. (3) Therefore, metal music contains highly complex, intricate, and subtle patterns. (4) Either these patterns are encoded in the extrinsic signal or in some other signal or signals. (5) But these intricate, subtle, and complex patterns are not compatible with the heavily distorted and dissonant sounds in the extrinsic signal. (6) If they are not compatible with the sounds in the extrinsic signal, then they are not encoded in that signal. (7) Therefore, they are encoded in some other signal(s) in metal music.

All three arguments justify the conclusion that black metal encodes at least one other signal besides its extrinsic signal. It encodes at least one other *intrinsic signal*, which explains the difficulty of black metal, the positive emotions felt by fans, and the interests of systematizers in the music. The most parsimonious approach asserts that *just one* intrinsic signal suffices to account for the difficulty of black metal, for the positive reactions of fans, and for the interests of systematizers. Assuming parsimony, there is no need to posit more than one intrinsic signal. So I will posit exactly one intrinsic signal here. Greenberg et al. (2015) use several sonic dimensions to analyze music. The *intense dimension* features sounds that are "distorted, loud, aggressive, and not relaxing" (2015, p. 3). The *sophisticated dimension* has sounds which are "inspiring, intelligent, complex, and dynamic" (2015, p. 3). This suggests that the extrinsic signal is encoded by sounds on the intense dimension, while the intrinsic signal is encoded by sounds on the sophisticated dimension. The intrinsic signal is encoded by *virtuosity*. It is encoded by features which indicate alertness, focus, speed, agility, and competence.

The intrinsic signal is positive and hard to process, while the extrinsic signal is negative and easy to process. Hence, these signals are complementary and oppositional. The thesis that black metal music contains multiple opposed signals is supported by the well-known fact that works of art often gain their aesthetic powers by encoding multiple opposed meanings and themes in dramatic conflict. According to Ollivier and colleagues, the extrinsic signal is processed by low-order perceptual circuits in our brains, while the intrinsic signal is processed by higher-order cognitive circuits. Thus metal fans "exhibit both 'typical' low-level processes that appraise rough sounds as negative and worthy of immediate attention . . . *as well as* high-order systems able to assert cognitive control over these responses and produce positive emotional experiences" (Ollivier et al. 2019, p. 8). Specifically, "fans' appreciation for metal music reflects a higher-order inhibition by cortical circuits of an otherwise normal, low-order response to auditory threat" (Ollivier et al. 2019, p. 2). Higher-order positive cognitive mastery of some lower-order perceptual negativity is the main feature of the Kantian *sublime*. Thus, black metal is sublime (Pohlmann 2015; Unger 2016; Shadrack 2021; Stevens 2022).

On the one hand, the extrinsic signal in black metal music symbolizes an attack on the listener by some predatory or dangerous animal(s). More abstractly, it symbolizes all the negativities of human life. These include biological negativities (deprivation, suffering, illness, injury, aging, death), as well as social negativities (solitude, unfairness, injustice, oppression), and existential negativities (anxieties about nothingness, fear of the abyss). All these negativities are produced by particular predators, and all these particular predators are instances of an ideal divine *Predator*, the causally powerful essence of predation. Hearing the extrinsic signal, low-order perceptual circuits trigger negative emotions and meanings. The extrinsic signal is the *first negation* in black metal music.

On the other hand, the intrinsic signal symbolizes a successful response to that predatory attack. The intrinsic signal symbolizes a human body that is biologically fit and competent. By hearing that intrinsic virtuosity signal, the listener *defies* and *defeats* the Predator. If the extrinsic signal signifies the first negation, then hearing the intrinsic signal signifies the *negation of that first negation*. To hear the intrinsic signal is to experience *victorious power* over the Predator. This is *joyful transcendence* of the negativities of life. This reasoning supports the predator defiance argument for the religiosity of black metal music: (1) Black metal music is *predator defiance music*. (2) Predator defiance music is religious music. (3) Therefore, black metal is religious music.

The Historical Dialectic of Black Metal

Black metal is often conceptualized as having three "waves" (Pohlmann 2015; Bivins 2017; see especially Cluness 2022, p. 59, n. 30). On my interpretation, these waves are driven by the negation of the negation. Each wave begins with some first negativity; that negativity negates itself; the product of that second negation enters the next wave. The logic of the negation of the negation is the *black metal dialectic*.

The *first wave* emerged in the 1980s in mostly Anglophone "heavy metal." This first wave treats God as the first negativity. First-wave black metal treats God as the Predator who preys on humanity. The extrinsic signal in the first-wave black metal signifies the predatory God. Hearing the intrinsic signal in the first-wave black metal negates that first negation. It is the second negation, the negation of the negation. It negates God's negation of humanity, and it also negates God. It rebels against God. By negating God, it affirms anti-God, that is, Satan, that is, Morningstar Lightbringer, that is, Lucifer.

The second wave occurred mainly in the 1990s in Norway and Sweden (so it is also called hyperborean black metal). The second wave is notorious for its Satanism (Granholm 2013). Along with Satan, second-wave black metal descends into the underworld at the center of the earth. It dwells in the abyss with Satan. Satanic black metal was deeply nihilistic, anti-social, and often criminal. But worshipping Satan is still slavish religious bondage. Satanic rebellion against established social institutions merely reaffirms the legitimacy of those institutions. Satanism turns out to be a negation which resurrects God by putting God in the abyss as Lucifer. But just as a cross turned upside down remains a cross, this inverted Christianity remains Christian.[6] The Predator is now Satan. Satan negates humanity. So Satan is the first negation in second-wave black metal. The extrinsic signal in second-wave black metal symbolizes the resurrection of God as Satan.

Hearing the intrinsic signal in second-wave black metal negates this resurrected first negation. It negates Satan, that is, it negates Lucifer. This negation of Satan is the second negation in the second wave. This second negation approaches Satan through an apophatic anti-theology (a *via negativa*). This *via negativa* leads eternally downward

[6] The cover art on Liturgy's *Aesthethica* (Thrill Jockey, 2011) has two relatively inverted crosses.

into the bottom of the abyss. This *harrowing of the abyss* strips Satan of all his properties. It strips Satan of his wickedness and his personhood. Eventually, it strips Satan of his very existence, leaving only nothingness behind.[7] This nothingness is absolute nonbeing. It is neither God nor Satan, neither God nor anti-God. It is pure absence. Second-wave black metal becomes trapped in the abyss, in the abyss of pure white snow. It becomes trapped in the hyperborean wasteland above the Arctic Circle, a wasteland which Hunt-Hendrix describes as "a dead static place, a polar land where there is no oscillation between day and night" (2010, p. 57). Third-wave black metal begins with this entrapment.

Third-wave black metal begins in the late 2000s. This third wave inherits its entrapment in the abyss from the second wave. It is entrapped in the pure negativity of the abyss (Stevens 2022). This entrapment is the first negation in third-wave black metal. But all that is entrapped in the abyss is the abyss itself. Hence, the first negation in third-wave black metal is the abyss itself. The extrinsic signal in third-wave black metal symbolizes this entrapment in the abyss. But in this identification of the abyss with its own negativity, third-wave black metal hears its intrinsic signal. If the abyss is identical with its own negativity, then, as Oliver and Smiley (2013) say, the abyss is (the x)($x \neq x$).

As that which is not identical with itself, the abyss negates itself. Apophatic anti-theology reaches its goal with the self-negation of nothingness. Scott correctly describes this as "The black metal curse, the negative negation of nothing" (2018, p. 190). Since black metal does not use the *via negativa* to find God, Scott says "black metal is more truly apophatic in its negative cursing of nothing" (2018, p. 191). The negation of nothingness, which is just its own self-negation, is the second negation in third-wave black metal. The self-negation of nothingness is being-itself; but being-itself is *the One*. Hence, the second negation in third-wave black metal reveals the One. The One is neither God nor Satan, but instead, after the first two waves, it has escaped from Christianity entirely.

Since the self-negation of the abyss occurs in the abyss, the One revealed by third-wave black metal is the One in the abyss. It is the dark One. Since nothingness is absolute impotence, the One is absolute power. Since nothingness is absolutely unproductive, the One is absolutely

[7] Scott writes that "Rather than a simple inversion, which could face the error of substituting Satan for God, the inversion [in second-wave Black Metal] is paired with a negation, a turning upside down and a departure" (2018, p. 189).

productive power. Since nothingness is absolutely negative, the One is absolutely positive productive power. Any such power aims at an absolutely perfect finality, which Platonists call *the Good*. If this power aims at the Good, then there exists something at which it aims, and so the Good exists. Since the One aims at the Good, the One is not identical with the Good. The One is the core at the center of the earth, while the Good is the sun in the sky. Hence third-wave black metal has solar ideals.

Through its second negation, third-wave black metal matures into *transcendental black metal*. Hunt-Hendrix writes that "Transcendental black metal is in fact nihilism, however it is a double nihilism and final nihilism, a once and for all negation of the entire series of negations" (2010, p. 61). The double negation of transcendental black metal produces an affirmation which is "white-knuckled, terrified, unsentimental, and courageous" (2010, p. 61, cf. 59). For Hunt-Hendrix, transcendental black metal is solar (2010, p. 62). It celebrates the solar cycle of life, death, and rebirth (ritualized in the Pagan wheel of the year).[8] It is oriented toward the sun as toward the "True, Good, and Beautiful" (2010, p. 64, cf. 62).[9]

Obviously enough, transcendental black metal is Platonic. But its Platonism differs from ancient Platonism by an inversion. While ancient Platonism identified the One with the Good, and placed the One-Good in heaven, transcendental black metal preserves the apophatic anti-theology which places the One in the abyss. The dark One in the abyss is not the Good, which remains in the sky as the sun. The dark One serves as the root of the great world tree, Yggdrasil, which grows up out of the earth. The branches of Yggdrasil grow upward toward the sun, that is, toward the Good. Ancient Platonism was top-down Platonism (Gerson 2005), but black metal Platonism is *bottom-up Platonism*.

The Good shines down on the One in the abyss. But if the Good shines on the One, then the One casts a shadow in the abyss. That shadow is *the Predator*. The Predator is the negativity which frees the beings from the One (this being is *not* the One) and from each other (this being is *not* that being). Thanks to the negativity in the Predator, every being surpasses itself into greater other beings. For organisms, the otherness in this self-surpassing entails death. The solar cycle (the wheel of the year) in transcendental black metal symbolizes the cycle of birth, life, death, and rebirth. Just as the sun dies and is reborn, so all things that die shall

[8] Listen here to Bootes Void, *C.O.L.D.*, that is, *Circle of Life and Death* (Ketzer Records, 2023).

[9] Listen here to Thumos, *The Republic* (Snow Wolf, 2022).

be reborn. As they are reborn, all things climb higher on Yggdrasil, the great world tree. The wheel of the year dramatizes how the negativities in nature negate themselves into positivities. After Ragnarok, the universe is reborn.

Pohlmann (2015) argues that third-wave American black metals (especially Cascadian black metal and its variants) use the self-renewal of nature to illustrate the self-surpassing of all things toward the Good. Pohlmann says Cascadian black metal adopts this concept of self-renewal from New England Transcendentalism (which was an American Platonism [Bregman 1990]). While second-wave black metal rejoiced in mere putrefaction, Pohlmann argues that third-wave black metal dramatizes "apocalypse and renewal" (23). The cycle of apocalypse and renewal is forcefully portrayed in *Two Hunters* by Wolves in the Throne Room (Southern Lord Recordings, 2007). Likewise, Skagos released tracks entitled "Blossoms will Sprout from the Carcass" and "A Night that Ends, as all Nights End, when the Sun Rises" (*Ast*, Eternal Warfare, 2009).[10] But there are other ways to thematize self-transcendence.

The Four Platonic Hypostases

To combine my two arguments for the religiosity of black metal, I will use a Platonic creation myth. I will stay very close to the ancient sources. However, Plato (and Leibniz) made up their own myths to serve their own philosophical purposes. Following their leads, I will take some poetic liberties in combining ancient ideas. My myth begins with nothingness, the abyss. Analytically, nothingness is the x such that x is not identical with x (Oliver and Smiley 2013). Nothingness is absolutely pure nonexistence; its absolute purity makes it holy.[11] Arithmetically, nothingness is the metaphysical *Zero*, the *Holy Zero*. As the Zero, nothingness is at the bottom of the vertical axis of existence, below and prior to all existing entities. Consequently, it is prior to all binaries; it is neither Good nor evil. Nothingness is wholly repulsive; its emotional

[10] The metal-adjacent band Earth produced an album, *The Bees Made Honey in the Lion's Skull* (Southern Lord Recordings, 2008). The Appalachian Black Metal project, Falls of Rauros, inspired by dark green nature-religion, released *The Light that Dwells in Rotten Wood* (Replenish Records, 2011). And Panopticon released . . . *and Again into the Light* (Bindrune Recordings, 2021).

[11] Rogerson (2003) reviews the classical associations of holiness with purity, cleanliness, and danger. Hence holiness here is *absolute purity*.

repulsiveness is *horror;* its aesthetic repulsiveness is its *hideousness*; and it is encountered in *stupefaction*.[12] It is night, cold, meaningless, and silent. In Egyptian mythology, nothingness is *Nun*, the primordial waters, the oceanic abyss (Van Dijk 1995; Fiala 2008). The Greek poets likewise equated the primordial waters of nothingness with Oceanus (Bernabe 2020). Turning to Norse mythology, nothingness is the waters beneath the world tree Yggdrassil.

Since the negativity of nothingness is absolute, it is universal; since it is universal, it applies to itself; hence nothingness negates itself (Priest 2001, p. 244; Moss 2022, p. 164; Steinhart 2022, ch. 2).[13] Black metal incorporates the self-negation of nothingness. Scott refers to "The black metal curse, the negative negation of nothing" (2018, p. 190). Noys says "Black metal still operates with the clashing elements it deploys to produce its own virtual 'negation of the negation' as affirmation" (2010, p. 120). Hunt-Hendrix confirms that this double negation is an affirmation (2010, pp. 59, 61). The self-negation of absolutely pure nonexistence is absolutely pure existence; it is *being-itself*.

Arithmetically, being-itself is the metaphysical *One*. As being-itself, the One is prior to all the beings among beings. Since the One is absolutely pure existence, its absolute purity makes it holy. The One is the *Holy One*. As such, it is wholly other; its otherness is *terror*, and it is encountered in *awe*. The absolute otherness of the One entails that it cloaks itself with its otherness, it *hides* within its terror as behind a paraconsistent veil of oblivion. The Pythagoreans pictured the One as a seed (Pseudo-Iamblichus, *Theology of Arithmetic*, 4–5). Speusippus said the One is a seed (Aristotle, *Metaphysics* VII.2, 1028b21-4, XII.7, 1072b30-1073a3). Plotinus often puts the One in the earth: the One is a root (E 3.3.7, 3.8.10, 6.8.15); or a seed (E 4.8.6.1-10); or a spring (E 3.8.10.1-5, 5.2.1, 5.7.12.23-7). The One in the earth is obscurity, darkness, and chaos (*Theology of Arithmetic*, 5). Turning to Egyptian mythology, the One is Atum, which rises up out of Nun like the primordial mound rises up out of the flooded Nile, or out of the oceanic abyss.[14] But the One is not a deity of any kind; on the contrary, the One is a Platonic hypostasis.

---

[12] Listening to Oranssi Pazuzu, *Varahtelija* (Svart Records, 2016).

[13] Listening to Blut aus Nord, *The Thematic Emanation of Archetypal Multiplicity* (Candlelight Records, 2005).

[14] Listening to Solbrud, *Solbrud* (Solbrud, 2012), *Vermod* (Vendetta Records, 2017).

Since the One is the first entity to emerge from the abyss, it remains below and beneath all the beings. The beings will rise up over and above the One, and it will support them from below. Using a Lovecraftian theonym, the One is *Azathoth*, the chaotic nucleus at the center of the abyss. As being-itself, the One is prior to all binaries; hence Azathoth is neither Good nor evil. Good and evil will appear only among the beings, which do not yet exist. Azathoth surrounds itself with the "muffled, maddening beating of vile drums and the thin monotonous whine of accursed flutes" (Lovecraft, CF 2.100).[15] I interpret this as black metal *drone* (Coggins 2018).[16] Azathoth begins the *music of creation*.[17]

The One *powers* (E 5.1.6.30-42, 5.2.1.5-10, 5.4.1.25-30). Since the One is super-abundant, it enfolds male and female principles within itself (*Theology of Arithmetic*, 4–5). If the One does not unfold these sexual principles, then it does not produce; but the One produces; therefore, it unfolds these principles. It unfolds them first as the two sides of its unity, that is, as an androgynous Two-in-One. In Egyptian mythology, Atum becomes the androgynous Two-in-One, whose male and female powers have sex with each other (Van Dijk 1995, p. 1700). The androgynous Two-in-One is found in Plato as well (*Symposium*, 189d-190b). The androgynous Two-in-One is the Dyad.

Porphyry, in his treatise on the River Styx, uses a statue of Shiva to portray the Dyad (Mastrocinque 2011; Brisson 2015). The right side of the statue has the form and parts of man, while the left side has the form and parts of a woman. Additionally, the arms were engraved with "the heavens, mountains, sea, rivers, ocean, plants, animals, in short, all that exists." The statue is a model for creation. The statue (the Dyad) has generated within itself images of all the beings among beings. But the images are still unrealized. So the Dyad is prior to the beings. Hence, the Dyad is neither good nor evil.

In Norse mythology, Ymir is the androgynous One, whose male leg has sex with its female leg. In the Cthulhu Mythos of Lovecraft, there are two reasons to think the androgynous Dyad is *Nyarlathotep*. First, Porphyry portrays the Dyad as the androgynous Shiva, but Price (1997) argues that Nyarlathotep is Shiva. Likewise, Clark Ashton Smith (1944)

---

[15] Lovecraft is standardly cited by volume and page number in the *Collected Fiction* (Lovecraft 2017). Thus, CF 2.100 is *Collected Fiction* volume 2 page 100. Azathoth surrounded by music (CF 1.205; 1.395; 2.100, 2.112-3, 2.204, 2.210-1; 3.244, 3.255; 3.471; "Fungi from Yuggoth" verse XXII).

[16] Listening to Darkspace; Mesarthim; and Echtra, *A War for Wonder* (20 Buck Spin, 2009), *BardO* (Temple of Torturous, 2018).

[17] Azathoth emanates the music of creation ("Fungi from Yuggoth," verse XXII).

says Azathoth asexually produces an androgynous entity, but Lovecraft portrays Nyarlathotep as a direct offspring of Azathoth (2014, p. 819). So here I will say that Nyarlathotep is the androgynous Dyad. Nyarlathotep is "the mad faceless god, [who] howls blindly in the darkness to the piping of two amorphous idiot flute-players" (CF 1.395; see CF 1.205). Nyarlathotep is the black metal scream. But Nyarlathotep is not a deity; like Azathoth, Nyarlathotep is a Platonic hypostasis.

If the two sexual sides of the Dyad remain bound together in one entity, then they are not fully sexually reproductive; therefore, they produce only images, not things. If the Dyad produces only images, then its power is not absolutely productive; so then the power of the One is not absolutely productive; but the power of the One is absolutely productive. Therefore, the two sexual sides of the Dyad separate. The Dyad unfolds its sexual powers into two distinct entities. Plato said Zeus separated the primal androgynous organisms (*Symposium*, 189d-193d). But here the Dyad tears itself apart, screaming in pain.

The self-diremption of the androgynous Dyad produces male and female fertility monsters. These two monsters are pure sexual powers; as such, they are holy. They are the *Holy Two*. Since they will produce the beings among beings, they are prior to those beings; since they are prior to those beings, they are neither good nor evil. Using theonyms from Lovecraft, the male power is *Yog-Sothoth*, while the female power is *The Black Goat of the Woods with a Thousand Young*. But here I will refer to her using Lord Dunsany's theonym *Sheol-Nugganoth*. On the one hand, Yog-Sothoth is a circle whose center is everywhere and whose circumference is nowhere. On the other hand, Sheol-Nugganoth is a circle whose circumference is everywhere and whose center is nowhere. But the center of Yog-Sothoth fits into the circumference of Sheol-Nugganoth. Like Azathoth and Nyarlathotep, Yog-Sothoth and Sheol-Nugganoth are hypostases. Using some vaguely Lovecraftian terminology, these four hypostases are the *Elder Powers*.

The Black Metal Music of Creation

It's time to do some Platonic myth-making. Here, I sketch a philosophical myth in which the music of creation and music of predator defiance come together. The creativity in this myth comes from Yog-Sothoth and Sheol-Nugganoth. They emanate, through their sexual interactions, all existing things. Whenever they have sex, they produce a batch of offspring.

Here, I follow the Platonic theme that mathematical emanations come before physical emanations. I have elsewhere defined five emanations (Steinhart 2025), but here I only sketch two of those five.

During their first emanation, the fertility monsters produce their first batch of offspring. These are all possible theories of mathematical objects. For precision, I'll say these are all possible axiomatic set theories. These theories have existence axioms. If those axioms are true, then the things they define exist. When they are born, these theories are immature. Since they are immature, they are neither true nor false. These theories are ranked according to their mathematical virtues. For example, inconsistent theories are worse than consistent theories, and less comprehensive theories are worse than more comprehensive theories. When all these virtues are taken together, they define the mathematical *fitness* of any theory. The different theories have different degrees of fitness.

When these theories were born, they were born into the abyss as beings among beings. Hence, they were separated from being-itself and separated from each other. These separations were painful, so these newborn theories cry out with pain. Their cries attract the Predator, who seeks to devour them all. The newborn theories hear the approaching Predator, and cry out even louder. Their cries, and the sounds of the approaching Predator, make the extrinsic signal in the first black metal music of creation.

Hearing the cries of their offspring, the Elder Powers all join in to produce a full black metal song. They produce an intrinsic signal to go with the extrinsic signal. This intrinsic signal contains themes of speed, skill, agility, virtuosity, and self-surpassing. This is the music of predator defiance. If any offspring hears this intrinsic signal, then it follows that signal. Guided by that predator defiance signal, it escapes from the Predator, and it grows to maturity. The ability to hear this intrinsic signal is equivalent to maximal fitness: the fittest offspring hear the intrinsic signal, while the others cannot hear it. The ability to hear this intrinsic signal acts as a filter which separates the best from the rest.

Only the best theories hear the music of predator defiance. For the sake of simplicity, I assume that exactly one theory is maximally fit. It is the best axiomatic set theory. This theory hears the music of predator defiance, which shows how to defeat the Predator. By following that predator defiance music, it defeats the Predator, and it grows to maturity. When it grows to maturity, it becomes *true*. Since it is true, the things defined by its axioms exist. That is, it acquires a model, which is its mature body. Call it the *Abstract Body*. But the other theories, which are not maximally fit, are devoured by the Predator. They are *false*. They do not grow to mature bodies; they do not have models.

The Abstract Body, which is the model of the best axiomatic set theory, contains all possible abstract structures. Some of these are the structures of possible physical universes, that is, they are cosmic forms. Cosmic forms are abstract universes. All possible abstract universes exist in the body of the best set theory. There are absolutely infinitely many (abstract) universes in that body. These universes are ordered by an improvement relation (Steinhart 2020, ch. 4, 2022, chs. 4–5). Every universe is surpassed by its improvements. If this universe is an improvement of that universe, then this universe is a better version of that universe. Since there are many universes in the Abstract Body, there are classes of these universes. Following Kraay (2011), say a class of abstract universes is an *abstract world*. The fertility monsters now enter the Abstract Body, which becomes an androgynous body like the statue of Shiva described by Porphyry. Animated by the fertility monsters, this body gives birth to its offspring. Each offspring is an abstract world. These offspring are born into the abyss. These abstract worlds have virtues which define their degrees of fitness. Exactly one abstract world is maximally fit.

These newborn worlds are crying in the abyss. Again, the Predator hears their cries and seeks to devour them. Their cries and the sounds of the approaching Predator make the extrinsic signal in the second black metal music of creation. Hearing the cries of their offspring, the Elder Powers all join in to produce a second full black metal song. They produce a second intrinsic signal to go with the second extrinsic signal. As before, if any offspring hears this intrinsic signal, then it follows it to safety. Only the fittest abstract world hears that signal, while the other abstract worlds do not hear it. The ability to hear this intrinsic signal acts as a filter which separates the best from the rest.

Exactly one abstract world is maximally fit; it is the best of all possible abstract worlds (Steinhart 2020, ch. 4.5, 2022, ch. 5). This world is defined by three laws. The *initial law* states that the least valuable abstract universe is the *initial universe* in the best abstract world. The *successor law* states that, for every universe in the best world, for every way to improve it, there exists a *successor universe* in the best world which is improved in that way. Hence, every universe is surpassed by at least one better successor. Every universe is *reborn* into each of its successors. The initial and successor laws define infinite progressions of ever-better universes. Now the *limit law* states that, for every progression in the best world, for every way to improve it, there exists a *limit universe* in the best world which is improved in that way. Hence, every progression is surpassed by at least one better limit. Every progression is *reborn* into each of its limits. The best abstract world is an infinitely ramified tree. It is the great world tree Yggdrasil. No universe in this tree is best. Every universe in Yggdrasil is surpassed by better universes.

Only the best abstract world hears the music of predator defiance which shows it how to defeat the Predator. By following that predator defiance music, it grows to maturity. When it grows to maturity, it becomes *concretized*. If any abstract world is concretized, then every abstract universe in that world gains a concrete physical model. Therefore, every abstract universe in the best abstract world gains a concrete physical model, which is a concrete physical universe. When it grows to maturity, the best abstract world gains a *Concrete Body*. This Concrete Body is the body of Yggdrasil. It is a class of physical universes ordered by the improvement relation. But the other abstract worlds, which are not maximally fit, are devoured by the Predator. They are *not concretized*. They do not grow to maturity, and so they do not gain concrete bodies. Consequently, the second black metal music of creation entails the existence of the best system of physical universes. Our universe is one of these, but it will be surpassed by many better versions of itself.

References

Atran, S. (2002). *In Gods We Trust: The Evolutionary Landscape of Religion*. New York: Oxford.

Bernabe, A. (2020). The primordial water: between myth and philosophy. In: *More than Homer Knew: Studies on Homer and His Ancient Commentators* (ed. A. Rengakos, B. Zimmermann, and P. Finglass), 417–437. Boston: de Gruyter.

Bivins, J. (2017). The weight of the world: religion and heavy metal music in four cases. In: *Religion and Popular Culture in America* (ed. B. Forbes and J. Mahan), 100–118. Berkeley, CA: University of California Press.

Bregman, J. (1990). The Neoplatonic revival in North America. *Hermathena* 149: 99–119.

Brisson, L. (2015). A description of an androgynous statue of Shiva by Porphyry, *on the Styx* (376 f Smith). *Antiquorum Philosophia* 8: 57–64.

Burkert, W. (1983). *Homo Necans: The Anthropology of Ancient Greek Sacrificial Ritual and Myth*. Berkeley: University of California.

Burkert, W. (1996). *The Creation of the Sacred: Tracks of Biology in Early Religions*. Cambridge, MA: Harvard.

Casarella, P. (2016). Trinity, simultaneity, and the music of creation in St. Bonaventure. In: *Time: Sense, Space, Structure* (ed. N. van Deusen and L. Koff), 141–159. Boston: Brill.

Cluness, B. (2022). From hyperborean darkness to transcendental light: on challenging masculinity, and the immanence of black metal through the esoteric Christianity of Hunter Hunt-Hendrix and Liturgy. *Correspondences* 10 (1): 49–85.

Coggins, O. (2018). *Mysticism, Ritual and Religion in Drone Metal.* New York: Bloomsbury.

Davis, H. (1982). The ainulindale: music of creation. *Mythlore* 9 (2): 6–10.

Demulder, B. (2020). Music and Plutarch's Platonic cosmos. In: *Music and Philosophy in the Roman Empire* (ed. F. Pelosi and F. Petrucci), 38–59. New York: Cambridge.

Fiala, A. (2008). Creation myths of the ancient world. In: *Encyclopedia of Religion and Nature* (ed. B. Taylor), 431–433. New York: Bloomsbury.

Fletcher, K. and Umurhan, O. (2019). *Classical Antiquity in Heavy Metal Music.* New York: Bloomsbury.

Gersh, S. (2009). The metaphysical unity of music, motion, and time in Augustine's *De Musica*. In: *Christian Humanism* (ed. A. MacDonald, Z. von Martels, and J. Veenstra), 303–316. Boston: Brill.

Gerson, L. (2005). What is Platonism? *Journal of the History of Philosophy* 43 (3): 253–276.

Granholm, K. (2013). Ritual black metal: popular music as occult mediation and practice. *Correspondences* 1 (1): 5–33.

Greenberg, D., Baron-Cohen, S., Stillwell, D. et al. (2015). Musical preferences are linked to cognitive styles. *PLoS One* 10 (7): e0131151.

Guthrie, S. (2002). Animal animism: evolutionary roots of religious cognition. In: *Current Approaches in the Cognitive Science of Religion* (ed. V. Anttonen and I. Pyysiäinen), 38–67. New York: Bloomsbury.

Hannan, C. (2018). Difficulty as heaviness: links between rhythmic difficulty and perceived heaviness in the music of Meshuggah and The Dillinger Escape Plan. *Metal Music Studies* 4 (3): 433–458.

Herbst, J.-P. and Mynett, M. (2023). Toward a systematic understanding of "heaviness" in metal music production. *Rock Music Studies* 10 (1): 16–37.

Houghton, J. (1995). Augustine and the Ainulindale. *Mythlore* 21 (1): 4–8.

Hunt-Hendrix, H. (2010). Transcendental black metal: a vision of apocalyptic humanism. In: *Hideous Gnosis: Black Metal Theory Symposium*, vol. 1 (ed. N. Masciandaro), 54–66.

Kraay, K. (2011). Theism and modal collapse. *American Philosophical Quarterly* 48 (4): 361–372.

Kuusela, T. (2015). "Dark Lord of Gorgoroth": black metal and the works of Tolkien. In: *Lembas Extra 2015: Unexplored Aspects of Tolkien and Arda* (ed. C. van Zon and R. Vink), 89–120. Amsterdam: Unquendor.

Leask, I. (2016). Performing cosmic music: notes on Plato's *Timaeus*. *REA: A Journal of Religion, Education and the Arts* 10: 14–27.
Levy, C. (2020). The *scala naturae* and music: two models in Philo's thought. In: *Music and Philosophy in the Roman Empire* (ed. F. Pelosi and F. Petrucci), 21–37. New York: Cambridge.
Lovecraft, H.P. (2014). *The New Annotated H. P. Lovecraft* (ed. L. Klinger). New York: W. W. Norton.
Lovecraft, H.P. (2017). *Collected Fiction* (ed. S.T. Joshi). In four volumes. New York: Hippocampus Press.
Martin, L.H. (2013). The ecology of threat detection and precautionary response from the perspectives of evolutionary psychology, cognitive science and historiography: the case of the roman cults of Mithras. *Method & Theory in the Study of Religion* 25 (4–5): 431–450.
Mastrocinque, A. (2011). Helios-Shiva: porphyry, Ardhanarisvara, and a magical gem in Naples. *Transactions of the American Philosophical Society* 101 (5): 67–93.
McIver, J. (2013). Black Sabbath and the sound of evil. In: *Black Sabbath and Philosophy* (ed. W. Irwin), 33–40. Malden, MA: Wiley-Blackwell.
Messick, K., Jong, J., van Mulukom, V., and Farias, M. (2023). The nontheistic sacred: the psychological functions of metal music and artifacts. *The International Journal for the Psychology of Religion* 33 (3): 198–213.
Moberg, M. (2012). Religion in popular music or popular music as religion? *Popular Music and Society* 35 (1): 113–130.
Moss, G. (2022). Transcending everything. In: *Everything and Nothing* (ed. M. Gabriel and G. Priest), 153–189. Hoboken, NJ: Polity Press.
Norman, J. (2013). "Sounds which filled me with an indefinable dread": the Cthulhu mythopoeia of H. P. Lovecraft in "extreme" metal. In: *New Critical Essays on H. P. Lovecraft* (ed. D. Simmons), 193–208. New York: Palgrave.
Noys, B. (2010). 'Remain true to the earth!': remarks on the politics of black metal. In: *Hideous Gnosis: Black Metal Theory Symposium*, vol. 1 (ed. N. Masciandaro), 105–128.
Oliver, A. and Smiley, T. (2013). Zilch. *Analysis* 73 (4): 601–613.
Ollivier, R., Goupil, L., Liuni, M., and Aucouturier, J. (2019). Enjoy the violence: is appreciation for extreme music the result of cognitive control over the threat response system? *Music Perception* 37 (2): 95–110.
Olsen, K., Terry, J., and Thompson, W. (2023). Psychosocial risks and benefits of exposure to heavy metal music with aggressive themes: current theory and evidence. *Current Psychology* 42 (24): 21133–21150.
Pelosi, F. (2017). Eight singing sirens: heavenly harmonies in Plato and the Neoplatonists. In: *Sing Aloud Harmonious Spheres* (ed. J. Prins and M. Vanhaelen), 15–30. New York: Routledge.
Petrucci, F. (2020). The harmoniser god: harmony as a cosmological model in middle platonist theology. In: *Music and Philosophy in the Roman Empire* (ed. F. Pelosi and F. Petrucci), 60–84. New York: Cambridge.

Pohlmann, S. (2015). Whitman's compost: the romantic posthuman futures of Cascadian black metal. *ACT: Zeitschrift fur Musik & Performance* 6: 2–30.
Price, R. (1997). Introduction: the theology of Nyarlathotep. In: *The Nyarlathotep Cycle* (ed. R. Price), vii–xii. Oakland, CA: Chaosium.
Priest, G. (2001). Heidegger and the grammar of being. In: *Grammar in Early Twentieth-Century Philosophy* (ed. R. Gaskin), 238–252. New York: Routledge.
Rogerson, J. (2003). What is holiness? In: *Holiness: Past and Present* (ed. S. Barton), 3–21. New York: Continuum.
Schmaltz, R., Watson, D., and Johnston, A. (2021). The thinking person's music: heavy metal and the need for cognition. *Psychology of Music* 49 (5): 1372–1380.
Scott, N. (2014). Seasons in the abyss: heavy metal as liturgy. *Diskus (Frankfurt Am Main, Germany)* 16 (1): 12–29.
Scott, N. (2018). Black metal's apophatic curse. *Theologiques* 26 (1): 185–206.
Sederholm, C. (2016). H. P. Lovecraft, heavy metal, and cosmicism. *Rock Music Studies* 3 (3): 266–280.
Shadrack, J. (2021). *Black Metal, Trauma, Subjectivity and Sound: Screaming the Abyss*. Bingley, UK: Emerald.
Sharman, L. and Dingle, G. (2015). Extreme metal music and anger processing. *Frontiers in Human Neuroscience* 9: 127226.
Smith, C.A. (1944). The family tree of the gods. *The Acolyte* 2 (3): 9–10.
Snaza, N. (2016). Leaving the self behind. In: *Helvete 3: Bleeding Black Noise* (ed. A. Ishmael), 81–98. Earth, Milky Way: Punctum Books.
Steinhart, E. (2020). *Believing in Dawkins: The New Spiritual Atheism*. New York: Palgrave.
Steinhart, E. (2022). *Atheistic Platonism: A Manifesto*. New York: Palgrave.
Steinhart, E. (2025). Non-theistic optimism in recent philosophy. In: *Optimism and the Best Possible World* (ed. J. Daeley), 161–185. New York: Routledge.
Stevens, F. (2022). Abyssal noise: representations of death and dying in extreme metal music. In: *Embodying the Music and Death Nexus* (ed. M. Bennett et al.), 75–87. Bingley, UK: Emerald.
Swallow, R. and Herbst, J.P. (2022). Dissonance in metal music: musical and sociocultural reasons for metal's appreciation of dissonance. *Metal Music Studies* 8 (3): 351–379.
Thompson, W. and Olsen, K. (2018). On the enjoyment of violence and aggression in music. Comment on "An integrative review of the enjoyment of sadness associated with music" by Tuomas Eerola et al. *Physics of Life Reviews* 25: 128–130.
Thompson, W., Geeves, A., and Olsen, K. (2019). Who enjoys listening to violent music and why? *Psychology of Popular Media Culture* 8 (3): 218–232.
Trout, P. (2011). *Deadly Powers: Animal Predators and the Mythic Imagination*. Amherst, NY: Prometheus Books.
Unger, M. (2016). *Sound, Symbol, Sociality: The Aesthetic Experience of Extreme Metal Music*. New York: Palgrave Pivot.

Van Dijk, J. (1995). Myth and mythmaking in ancient Egypt. *Civilizations of the Ancient Near East* 3: 1697–1709.

Watier, N. (2022). Threat cues in metal's visual code. *Metal Music Studies* 8 (2): 205–223.

Wiebe, D. (2013). Pseudo-speciation of the human race: religions as hazard-precaution systems. *Method & Theory in the Study of Religion* 25 (4–5): 410–430.

Xhignesse, M.-A. (2024). The heaviest metal. *Philosophia* 52: 681–697.

Part III

The Science of Noise: On Aesthetics

Chapter 8
The Role of Performance Personae in Black Metal Aesthetics

Ley David Elliette Cray
Department of Philosophy, New Mexico State University, Las Cruces, NM, USA

Introduction

In terms of visibility and recognizability outside of metal subcultures, the *aesthetics* of black metal have arguably surpassed the actual music. These aesthetics include not just the leather, spikes, and "corpse paint"—starkly contrasting black-and-white makeup designed to make the wearer appear as a living corpse or some variety of demonic entity—but also the "evil" or "inhuman" personae of black metal musicians. Feeding into these personae have, historically, been criminal acts such as church burnings and homicides (including killings of bandmates) as well as anti-social acts such as animal sacrifice and overtly fascist gestures and symbols. While certainly far from universal among black metal subculture, the combination of all of the above has undeniably shaped the public perception of the subculture—even for those who have no sense of the musical characteristics common to the genre.

Shifting focus to those familiar with the genre, one could make the case that there have come to be aesthetic expectations of black metal that go beyond the music and extend to the performers. Performers typically reveal very little about their private, personal selves and instead retain a sense of anonymity reinforced by the construction of a public-facing persona. Quite often, this persona maintains a particular look—perhaps donning the aforementioned leather, spikes, and corpse paint, or even just remaining ominously obscured by shadows (or bad lighting) in promotional photos—and adopts a pseudonym that invokes some variety of Satanic, confrontational, or otherworldly character; see, for example, *Lord Angelslayer* (vocalist and guitarist of Finland's Archgoat), *Nocturnal Grave Desecrator and Black Winds* (vocalist and former bassist of Canada's Blasphemy), or *Vindsval* (vocalist, guitarist, and overall conceptual leader of France's Blut Aus Nord). In adopting and operating under these personae, the musicians distance themselves from concrete reality and become as if something other than human.

Throughout this chapter, I'll argue that—contrary to common protestations of being "all about the music"—such personae are not an incidental aesthetic feature of black metal subculture, but are instead quite relevant to aesthetic engagement and evaluation of the music itself. Indeed, this relevance goes beyond the role personae in general play in such engagement and evaluation of music across genres, and is instead a *central* component of black metal. In making the case for this claim, I first look at scholarship on personae from within the philosophy of music before moving on to a critical, historical analysis of black metal as both a musical genre and a subculture. I'll conclude by exploring the role of personae within black metal with the aim of demonstrating their peculiar centrality as an aesthetic device.

Regarding Performance Personae

The notion of performance personae as aesthetic devices originates outside of the context of black metal, of course. In positing and subsequently developing this notion, philosophers such as Stanley Godlovitch (1998), Jeanette Bicknell (2005, 2015), Theodore Gracyk (2017), and myself (2019, 2024, 2025) have made the case that such personae are, in fact, ineliminable components of both live musical performance *and* efforts to aesthetically engage with and evaluate such performances.

Focusing just on the personae of performers engaged in live singing performances, Bicknell (2005, p. 263) clarifies that:

> A singer's public persona is the face, body, and personal history he or she presents to the audience. It includes such factors as gender, race, age, and ethnicity, as well as quirks of personality such as those described by Godlovich. This information is conveyed by the singer's appearance, clothing choices, and the statements and activities reported by the media or circulated among fans.

Here, Bicknell refers to remarks by Godlovich (1998, p. 143) regarding live performers more generally:

> We are drawn to personal details, and these seamlessly intertwine with our aesthetic expectations; for example, the riotous life of the performer, his cranky, immature conduct at august gatherings, his wayward attitude to his listeners, his crippling depressions, his bitter envy of his colleagues, his rapt intensity on stage, his savage career ambitions, and the like.

All of these details inform the lens through which we view and interpret the performer's performance, with this lens—the *persona*—playing a role in the degree to which audiences will plausibly receive the performance as *authentic*, *believable*, *convincing*, *compelling*, *honest*, and so on. Insofar as such judgments are ultimately *aesthetic* judgments, the case is thereby made that performance personae are relevant to the aesthetic engagement and evaluation of live music performance.

To elucidate this framework through examples, consider someone like the late Toby Keith performing Coolio's 1995 hip-hop hit, "Gangsta's Paradise" or Taylor Swift offering a rendition of Cannibal Corpse's 1991 death metal classic, "Butchered at Birth." Even if performed earnestly, both would likely be experienced by audiences as incongruent with the personae of the performers in question, with the performances themselves seeming *awkward*, *unconvincing*, or perhaps even *silly* or *mocking*. Insofar as these traits constitute aesthetic deficiencies in the performance, we might conclude that when it comes to Keith and Swift, performances of such songs are simply "outside of their range" in the sense that they are not plausible candidates for believable and compelling performances.

Bicknell observes that personae "may transparently reflect a singer's true personality; more likely, it will be highly mediated and constructed" (2005, p. 263). I have developed this point further (see Cray 2019) by exploring the distinction between *transparent* and *opaque* performance personae. In short: a persona is *transparent* to the degree that inferences about the performer's persona also apply to the performer as a private individual (and *vice versa*), and *opaque* to the degree that they do not. So the personae of such "persona-less" performers as, say, Eddie Vedder, Tori Amos, or Aretha Franklin are simply transparent personae, whereas those of performers such as Ethel Cain (the character portrayed through performance by Hayden Silas Anhedönia), Ronald Osbourne (portrayed by the anonymous singer of McDonalds-themed Black Sabbath parody band, Mac Sabbath), or David St. Hubbins (portrayed by Michael McKean of Spinal Tap) are, to various degrees, opaque. In the case of opaque personae, it is appropriate to engage in a sort of "pretending," *screening off* facts about the performer as a private individual and instead considering only those of the opaque persona.

This framework can be enriched and expanded in several ways. Consider the distinction between *performance personae* (adopted consistently by a performer) versus *song personae* (adopted for the performance of particular songs, such as Shel Silverstein's 1969 "A Boy Named Sue," made famous by Johnny Cash) (Cray 2019). Alternatively, we might draw distinctions between individual personae and *group personae*, adopted collectively by a line-up in formation as a band (see Cray 2024). More recently, I have extended this framework so as to apply to not just live performance but also studio recordings by carving out a distinction between *performance personae* and *recording personae* (Cray 2025). Though for the sake of simplicity we won't consider these distinctions further here, they collectively provide an enriched and more comprehensive framework that can helpfully apply to all still to be discussed throughout this chapter.

Regarding Black Metal

With our foundation set through this discussion of the underlying framework of performance personae, we can now move on to the characterization of *black metal* we'll be adopting throughout the rest of the chapter. As with any attempt to characterize any genre or subculture—or *anything at all*, for that matter—the account here will inevitably have its detractors. I ask devout fans to interpret what follows not as a dictate about how *they* should understand black metal, but instead how *I* understand it within the context of this discussion.

Characterizing any genre is a task fraught with difficulty. As Gracyk (2016, p. 776) points out in the context of attempts to define metal as a whole, "the answer is neither obvious nor settled." Gracyk continues: "it appears that both the music and the fan base are so varied that the label involves significant conceptual drift: the meaning shifts, given the context of use, among the categories of genre, style, and subculture" (2016, p. 776). What is true of metal as a whole in this case seems to be true also of black metal, which itself contains substantial stylistic and subcultural diversity. On this front, consider, for example, so-called "first-wave" acts such as Venom and Mercyful Fate in contrast to "second-wave" Norwegian acts like Mayhem or Burzum, and both in contrast to the Finnish community comprising bands such as Archgoat or Beherit or the American Cascadian "scene" with which groups such as Alda, Fauna, and Wolves in the Throne Room are often identified. These subcultures are as varied as the music they center on, and attempting to find some musical feature universal (and exclusive) to the acts just mentioned would likely not be the best use of our time.

With that all said, we *can* distinguish between *musical features* in the form of characteristic (though short of universal or essential) stylistic tendencies, and *extramusical features* such as characteristic subcultural tendencies (similarly qualified). To illuminate both of these, it would be fruitful to consider black metal through a primarily historical lens.

Venom and the First Wave

Many aficionados trace the roots of black metal back to English band Venom, formed in Newcastle in 1978. As part of the New Wave British Heavy Metal (NWOBHM) movement of mid-to-late 1970s and early 1980s, Venom explored a style informed by foundational heavy metal acts such as Black Sabbath and Judas Priest in conversation with the speed, intensity, and anti-establishment ethos of early British punk acts such as the Sex Pistols, the Clash, and the Damned. Of particular influence were celebrated precursors to this hybrid style, Motörhead.

Though they were far from the first to incorporate Satanic lyrics and imagery (see, for example, Black Widow's 1970 debut *Sacrifice* or Coven's 1969 debut *Witchcraft Destroys Minds & Reaps Souls*), Venom arguably centered such "shocking" elements more so than any other contributor to the NWOBHM. Though their 1981 debut *Welcome to Hell* laid the foundations, it was 1982s *Black Metal* that many fans will cite as the catalyst for what would become black metal as we now know it.

Aspects of both Venom's musical style—a raw, somewhat sloppy form of speed metal—and presentation—leather, spikes, and the use of esoteric stage names such as Cronos, Mantas, and Abaddon—would go on to influence other progenitors of what is now known, retroactively, as the *first wave* of black metal. Acts most commonly associated with the first wave include Denmark's Mercyful Fate, Switzerland's Hellhammer (who quickly evolved into first-wavers Celtic Frost), and Sweden's Bathory. While these groups varied substantially in terms of musical style—with Mercyful Fate exploring a more polished, traditional heavy metal sound while Hellhammer and Bathory drew more from the emerging crust and d-beat scenes in adjacent punk communities—each continued Venom's focus on Satanic (or occult) imagery in terms of both lyrics and presentation, adopting pseudonyms and exploring more and more "extreme" forms of adornment. Drawing inspiration from earlier acts such as Alice Cooper and KISS, members of Hellhammer, Mercyful Fate, and Venom began painting their faces with stark black-and-white makeup, laying the foundation for what would become solidified—through a photo on the cover of Brazilian first-wavers Sarcófago's 1987 LP *I.N.R.I.*—as *corpse paint*. This photo, with its depiction of the band members in studded black leather with bullet belts and wielding inverted crosses, would go on to heavily influence the visual presentation of black metal musicians from then on.

Consideration of Sarcófago is also a healthy reminder that—despite the typical focus on Venom, Hellhammer, Mercyful Fate, and Bathory—what we now think of as the first wave of black metal was far more than a European phenomenon, with bands such as Blasphemy (Canada), Parabellum (Colombia), Von (United States), and Sabbat (Japan) often included as important contributors that demonstrate a more global reach.

Norway and the "Second Wave"

Taking cues and influence from the more musically and culturally diverse first-wave, black metal began to solidify into its more typical and familiar contemporary form through the so-called "second wave," centered in Norway during the early 1990s. Beyond deriving influence from the Satanic themes and imagery of the first wave, the second wave congealed around a distilled subset of musical traits found among some first-wave bands, along with the "raw" and amateurish production of key acts such as Venom, Hellhammer, and Bathory. Among these musical traits include the use of the blast beat (a repetitive rhythm that most commonly takes the form of "blasts" incorporating bass drum, snare, and either hi-hat or ride cymbal—purportedly named by Mick Harris, former drummer of British grindcore band Napalm Death), distorted guitars emphasizing tremolo-picking (rapid and steady, alternate up-and-down picking often utilizing a single note or string, typically employed for melodic effect), and harshly shrieked vocals. While the topic remains a source of debate among black metal musicians and fans, the evolution of tremolo-picked guitar riffs into the angular, hypnotic, and often dissonant form iconic of the second wave is widely attributed to guitarist Snorre Ruch, especially with respect to the guitar work on the 1991 demo *Grymyrk* by his band, Thorns.

One cannot speak of the second wave without a discussion of Helvete ("Hell"), a record shop in Oslo opened by Øystein Aarseth (also known as Euronymous, in reference to the Hellhammer song, "Eurynomos") in 1991. Aarseth had formed the band Mayhem in 1984 and acted as a sort of ringleader of the so-called "Black Circle," a loosely connected group of black metal musicians who gathered in and around Helvete and shared—to various degrees—a misanthropic and specifically anti-Christian ideology. While the violent and Satanic imagery and lyrics of the first wave were somewhat explicitly just for show, many musicians of the Black Circle sought to live such things out in their lives off stage and camera, resulting in a string of fabled criminal acts. Such acts comprise (at least) a string of church burnings, one suicide (Per Ohlin, also known as Dead, the former vocalist of Mayhem), and two murders, including the murder of Aarseth himself by Varg Vikernes (one of the aliases of Louis Cachet, formerly Kristian Vikernes and also once operating as "Count Grishnackh"), former session bassist for Mayhem and sole member of Burzum. Due to extensive media coverage, these acts (and others in their vicinity) alongside the anti-social ideology inherent in them became nearly synonymous with black metal, arguably even going on to overshadow the music itself.

While the first wave largely fashioned itself as apolitical, the image of the ideology-driven second wave has become tied in public consciousness to fascism, racism, and anti-semitism. Aside from Vikernes's explicitly far-right, racist, and anti-semitic views and Neo-Nazi ties, Mayhem drummer (and prolific collaborator of more bands than need be listed here) Jan Axel Blomberg (also known as Hellhammer) is quoted in *Lords of Chaos:*

The Bloody Rise of the Satanic Metal Underground—written by Didrik Søderlind and far-right sympathizer Michael Moynihan—as saying:

> I'll put it this way, we don't like black people here. Black metal is for white people. . .. I'm pretty convinced that there are differences between races as well as everything else. I think that like animals, some races are more . . . you know, like a cat is much more intelligent than a bird or a cow, or even a dog, and I think that's also the case with different races.
> (Moynihan and Søderlind 2003, p. 259)

In the 2008 black metal documentary *Until the Light Takes Us* (directed by Aaron Aites and Audrey Ewell), Blomberg declares that he "honors" Bård G. Eithun (also known as Faust, drummer of the band Emperor, and many others) for killing a "fucking faggot," in reference to Eithun's brutal and homophobic stabbing of Magne Andreasson in Lillehammer in 1992.

Darkthrone's fourth album, 1994s *Transilvanian Hunger*, featured guest lyrics by Vikernes on four out of eight songs while also containing the phrase "Norsk Arisk Black Metal" ("Norwegian Aryan Black Metal") on the original back cover, with the press release penned by the band and issued by record label Peaceville (with accompanying criticism) stating that the band would "like to state that *Transilvanian Hunger* stands beyond any criticism. If any man should attempt to criticize this LP, he should be thoroughly patronized for his obviously Jewish behavior." While Gylve Nagel (also known as Fenriz, of Darkthrone) would later express regret about these statements and characterize them as "disgusting" (Patterson 2013, pp. 202–203), the statements themselves have become part of the common lore emphasizing the underlying fascist sympathies of black metal.

Much more could be written about the crimes and unsavory statements, viewpoints, and ties of the second-wave black metal community in Norway during the 1990s, but further focus on those topics here would prove to be gratuitous. The relevant point, I take it, has been made: it would be hard to deny that such extramusical components of the Norwegian scene have left a stain on the history—and arguably even the future development—of black metal as a whole.

Before moving on from the second wave, it would be prudent to extend our focus to outside of Norway in order to truly acknowledge and appreciate black metal's wider and continuing reach. Despite many of the characteristic second-wave bands—Arcturus, Burzum, Carpathian Forest, Darkthrone, Dimmu Borgir, Emperor, Enslaved, Immortal, Gorgoroth,

Mayhem, Mysticum, Satyricon, Thorns, Ulver, and others—all originating in Norway, clusters of second-wave bands can also be found in Finland (Archgoat, Barathrum, Beherit, Impaled Nazarene), France (Belkètre, Mutiilation, Vlad Tepes), Greece (Rotting Christ, Varathron), Sweden (Dissection, Marduk, Nifelheim), Switzerland (Samael), and the United States (Judas Iscariot, Profanatica). Some of these regional scenes developed their own analogues of Helvete's "Black Circle," such as France's Les Légiones Noires, while others—such as the particularly primitive and bestial bands of early Finnish black metal—developed regional "sounds."

Continuing Development

Black metal has continued to develop and expand even with the fading of the second wave during the late 1990s and early 2000s. What some characterize as a "third wave" is really more akin to multiple branches diverging from the more unified trunk of the second wave, itself a coalesced product of the comparatively variegated first wave. While it would be foolishly ambitious to even attempt to informatively circumscribe the continued—and continuing—growth of black metal as a whole, there are several developments and phenomena of particular note.

Growing out of the fascistic tendencies of some members of the Norwegian second wave is National Socialist Black Metal (NSBM), consisting of bands such as Absurd (Germany), Clandestine Blaze (Finland), Grand Belial's Key (United States), Graveland (Poland), Nokturnal Mortum (Ukraine), Peste Noire (France), and Temnozor (Ukraine), all of which are overtly or covertly connected with the "movement"—which itself has ties to other far-right, racist conduits such as Rock Against Communism (RAC). It is not uncommon for black metal musicians to be asked their stance on NSBM in interviews, with many bands rejecting such explicit far-right sympathies by (sometimes somewhat half-heartedly) declaring themselves to be "apolitical."

In reaction to the growth of NSBM, some bands—such as Ashenspire (Scotland), Bull of Apis Bull of Bronze (United States), Dawn Ray'd (England), Iskra (Canada), Feminazgûl (United States), and Panopticon (United States)—have become associated (by self-identification or by fans) as part of a left-wing Red and Anarchist Black Metal (RABM) movement. A few RABM bands even adopt a mocking anti-fascist tone that borders on trolling, as can be seen in song titles such as British band Gaylord's "Odin Doesn't Listen to NSBM You Inbred Alt-Right Shitheels" off of their 2018 debut LP, *The Black Metal Scene Needs to Be Destroyed*; or satirical US band Neckbeard Deathcamp's "Incel Warfare" from their respective debut LP from the same year, *White Nationalism is for Basement Dwelling Losers*.

Closely related to—and occasionally overlapping with—RABM is the so-called "Cascadian Black Metal" scene, named in reference to the association of such acts with the Pacific Northwest region of the United States. Bands such as Addaura, Alda, Ash Borer, Fall of Rauros, Fauna, Fell Voices, Skagos, Weakling, and Wolves in the Throne Room (all from the United States) draw heavy influence from the Norwegian second wave (particularly the raw and hypnotic atmospherics of Burzum) combined with various incorporations of crust punk, drone metal, post-rock, and regional folk music traditions alongside typically left-leaning and ecologically driven or sometimes anarchist ideology.

A more inwardly focused and overtly self-loathing approach can be found in so-called "Depressive Suicidal Black Metal" (DSBM), with acts such as Animus (Israel), Leviathan (United States), Lifelover (Sweden), Silencer (Sweden), Shining (Sweden), and Xasthur (United States) focusing on a raw, somber, and painful sound, paired with particularly depressive and despairing lyrics. Some acts, such as Brazil's Pessimista, have a foot in both DSBM and RABM.

We could continue in various directions, honing in on various other branches off of the black metal tree: the industrial black metal of Blut Aus Nord or the dissonant technical black metal of Deathspell Omega, both from France; the folk black metal approach of Agalloch (United States) or Drudkh (Ukraine); the so-called "avant-garde" black metal stylings of Norway's Solefald or Ven Buens Ende; the viking black metal of Falkenbach (Germany) or Windir (Norway); or the comparatively more accessible post-black style of Alcest (France) or Deafheaven (United States). What has been established by this point, though, is simply that there is a complex though tractable story to tell about the history and development of black metal—the establishment of which is sufficient for forward movement into the next phase of our discussion.

Toward a Unified Characterization

In his discussion of heavy metal, Gracyk (2016) argues that—rather than fruitlessly attempting to offer some sort of necessary and jointly sufficient set of conditions for status as *heavy metal*—it would be best to characterize the genre *historically*. Taking inspiration from, *inter alia*, Jerrold Levinson's (1979, 1989) discussion of a *historical theory* of art (cf. Stecker 2003, pp. 148–153), the idea is that something is appropriately categorized as "heavy metal" to the extent that it plays certain central roles in the history of heavy metal, is created with intentional connection or certain kinds of response to that history, etc. Insofar as this is a plausible method of characterizing heavy metal, it also seems a promising candidate in terms of characterizing black metal.

On a historical characterization, we can understand why acts as musically, lyrically, and ideologically different as Venom and Gaylord are both rightfully grouped together under the umbrella of black metal: though Venom is at the root and Gaylord is on the tip of one of the branches, both have substantial and sufficient connection to (and dialogue with) the history of the genre. Toby Keith and Taylor Swift, on the other hand, do not, leading to the obvious absurdity of even entertaining the thought that such artists could qualify as black metal. Some cases—such as the early work of thrash titans Slayer or death metal pioneers Possessed, both from the United States—are rightly affirmed as borderline cases through this historical approach by noting their relevance to, but comparative distance from, the center of the story of black metal. This distance becomes especially clear when such cases are contrasted with paradigm examples such as Venom and Mayhem, as well as more recent contributors such as Wolves in the Throne Room.

In short, then, we might conclude that a band is rightly classified as black metal to the degree that a plausible and compelling case can be made that they play some part—from the central to the peripheral (or perhaps near-peripheral)—in the ongoing *story* of black metal: a story that tells us of the roots, the trunk, and the branches.

Black Metal and Performance Personae

With an understanding of the framework of performance personae and a working characterization of black metal on the table, we can start to explore the intersection of both topics in a manner that will, I argue, further illuminate our aesthetic understanding of the music itself. To begin, we can excavate and extract certain consistent (and interrelated) themes throughout the history of black metal, as sketched in the previous section. These themes are: *an opposition to worldly modernity, a wedding to value systems, a comparative foregrounding of physical presentation, an affectation of sound sources to suggest a harsh inhumanity or otherworldliness,* and, finally, *a pretense of authenticity*. These are clearly not the only themes that could be said to emerge; that said, they are the ones we will focus on here.

Opposition to Worldly Modernity

To say that, historically, black metal has stood in opposition to worldly modernity is to say that it has either implicitly or explicitly resisted the mundane, material focus that permeates much of contemporary life. We see this in the escapist ("shocking") imagery of the first wave, as well as the anti-Christian ideology and juvenile fascism common to the second wave. Looking to more contemporary black metal, both NSBM and RABM reject this worldly modernity, the former in the direction of fascism and the latter in the direction of anarchy (or anarcho-communism). It could be argued, too, that even DSBM continues this theme by centering and arguably glorifying suicide as a legitimate means of "escape" or "release." A black metal musician cultivating a persona in contrast to this theme—that is, one that embraced worldly modernity—would certainly be received as an odd fit within the subgenre and subculture. Similarly, the revelation that a performer who, contrary to persona, is actually a life-affirming, fun-loving citizen of the world with a mundane job might, as it were, "break the spell."

Consider, for example, both the case of Tom Cato Visnes (also known as King, formerly King Ov Hell, of a range of acts including Gorgoroth, Sahg, I, Ov Hell, and others), who is a former primary school teacher, and that of Ted Skjellum (also known as Nocturno Culto, most famously the vocalist and guitarist of Darkthrone), who retains his school teacher position to this day. Looking also at Darkthrone, we see the case of Fenriz, who has famously worked for most of his musical career as a part-time employee of the postal service and has served a term as an elected political official in the form of substitute councilor for the Liberal Party in Oppengård. A foregrounding of these far-less-than-ominous, mundane facts of employment during performance (or in the context of absorbing a recording) would clash with a central theme of black metal and hence run the risk of pulling the audience "out of it," as it were, resulting in a detriment to aesthetic experience and evaluation. (Some later Darkthrone tracks, such as 2010s "I Am the Working Class," might prove to be somewhat novel exceptions to this claim.)

Wedding to Value Systems

Related to the theme of opposition to worldly modernity—and gestured at through the above contrast between NSBM and RABM bands—is the theme of being wedded to a particular value system, which seems to have taken hold more so around the onset of the second wave. Whereas other areas of metal typically focus on some combination of sound and mood (with death metal being abrasive and horrifying, doom metal being crushingly slow and drenched in despair, power metal being vibrant and triumphant, etc.), black metal is historically and perhaps uniquely ideological, with the ideology adopted by a particular band steering how that band will actualize their resistance to worldly modernity. Performers in NSBM bands are expected, insofar as they are NSBM bands, to embody fascist ideology. An "NSBM" band consisting solely of anti-fascist performers would perhaps be reduced to an aesthetically impotent artistic absurdity, with the same being said of an "RABM" band consisting entirely of fascists.

NSBM and RABM both resist worldly modernity by resisting the *modernity* component, in particular. Satanic bands—Deathspell Omega, Dissection, Gorgoroth, etc.—also reject the *worldly* component, with a focus more on the intellectual and spiritual. The supposed "core" members of Deathspell Omega (excluding purported vocalist, Mikko Aspa) cultivate mysterious, otherworldly personae by remaining in relative obscurity, foregoing live performances, social media presence, and promotional band photos. The few interviews they agree to give are consistently stuffed (one might say *bloated*) with attempts at demonstrating a sort of detached and elevated philosophical and intellectual vantage point. Together, these tendencies help to construct and maintain their "otherworldly" personae. In the case of Dissection, a few would argue that core member Jon Nödtveidt failed to live up to the Satanic persona he embodied on stage, having cofounded a Satanic cult (the Misanthropic Luciferian Order) and died by ritual suicide after having self-assessed as having achieved his spiritual and philosophical purpose in the mundane, material world.

The cases of Fenriz and Nocturno Culto of Darkthrone are again of interest here, as well, insofar as one might take it to be difficult to "lose yourself" in a song performed as if by agents of evil while simultaneously holding in mind the incongruent vision of those performers exemplifying the virtues associated with being public servants.

Foregrounding the Physical

Insofar as black metal performers are expected to embody the values they espouse through their music and the performance of such, black metal also has a consistent theme of foregrounding physical presentation—to a higher degree than perhaps most other musical traditions.

In a discussion of musical performance (which also extends quite naturally to that of recordings), Gracyk (2001, p. 181) argues that we tend to experience a song as if authored by the embodied being giving voice to it (see also Bicknell 2005, p. 264). Incongruence between the content or character of the song and the embodied performer, then, can lead to aesthetic detriment in the manner discussed previously in this chapter. It is a norm of black metal, then, for at least the singer (and ideally the other performers) to present physically in a way (whether during live performances or for promotional band photos, during interviews, etc.) that reinforces rather than strains the connection between ideology and embodiment. The typical black metal "uniform" of leather, spikes, and corpse paint—sometimes accompanied by various medieval weaponry or other such LARP-esque implements—serves, then, to distance the performer from worldly modernity, giving them the appearance instead as if some kind of confrontational *other*.

Of course, not all black metal bands adopt the aforementioned "uniform." Brothers Aaron and Nathan Weaver—the two consistent members of Wolves in the Throne Room—eschew corpse paint, as do most Cascadian and RABM bands that position themselves against the implicit or explicit fascism found in some other pockets of black metal. The fact that it is a noteworthy feature that a band foregoes corpsepaint (and, in Wolves in the Throne Room's case, esoteric or confrontational pseudonyms, as well), reinforces the claim that this supposed black metal "uniform" remains thematically centered.

The Weavers, still look like what the average person might call "metalheads," however, and like virtually all black metal bands, their black metal aesthetic extends to their album art, stage design, logo, etc. By contrast, we might contextualize and understand some of the claims that Deafheaven isn't "real" black metal by situating them within the norms under discussion so far: the band members present as "normal dudes" (rather than metalheads, and certainly not in any variation of black metal "uniform"), with their breakthrough album (2013s *Sunbather*) sporting a decidedly warm and sleekly designed, peach-pink cover. In this, their personae do not embody or exemplify a value system in opposition to worldly modernity, violating a key norm and hence leading to the resistance among many die-hard black metal fans to even categorize them as such in the first place.

Affectation of Sound Sources

The theme of embodiment continues in a fourth norm, this time centering the affectation of sound sources so as to suggest a harsh inhumanity or sense of otherworldliness. We see such affectation in the extreme distortion on typical black metal guitars, the often overwhelming force and speed of the drums, sometimes in the harsh or raw production quality of a recording, and perhaps most strikingly, in the vocal style emblematic of the style. Though the characteristic harsh black metal shriek was still taking shape during the first wave (employed not at all by some vocalists, such as Mercyful Fate's Kim Petersen, also known as King Diamond), it was omnipresent in the second wave and has remained a staple ingredient of black metal in all of its forms ever since.

This vocal style helps to construct and reinforce the inhuman or otherworldly personae of the vocalist, reinforcing their image as if in opposition to worldly modernity. Whether sounding like a demonic being or, perhaps in the case of Cascadian black metal bands, the raw voice of an angry nature itself, this vocal affectation—especially in conjunction with the aforementioned black metal "uniform"—serves to stifle reminders to audiences that they are listening, after all, to a human person born of this mundane, modern world. It's noteworthy, too, that even those that eschew conventional black metal shrieking—as in, perhaps most famously, the case of Attila Csihar's operatic and ghoulish session vocal performance during the recording of Mayhem's landmark 1994 album, *De Mysteriis Dom Sathanas*—still most often aim for an inhuman and otherworldly approach, even if through different means.

Pretense of Authenticity

It's sometimes said of Batman that his Dark Knight, Caped Crusader, etc., persona is actually not a persona at all, but his true self. The "Bruce Wayne" persona, according to this view, is the *real* mask. The same might be thought of typical black metal performers: Archgoat's Lord Angelslayer is the *real* person, with Rainer Puolakanaho being the mask worn in the world of the mundane. When Gorgoroth's Roger Tiegs removes his mask, he *is* Infernus. Approaching things this way leads us to a picture of black metal according to which the intuitive assignment of *persona* and *private individual* is reversed. To return to the earlier distinction drawn between *transparent* and *opaque* personae (cf. Cray 2019), Lord Angelslayer and Infernus are presented as the transparent personae, while Puolakanaho and Tiegs are the opaque.

Though it might strike some as a bit of a stretch, this thought could even be extended to black metal performers who seem to have consistent personae on and off stage, such as the Weavers of Wolves in the Throne Room, Nödtveidt of Dissection, or Mikko Aspa of Clandestine Blaze and Deathspell Omega. The reason for this has to do with the affected vocal style, through which these performers "unmask" and present their true inhuman or otherworldly selves as embodying opposition to worldly modernity. While an interesting consideration, this extension need not be accepted for what follows to still hold true.

When one attends a show by GWAR, Ghost, or Gorillaz, you know that you are engaging in something like a fiction. The band knows that you know that, too, and you know that the band knows that you know that. But the typical intended phenomenology of a black metal show—or the listening-to of a black metal recording—is aimed at getting at something *deeper*, something somehow *more real* than the mundane world. Of course, it's *not*—it's a stage show often involving fellow humans sporting grotesquely unsubtle makeup and pseudonyms while vocalizing demonic impressions into a microphone—but there does seem to be a norm of a sort of *pretense of authenticity*. In other words, there seems to be a sort of expectation to act as if you are *not* engaging in something like a fiction and to treat opaque personae as if they are transparent.

I have offered a contrasting, more general norm elsewhere:

> When adopting an opaque performance persona, it is a matter of custom for a singer to signal to audiences, in some explicit or implicit manner, that the persona is, in fact, opaque. Failure to do so runs the risk of undermining, perhaps categorically, the singer's convincingness and sincerity. Insofar as convincingness and sincerity are aesthetically relevant features of particular performances, a categorical undermining of such traits might lead to lingering aesthetic frustration of that singer's performances across the board.
>
> (Cray 2019, pp. 188–189)

To say that black metal musicians characteristically (or at least commonly) transgress and invert this more general norm is perhaps to—as they say—say the quiet part out loud.

Conclusions

Throughout this chapter, I've offered an overview of a framework for thinking about the aesthetic relevance of performance personae when it comes to engagement and evaluation alongside a historical characterization of black metal, converging into an exploration of the relation between various prominent themes in black metal and their connections to such personae. In doing so, I've undoubtedly omitted mention or consideration of some band, performer, album, scene, event, or case that die-hard fans would consider essential to any discussion of this sort. Given the breadth of this discussion and its associated subject matter, such omissions are a fact of life.

That said, from all of the above, I conclude that considerations of performance personae play not just a role in the aesthetic engagement with and evaluation of black metal, but also a role that is particularly central and important. Accepting this claim enriches our understanding and appreciation of black metal, and should inspire anyone who insists that black metal is "all about the music" to rethink their stance.

A key observation made late in the discussion was that one of the norms of black metal—the pretense of authenticity—can frequently come into conflict with the more general norm that opaque personae ought not be passed off to audiences as if transparent. From the perspective of this more general norm, doing so makes one—to speak with the vulgar—somewhat of a *poser.*

This all leaves us at a fork in the road. Black metal is no stranger to transgressive inversions, so is this "inversion" of the more general norm simply another transgressive mark in black metal's confrontational favor? Or should it perhaps lead us to conclude instead that black metal is, at least in part, somewhat of an inherently or characteristically *poser genre*—or, at least, a safe space for poserdom? For now, at least, I'll leave any robust attempt at solving this dilemma as an exercise for the reader.

References

Bicknell, J. (2005). Just a song? Exploring the aesthetics of popular song performance. *The Journal of Aesthetics and Art Criticism* 63 (3): 261–270.

Bicknell, J. (2015). *Philosophy of Song and Singing: An Introduction.* Routledge.

Cray, W. (2019). Transparent and opaque performance personas. *Journal of Aesthetics and Art Criticism* 77 (2): 181–191.

Cray, L.D.E. (2024). Bands, personas, and the evaluative import of (some) social ontology. In: *The Ontology of Musical Groups: Identity, Agency, and Persistence of Creative Groups* (ed. T. Peterson and L. Janson), 61–73. Routledge.

Cray, L.D.E. (2025). Taylor's versions and versions of taylor. In: *Taylor Swift and the Philosophy of Re-Recording: The Art of Taylor's Versions* (ed. Polite), 153–167. Bloomsbury Publishing Plc.

Godlovitch, S. (1998). *Musical Performance: A Philosophical Study.* Routledge.

Gracyk, T. (2001). *I Wanna Be Me: Rock Music and the Politics of Identity.* Temple University Press.

Gracyk, T. (2016). Heavy metal: genre? Style? Subculture? *Philosophy Compass* 11 (12): 775–785.

Gracyk, T. (2017). Performer, persona, and the evaluation of musical performance. *Contemporary Aesthetics* 15.

Levinson, J. (1979). Defining art historically. *British Journal of Aesthetics* 19 (3): 232–250.

Levinson, J. (1989). Refining art historically. *The Journal of Aesthetics and Art Criticism* 47 (1): 21–33.

Moynihan, M. and Søderlind, D. (2003). *Lords of Chaos: The Bloody Rise of the Satanic Metal Underground*, revised edition. Feral House.

Patterson, D. (2013). *Black Metal: Evolution of the Cult.* Cult Never Dies.

Stecker, R. (2003). Definition of art. In: *The Oxford Handbook of Aesthetics* (ed. Levinson), 136–154. Oxford University Press.

Chapter 9
Freedom—Nature—Satan: On the Beauty of Black Metal

Daisy Dixon and Panos Paris
School of English, Communication and Philosophy, Cardiff University, Cardiff, UK

Content warning: expletives, and descriptions of sexual violence

Introduction

Black metal is an extreme subgenre of heavy metal which originated in the 1980s. Its first wave emerged with the English band Venom's album *Black Metal* (Neat Records, 1982). This album's raw and heavy sound, characterized by "a rough low-budget production like a gig in the cellar" (Dimery 2005, p. 498), was hugely influential and paved the way for the Swedish band Bathory, who spearheaded a second wave which largely developed in Norway. There, in the early 1990s, black metal developed its signature sound, led by bands such as Mayhem, Burzum, Gorgoroth, and Darkthrone. This "early Norwegian black metal" scene was characterized by low-fi, raw, "necro" soundscapes, composed of trebly buzz and tremolo-picking guitar techniques, screeching obscure vocals, blast-beat percussion, and a thematic concern with pagan religion, Nordic folklore, the occult, Satanism, and the natural world (Coggins 2021).

Since the early 1990s, black metal has spread across the world and has come to vary widely in its thematic content and style, ranging from the orthodox (or "kvlt") style, to heavily atmospheric "post"-black metal subgenres, which blend black metal offshoots such as "dungeon-synth," and other rock genres such as "shoegaze" (forming "blackgaze"), which have more complex sonic layering.

Despite its evolution and branching, black metal today is still considered as a more or less unified genre or style; one which is preoccupied with humans' relationship to the natural world and the self, and which expresses this broad theme via stark Satanic aesthetics and chaotic walls of sound. One thing to notice about good black metal is its powerfully immersive atmosphere. According to Ihsahn (previously of the band Emperor), for instance, "black metal is an abstract feeling, an atmosphere . . . It doesn't rely on any specific sound. Jerry Goldsmith's score for *The Omen* can sound as black metal as *Bathory*."[1]

Black metal shares some of its aesthetic features with other extreme subgenres of metal, like thrash and death; most notably, its heaviness and guttural vocals. Unlike these other subgenres, however, black metal is distinctive in that—with only a few exceptions—much of it is characterized by a kind of *beauty*. Some beauty in black metal is obvious. Black metal works often contain mellifluous and melancholic interludes, even whole musical voices. Sometimes this is captured with classical symphonic orchestration, like in the music of bands like Cradle of Filth or Dimmu Borgir, and other times captured by ethereal folk tunes like in Amalie Bruun's Myrkur. But this is only the tip of the iceberg, for there is a kind of beauty, too, in the less melodic, often chaotic, haunting, obscure, and discordant soundscapes of bands like Darkthrone, Burzum, Satyricon, Emperor, Wolves in the Throne Room, or Panopticon. Such beauty is not immediately obvious, and yet it does seem to characterize black metal, and to set it apart from, say, death metal, which is, at least in most cases, characteristically *un*beautiful if not outright, and purposely, ugly (cf. Gracyk 2016, p. 776)—the music of

[1] Quoted on Apple Music album notes for *IHSAHN* (Candlelight Records, 2024).

Obituary, Morbid Angel, and Cannibal Corpse may be aesthetically valuable in many ways; but *beautiful*, it is not.

The aim of this chapter is to trace the beauty of black metal to a surprising source: its ethical dimension. We argue that the less "conventionally" beautiful black metal music, in fact, embodies an ethically laden kind of beauty; specifically, what we call a "Miltonian-Satanic ecological sensibility." This core ethic comprises a rejection of societal mores such as monotheistic religion, patriarchy, and capitalism, and a preoccupation with freedom and nature. As we'll show, this core ethic and its accompanying themes are expressed in black metal in various ways, from its lyricism and sonic properties to the motivations of the artists themselves. We reveal that much black metal, which prima facie *appears* unethical because of its subversive "Satanist" aesthetics and obscure sonic character, is in fact a seductive conduit to resist authoritarian worldviews and embrace a love and respect of nature in its raw, wild form.

The chapter is structured as follows. First, we will do ground-clearing and clarify the notions of beauty we're concerned with. Then, we will explore the immorality of black metal and consider this in light of the moralism debate in aesthetics. Finally, we will outline black metal's surprisingly ethical outlook, which affords it a distinctive kind of beauty.

What Kind of Beauty?

When we say that the music of, say, Wolves in the Throne Room is beautiful and that that of, say, Dead Congregation is not, we are not saying that Wolves in the Throne Room are *better* than Dead Congregation, or that they are more aesthetically valuable. This clarification is important because "beauty" in regard to art is often used in different senses. One is a broad sense, in which "beauty" means something like aesthetic success or artistic value in general. For instance, critics might describe Damien Hirst's formaldehyde animal artworks as "beautiful" because of their arresting effects on audiences, as well as their progressive takes on the artworld itself by calling into question what art even is. They are beautiful in the sense that they (arguably) have positive artistic value. Call this broad sense $\textit{Beauty}_B$.

In a narrower sense, "beauty" refers to a specific kind of aesthetic value or property, and a certain form of aesthetic success only, which may or may not be present alongside other aesthetic qualities (Paris 2025b).

One narrow sense of beauty—the traditional sense, if you will—involves the aesthetic quality *par excellence* that is associated with form: order, harmony, balance, and clarity (Paris 2025a; Tatarkiewicz 1972). This ancient view of beauty found expression in the works of the Pythagoreans (6th C. BCE), who saw beauty as a matter of mathematical proportion, such as harmony and symmetry, and it persisted throughout most of pre-Modern thinking, both in philosophy and art theory. Call this narrow sense $Beauty_F$.

A work that is beautiful in this sense will, of course, be aesthetically valuable to that extent. But there are other ways of being aesthetically valuable other than by being formally beautiful, and it's certainly possible for an artwork that is not formally beautiful (or $beautiful_F$) to be more aesthetically valuable than one that is $beautiful_F$. For instance, Picasso's *Guernica* (1937), hardly a $beautiful_F$ work of art, is arguably artistically greater than his more $beautiful_F$, but somewhat sentimental and boring, *The Old Guitarist* (1903–1904).

Even with this clarification in place, however, one may wonder why or how black metal can be beautiful, given how chaotic-sounding, or even dissonant, it can sometimes be, and given the darkness and sometimes blatant vulgarity of its lyrical and thematic content. After all, though there are now more inclusive and flexible accounts of beauty available, isn't the narrow and traditional sense of beauty the aesthetic quality *par excellence*? And aren't these formal qualities the near-opposites of the ones one might use to describe, say, Darkthrone's *Transylvanian Hunger* (Modern Invasion Music, 1994), with its simple and raw minimalist sound and its use of unresolved dissonances and disharmonies?

Even if there's a way out of this conundrum, the respite seems only momentary. For another quality traditionally associated with beauty, and one whose association is well-demonstrated as a staple of human psychology, is its link to other values, notably moral goodness. On this other narrow view of beauty, beauty is a property intimately connected with the ethical. Also an ancient view, it can be found in the ideas that Plato's Socrates attributes to Diotima: "the beauty of people's souls is more valuable than the beauty of their bodies" (1989, 210b), and Plotinus, following Plato: "all virtues are a beauty of the Soul, a beauty authentic beyond any of these others. . .Beauty, this Beauty which is also The Good" (2020, I, 6.1 and 6.6; V, 8.1). This identification of beauty with the good continues into Early Modern thought, and is to be found in David Hume's writings, among the writings of others during that period. A person's virtue, thinks Hume, is defined as "whatever mental action or quality gives to a spectator the pleasing sentiment of approbation; and vice the contrary" (1777, p. 289). Hence, Hume frequently refers to "moral beauty," noting both that it "bears so near a resemblance" to natural beauty (p. 291), but also that, like "many orders of beauty, particularly those of the finer arts, it is requisite to employ much reasoning, in order to feel the proper Sentiment," "moral beauty . . . demands the assistance of our intellectual faculties, in order to give it a suitable influence on the human mind" (p. 173).

The central idea here is that moral virtues or other ethically meritorious traits, when expressed or otherwise manifested, are beautiful or, put somewhat differently, their expression or manifestation is a kind of beauty. And it does seem correct that nonsensorial things can be beautiful, such as mathematical proofs and theories (Paris 2024). So the idea that a virtue or morally good action can be beautiful is not immediately incoherent. Indeed, it has recently received considerable attention and support (see Scarry 1999; Gaut 2007, ch. 6; Paris 2018a,b, 2019a; Doran 2021, 2022, 2024). Call this other narrow sense of beauty $Beauty_E$.

Returning to Picasso's *Guernica*, we may judge that it has broad aesthetic value that goes beyond beauty, but it may also have some beauty in the ethical sense just outlined. Its moral perspective on the nature of war and suffering is a laudable one, and its success as an anti-war protest artwork may be in part due to its $Beauty_E$.

What does all this mean for black metal? Alas, as a genre, its morals are notorious—Satanism is its official religion, and the moral record of some of its artists is grim, ranging from assault, arson, and murder, to racism, nationalism, and neo-Nazi ideologies. That is, black metal seems to be intimately connected with vice, not virtue. So, most black metal appears not to be beautiful in either sense: it is not $beautiful_F$ or $beautiful_E$. To consider the tenability of this grim view, we must consider what (im) morality in art, including black metal, can even look like.

The Immorality of Black Metal

Morality and Art

There is an ambiguity in the above discussion. Some of the charges of immorality in black metal above are not to be directed to the overall musical content of black metal, but only to either its lyrical content, its artists' actual lives, or unfortunate consequences that seem to flow from listening to it. It is worth making some important distinctions so that we can clarify the kind of moral features we're concerned with when it comes to black metal.

Art—including black metal—can relate to morality in at least five ways. The first is where the artwork simply represents some moral state of affairs, such as murder. This can be done either neutrally or in a substantive way: the artwork might be a straightforward portrayal of an event, or it might also express a *perspective* about that event or object. This pertains to the second relation, where an artwork implicitly or explicitly invites the viewer or listener to engage with the representation in a morally significant way—for instance, to find glory (or baseness) in depicted fascism, or erotic arousal (or disgust) in depicted sexual violence. The third relation is where the artwork is created by an artist with a certain moral character—the extent to which this character affects the artwork itself will be addressed momentarily. The fourth relation is where the artwork's creation involved ethically significant means of production—perhaps it was created by abusing (or caring for) a real model, or its creation incurred a large (or zero) carbon footprint. The last is a consequentialist relation: engaging with the artwork might cause or trigger the consumer to go out into the world and commit a heinous offense (or good acts of charity).

These various relations can come apart, and be aesthetically significant in different ways, or, in some cases, not at all. That is, a moral property that a work of art might happen to have may or may not form part of that artwork's content and artistic properties.

For instance, an artwork might be created by a terrible person, but it's a further question as to whether or how the artist's immoral character bleeds into or affects the content of their art (Matthes 2021; Dixon 2023, forthcoming). Consider two pedophilic artists. Eric Gill sexually abused his own daughters, who are also the subject of many of his famous sculptures. Here, there is a direct link between the artist's immorality and his art—for his art literally portrays the subject of his misdeeds; his works' perspectives are inflected by his immoral character. But consider Rolf Harris, a convicted child sex offender. His famous paintings mainly consist of innocuous landscapes and a portrait of Queen Elizabeth II. In these cases, at least, there is no clear link between his pedophilic proclivities and the content of these artworks, so it is far less clear how the perspective of these works is inflected by Harris's life. As Berys Gaut notes, "it is the *way* that a work conveys its ethical or other insights that makes them of aesthetic relevance" (2007, p. 84). An artist's moral character won't always be aesthetically relevant to the artworks they create.

Moreover, an artwork might be part of the causal explanation of its consumer's terrible acts, but without inciting that consumer to do so. There is a difference between an artwork that happens to trigger a bad reaction in someone and an artwork which explicitly urges its viewers to commit a hate crime. The antisemitic films produced under Joseph Goebbels' Ministry of Propaganda, for instance, actively and intentionally encouraged antisemitic violence in its wider bid to justify the Holocaust. This incitement was part of the very nature and intended function of these films. A documentary about a serial killer, however, is unlikely to be intended to inspire future serial killers, even if it happens to do so.

These five relations are distinct, then, but often blend into one another. A work of art might be immoral because its artist expresses their immoral character through their art, which in turn expresses an immoral perspective via its unethical production, and which in turn has negative consequences in the wider world. Importantly, though, this needn't be the case.

"Total Fucking Darkness"[2]

Black metal as a whole genre notoriously exhibits all five of these relations between art and morality, and in a way that compounds its seeming barbarity. First, lyrics in black metal songs often portray immoral states of affairs, to put it mildly. For instance, Mayhem's "Chainsaw Gutsfuck" (Deathcrush. Posercorpse Music, 1993) describes necrophilia and sexual violence: "Chainsaw in my bleeding hands/As I start to cut you in two/Your guts are steaming out/And I just love the sight/Maggots crawling in her cunt/I just love to lick that shit/Bury you in a slimy grave/You will rot forever there."

Second and relatedly, much black metal music expresses immoral perspectives about the world, which can easily be found in its lyrics, the band's overall image, and their overt influences and artistic motivations. Some openly National Socialist black metal (NSBM) bands such as Asenheim feature anti-Muslim lyrics, and some explicit album names,

[2] The title of a self-released Cradle of Filth demo from 1992.

manifestos, and cover art leave little to the imagination: *Fuck You All, We Are NSBM!!!* (Self- or Unofficial Release, 2012) by 1389 and Tank Genocide, and Hate Forest's album dedications to white supremacists, being just a few unambiguous examples.

Third, as is obvious in the above examples, several black metal works are created by immoral artists. Sometimes this moral property is clearly aesthetically relevant because it is wholeheartedly and literally expressed in the songs—consider the lyrics in 1389s song "Hail Fuhrer" (Windhorst, Winterkalt Records, 2012): "Hail Fuhrer/True Leader!/Hail Fuhrer/True Imperator/Protector of White Men & Women/Proud to be/White People!" But sometimes it is not so obviously aesthetically relevant. Burzum, for instance, is the product of the openly neo-Nazi Kristian "Varg" Vikernes, who is also the convicted murderer of Mayhem's original lead vocalist Øystein "Euronymous" Aarseth. And yet, Burzum's lyricism and thematic imagery are not explicitly political (Lukes and Panayotov 2023). Some Burzum fans, therefore, have an easier time separating the art from the artist, for Burzum as a musical project might arguably be untainted by its homophobic, white supremacist creator.

However, it is worth noting that even in cases where the artist's moral character is not detectable in the lyrics or depiction in their works, their artistic motivations in making the work, and their overall musical style and practice, may suggest a significant albeit subtler link between their moral character and their art. For instance, as Ted Nannicelli (2020) suggests, the evidence required to establish a conceptual link between the artist's moral character and their art needn't be so explicit and literal as in the case of lyrics or depiction. Rather, if we know that an artist had an immoral motivation in *making* a work, this can plausibly shape that work's artistic properties. Consider, for instance, a portrait of a girl that is not visually sexualized. But suppose the painting was made by the pedophilic artist Graham Ovenden, and that he had the aim of attaining sexual arousal in making the painting. This fact would bear on the properties of his painting—it would be a piece of child pornography, rather than an innocent picture of a girl (2020, p. 231).

Similarly, even if Burzum's lyrics and themes are not *explicitly* white supremacist, Varg Vikernes may well have had immoral motivations surrounding the creation of his musical works. More specifically, he may have been harnessing a familiar artistic-intellectual theme co-opted (or hijacked) by the Nazis as part of their myth-making in the 19th and 20th centuries, namely, a romantic nostalgia for the pastoral

(Dixon 2023, forthcoming). Embracing the sublime power of nature was central to the romantic movement in the 19th century, and the Nazis later used romantic ecological aesthetics—specifically the German forest—to distill their national identity and promote their ideology of "blood and soil": a call for "racially pure" citizens to embrace and settle in their homeland.[3] As Johannes Zechner writes: "Inherent in this forest ideology [. . .] was a strong racist component: the capability to care for nature was exclusively attributed to Aryan racial ancestry" (2011, pp. 22–23).

Now, Vikernes—a neo-Nazi—screeches a lot about forests. Burzum's lyrical and sonic themes therefore do evoke the general power of nature, and so express at least some morally wholesome romantic ideals. But perhaps it's not a huge leap, then, to judge that his musical works also have an implicit neo-Nazi style or content, in part because of his fascist-romantic creative motivations as an artist.[4] Burzum may well be a case where its creator's moral character manifests as an aesthetic (dis)value of his musical works in their passion for nature because "artistic means . . . are employed to convey these ethical qualities" (Gaut 2007, p. 88).

Fourth and fifth (and finally), the black metal scene has gathered its notoriety in part because of its violent methods of production and its supposed consequences on people's actions and mindsets. Regarding the first, the shocking performances in black metal music have frequently featured displays of dead animal parts and consumption of pigs' blood (as, for instance, practiced by Watain), as well as self-harm on stage (Per "Dead" Ohlin being a classic example).[5] Much of the genre's aesthetic characteristics are galvanized by the historic bloodshed and violence that has surrounded it since its inception (Dixon forthcoming). Regarding the second, there were at least thirty church burnings across Norway responding to the emerging scene in the early 1990s. Generally, the genre's core artists and fans—sometimes referred to as the "Black Metal Inner Circle"—have committed assault, murder, and arson (this may arguably be an example of the fourth relation too).

---

[3] For more on the German forest metaphor in the Third Reich, see Wilson (2012). For more on the general ecological element of the Nazis, see Bramwell (1989).

[4] If true, then this may affect our listening practices. For instance, it might be argued that we can still appreciate a piece of music without bothering too much about its lyrics, and that we can psychologically separate the morality of artists from our valuing of their art. Whether we *ought* to do so, though, is a further question that we won't address here.

[5] https://rateyourmusic.com/list/HelloInquisitor/black-metal-bands-and-their-politics/. For more on Dead's performances, see Carey (2023).

The above suggests that black metal has earned its place at Satan's table. It often portrays barbaric actions, expresses despicable worldviews, is created by outright neo-Nazis and homophobes, and has been physically created in troubling circumstances. It therefore looks like a very poor contender for the ethical sense of beauty we've outlined.

"Bloodlust and Perversion"[6]

The prospects for developing an account of the beauty of black metal, then, are looking dim. If anything, black metal seems much better suited to lend plausibility to views such as aesthetic immoralism. Immoralism is one of two central theories in the so-called moralism debate in aesthetics, concerning how the broad aesthetic value of a work of art can be influenced by its ethical value.[7] As the name suggests, immoralism holds that a work's aesthetic value can be improved by, and *in virtue* of, that work's immorality. The other major theory—ethicism—denies immoralism's central claim, holding instead that a work's moral defects always detract from its aesthetic value, while its moral merits always contribute to its aesthetic value (Gaut 2007).

So, black metal seems like grist to the immoralist's mill. If black metal is beautiful or otherwise aesthetically valuable, and given how immoral it is, it seems plausible that its immorality forms part of the explanation of its aesthetic appeal: its immorality is a source of its overall aesthetic value. And it does seem right that many people are drawn to the morbid and obscene; phenomena that can be cognitively valuable or afford intense aesthetic experiences of disgust. Obscene and morally repugnant artworks can indulge desires that may be considered morally deviant, or at least fulfill a "meta-desire" to be morally transgressive—the desire to desire the repulsive (Kieran 2003). As Gaut notes of the immoralist position, "beauty can subsist in cruelty and violence" (2007, p. 129).

While perhaps there is something to this claim, the truth, we think, is more complicated. In the first place, there are some serious objections to immoralism, which stem from the fact that it's difficult to imagine

---

[6] A Carpathian Forest album from 1992 (No Label).

[7] We take the moralism debate to be the debate described above. Another related debate concerns whether aesthetic and ethical value ever interact at all. On this broader debate, the above views count as "interactionist," whereas other views, such as "moderate autonomism," which holds that the ethical value of a work never affects its aesthetic value, count as "separatist" (cf. Harold 2011).

how immorality *in itself and for its own sake* can really make any artwork better (Paris 2019b). Just because there might be beauty found in immoral works of art, it does not follow that the work is beautiful *insofar* as it expresses a morally repugnant attitude. All it shows is that we can have beautiful *presentations* of immorality, not that immorality itself can be beautiful (Gaut 2007, p. 130). That is, the visual or sonic features of a work might compose a formal beauty, but these are distinct from the debased perspective being expressed via those features. The image or sound of death and blood spatters might be "beautiful" in a formal sense (and there is nothing *inherently* wrong with death or blood), but the musical or cinematic scene would not be beautiful because of its manifested *immoral* perspective (for instance, if the death being described is one of glorified gender-based violence and femicide).[8] Moreover, immoralists in general tend to appeal to artworks that in fact turn out to not be immoral in the relevant sense anyway, because they do not actually adopt an immoral perspective but merely present us with one which is critiqued on a deeper level (Gaut 2007, pp. 192–201; Paris 2019b).

Regardless of these difficulties, it's nonetheless far from clear—indeed, we think it is highly implausible—that even a sensible immoralist would think that immorality in the form of full-blown fascist ideology, for instance, can ever *improve* a work of art, let alone make it more beautiful. It is of course true that NSBM will offer an important source of appeal to neo-Nazis and others who espouse the ideology of the extreme right. But, if we assume that such an ideology is flawed, there is little reason, it seems, to take their appreciation as somehow instructive on the question we are addressing. Because it's likely that, far from comprising black metal's core audience, the share of genuine neo-Nazis and national socialists who are serious appreciators of black metal (including NSBM) is probably a small minority (cf. Shadrack 2020), and *we* are most certainly *not* part of that minority.

So, immoralism doesn't look like a plausible avenue to take here. And yet, we want to argue that black metal is beautiful and infectious in its appeal, and we suspect that others who are interested in this and related subgenres share our experience of it. Moreover, reflecting on our own experience, we feel that the beauty_F of some black metal is something we

[8] This of course relies on accepting a broadly objectivist stance about morality. For the purposes of this paper, we remain neutral on the nature of moral facts per se, but we do assume (and endorse) the claim that there are such things as moral facts: something can objectively be right or wrong.

appreciate *in spite of*, rather than in virtue of, any fascist or other abhorrent ideologies that may be involved in it. Indeed, we find the beauty$_F$ in question less often in works that seem seriously to entertain such ideologies (such as Ildjarn and Hate Forest), though we grant that in some cases beauty$_F$ can be found there too (Marduk). So, when listening to immoral black metal, we can appeal to the ethicist's "pro tanto" principles (Gaut 2007, p. 128): while there might be beauty$_F$ in a work, its immorality composes a deep aesthetic flaw which might make the work *overall* an aesthetic failure. Or, the beauty$_F$ might outweigh these flaws such that the work is overall an aesthetic success.

However, as we outline above, beauty$_F$ is only a small subset of beauty in general, and not the distinctive kind of beauty we find in black metal. So where does black metal's beauty lie?

Of the Devil's Party: The Ethically Sound Core of Black Metal

Let us summarize the problem. On the one hand, much of the formal aesthetic in black metal resists being characterized, on the whole, in terms of the beautiful$_F$, embracing as it does the chaotic and the haunting through its extremely distorted and blurred sound. While, on the other hand, its notorious immoral content is not one to be associated with beauty either.

But this is too quick. Besides its most controversial brushes with fascistic, homophobic, and racist ideologies, a closer look reveals that black metal is, even more characteristically, focused on concerns and themes that are best described as *ethical*.

Black metal's most notorious themes are a preoccupation with anti-Christian sentiments, Satan and Satanism, and misanthropic attitudes. Band names like Rotting Christ, Impaled Nazarene, and Blasphemy, and album titles like *Puritanical Euphoric Misanthropia* (Dimmu Borgir, Nuclear Blast, 2001) and *Fuck Me Jesus* (Marduk, Osmose Productions, 1991) seem to the point. While these features may seem to make the gap between black metal and beauty even wider, we want to suggest that black metal's musical expression and development of such preoccupations may be more than they appear at a superficial glance. Indeed, Satanism, anti-Christianity, and even misanthropy form the core of an ethic that is a staple of black metal. Central to this ethic is, in fact, a concern for humankind and its lost potential, expressed as a profound disappointment with its development (misanthropy) and a preoccupation with freedom and autonomy in the form of self-legislation (Satanism)—all interwoven with an ecological sensibility—which can be seen as encompassing an over-arching philosophical outlook.

Perhaps quelling the moral panic that has surrounded the black metal genre for decades, we will now highlight its surprisingly ethical content and wholesome relationship to the world. First, we will outline the ethical core of black metal, which we describe as a *Miltonian-Satanic ecological sensibility*. Second, we will identify concrete and substantive expressions of that ethical core, namely, a concern for ecological and social justice. Throughout, we show how black metal's artistic and aesthetic character is particularly adept at evoking these ethical themes.

*

More than any nationalistic or fascistic ideologies—which, as explained above, remain on the fringe of black metal—perhaps the most widespread and distinctive ethical trait to characterize black metal is its preoccupation with "evil." This often takes the form of Satan and their worship, viz., Satanism, and related attitudes, particularly misanthropy. Now, it is easy to see this aspect of black metal as just another source of evidence for its immorality. And yet, here too, things are not what they seem. For while there are some instances where black metal's devotion to evil and Satan take what can only be described as a crude form—including genuine devotees reading Satanic Bibles and performing rituals, or committing genuinely bad deeds, like murder, arson, and the like—much of black metal is also characterized by what may be described as a *Miltonian* form of Satanism and a humanitarian misanthropy. Allow us to explain.

First, consider Satan. For most people, Satan simply epitomizes evil as the enemy of the Abrahamic God, the trickster who seeks to perpetuate the fall from Eden, and who tempts Christ and tries to turn him against his Father. Even on this received narrative, however, it's easy to see that Satan stands in for a lot more than just evil, since part of his role is to awaken the temptation to know and understand, to embrace embodied desires, etc. Indeed, there is a reading of Satan's role in the Fall narrative that is difficult to resist from a contemporary perspective, and which might present Satan as the liberator of the oppressed (Eve), through the acquisition of knowledge and understanding (the apple), and thereby the freedom and autonomy to live out her life, even if the cost of this would be a mortal life in an imperfect world (the Fall).

Simplistic as this is, it also captures something in the character of Satan that has not escaped some of the greats. Although this reading is mostly resisted today, it was none other than William Blake who noted that, in *Paradise Lost* (1667), "Milton wrote in fetters when he wrote of Angels and God, and at liberty when of Devils and Hell, . . . because he was a true poet, and of the Devil's party without knowing it" (1906, p. 11). Whether or not this is an accurate reading, there is no question that when reading *Paradise Lost*, it's hard not to think that God is often all too authoritarian and arrogant, and that Satan increasingly adopts attitudes that are to be expected from those whose oppression leaves them with little else with which to retaliate other than their wit and cunning.

Thus, Satan chooses the path of autonomy and power, albeit limited, in place of servitude to a God that seems to care more than he should about the subjection of his subjects. And, in doing so, Satan gets some of the best lines in the poem (hence, no doubt, Blake's witticism), not least:

> The mind is its own place, and in itself Can make a heav'n of hell, a hell of heav'n. What matter where, if I be still the same, And what I should be, all but less than he Whom thunder hath made greater? Here at least We shall be free: th'Almighty hath not built Here for his envy, will not drive us hence: Here we may reign secure, and in my choice To reign is worth ambition, though in hell; Better to reign in hell than serve in heav'n.
>
> (Milton 1877, pp. 9–10)

All the relevant notions that Satan embraces here—including self-creation, freedom, and ambition—are part and parcel of a post-Enlightenment virtuous individual. Of course, part of Satan's allure in *Paradise Lost* stems from his great rhetorical power—it is not clear what lies underneath, and whether or not it is of genuine value.

Satan's rhetoric itself provides us with the tools of self-creation and self-examination that will allow us to unearth the truth if only we set our minds to it. But this, of course, often involves going against the norm. It is thus unsurprising that Behemoth, in their *The Satanist's* (Nuclear Blast, 2014) eponymous track, proclaim: "I am the Great Rebellion/ 'Neath Milton's tomb I dwell," after having expressed that: "This universe has never been enough/Compelled to liberate the spring of life." For it turns out that Satan, no less in black metal than in Milton's epic, is Lucifer—bringer of light—and stands for a kind of freedom. Indeed, when Gorgoroth's Gaahl was asked in a 2005 interview what the main ideology of Gorgoroth is, his answer was simply "Satan." Upon being asked to elaborate on what Satan embodies or represents, he simply said, following a leisurely sip of red wine: "Freedom."[9]

This, then, brings us to the second point, which is that black metal's Satanism, *qua* Miltonian (or at least the one Blake reads in Milton), consists in going against authority and fighting against oppression,[10] but goes beyond this to highlight the importance of the courage and freedom to know, question, understand, explore, and self-legislate.[11] In fact, it may even go beyond that toward a quest for self-improvement and self-perfection, as Thorgersen and Von Wachenfeldt (2022) argue on the basis of qualitative interviews with black metal artists. According to Thorgersen and Von Wachenfeldt, black metal adopts what they call a *Luciferian Principle*, which is a "role model for idealism, personal development, and individual freedom" (190), consisting in "the search for knowledge and enlightenment" (184).

Thorgersen and Von Wachenfeldt go so far as to argue that black metal offers a contemporary culture that closely resembles the Enlightenment-fueled romantic ideal of *Bildung*, which consists in, *inter alia*, developing "individuality in completeness, as a whole or holistic human being. The development should not only be of private interest, but have universal value, and thereby attain a status and sense of trustworthiness, authority, and security, or Mündigkeit" (186).

Admirable as this may seem, Thorgersen and Von Wachenfeldt caution that this preoccupation with self-development in black-metal-*Bildung* also has a controversial underside, for it often comes with an elitist side. This, as they point out, "creates competition and thereby strengthens the incentives for personal growth and cultivation" (192). It can also be the basis of a "somewhat arrogant attitude towards simplistic and superficial music and art and therefore go to the canonized, pre-modernist classics, and also beyond the classics to be inspired to develop as human beings

[9] Available at: https://www.youtube.com/watch?v=ROmkJAl96BU (accessed 4 March 2025).

[10] It may be worth pointing out here that, although on certain literary and popular conceptions Satan is the *ruler* of Hell, in the Book of Revelation, he is placed in Hell to suffer eternally. We'd like to thank Jonathan Mitchell for this point.

[11] Philosophers often distinguish between negative and positive freedom (Berlin 1969), where the former refers to freedom from external constraints and the latter to a kind of freedom to live according to self-imposed principles even if these appear to be constraining. Though these are not mutually exclusive, it seems that it's mostly positive freedom that the place of Lucifer in black metal is intended to hold.

and artists" (193). And this is not all, for it can also arguably further develop into either a form of disillusion or even contempt for others, especially those who sheepishly follow trends and do not (or appear to the black metal crowd not to) live up to the ideals of *Bildung*, or live up to their potential.

Such disillusion or contempt can, in turn, lead to the third feature of black metal ethics mentioned above, viz., the theme of *misanthropy*. This is perhaps a less palatable feature, which, however, undeniably characterizes a considerable share of the black metal works we're interested in. Again, it's a feature of black metal that can easily be illustrated explicitly through lyrics, as witness Satyricon's line from their "Immortality Passion": "Where the howling winds rage/And the mountains are majestic/I can breathe and where there is/Human flesh I feel strangled" (*Nemesis Divina*, Moonfog Productions, 1996).[12]

Fortunately for the argument we're advancing, it seems that this too, at least in its nonviolent and nonmalicious guises,[13] can be traced to ethically salubrious sources, as we've already hinted. For the kind of misanthropy at stake appears to often find expression in one of the following ways: either as a retreat from the human to the natural world; or as a reaction to populist authority, human greed, or weakness; or again from aspects of humanity that are in violation of the Luciferian Principle: blind submission, complacency, shirking from the painful or difficult,

[12] Our argument here is complicated by, and may be resisted on the grounds that, first of all, black metal is explicitly aggressive and often expresses emotions like anger, disgust, etc., toward humanity. This may suggest that its misanthropy is an objectionable kind, namely affective (expressed through emotions, etc.) as opposed to cognitive (expressed in thoughts or beliefs about the regretability or sorry state of the human condition). This is not the place to explore this issue, but it may be worth noting that, on the one hand, it is not clear whether affective misanthropy is, in fact, to be avoided, especially when it is channeled through ethically appropriate modes (of which music is an excellent example). On the other hand, misanthropy probably has little value if it is not associated with motivations to improve, help, etc., and it's unlikely that such motivations can be sustained through purely cognitive misanthropy. If this is right, it may seem that an appropriately channeled affective-cognitive misanthropy may be the more valuable option. A second objection may target precisely this latter point by pointing out that channeling the relevant emotions and encouraging a pessimistic outlook may, in fact, end up promoting quietism. Indeed, it is true that many black metal artists and audience members are explicitly *a*political. Be that as it may, as will be seen in this section, this is neither true of all black metal artists and audience members, and, for those of whom it is true, it can be accounted for by the other dimension of black metal's ethical outlook, namely the focus on autonomy, freedom, self-creation, and development.

[13] Which (like other problematic aspects of black metal such as national socialism) do exist but constitute a fringe minority.

and, ultimately, the unexamined life. As Erik Davis puts it when discussing the music of Wolves in the Throne Room,

> [l]ots of people who open their souls to today's seemingly relentless assault on wild creatures and wild places find themselves gripped by bitterness, melancholy, and misanthropy. For the Wolves, black metal just makes sense; it's melodramatic Satanism transformed into an angry lament for human folly.
>
> (2007; cf. Robbins 2014)

The above principles are nicely encapsulated, albeit under the label of "Cynic philosophy," by certain lyrics of Rotting Christ's "The Apostate" from their *Pro Xristou* (2024):

> The end and aim of the Cynic philosophy/As indeed of every philosophy, is happiness/But happiness that consists in living according to nature/And not according to the opinions of the multitude/No wild beasts are so dangerous to men/As Christians are to one another/And concerning the book you gave me to read/I read/I understood/I condemned.

While much of the argument above has been supported by appeal to lyrics, these themes are also expressed and developed at the sonic level. As Thorgersen and Von Wachenfeldt note, the so-called Luciferan Principle is "revealed through the eerie and chaotic sonic and artistic expressions in Black Metal" (2022, p. 184). Admittedly, with any attempt to verbally capture how certain works of art articulate particular ideas through abstract, stylistic means, it is difficult to show this with great precision. Still, black metal shares with other metal qualities of heaviness, loudness, and aggressiveness, which tend to go against both more popular genres of music and also the unreflective preferences of many people. These qualities serve not only to gate-keep and resist commercialization, but also to ensure that those who develop an interest in the genre are not attracted to it on the basis of any easy, common, or superficial pleasure.[14]

Moreover, black metal's freedom is articulated in the myriad ways in which its sound has been developed, not only in terms of its complex

[14] This does not guarantee depth or profundity, but it does suggest a self-conscious attempt to distance the genre from the mainstream and, at least in the early days of black metal, commercialization. Whether or not there is depth or profundity is, in a way, what our argument in this section is about.

branching into multiple subgenres or styles, but also in the varying thematic and stylistic preoccupations of its different artists. Where Ancient Rites, for instance, focus on the folklore and tradition of Scandinavia, Immortal are transfixed by ice, snow, and the landscapes of "grim and frostbitten kingdoms." Others, like Rotting Christ, explore anti-Christianity and Paganism, while Bathory, Ulver, and Ihsann have exercised the freedom and self-stylization that characterizes black metal to virtually leave the genre behind them altogether, paving their way into distinct sonic territories (Bathory by inaugurating Viking metal, Ulver into the realms of ambient, electronica, and avant-garde, and Ihsann into a post-black metal hybrid comprising electronic and orchestral elements).

This kind of self-styling freedom and creativity also supports Thorgersen and Von Wachenfelds's *Bildung* argument for, among other things, black metal, both as a whole genre but also within the musical trajectory of many of its artists, clearly evinces the principles of self-improvement and exploration. The sophistication of the music, the complexity of sonic landscapes, and of the atmospheres crafted by artists, like Mayhem, Satyricon, Rotting Christ, Immortal, Mgla, Emperor's Ihsann, or Behemoth's Gaahl, have been on an expanding dynamic trajectory, even while maintaining distinctive identities (somehow, despite the examples mentioned below, it's still possible to identify the distinctive sound of different bands/artists throughout their expansive and experimental oeuvres).

For instance, Mayhem's *Grand Declaration of War* (Season of Mist & Necropolis Records, 2000) seamlessly blends ambient and electronic sounds with relentless blast-beat passages to create something that seems hard to believe came from the same band that created *De Mysteriis dom Satanas* (Deathlike Silence, 1994). Rotting Christ's sound has evolved to embrace more and more of traditional Greek music, something that can be most clearly heard in songs like "Nemecic" from *Theogonia* (Season of Mist, 2007) or "Tou Thanatou" from *Rituals* (Season of Mist, 2016),[15] but also characterizes the rhythms and chords used in many other songs like their recent "The Apostate" from *Pro Xristou* (Season of Mist, 2024). Perhaps this self-stylization and experimentation is best exemplified by

[15] Indeed, Rotting Christ have developed a signature Greek black metal sound that can be heard both in other Greek black metal bands, and also in bands of related genres, like the melodic death metal band Aetherian, which, though classified as death metal, shares many of the qualities discussed in this paper, as witness their song Primordial Woods (featuring Rotting Christ's Sakis Tollis).

Batushka's radical choice of using Russian Orthodox liturgical chants to conjure an atmosphere of darkness and freedom, but also chaos, that many would struggle to achieve using Satanic aesthetics.

Running through these core themes of the Miltonian-Satan, freedom, self-improvement, and misanthropy is a penchant for nature: a staple of black metal is its simultaneous enchantment and disenchantment with the natural world. This focus has origins in the romantic and modernist turn to nature, and so is rooted in an ethical orientation against societal mores and toward a wilder, more elemental approach to life.

Characterizing much of this concern is a lament and sorrow about humans' ruined communion with nature. As Coggins notes,

> [. . .] Wolves in the Throne Room, known for bringing twigs and branches into indoor performance spaces, have spoken of a 'deep woe' in black metal which is 'about fear – that we can never return to the mythic, pastoral world that we crave on a deep subconscious level', as well as about self loathing, for modernity has transformed us, our minds, bodies and spirit, into an alien life form; one not suited to life on earth without the mediating forces of technology, culture and organized religion.
>
> (2021, p. 39)

This ecological thread, which binds the above themes together into an overall ethical core, is again intimately connected to the distinctive aesthetic of black metal. First, it can be found in lyrics from all over the genre. For instance, the indigenous black metal band Blackbraid's "The River of Time Runs Through Me" has passages describing and personifying parts of the natural world which reflect on the experience of deep time: "Deep in the heart of a forgotten hemlock forest/Your stream flows swiftly over ancient weathered stones /Beneath her surface an ancient current whispers/The memories of a thousand dreams converging deep below" (Blackbraid I, Neuropa, 2022).

Second, the artwork of black metal album covers is famously characterized too by idealized landscapes, from painterly forests (like Ulver's *Bergtatt*, Head Not Found, 1995) to icy fjords and fantasy lands with ruined medieval towers and castles (like Immortal's *At the Heart of Winter*, Osmose Productions, 1999). Some bands infuse their work with local places, whereas others invent whole new worlds, such as Immortal's invented winter kingdom of Blashyrkh. Such scenes and imaginaries represent a longing for nature, but also our alienation from it since the rise of modernity.

Third, while requiring more support than we can give here, we wish to claim that the natural world is also evoked *sonically*. That is, black metal's staple sonic characteristics, such as its blast-beat distortion and frenetic walls of sound, formally reflect and metaphorically express the natural world, particularly when interpreted against background knowledge, including the artist's motivations and the music's explicit thematic content. Sometimes this conceptual link with nature is done literally: many black metal songs include field recordings of natural phenomena like wind, rain, flowing water, birdsong, and snowy footfall (Agalloch's *Marrow of the Spirit* [Dämmerung Arts, 2010] is an exemplar of this). But sometimes the link with nature is achieved more abstractly. Darkthrone's "unholy trinity" albums, for instance, are rife with melodies and riffs that seem to replicate the interlocking branches of trees, the darkness of canopies, the force of the elements; Immortal's guitar style evokes thoughts and images of cold and ice; and Agalloch's crying screams lament the disappearance of pagan belief systems and capture the sorrow of humanity's destruction of earth.

To see this, try an experiment: listening to black metal while exploring a wild natural space, like a forest. Such a hybrid audiovisual experience can, we think, reveal what the music in question relates to or at least fits well with. We hope that it will be clear from conducting this experiment that, say, listening to Darkthrone, Panopticon, or Wolves in the Throne Room in the woods is far more *fitting* than, say, Abba or The Beatles.[16] And for those who do not have such easy access to natural world spaces (and this can sometimes be because of the inequalities of gender, race, ability, and class), black metal may be an effective form of mental transportation, or even "world-traveling," offering as it does immersive soundscapes and ecological imaginaries. As articulated by Maria Lugones (1987), world-traveling offers a route to understand ourselves and others from different worlds by taking on their perspectives in new environments, which can deepen our sense of self and belonging—in this case, how "the self" relates to the wildness of nature.

These are not mere eccentric reactions—after all, the visual artwork accompanying the music in question facilitates these associations. But this, of course, raises the question of whether the artwork biases listeners into drawing these connections. While this may be possible,

[16] To run this experiment, of course, it is important to already be able to hear black metal as more than just loud noise.

it is far more plausible that the supporting art encourages or strengthens the relevant affective links, than that it's solely responsible for them. For it's far more plausible that these links were intended by artists like Darkthrone or Immortal, and that they chose the relevant visual accompaniment to reinforce and to give more shape to their acoustic vision than to trick listeners into thinking that this music is linked to themes revolving around nature, forests, snow, etc. Put it this way: an image of a Viking ship amidst majestic fjords is unlikely to have a similar effect if gracing a Beyoncé album cover.

All these elements combine into a distinctively black metal ecological ethic which aggressively rejects anthropocentrism but also grieves its relentless inevitability. Morphing as it did from the Satanist leanings of its earlier scene into an interest in Nordic pagan folklore, black metal is defined not only by its desire to reconnect humanity to nature, but also by its insistence that we confront our violent destruction of this nature. This makes sense of the genre's core aspects of Satanism and misanthropy.

In fact, as indicated previously, black metal's National Socialist branches (NSBM) are also explained as a side effect of this ecological ethic, as they are an outlier/side effect of such Romanticism as part of early (nationalist) modernism. As Coggins warns:

> [Black metal's] Ideas of setting apart nature from the perceived corruption of the modern world may be an attempt to sacralise the environment, but care must always be taken that this does not incorporate violent essentialisms about who should and should not be 'allowed' to identify with any particular land: assessments of black metal's protectionism and gatekeeping must always be wary of where such tendencies can lead.
>
> (2021, p. 136)

Locating NSBM within or around the ethical core of black metal in general remains a problem, and one that we cannot entirely solve here. However, some brief remarks can begin to carve out an explanation as to why NSBM is on the fringe of the genre, and arguably *fails* to live up to the genre's ethical core and ideal of a Miltonian-Satanic ecology.

For one thing, while much of NSBM utilizes Satanic-ecological aesthetics—through its lyrics and imagery—we would argue that this link is a faulty one. This is because the neo-Nazi core of NSBM is incompatible with the Miltonian-Satanic ethic. To be a fascist—to be racist and support social hierarchies—is (to our minds) to have a false philosophical outlook, and one that goes against freedom in the truer sense. In some way, fascists imprison themselves by having a false worldview, and moreover, their ideology depends on the subjection and enslavement of others. And so, *their* core ethic is one that conflicts with the Miltonian-Satanic ethic, and their use of it might arguably reduce to mere appropriation. More specifically, NSBM uses Miltonian-Satanic ecological aesthetics only *superficially*; in a sense, it hijacks them. Indeed, this explains why NSBM is considered a fringe subgenre of black metal and has largely been rejected by the wider black metal community: it fails to embody the distinctive ideal of black metal.[17]

*

The Miltonian-Satanic ecological sensibility that we've argued forms the ethical core of black metal gives rise to sophisticated and varied interpretations, where key aspects of that core are distilled into specific concerns for ecological and social justice.

The fact that black metal has had a bad reputation for the immorality described earlier is not so much an objection to this claim, but may, surprisingly, lend support to it. A passionate but mishandled or misguided attitude for social justice is often far more dangerous than complete indifference to social justice issues. Be that as it may, the evolution of black metal has arguably distilled the central features we've traced so far into clearer, more substantive concerns and themes. Putatively ethically good themes ranging from eco-activism, feminism, anti-racism, and postcolonial critique are nowadays common, and explicitly expressed in black metal works, via their lyrics, soundscapes, manifestos, and overt creative motivations.

For instance, some black metal bands distill the ecological aspect of black metal's ethical core into a form of eco-activism. The band Botanist, for instance, moves "away from the nexus of Satanism/(neo)-Paganism, nature worship and white nationalism, and towards lamentation and anger over

[17] Black metal works that are deemed NSBM but lack *explicit* markers of this ideology form trickier cases. Burzum, for instance, partakes in the Miltonian-Satanic ethical core to some extent, namely, in its ecological sensibility and embrace of anti-Christian belief systems. However, if it's true that Burzum possesses an *implicit* neo-Nazi meaning as outlined previously—if Vikernes is co-opting a romantic embrace of nature for neo-Nazi aims—then his music would be ethically and aesthetically flawed to this extent. So, on our account, some black metal works will turn out to be both morally beautiful and ugly at differing levels.

the failures of the human-nature relationship" (Lucas 2019, pp. 484–485). Similar attitudes are explicit in the music of bands like Panopticon, as witness their "The Scars of Man Upon the Once Nameless Wilderness (Pt. 1)" (Nordvis, 2018). Others blend this eco-activism into their broader social justice projects: Blackbraid's songs weave indigenous narratives about nature, as well as refer to the genocide of indigenous peoples, referencing specific events such as the Wounded Knee Massacre in 1890.

Other bands lean more toward the Satanic aspect of black metal's ethical core, to explore themes such as feminism and anti-racism. As articulated above, what defines the Miltonian-Satanic ethic is *freedom*; not just for the privileged few, but for all. A prime example of distilling Satanic aesthetics into a concern for social justice is Manuel Gagneux's Zeal & Ardor, which blends black metal with African-American work/slave and spiritual songs from the era of slavery. In a 2017 interview, Gagneux stated that the band's conceptual basis arose out of the question: "what if American slaves had embraced Satan instead of Jesus?" (where this question itself emerged after Gagneux was submitted to a racist joke on a 4chan message board). Embracing Satan as a metaphor rather than literal worship of the biblical horned figure, Gagneux—who is black—has stated that he finds it "odd that American slaves adopted the beliefs of their oppressors and masters in their very personal music," and that embracing Satan in his own music is an act of rebellion from such egregious oppression.[18]

Much feminist black metal also takes Satan as its central focal point as the liberator of the oppressed: in this case, Eve. Satanism—much like third-wave feminism today—rejects traditional Christian values such as patriarchal control, chastity, and fetishized virginity. By harnessing Satan as a metaphor in all their "deviance" and carnality, bands such as Witch Club Satan and Feminazgûl embrace the empowerment of women, and resist and reject gendered binaries and body-shaming in their subversion of patriarchal ideology.

As articulated above, black metal's frequent embrace of such putative moral goodness is not incidental to it as a genre. Rather, its distinctive musical qualities are particularly adept at expressing or evoking anger toward oppression and injustice. Its aesthetic features and techniques,

[18] Available at: https://www.revolvermag.com/music/slavery-and-satanism-inside-zeal-ardors-controversial-take-black-metal/ (accessed 23 May 2025).

such as its blast-beat distortion, lyricism, and guttural vocals, arguably express anger and resistance to capitalist, white patriarchy.

For instance, consider the lyrics in Feminazgûl's "A Mallacht (A Keening) (Birds Before the Storm, 2021)": "Subjugated to the laws of man/Of progenitor/Of spouse/And of Lord . . . /Hell hath no fury/May they all wither." And consider Witch Club Satan's "Fresh Blood, Fresh Pussy" (2024): "I eat a man every fourth week/I like my men medium rare/Cum shots from an ox/All I can think about is/I need blood." The raw and guttural presentation of these themes expresses female anger and subverts gender stereotypes in a cacophony of distortion.

Crucially, bathing feminist themes in such obscure and illegible expression may well offer an effective feminist aesthetic to reject "phallocentrism," that is, the dominant symbolic order or organization of social arrangements which subordinate women and prioritize masculine ways of seeing and navigating the world. Taking, for instance, a poststructuralist Irigarayian approach toward phallocentrism means rejecting and resisting the traditionally male view of the world, which has inscribed our language and culture with a solely masculine lens, rendering women's minds, bodies, and communication as ineffable and alien, as well as inferior (1985). As part of Luce Irigaray's critique, she herself writes in an almost inaccessible style, performing the unintelligibility of women's experience when being categorized in a dominant system of meaning and binary structures.

Given black metal's obscure and ferocious Satanic aesthetic, it is arguably a perfect vehicle to resist phallocentrism in a similar way, express female rage, and subvert feminine stereotypes—women especially are not supposed to be loud, vulgar, or shameless. As Witch Club Satan drummer Johanna Klieve recently said in an interview:

> I feel that black metal is a really feminine genre [. . .] Because women have screamed throughout history. Many people who have seen us perform tell us it feels like we scream not just one woman's scream, but every woman's scream.[19]

The feminist future of black metal—and its disruption of the jaded image of heavy metal being a white man's pursuit—therefore knows

[19] Available at: https://www.loudersound.com/features/witch-club-satan-interview-2024 (accessed 25 April 2025).

no bounds. As the content creator Kim Diaz Holm said in a recent Instagram video, "feminist black metal is how black metal always should have been." Commenting on their raw aggression and lyrics that are "especially for us men, *really* uncomfortable," Holm praises Witch Club Satan as truly embodying what we've delineated as the ethical core of black metal:

> Satanism in black metal was always about the inversion of Christianity. Unfortunately, in the obscene romanticisation of the fictional pagan warrior spirit of old, so many bands seem blind to the fact that a patriarchal machismo that they're screaming about is different from the Christian patriarchy only in aesthetic. The Satanic should be an inversal [*sic*] of the patriarchy, not a conservative reinforcement [. . .] *Black metal should be - obscenely and violently - feminist.*[20]

*

Combined with the extraordinary skills required to perform them, the musical qualities of black metal and the artistic trajectories of many of its artists testify to the ideological dimensions of black metal explored here, namely, its anti-authoritarian attitude that fuels a freedom focused on self-fashioning and self-creation, self-improvement, and ecological preservation and cultivation.

If our analysis here is accurate, then a distinctive feature of black metal is its expression of an ethical outlook based on freedom and a closeness to nature—an ecological ethic where humans do not occupy a privileged position. This, we think, is not just an acceptable ethical outlook, but an attractive one, especially in today's nature-depleted, divided, and polluted world, where many are driven by extreme self-interest and only see in nature opportunities for income generation or for social media selfies.

And if we are right that black metal gives such a set of outlooks a distinctive musical expression, it would be not surprising if its audience—who are best equipped to discern such an expression, even if not always in a manner fine-grained enough to render it articulable—experience this as a form of beauty, however dark or haunting that beauty might formally sound. The peculiar beauty of back metal, then, on our account, turns out

[20] Available at: https://www.instagram.com/p/DGiQMcCiDEQ/ (accessed 26 February 2025, our emphasis).

to be an ethically inflected one. But, as per Hume's earlier claim, it may take practice, experience, and reflection to discern this ethical dimension.

And so, we find much beauty in black metal. As explained earlier, besides its association with certain formal qualities like order, proportion, harmony, etc., beauty has also long been associated with central—notably ethical—values. While this view of beauty is not very popular today, it would not be surprising if appreciators of a likewise unpopular, marginal subculture were attuned to its central feature.

Conclusion

On first listening, black metal as a genre does not strike one as beautiful. In the formal sense of beauty, this is often true. But if we turn to another, deeper, and equally historically influential view of beauty, which finds beauty in virtue and related ethical dispositions, black metal is not doomed at all; in fact, the truth turns out to be the opposite. Black metal works may be among the most beautiful examples of contemporary music, with their sonic enchantment of the natural world and provocative rejection of and resistance to social injustice.

We have argued that, while some examples of black metal arguably possess hardly any beauty at all, being both formally uninviting and ethically bankrupt, there are black metal works that possess formal but no ethical beauty. But in a great many cases, black metal comprises a deeper, ethical beauty, whether or not this is sometimes combined with charming formal adornment. This beauty can surprisingly be traced to its thematic preoccupation with Satanism, freedom, and misanthropy—all interwoven with an ecological sensibility—and has increasingly been channeled into more concrete ethical concerns with social justice. This Miltonian-Satanic ecological sensibility forms an ideal of the genre—not all black metal music fully partakes in it, but it ought to.

Thus, our approach captures not only many of the formal aspects of black metal and its historical development, but also its peculiar beauty, which has been largely ignored in examinations of black metal to date—one which is deep, difficult, and often violent.[21]

---

[21] We're grateful to Patrick Hassan and Jonathan Mitchell for very helpful comments on an earlier draft.

References

Berlin, I. (1969). Two concepts of liberty'. In his. In: *Four Essays on Liberty*, 118–172. London: Oxford University Press.

Blake, W. (1906). *The Marriage of Heaven and Hell*. Boston: John W. Luce and Company.

Bramwell, A. (1989). *Ecology in the 20th Century: A History*. Yale University Press.

Carey, J. (2023). Pure fucking art: self-harm and performance art in Per 'Dead' Ohlin's musical legacy. *Metal Music Studies* 9 (1): 101–118.

Coggins, O. (2021). Ecology, estrangement and enhancement in Black Metal's dark heaven. *Green Letters: Studies in Ecocriticism* 25 (2): 130–142.

Davis,Erik.(2007).Deepeco-metal.*Slate*(November2007).https://slate.com/culture/2007/11/heavy-metal-environmentalists.html (accessed 5 October 2025).

Dimery, R. (2005). *1001 Albums You Must Hear Before You Die*. Universe Publishing.

Dixon, D. (2023). Honouring and admiring the immoral: an ethical guide. Drawing the line: what to do with the work of immoral artists from museums to the movies. *The Philosophical Quarterly* 73 (3): 831–837.

Dixon, D. (forthcoming). *Depraved: The Story of Dangerous Art*. Faber and Faber.

Doran, R.P. (2021). Moral Beauty, Inside and Out. *Australasian Journal of Philosophy* 99: 396–414.

Doran, R.P. (2022). Thick and perceptual moral beauty. *Australasian Journal of Philosophy* 101 (3): 704–721.

Doran, R.P. (2024). Freedom, harmony, and moral beauty. Forthcoming in Philosophers' Imprint. https://doi.org/10.3998/phimp.3954

Gaut, B. (2007). *Art, Emotion and Ethics*. Oxford: Oxford University Press.

Gracyk, T. (2016). Heavy metal: genre, style, or subculture? *Philosophy Compass* 11 (12): 775–785.

Harold, J. (2011). Autonomism reconsidered. *British Journal of Aesthetics* 51 (2): 137–147.

Hume, D. (1777 (1902)). *Enquiries Concerning Human Understanding and Concerning the Principles of Morals*. Ed. L.A. Selby-Bigge. Oxford: Clarendon Press.

Irigaray, L. (1985). *This Sex which is Not One*. Cornell University Press.

Kieran, M. (2003). Art and morality. In: *The Oxford Handbook of Aesthetics* (ed. J. Levinson), 451–470. New York: Oxford University Press.

Lucas, O.R. (2019). "Shrieking soldiers . . . wiping clean the earth": hearing apocalyptic environmentalism in the music of Botanist. *Popular Music* 38 (3): 481–497.

Lugones, M. (1987). Playfulness, "World"-travelling, and loving perception. *Hypatia* 2 (2): 3–19.

Lukes, D. and Panayotov, S. (2023). Introduction: somewhere over a Black metal rainbow. In: *Black Metal Rainbows* (ed. D. Lukes and S. Panayotov), 21–22. Toronto: PM Press.

Matthes, E. and Hatala (2021). *Drawing the Line: What to Do with the Work of Immoral Artists from Museums to the Movies*. Oxford University Press.

Milton, J. (1877). *Paradise Lost*. Boston: James R. Osgood and Company.

Nannicelli, T. (2020). *Artistic Creation and Ethical Criticism*. Oxford University Press.

Paris, P. (2018a). On form, and the possibility of moral beauty. *Metaphilosophy* 49 (5): 711–729.

Paris, P. (2018b). The empirical case for moral beauty. *Australasian Journal of Philosophy* 96 (4): 642–656.

Paris, P. (2019a). Moral beauty and education. *Journal of Moral Education* 48 (4): 395–411.

Paris, P. (2019b). The 'Moralism' in immoralism: a critique of immoralism in aesthetics. *British Journal of Aesthetics* 59 (1): 13–33.

Paris, P. (2024). Delineating beauty: on form and the boundaries of the aesthetic. *Ratio* 37 (1): 76–87.

Paris, P. (2025a). On beauty and wellformedness. *British Journal of Aesthetics* 65 (2): 257–282.

Paris, P. (2025b). Which beauty? What taste? Reflections on the importance of the philosophy of beauty and taste. *Debates in Aesthetics* 19 (2): 9–32.

Plato (1989). *Symposium*. Indianapolis: Hackett.

Plotinus (2020). *The Plotinus Reader*. Ed. and trans. Lloyd P. Gerson. Indianapolis: Hackett.

Robbins, Michael. (2014). Destroy your safe and happy lives: A poet's guide to metal. *Harper's* (May issue). https://harpers.org/archive/2014/05/destroy-your-safe-and-happy-lives/ (accessed 5 October 2025).

Scarry, E. (1999). *On Beauty and Being Just*. Princeton: Princeton University Press.

Shadrack, J.H. (ed.) (2020). *Black Metal, Trauma, Subjectivity and Sound: Screaming the Abyss*. Emerald Publishing Limited.

Tatarkiewicz, W. (1972). The great theory of beauty and its decline. *The Journal of Aesthetics and Art Criticism* 31: 165–180.

Thorgersen, K. and von Wachenfeldt, T. (2022). Black metal *Bildung*. *Philosophy of Music Education Review* 30 (2): 183–201.

Wilson, J.K. (2012). *The German Forest: Nature, Identity, and the Contestation of a National Symbol, 1871–1914*, vol. 11. University of Toronto Press.

Zechner, J. (2011). Politicized Timber: The German Forest and the Nature of the Nation 1800–1945. *The Brock Review* 11 (2): 19–32.

Chapter 10
From Drumheads to Platonic Forms: Enecstatic Considerations of Metal

Jim Kanaris
School of Religious Studies, McGill University, Quebec, Canada

Einstein is said to have thought in musical shapes (McGilchrist 2021, p. I:612). This is a concise description of what I adumbrate in this chapter, to wit, the convergence of an artistic predilection with the act of thought. More concretely, I tie this to a symmetry experienced in my own journey to philosophy that began with and continues to be, *mutatis mutandis*, viscerally sustained by the unconventional genre of heavy metal. The overview is more involving, of course, with autobiographical twists and turns arranged philosophically to add substance to principal claims. Though not exactly a memoir, that dimension of the exposition is offered to mitigate unnecessary assumptions concerning the theme on which those claims are based: the relation of heavy metal to philosophy and, eo ipso, vice versa. The unconventional nature of the theme is bound to attract and repel at the same time. However, I do not wish to disappoint. I commit no one to the connections made with the genre of metal, readers, and, obviously, the pantheon of figures I invoke. In fact, I see this as incidental to, though weighty in (pun intended), my understanding of what it might mean to think in musical shapes and the degree to which my experience then *shapes* that understanding.

Announced toward the end of the chapter, I deem this process, with metaphorical intention, a jig, a supple gyration within the decision-making process to correlate different concerns and goals. I further describe this jig more enigmatically as "enecstatic," which is an amalgam of sentiments culled from the philosophers discussed serially throughout. Significant here is that enecstasis is contoured to surface a ruling element in music—in a word, individuality, irreducibility (to use phenomenological parlance), whether creatively "hammering out" tunes or contemplating general relativity. Enecstasis is shorthand for this inclination caught in a contest of voices to determine how one is to sound one's own. I offer the following considerations to this end in deference to those unable to glimpse the light in the sky as refracted in my window.

Setting the Stage: An Early Journey

It is a primal thing with many explanatory routes. Mine reaches back to *The Beatles' Second Album*, released by Capital Records just months before my birth. A few years later, I would be hypnotized by diverse spinning vinyl on a cherished record player, followed still later by dress rehearsals in front of a bedroom mirror with swirling mock-guitar hockey sticks. My elder brother and I were aiming to master Lennon-McCartney harmonies as he became adept on the six-string. Not exactly metal, but an important *sine qua non* for boomers who entered the fray of the heavy.[1]

[1] The influence of the British Invasion, spearheaded by the Beatles, on what later would become far edgier music is well known. For purposes of convenience, allow me to reference the simple report from the so-called "Prince of Darkness" himself, Ozzy Osbourne. Focusing on the Beatles and the impact they had on him and his generation of metal heads, it may strike a (power)chord with Millennials and subsequent age groups at pains to circumvent the rift between early rock and metal: "I'd go to bed in a black and white world and [wake] up in [a world] turned to color. That's exactly what it felt like" (https://www.instagram.com/p/C4ay8xULp5v/?utm_source=ig_embed&utm_campaign=embed_video_watch_again). The impact was real.

What seemed like a teenage passing phase slowly turned into a career path, as I eventually accompanied my brother's ear-piercing Marshall stack with my reputed thunderous drumming. Led Zeppelin, Black Sabbath, and Van Halen, to name only the more dominant classic influences, spoiled our parents' aspirations for us and robbed them of any hope of completing my high-school education. Like cannon balls, we catapulted into the clubs, honing our craft while numbing our morals. It was the 1980s!

As Judas Priest encouraged us:

> Hold life, I'm gonna live it up
> I'm takin' flight, I said I'll never give it up
> Stand tall, I'm the only kind of proud
> I'm on the top as long as the music's loud.[2]

The relation of metal to philosophy seems a stretch, as if the relation of metal to the Beatles wasn't enough of one. However, like life, insight has its idiosyncrasies. In terms of approach, mine is that, too: idiosyncratic. "A headbanger's journey" can take many forms.[3] For reasons of authenticity, due to a lack of erudition about the subject matter, I pursue here an approach that is general in scope and personal in shape—my life experience that, to put it flippantly, took me from drumheads to Platonic forms. As I reflect on the connection, the impact was more direct than my scholarly sensibilities allow me to admit at times. Alas, philosophy can be so drab, "out of touch" really, desirous of an Archimedean point that deflates all things pulsating and real into representations bested perhaps by thriller series like the British *Black Mirror*. While the advice of Bertrand Russell (1959, p. 20) over a century ago continues to ring true, it can also sadly mask a pathology: ". . . whoever wishes to become a philosopher must learn not to be frightened by absurdities." I am hedging my bets that the consideration of metal to philosophy, while not part of the orthodoxy, is less absurd than other philosophical considerations presumed to be pertinent. Eliminative materialism niggles me lately. It is at variance, to put it mildly, with many of the considerations here. Luckily,

---

[2] Judas Priest, "You've Got Another Thing Comin'" from the album *Screaming for Vengeance* (Columbia Records, 1982).

[3] See, for example, the pioneering documentary of Sam Dunn et al. (2005) for journeys as theirs.

that battle is being fought, successfully in my view, by others requiring no assistance from me.[4]

Music, first in the form of rock and then metal, was my gateway. The child of parents who migrated from Greece to Montreal in the late 1950s, I struggled, admittedly less than they, to assimilate into North American culture. Education, let alone basic literacy, was as elusive to me as a CEO's paycheck is to a burger flipper. I could barely string a sentence together without the overuse of punctuation of the expletive variety. Not meaning to be a linguistic prude, my point is that my desire to self-transcend, however fragmentary and elementary, did not include anything from the sciences or the arts. The only thing I permitted through the Scylla and Charybdis of my consciousness would be that which was amenable to being self-taught and what resonated at a personal level. Music became that outlet for me, as it does for many: the satisfaction of a desire that eludes representation and concept, another term for which, pretentious though it is, is "high" culture.

At a Goal and on a Wheel: Schopenhauer

Arthur Schopenhauer, unique in his philosophical appreciation of the insuperability of artistic expression, captures the primal nature of the experience with unprecedented clarity, even if heavy metal might chafe his quill. Schopenhauer (2010, p. I:283) accords to music a *sui generis* form of mimesis that, unlike the other arts (architecture, sculpture, painting, poetry, and literature), mediates the underlying force of reality, the will, directly. "[I]t is not an imitation or repetition of some Idea of the essence of the world" in, say, a sonnet of Shakespeare, a painting of Caravaggio, Michelangelo's David, or what have you. Music "is an *unmediated* objectivation and copy of the entire *will*" (2010, p. I:285). A few lines later, Schopenhauer repeats himself, but more emphatically: "music is in no way a copy of the Ideas; instead, it is a *copy of the will itself*." As Schopenhauer (2010, p. 287) points out, the idea, at least in the west, goes back to Plato, who clearly distinguishes between the "language" of the soul

[4] In the naturalist battalion, John R. Searle, David Chalmers, and Galen Strawson deserve honorable mention. Their critiques of this late modern philosophy are especially effective. My own directives, however, are supplied, informed rather, by philosophers such as David Bentley Hart, Iain McGilchrist, and Bernard Lonergan. Their views are more ambitious in range, suitable to individuals like me, utterly spent by the vicissitudes of naturalism.

and its reasoning capacity, music being "the movement of melodies that imitates the emotions of the soul." Is it any wonder that a few notes of melody can disarm the brute infinitely more effectively than a library or gallery, not to diminish the value of the latter, of course (1 Samuel 16:23). It can also equally excite. A handy example is the mosh pit.

This experience itself, I wager, may be that which instills that irrepressible sense of the phenomenally real, our awareness of the self, to wit, what "authentic" means to many. I assume this from the following. After Schopenhauer (2010, p. I:289) discusses the modulation of melodies and how it moves us in specific ways on a spectrum, he is careful to draw this important distinction:

> [M]usic [. . .] never expresses appearance but only the inner essence, the in-itself of all appearance, the will itself. Therefore it does not express this or that individual and particular joy, this or that sorrow or pain or horror or exaltation or cheerfulness or peace of mind, but rather joy, sorrow, pain, horror, exaltation, cheerfulness and peace of mind as such *in themselves*, abstractly, as it were, the essential in all these without anything superfluous, and thus also in the absence of any motives for them. Nevertheless, we understand them perfectly in this pared-down quintessence. This is why our imagination is so easily excited by them and tries to take that invisible and yet so vividly aroused spiritual world, a world that speaks to us directly, and to form it, to clothe it in flesh and bone and thus embody it in an analogous example [. . .] For music everywhere expresses only the quintessence of life and of the events taking place in it, never these themselves, and so distinctions within these do not always influence it.

Schopenhauer, Kantian Platonist that he was, is careful to avoid conflating instantiations of taste with the being of tasting as such. I cannot speak for everyone, but this accurately conveys my memory of an experience I wish to exploit for present purposes. It approximates something of an existential awakening. To Schopenhauer, and to any self-respecting nonreductionist, the "language" that attaches to the experience concretizes form, set to this or that creative representation or medium of expression (representations of Ideas), to which one does or does not gravitate for whatever reason.

To my inarticulate young mind, rock became the primary means of articulation, my participation, if you like, in that great score of the universe: the Pythagorean *musica universalis*. I have no interest to psychologize why *that* form or to indulge in (to my mind) useless apologetics concerning it, pro and con. Rock simply is what seized my young imagination, inaugurating it into a process that lifted me from the drudgery of individuality and representation to the universality and objectivity of Schopenhauer's (2010, p. I:221) "*one* eye of the world that gazes out from all cognizing creatures." Music, whatever its particular form, mediated principally[5] by genius for Schopenhauer (2010, p. I:220), is the artistic vehicle *par excellence* that emancipates from the rational appetite of the will, providing some temporal respite. How unsurprising, then, that a philosopher's esteem of art, music especially, is considered unique, upstaging that otherwise significant aspect of the objectivizing will impelled ceaselessly onward by the principle of sufficient reason.[6] To what mode of cognition does Schopenhauer (2010, p. I:207) attribute concern "with the truly essential aspect of the world alone," an essence "not subjected to change and is thus cognized at all times with the same degree of truth"? To science? No. To philosophy? No again. To art!

Art, and (I must hasten to add each time) music in particular, for Schopenhauer (2010, p. I:208) is always "at its goal," released from the vicissitudes of reason's ever onward, ever unattainable goal of complete intelligibility. Before a totality, calmly resistant to contemplation and sutured to the composite relations in "the wheel of time," artful awareness "remains at rest," facing its object "in isolation," in (ideally) rapturous union. Artists of all casts are intimately aware of the experience as they move from the mechanical execution of what they skillfully convey to what this supple movement inculcates. In *All Things are Full of Gods: The Mysteries of Mind and Life*, David Bentley Hart (2024, p. 254) notes this in the guise of his principal protagonist, Psyche:

> At times, they [*qualia*] can even be disruptive of one's preoccupation with oneself. A ballerina may lose herself in her dance, precisely

[5] I qualify genius to flag Schopenhauer's hero character, not to limit the affectivity of art, music in particular, to "pure" mediation. Such a qualification may be permitted in Schopenhauer himself if I am granted some liberty in instances like the following: "the essence of *genius* consists simply *in the prevalence of* a capacity for such contemplation" (2010, p. I:208, italics mine) and also "*genius* is nothing other than *the most* [my italics] perfect *objectivity*" (2010, pp. I:208–209). Genius is a quality suffered by few. Since, as the saying goes, it takes one to know one, I refrain from being doctrinaire, identifying possible instances. For more on genius, see Jerry S. Clegg (1994).

[6] This principle is central to Schopenhauer's philosophy, which was the subject-matter of his PhD dissertation, *The Fourfold Root of the Principle of Sufficient Reason* (1813).

> because her qualitative awareness has in a sense liberated her from herself, and allowed her to submerge her consciousness in the pure flow of sensuous and emotional impressions, and to achieve a rare immediacy of encounter with the phenomenal realm. There are moments of transport—artistic, mystical, what have you—that utterly subsume function in experience; but the qualitative privacy of the experience remains constant.

This transport into the private, to return to my outline, deadened reason to my younger self through a two-decade-long trance of rock and metal, much like a delicious meal might sate a dog. And this applies to any genre that elicits the experience. "At its goal," the chase is an expenditure of energy unequal to what is achieved in the encounter. And thus my story begins.

Epistemic Emancipation as Artistically Contoured: Plato

As any trained or diligent musician will recognize, the union about which Schopenhauer writes, while intensely private, buried in a qualitatively relationless relation, is nonetheless inextricably linked to a communicative efficiency. In the context of music, this means inculcating a skill through which the experiential semiotic is carried, conveyed, and summoned, that is, summoning involvement. The *communio* is between oneself, one's instrument and, merged as such, one's audience. This network of relations can be detected in Plato's well-known "figure of the cave," even if explicitly correlated with knowledge. A brief detour may be instructive.

Wandering through a dim, densely populated den, an escapee discovers the source of the shadows of which he has no prior knowledge. His mobility has been compromised since childhood, to view only animated figures on a wall. Loosed from his chains, he comes to recognize that the objects casting the shadows are truer than the objects, the shadows, to which he formerly affixed the label "truth." Venturing out more still, he is dazzled by the significantly more brilliant light illuminating his newfound surroundings. Whether those surroundings are extra-cavernous depends, analogous to what occurred in the cave, on the escapee turning his gaze from the reflections caused by the sun to the source of that light, the sun itself. Besides Plato's protagonist being relentless, he is no fool.

He rightly gathers that the sun "is the source of the seasons and the years, and is the steward of all things in the visible place, and is in a certain way the cause of all those things he and his companions had been seeing" (*Republic*, 516b-c). The realization (imagine for dramatic effect) forces him to his knees. An irresistible urge to return to his former shadowy estate overtakes him. He must convey the news so that fellow inmates share in the experience.

The story is about the emancipatory nature of veridical *knowledge*. It corresponds to Schopenhauer's principle of sufficient reason, to the a priori category of human consciousness in servile relation, as it were, to Ideas prompted by the will.[7] And yet, as suggested by the invocation, the story permits a structural significance tethered existentially to that which is achieved in a musically patterned experience. It is a form-filled intimacy extended in and captured by an instrumentality that resonates with the will that attracts participation. The time put into what is describable in terms of musical ecstasy inspires a journey of becoming adept at summoning an experience that may elude Plato's otherwise preoccupied protagonist. In my experience, at least Schopenhauer's description of these distinct forms of intentionality, in art and reason, has been confirmed. It speaks to an intelligence embodied already in the orientation made manifest through instrumentation. For roughly two decades, the principles of logic, intrinsic to unearthing the world's intelligibility, were muted in my formative young life. I forfeited the haughty halls of academia—my entrepreneurial immigrant parents never forcing education anyway—for the beer-scented, acoustically compromised halls of nightclubs. There is a very good reason this and any related formative experience is called "paying one's dues."

Learning to Dance on a Wheel

A relatively long apprenticeship followed, via vinyl, of course. Learning "the chops" of masters such as John Bonham, Ian Paice, Cozy Powell, Alex Van Halen, and Bill Ward, to name my more dominant influences,

[7] I should note in passing that, by invoking Schopenhauer in this chapter, I am not in any way embracing his understanding of the will as blind and impersonal. Schopenhauer serves my purpose in that he uniquely represents the philosopher with a high estimation of knowledge dwarfed by the higher operation of art, the supereminent manifestation of will in human form that deposes blind will.

provided the determination to surface the experienced intimacy supported by music. This "philosophy of life" was as close to the shores of philosophy as I would sail. In hindsight, I can comfortably admit that it was an enviable right-hemispheric thinking, to put it neuroanatomically. My modality was sharply at odds with the predilection directed toward knowledge proper, a characteristically left-hemisphere fixation. And yet it was that very orientation, after metaphorically tripping on a flight of stairs, that siphoned a philosophic propensity in me that I didn't know existed.

The experience named in musical encounter, though vectorially dissimilar to philosophy, shares a scalar similarity in terms of artifice, which I have been correlating with skill, communication, and so on. A clever rhythmic pattern or melodic polyphony of notes is not so very different structurally from a finely sculpted syllogism. An experience, worthy of the name, is usually summoned through and with finesse. Our ballerina, submerged "in the pure flow of sensuous and emotional impressions," knows the experience only too well as she executes an amnesic ritual uniting body with that pure flow. Other examples in closer proximity might include Edward Van Halen exquisitely fretboarding "Little Guitars" or Bonham's equally exquisite shuffle in "Fool in the Rain." Technique blending with soul "at its goal."

This connection I wish to make underscores the relation of a union at the different poles of experience, which I am borrowing from Schopenhauer. It began with music for me and doubtless many others, at first to and in a world of intimacy that my ego could root its tendrils, and then to the habits of instrumentation rhythmically mimicking expressions. In time and as personal interest coalesced with forces in the service of Schopenhauer's "wheel of time" (Ideas and being's intelligibility), I applied myself in a manner that resembled or was contiguous with my experience of music but whose aims and cadence were essentially different, though, not in my estimation, irreconcilable or incommensurate. In a word, I redirected the intentionality that galvanized my acquired skillset to another, one united to my manner of being, which is central to my proposal of a possible relationship between metal and philosophy. It is tied to a phenomenology of music and reason, but ignited by a different desire, one to know.[8] In me (not, I imagine, as a special case), these two desires—one at its goal, the

[8] One of the more illuminating expositions of "the desire to know" is Bernard Lonergan (1992).

other perpetually awakened to intend an end of complete intelligibility—have combined in ways that, to my surprise, unwittingly configured my own research program: one that both holds them in tension and continues to sustain the genre that first ignited them.

The Ascetic Connection Between Two Poles of Knowing

The experience of technique in communicating what unites "at its goal" became for me a habit that slipstreamed the variety apropos to that on "the wheel of time," by now serviceable phrases for which I beg the reader's continued indulgence. Qualitatively distinct modes of being, their expression shares a similarity, that of application, execution, passion, singularity of focus, and so on. "Practice makes perfect," as the colloquial expression has it. The one mode, the musical, abets an undifferentiated union, a *communio* at its goal; the other, the philosophical, services differentiations of correspondence on the wheel of time, or, if one prefers, coherence. Whatever the preference, correspondence or coherence, it's not a hill worth dying on. A paraphrase of Heidegger (1962, pp. 258–260) quickly allows me to wave it off: the "truth-relation" or *adaequatio* between intellect and thing (*res*) must be released from the fetters of Cartesian epistemology. More on the significance of this later.

The demands of philosophical reflection, when awakened to its relevance, did not strike me as something alien. I credit this to cutting my teeth on a boisterous era famous not only for its shredding drums and wailing guitars, but also its tolerance for the obstreperous. Were I reared on dominant, popular genres today, I cannot be sure that the transition would have been as seamless. I have my doubts.[9] In any case, the appreciation of the creative process made sentiments as Russell's noted earlier concerning the forbearance and resolve of the philosopher seem commonplace. While philosophical absurdities too often become standard, their consideration is, alas, basic to thought ambitious for the circumspect. I avail myself of allaying suspicions concerning what the nature of that circumspection is. My intentions are not so ambitious. I am simply

[9] I find YouTuber Rick Beato insightful about such matters (i.e. today's music). See https://www.youtube.com/watch?v=Ks4c_A0Ach8&t=10s; https://www.youtube.com/watch?v=1bZ0OSEViyo; https://www.youtube.com/watch?v=KphPa_i2VXE. However, being of the same generation, we may be in the same echo chamber.

drawing a phenomenological parallel: musicians share with the philosopher this acuity. The obvious example would be the cavillous sensibility of spotting, for instance, a "good take" in the studio or an ill-chosen rudiment or scale in a live performance. Perhaps less obvious, but related and equally significant, is the rapturous devotion to "getting it right," to eliminate, to be precise, whatever curtails the process. To be "in the zone" is more shorthand, which conveys the idea of due diligence one finds in other walks of life as well—sports, politics, business, and what have you. What allows for this earnestness is harnessed by a desire at its goal or on the wheel. I often wonder if my own aptitude (tolerance?) for philosophy was bolstered by something analogous. It bestowed on me a kind of resilience to entertain, endure, what society typically scorns—too often, I'm afraid, with good reason.

Is it reasonable to make what resembles an ascetic connection? Metal culture is legendary for deliberately subverting the ascetic ideal. In fact, early forms made this their platform. To document it would be redundant, albeit probably more entertaining than this exposition. Metal as a culture quintessentially embodies an attitude of repugnance toward all forms of denial, equating it with life-suffocating repression, religious forms notwithstanding. But it does involve self-discipline, a great deal of it in fact. Excellence of delivery depends on it. Just as I had to apply myself in mastering rudiments, excluding distractions that obstructed my register, I aimed to do the same when voicing the initially strange desire to know. It may be pedestrian to point out, but how these oscillating desires syncopated in my experience contoured what I came to understand by the practice of philosophy.[10] Such self-mastery would prove beneficial when navigating the challenges of seemingly incommensurable philosophical styles and agendas, namely, how to keep them prudently in creative tension.

In this respect, then, and only in this respect, the discipline involved in habituated experience "at its goal" provides for the acclimation to a

---

[10] Unsurprising to me now is why contemporary estimations of the value of early philosophy as "a way of life" (P. Hadot) or "art of living" (A. Nehamas) instinctively resonated with me. I had concrete exposure to such a pre-Cartesian view of philosophy early in my academic formation through the dazzling, though underappreciated, works of Jesuit philosopher-theologian Bernard Lonergan. The spirit of his offering somewhat obliquely combines the intensely personal, self-realizing spiritual exercises of St. Ignatius of Loyola, the founder of Lonergan's religious order, with a rhetoric of human action that goes back to, *inter alia*, Aristotle, Giambattista Vico, John Henry Newman, and Kenneth Burke. For a recent treatment regarding the Ignatian connection, see Patrick H. Byrne (2020). For the wider context of the "rhetoric of human action," see Kanaris (2002, pp. 27–29).

discipline, different in aim, requisite "on the wheel." The only continuity, in other words, is the act of self-discipline in mediating different goals. Moreover, both acts target individual objectives susceptible to an impediment, one that both practices seek to allay: conflating hard-earned technical prowess with its end. Having fought hard to get into "the zone," musicians and philosophers alike must paradoxically relax the grip by which they shape their respective teleologies. I cannot say whether the musician has it easier in this regard since her craft is not immune to disruptions of an overactive region of the brain dominated by mechanization. The highly trained musician, for instance, experiences the challenge far more than the amateur uninterested in the understanding of music. The objective is to dissociate from the knowledge and awareness that the skill executes. Such withdrawal provides for a merger with and in the encounter being shaped. Herein lies the more egregious challenge facing the philosopher.

The philosopher's instrument *is* the understanding. It pushes the immediacy in artistic realization into the mediacy of rational apprehension. Even if, technically speaking, the understanding does not reduce to reason, especially a condensed form of reason, it is ingredient to it. And so, both musician and philosopher participate in understanding, but in the former, the understanding services the immediate goal, in the latter, the understanding mediates to itself the goal forever being serviced on the wheel. When that reflex is assumed by the musician, the goal is inhibited, as pointed out earlier, which marks the point of departure of the musician's and the philosopher's respective asceticisms.

Iain McGilchrist (2009) gets at this by distinguishing two kinds of *knowing*, which he flags by the German *kennen* and *wissen*, among other terms in different languages. The first, known by the musician, *kennen*, is relational and qualitatively empathic, as in an acquaintance or encounter with something or someone "other" that is simultaneously personal.

> It's the way we naturally approach knowledge of a *living being*; it's to do with *individuals*, and permits a sense of *uniqueness*; it's "mine", *personal*, not something I can just hand on to someone else unchanged; and it not *fixed* or *certain*. It's not easily captured in *words*; the *whole* is not captured by trying to list the *parts* ("quick-tempered", "lively", etc); it has at least something to do with the *embodied* person (the photograph); it resists *general* terms; it has to be *experienced*; and the knowledge depends on *betweenness* (an encounter).
>
> (McGilchrist 2009, p. 95)

McGilchrist (2009, p. 96) directly relates this knowing to music:

> The approach to music is like entering into relation with another living individual, and research suggests that understanding music is perceived as similar to knowing a person; we freely attribute human qualities to music, including age, sex, personality characteristics and feelings. The empathic nature of the experience means that it has more in common with encountering a person than a concept or an idea that could be expressed in words. It is important to recognize that music does not *symbolise* emotional meaning, which would require that it be interpreted; it *metaphorises* it—"carries it over" direct to our unconscious minds. Equally it does not symbolise human qualities; it conveys them direct, so that it acts on us, and we respond to it, as in a human encounter.

Stark is the contrast with the philosophical inclination or just plain knowing on the wheel. Unlike the relational in music, this apprehending mode of acquaintance (*wissen*) is locative in nature. Currently, for example, I am tantalized by a steamy cup of coffee on my desk as everything dims around me while ushering the cup to my open lips. Keyboard, computer, screen, desk, room, house, town, *und so weiter*, virtually disappears as I exhale to cool the liquid substance about to taper my addiction. McGilchrist (2009, p. 96) characterizes the activity in terms of "an affinity with the non-living; with 'pieces' of information; general, impersonal, fixed, certain and disengaged." Extreme instances of this occur in individuals who have suffered a right-hemisphere stroke.[11]

Acquaintance of this kind can and wondrously does come as a "release to the tension of inquiry," taking on "a selective alertness that keeps pace with the refinements of elaborate and subtle classifications," an act, incidentally, that occurs "frequently in the intelligent and rarely in the stupid" (Lonergan 1992, p 28, 29, 209). And yet, as locative knowing, to which the understanding is alloyed, this "meddling intellect" is constantly menaced by an uncalm desire to "murder to dissect," as Wordsworth harrowingly puts it in *The Tables Turned*. It's an old, old story mitigated, it seems to me, by a conscious awareness shaped and captivated by the two different poles of experience, one at its goal, the other on the wheel. With its innumerable pathologies, an aberrant laterality would

[11] For an illustrative catalogue of symptoms, see McGilchrist (2021, pp. I:67–104).

easily test so boundless a reality as the cloud, virtual though it be. Without being too sanguine about the deliverances of metal, to return to my principal theme, the genre and my appreciation of music more generally instilled the importance of harnessing the vital sensibility of relational involvement, unencumbered by the “selective alertness” *ipso facto*, taking stock of a gestalt composed of parts.

An example may prove solvent. Although susceptible to mood, Ozzy’s song “No More Tears”[12] almost unfailingly pulls me into a fascinating orbit of undifferentiated delights. Its opening fluid, almost hypnotic bass line inaugurates the experience. The crashing entry of gloriously overproduced drums patterns the mood, supported by a foreboding synthesized soundscape. And then, like a Diablo wind in Northern California, Zakk Wylde’s perfectly distorted slide guitar heightens the regression. “Classic!”, as they say. Once I transition to the verses, Wylde’s biting antiphonal response to each of Ozzy’s somewhat charming nasal oscillations winds me as each delivery is punctuated by Wylde’s signature pinch harmonic or bottleneck decreasing pitch. “The light in the window is a crack in the sky.” From bridge to chorus to verse, much of the same. It is effective, too, since the measure repeats until the keyboard break and guitar solo in the middle, after which the cycle repeats one last time. By today’s standards, the song is long—coming in at over seven minutes. It is a fabulous length, though, if the genre resonates.

The description alone is a demonstration of how both types of knowing can come together, thanks to phenomenological configurations of *wissen*. However, what I have come to understand as a lateralized production typically approaches experience through psychological, physiological, or sociological points of reference. Such accounts, while not without validity, fail to supply the living encounter (*kennen*), and with it the significance that is siphoned off in explanation (*wissen*). The explanations are especially ineffectual when thought to account for or substitute for my predilection or that of others who happen to share a similar experience or disagree entirely with me based on their own preferences.[13] The experience in its undifferentiated simplicity, intentional unity, eludes the otherwise insightful differentiations that mean to fix some composite

[12] Ozzy Osbourne, “No More Tears” from the album *No More Tears* (Epic Records, 1991).

[13] In academic circles, what I am describing might be relegated to that dejected bin of “theories” judged as “folk psychology.” However, I have become progressively convinced that such a diagnosis is itself a symptom of a malaise characteristic of modern, physicalist assumptions about the world, one that contributes to our sense of alienation, clinging ever tightly to promises concerning the deliverances of the calculating mind. See Hart (2024, pp. 200–201). See also McGilchrist (2009, pp. 330–427).

delineation. Zakk Wylde's perfectly timed, perfectly distorted pinch harmonics, ensconced in the overall soundscape of the song, must be experienced to be understood. It has a formal causality of its own that resonates (or does not) with a first-person perspective irreducible to third-person descriptions about its nature.[14]

The Dream of Morning: Heidegger Reconsidered

Whatever the shortcomings of Heidegger, infamously one racist failure in particular, he managed to pinpoint a sensibility lost in the reflex of modernity related to our particular being-in-the-world. Cogent here is the sheer sense that that being, in Heidegger's estimation, requires a special form of analysis, unlike what the sciences represent, reliant, both indirectly and critically, on ancient Greek metaphysics. Without getting sidetracked by hermeneutical issues related to the solvency of Heidegger's reading of the heritage, my point is to invoke him, like Schopenhauer, as representative of a pole in the tension I have been building since the outset, to wit, a gesture at its goal and another on the wheel.

A surface reading of Heidegger would hardly reveal this gesture as artistic, the pole in question I take him to represent. In one sense, that reflex would not be completely gratuitous. Heidegger, no less than his nemesis, western metaphysics, is involved, albeit idiosyncratically, in a concern with intelligibility forever elusive on the wheel of determinations. It is his style and the configuration of his phenomenological objectives, however, that merit pause. Heidegger flags a forgetfulness (*Seinsvergessenheit*) in the understanding represented here by *wissen*, always prone to conflate what it knows with the being of its knowing, *kennen*. Like the trained musician, who understands her goal, which, conveniently put, is to forget the scales she must learn to summon what awaits, Heidegger's existential analytic, *a fortiori* in its late "post-metaphysical" phase, is functionally identical. He, too, advances a forgetfulness, albeit productive, artistic, in his deconstruction of conflating being (*Sein*) with its entitative status (*Seiende*). In effect, his philosophy is advanced precisely with this in mind: to negotiate the inauthentic varieties of forgetfulness, especially in their irresistible

[14] I am indebted, once again, to David Bentley Hart for his insightful reading of Aristotle's notion of causality. See especially Hart (2024, pp. 59–74) for a systematic outline invoked throughout the entire volume of *All Things are Full of Gods*.

objectification of being. It does so through a thinking practice (andenkendes Denken) attuned to the intimate strangeness that haunts our being-in-the-world—an attunement regularly eclipsed by its differentiations. That is why Heidegger fashions a peculiar language—language being the house of being for him—to fissure prospects of authentic reception of being's ever-eventful manifestation. Is this not the artist's tactic, the predilection to create fissures into that which obstructs experience at its goal? My hunch is that it is.

It was a published lecture on art by the Canadian philosopher Bernard Lonergan (1993, pp. 208–232) that cleared a path for me in this respect. Lonergan himself was apprised of the understanding through the work of Ludwig Binswanger, his appreciation of Heidegger in the context of psychiatry and existential psychology, and philosopher Susanne K. Langer, her theory of art. Binswanger detects in Heidegger's notion of *Dasein* the existential subject transitioning from the organically influenced dream of night, of inconsequential existential significance (e.g. digestion), into that of morning, the contrast of a consequentially elemental wakefulness in which the subject enters the intentional order of meaning, a world "simultaneous and correlative" to her state of being (Lonergan 1993, p. 210). Heidegger's early gesture to relax the grip of Cartesian dualism is given an alternative form by Binswanger. This provides us with an extension of Schopenhauer's appreciation of art, but as a thinking (*kennen*), the philosophy connection, an interstice between art at its goal *and* on the wheel.

In Langer's case, the connection is the intentional order of what Lonergan calls "elemental meaning," a purely experiential pattern of meaning in which subject in act and object in act are one and the same, Binswanger's dream of morning, and artistic objectifications in spatial, temporal, and poetic forms. Respective examples include the objectified relationality of patterning in a painting (space), a musical score (time), and a narrative (poetry). A crucial function of these forms, in their convergence with their individual, undifferentiated acts of meaning, is to exclude alien patterns that instrumentalize experience, hence the qualifier "pure" in elemental meaning. Thus, Lonergan (1993, p. 216) can view Heidegger's philosophic intentions as "another way of indicating what is meant by elemental meaning." The gesture in Heidegger purposely unsettles what Lonergan calls the "fuller development" of meaning found in the sciences, which instrumentalize experience toward significantly different aims, those of description and explanation. I have been delineating these in this chapter in the terms of Schopenhauer, specifically, reason on the wheel.

In philosophy circles in the English-speaking world, one finds representations of these different objectives in the popular, once rigid distinction between continental philosophy and its analytic counterparts. The former is taken to be conceptually more fluid and political, psychoanalytic, than the latter, which tends to mirror the scientific disposition that gained ascendency after Descartes by way of foundational thinkers as Gottlob Frege, Bertrand Russell, the young Ludwig Wittgenstein, and G.E. Moore. The artistic underpinning in Heidegger famously aligns with the continental tradition, its self-reflexive strand subversive of the specter detected in systems engendered by its founding father, Hegel. As interesting as this subversive trajectory is, from Heidegger to his "postmodern" children and grandchildren, I forego an outline to pursue my pedestrian aims.

My transition from drumheads to Platonic forms, to use the trusty imagery from earlier, sustained an inclination, albeit governed by formally different concerns. As ciphers, Schopenhauer's traditional configuration of the arts covers that inclination as discontinuous with, distinct from, what eventually would become my primary, professional concern with reason and philosophy; Heidegger's revamping of the philosophical landscape, when visiting me later in life, aided in the realization that that inclination was continuous with the lure of elemental meaning coincident with *thought* as *kennen* contrasted to *wissen*. In the context of a larger conversation, continental and analytic thought become somewhat representative of these respective traits, which is why I mention them. However, it is important to point out that nothing prevents either knowing style from slipping into shopworn characterizations of philosophy as existentially dissociative, *wissen*, if you like, usurping *kennen*. To put matters more plainly, nothing in analytic thinking makes it intrinsically inimical to *kennen*. That privilege, as it were, is afforded by the metaphysical horizon of its practitioner. In any case, the topic is best left for another occasion, although I will touch on it below.

Creative Tensions: Lonergan's Gift of Differentiated Consciousness

My relationship to this entire dynamic has both past and present application. Regarding the past, I see, in retrospect, how music (rock then metal) could siphon my attraction to elemental meaning in its philosophic form. Although I make no claims about this eventuality being explicit with my awareness at the time, it is reasonable to assume it was tacit and continues to be indirect. Its relation to my experience of music as emancipatory, together with the earlier connection to Plato's prisoner and the corollary of sustained effort as ascetic-like, shaped my later, viscerally measured admiration of philosophy in the guise of *kennen*. This admiration takes the form of an encounter—at times a skirmish—with elemental meaning. *Wissen* is a part of it, to be sure—some would, in my estimation (and in McGilchrist's incidentally) wrongly contend: is all of it—but as a potentially "fuller development," *wissen* is, if it is to be vibrant and fruitful, in creative tension with *kennen* ideally.

"Enecstasis" is a term I have devised to capture this sensibility caught in the interstice between artistic and philosophic negotiations of elemental meaning on the one hand (*kennen*) and its more granular instantiations of systematic meaning on the other (*wissen*). Even though the term and its idiosyncratic connotation were inspired by Heidegger, his early thinking concerning ecstatic *Dasein*, whose contours I outline elsewhere (Kanaris 2023, pp. 11–36), it took shape rooted in my apprenticeship to music, which I am comfortable to call its *sine qua non*. I confess that that influence has fluctuated in importance over the years. Still, in moments of disruption, visceral connection to older forms of metal already mentioned—Lamb of God for me being a newer variety followed by tamer, more melodic installments as, for example, Alter Bridge and Big Wreck—reminds me of the artistry that provided for and continues to generate the artistic constitution of the enecstatic in me.

Why "enecstatic"? The term signals a Heideggerian appreciation of engaged agency, although distinct from and sometimes contrary to the framework of fundamental ontology. Heidegger's treatment is tied to a notion of being, the formulation of which is sutured to a neutralizing agent peculiar to Heidegger's diagnosis of western metaphysics. Enecstasis is distilled from this programmatic, indicated by the Greek prefix "en" (in) added to that of "ek" (out, from) in the form advanced by Heidegger (1962, pp. 377–388), namely, *ekstatikon*. For reasons of space, I refrain from further comment on this specific tension with the Heideggerian system to turn to two others more pertinent to this exposition.

The "enec" of enecstasis is a play on an inextricable relationality of subjective and objective agency captured in the phrase elemental meaning. It speaks to the intimacy, dream of morning, of subjective involvement in a goal it, the subject, participates in and mediates but does not precipitate. It is an in-standing, if you will, *in* what the subject simultaneously reaches *out* for. Put otherwise, this in- and out-standing (en-ec-stasis) of subjective involvement is premised on a relational relation that conditions the otherwise irreducible individuality of the standing.[15] For this reason, Schopenhauer's "at its goal" has appealed to me as does Lonergan's reading of fundamental ontology as concern with compact elemental meaning, if the descriptive qualification ("compact") be permitted. In a paragraph that outlines Binswanger's reading, Lonergan (1993, p. 210) writes: "The reason Heidegger speaks of *Dasein* is that he does not want any split between subject and object." The desire is indicative in compressed form to touch the face of reality. In terms reminiscent of Binswanger's, Hart captures this dynamic beautifully at the end of a chapter on being, which exposes, unwittingly, the element of the mystical in Heidegger that is hard to shirk despite Heidegger's efforts.[16] Consider Hart's (2013, p. 151) account:

> That sudden instant of existential surprise is [. . .] one of wakefulness, of attentiveness to reality as such, rather than to the impulses [instrumentalizations] of the ego or of desire or of ambition; and it opens up upon the limitless beauty of being, which is to say, upon the beauty of being seen as a gift that comes from beyond all possible beings. This wakefulness can, moreover, become habitual, a kind of sustained awareness of the surfeit of being over the beings it sustains, though this may be truly possible only for saints. For anyone who experiences only fleeting intimations of that kind of vision, however, those shining instants are reminders that the encounter with the mystery of being as such occurs within every encounter with the things of the world; one knows the extraordinary within the ordinary, the supernatural within the natural. The highest vocation of reason and of the will is to seek to know the ultimate source of that mystery. Above all, one should wish to know whether our consciousness of that mystery directs us toward a reality that is, in its turn, conscious of us.

[15] Heidegger's (1992, p. 255) formulation, after which my notion of enecstasis is modeled, is: a "standing in" in the openness of Being, "of enduring and out-standing this standing-in (care), and of outbraving the utmost (Being-toward-death)."

[16] See Heidegger (2002, pp. 49–75). Derrida, Heidegger's famous close reader is not convinced, who writes of "a Heidegger who seems unable to stop either settling accounts with Christianity or distancing himself from it—with all the more violence in so far as it is already too late, perhaps, for him to deny certain proto-Christian motifs in the ontological repetition and existential analytics" (Derrida 2002, p. 51).

I personally have no problem with the reference Hart makes to the ultimate mystery and even to the supernatural. However, what is illustrative in the quotation are all the elements of the pre-egoic that fuse together nicely with the existential, artistic inclination, which both Binswanger and Lonergan tie to thinking. Incidentally, I believe Hart himself would welcome the connection. In any case, enecstasis is my vocabulary for this, made possible initially by a wakefulness experienced in music that detoured, I am comfortable stating, into philosophy. That detour, long and sustained, involved a tenuous relationship to a self, the self, at its goal impacted, sometimes deeply, sometimes incidentally, by traffic on the wheel. The balance act was and is delicate. It requires a pliability—better still: supple movement—that can adapt to inevitable disturbances that give it shape, which is why I whimsically call enecstasis a jig (Kanaris 2023, pp. 23–36).

This brings me to the third and final tension, mentioned already *en passant*. Not only is the porosity of enecstasis in reciprocal relation to a tension at its goal, between that of music and artistic thinking, but also one in whose philosophical interaction on the wheel, between *kennen* and *wissen*, can at the very least preserve a productive configuration. The preoccupation has followed me since the early 1990s in graduate school, when the contest between continental and analytic philosophy was at its zenith. While Jacques Derrida certainly cannot be taken to represent the entirety of the continental tradition, let alone that pocket ambivalently earmarked postmodern, the 1992 Cambridge affair is emblematic of this deep rift between the different aims and thinking styles these philosophical traditions represent. They arguably, though broadly, align with McGilchrist's two types of knowing. Still, while the tension has abated, it continues to reverberate.[17] Whatever the case, enecstasis came to fruition due to my appreciation of the "differentiations of consciousness" that these aims and styles reflect.

I borrow the expression from Lonergan's conceptual landscape. In his phenomenological overview of insight—too often overlooked in the literature—he correlates the unity of understanding, insight, with patterns of experience directed by conscious exigencies that give rise to different realms of meaning.[18] This is a highly condensed summary of a

[17] One sees this in outcries against "postmodernity" in speculative realism, new materialism, object-oriented ontology, process philosophy, etc. In my own field, religious studies, two recent installments serve as examples of sober appreciations of canonical figures while advocating for alternatives of their own. See Josephson Storm (2021) and Craig Martin (2022).

[18] See Lonergan (1992, pp. 27–371), especially pp. 196–215 in connection with my summary, and Lonergan (1972, pp. 57–99).

very complex organization of elements. I propose it only with a view to underline one of Lonergan's many important points about consciousness: that it is in constant state of tension with itself in and through various realms of meaning that facilitate its development. Theory, interiority, art, and scholarship, to name some of the more pertinent realms for our purposes, become avenues of intentional consciousness to become increasingly differentiated, to understand, that is, the different realms, their differentiations, and to know how to shift from one to the other (Lonergan 1972, p. 84). A differentiation, roughly, consists in a procedural adaptation of consciousness through a self-correcting process of learning. As differentiated, in its enhancements through apprehended content, consciousness inhabits a definite field of relations that "develops its own language, its own distinct mode of apprehension, and its own cultural, social, or professional group speaking in that fashion and apprehending in that manner" (Lonergan 1972, p. 272). The apprehending of the artist is not that of the scholar or scientist, but it might include aspects of those individual differentiations toward a differentiated perspective of the artist's own. Although that achievement may involve different rules of interaction, they need not violate those of the differentiations being compared or integrated. A caveat, of course, is that a violation is bound to occur when or if perceived as such by an undifferentiated perspective, an indiscriminate mind already convinced by what is obviously the case, and, even more egregiously, a highly differentiated consciousness tethered to an exploratory efficiency turned self-sufficient.

The arrangements are overabundant. Lonergan (1972, p. 272) himself halfheartedly notes thirty-one possible combinations, stratified and duplicated as mathematically feasible. But it is to the dynamic of relation that I am particularly drawn. In its form as artistry, a plasticity is present that facilitates different types of knowing structured procedurally as *kennen* or *wissen*, to invoke McGilchrist one last time. In Lonergan's imagery, it is to know how to shift from one realm of differentiated achievement to another in transitive or duplicative form. This, now in my terms, is to be in enecstatic relation to different content enticed by and toward different types of unity that utilize a tension, one at its goal, the other, indeterminately future, on the wheel. A differentiated consciousness can bring both types of tension into productive relief. Music, in its admittedly debatable accent as metal (consensus on the matter would be delusional), mitigated the tensions for me via the notion of enecstasis.

If practice is any indication, I continue to drum while erecting bridges between continental and analytic pathways of thought.

Conclusion

I end with a blush, perhaps not making the reader all the wiser about the relation of metal to philosophy. Having said that, I also end as I started, without pretense to doing so. Like the reader, I am eager to learn from contributors to this volume how philosophy can and does interface with the genre.

Greeks have a term that captures what enecstasis formally conveys. The term is *meraki*. It means to do something with spirit, with heart, to imbue an activity with a quality of love. When something is done with *meraki*, skill meets passion. While skill surfaces the activity as performed with or containing *meraki*, *meraki* does not reduce to skill. Something can be skillfully executed but lack *meraki*. Spirit is the *je ne sais quoi* of the activity, translating skill into something that is alive, something beautiful, a staging, if you will, of *meraki*. McGilchrist might put it in the following terms. *Meraki* is performed or can be spotted when the left hemisphere of the brain relinquishes its role as master.

While enecstasis as a formal concept can never capture such a quality, it points to *meraki*, surrounds itself with it, guarding its occasion, its irreducible possibility. Such a sensibility was gifted to me, as narrated here, through my encounter with music (yes, metal) and an ineluctable desire to know. Hopefully, its limited scope resonates. At the very least, perhaps the light in the window of this exposition refracts a crack in the sky.

References

Byrne, P.H. (2020). Discernment and self-appropriation. *Revista Portuguesa de Filosofia* 76 (4): 1399–1424.

Clegg, J.S. (1994). *On Genius: Affirmation and Denial from Schopenhauer to Wittgenstein*. New York: Peter Lang Publishing.

Derrida, J. (2002). Faith and knowledge: the two sources of 'Religion' at the limits of reason alone. In: *Acts of Religion* (ed. G. Anidjar), 42–101. New York: Routledge.

Dunn, S., McFadyen, S., and Wise, J.J. (2005). *Metal: A Headbanger's Journey*. Seville Pictures and Warner Home Video.

Hart, D.B. (2024). *All Things are Full of Gods: The Mysteries of Mind and Life*. New Haven and London: Yale University Press.

Hart, D.B. (2013). *The Experience of God: Being, Consciousness, Bliss*. New Haven and London: Yale University Press.

Heidegger, M. (1962). *Being and Time*. Translated by John Macquarrie and Edward Robinson. Oxford: Blackwell.

Heidegger, M. (2002). "Phenomenology and theology" and "The Onto-theological constitution of metaphysics". In: *The Religious* (ed. J.D. Caputo), 49–75. Blackwell Publishers.

Heidegger, M. (1992). The way back into the ground of metaphysics. In: *Primary Readings in Philosophy for Understanding Theology* (ed. D. Allen and E.O. Springstead), 248–262. Louisville: Westminster/John Knox Press.

Jason Ānanda, J.S. (2021). *Metamodernism: The Future of Theory*. Chicago: University of Chicago Press.

Kanaris, J. (2002). *Bernard Lonergan's Philosophy of Religion: From Philosophy of God to Philosophy of Religious Studies*. Albany, NY: The State University of New York Press.

Kanaris, J. (2023). *Toward a Philosophy of Religious Studies: Enecstatic Explorations*. Albany, NY: The State University of New York Press.

Lonergan, B. (1992). *Insight: A Study of Human Understanding*. Volume 3 of *Collected Works of Bernard Lonergan*. Edited by Frederick E. Crowe and Robert M. Doran. Toronto: University of Toronto Press.

Lonergan, B. (1972). *Method in Theology*. New York: Herder and Herder.

Lonergan, B. (1993). *Topics in Education: The Cincinnati Lectures of 1959 on the Philosophy of Education*. Volume 10 of *Collected Works of Bernard Lonergan*. Edited by Robert M. Doran and Frederick E. Crowe. Toronto: University of Toronto Press.

Martin, C. (2022). *Discourse and Ideology: A Critique of the Study of Culture*. London: Bloomsbury Academic.

McGilchrist, I. (2009). *The Master and His Emissary: The Divided Brain and the Making of the Western World*. New Expanded Edition. New Haven and London: Yale University Press.

McGilchrist, Iain. 2021. *The Matter with Things: Our Brains, Our Delusions, and the Unmaking of the World*. 2 vols. London: Perspectiva Press.Russell, Bertrant. 1959. The Problems of Philosophy. New York: Oxford University Press.

Schopenhauer, A. (2010). *The World as Will and Idea*. Volume 1. Translated and edited by Judith Norman, Alistair Welchman and Christopher Janaway. Cambridge: Cambridge University Press.

Chapter 11
Headbanging as Kinaesthetic Judgment

Jason Miller
Public Humanities, Warren Wilson College, Swannanoa, NC, USA

Introduction: What Is Headbanging, Really?

For much of the modern Western world, we have MTV to thank for bringing the term "headbanging" into common currency. Premiering in 1981 and hosted by Riki Rachtman, *Headbangers Ball* featured hair-metal favorites like Whitesnake, Motley Crüe, and Twisted Sister as well as heavier, more fringe acts like Motörhead and Iron Maiden. Much of the rest of the world, however, has come to know about headbanging from a YouTube video of Snowball, the yellow-crested cockatoo who bobs its head dramatically up and down to the beat of music.

But what is headbanging, really? What, indeed, is a headbanger? Often dismissed as an uncouth, even self-destructive display of fandom—wild, violent, and anarchic—many fans of heavy metal or "metalheads" love it for precisely this reason. At best, it is seen as an eccentric by-product of heavy metal culture; at worst, a medical hazard. But these interpretations not only misunderstand the act itself, but they also misidentify its aesthetic and philosophical significance. In this chapter, I will argue that headbanging is best understood as a form of *kinaesthetic judgment*: a bodily, aesthetic response to the heaviness of heavy metal music. More than ritual, more than catharsis, and more than mere dance for metalheads, headbanging is an embodied expression of appreciation—an act through which listeners not only process but evaluate music via physical movement.

Nor do I think this inquiry into headbanging is of interest exclusively to metalheads. The questions it raises may be of equal interest to headbangers and nonheadbangers alike. It offers an account of a phenomenon so familiar and seemingly straightforward that its more nuanced significance might easily be overlooked by even its most ardent practitioners. For those with little to no interest in heavy metal music and its attendant practices, this account of headbanging raises a broader and more interesting set of questions about the relation between art, aesthetic appreciation of art, and the physical, bodily response to art.

The Genealogy of Headbanging: Beyond Heavy Metal

For most, the term "headbanging" readily conjures images of rowdy crowds (mostly long-haired young men) in front of a stage where music (probably heavy metal) is being played (probably very loudly). But what is actually going on with headbanging is much harder to put into a crisp definition. Wikipedia has it that headbanging is "the action of violently shaking one's head in rhythm to the music." Cambridge Dictionary defines it as "the activity of shaking your head up and down with great force to the beat of rock music."[1] Probably the most compelling description, however, comes from the Urban Dictionary, which explains that headbanging means "swinging your head up and down as hard as you can as if to almost rip it off, while listening to heavy metal."[2]

But if we're serious about gaining a better understanding of the widely practiced phenomenon of headbanging, it's important to sort out what's useful and what's not in these and similar definitions. To begin with, although headbanging is most closely associated with heavy metal,

[1] https://en.wikipedia.org/wiki/Headbanging
[2] https://www.urbandictionary.com/define.php?term=headbanging

it neither originates with the genre nor remains exclusive to it. Indeed, similar practices are observable in ritualistic and devotional traditions dating back centuries. Traditional Sufi music in India, Kurdish dervishes in Iran, and the Berber *Nakh* dance of the Maghreb region all involve rhythmic, repetitive motions of the head as a response to music. These activities, though not genealogically linked to headbanging in metal culture, suggest a long-standing human impulse to engage the body—especially the head—in rhythmically felt music.

Focusing specifically on the modern meaning and significance of headbanging, namely as a bodily accompaniment to music, it's important to link it specifically with the musical genre of heavy metal. It is true that the modern practice of headbanging finds its speculative origins in the somewhat undefined boundary between hard rock and heavy metal. But even there, it is difficult to identify its precise origins. Some accounts trace it back to the fans of Led Zeppelin who reportedly "banged" their heads against the stage in ecstasy at the Royal Albert Hall in London. Black Sabbath's 1970 Paris concert likewise features footage of band members and fans moving violently to the music, offering a slightly different origin story. Likewise, Motörhead's followers were dubbed "Motörheadbangers," signaling a growing self-awareness of the practice. Yet even as its cultural lineage becomes entangled with the development of heavy metal, headbanging resists easy historicization. It is not a derivative tradition but a distinct *aesthetic response*—one that is rediscovered, rather than inherited, somewhere in the evolution from rock music to heavy metal.

Further, the common characterization of headbanging as violent or self-destructive is problematic. Granted, researchers have found that, in fact, intense headbanging can lead to chronic subdural hematoma (for at least one 50-year-old man at a Motörhead concert, anyway) (see Mackenzie 1991; Islamian et al. 2014). Typically speaking, however, there is no intention to cause any harm to oneself or others in headbanging, and indeed, there is a tacit code of ethics adopted and enforced in almost any sanctioned space where headbanging and similar activities are practiced to ensure the safety of everyone involved. Moreover, headbanging varies greatly in intensity, and can be performed as mildly as a gentle nodding of the head.

Moreover, it's worth pointing out that headbanging is primarily conducted in response to *live* music. This is because (as I'll explain more fully below) headbanging is a deeply social phenomenon, most often conducted in the presence of other fans. This doesn't mean headbanging doesn't happen along with music channeled through speakers, or even more privately, through headphones. This kind of audio experience might even be done in a communal setting. But I think any metalhead will allow that this is at best a secondary, derivative form of headbanging intended to approximate the real deal of headbanging to music at a live show or concert. Generally speaking, the philosophically interesting thing about rock music, as Ted Gracyk (1996) has argued, is that the music is ontologically situated in the allographic recording of the music. Given the significance of headbanging in listening to heavy metal, however, one could argue that headbanging to some extent reclaims the priority of the live performance. The point I want to emphasize here, however, is simply that headbanging has its fullest expression in the experience of live music.

Finally—and this is a bit of a hot take—it seems to me that the common association between headbanging and long hair is vastly overstated. Deena Weinstein, one of the leading scholars of heavy metal music, suggests that the length of hair is even correlated with the quality of the headbanging:

> Done correctly and with long, loose hair, the downward thrust repositions the hair so that it falls down around the face as one faces the folklore. The upthrust neatly repositions it down the back. As one headbanger remarks, the feeling achieved by headbanging is diminished if one does not have long hair.
>
> (Weinstein 2000, pp. 131–32)

Headbanging is of course a fundamentally physical, bodily activity. But the ability and quality of the experience need not depend on any particular bodily attribute. Instead, it has to do with the way the activity is performed, which, as musicologist Stephen Hudson points out, can actually *enhance* the listening experience. "Headbanging," Hudson explains:

> [. . .] thrusts the body's central organs of aural and visual perception downward, with a felt beat occurring at the nadir when the head's descending motion is arrested by jerking the neck muscles, creating a sensation of heavy impact in the head as the brain pushes against the inside of the skull. In other words, headbanging creates heaviness by adding an additional layer of physical impact to whatever is heard or imagined in the sound alone.
>
> (Hudson 2022, p. 123)

But what, more specifically, is it about headbanging that could explain its connection to the *aesthetic* quality of heavy metal music? What kind of practice is headbanging, such that engaging in that practice has a positive bearing on the quality of the music listening experience? Is it a kind of ritual, an activity performed as a traditional accompaniment to the music? Is it a kind of dance, a physical expression of engaging with the music? Is it a means of emotional or psychological release? Or is it something else?

Some Close Contenders: Ritual? Dance? Catharsis?

To better understand what headbanging is, it may be useful to begin by clarifying what it is not. In the case of headbanging, an indirect ontology may be the most useful approach, specifically because headbanging can easily appear as a subspecies of similar practices. Clarifying distinctions between them will highlight what is distinctive about the practice of headbanging.

First, headbanging is not a *ritual*, at least not in the traditional sense. Of course, there is a ritualistic aspect to headbanging, in the sense that it is a familiar and common practice in listening to heavy metal, particularly when performed live. But in contrast to, say, religious or cultural rituals, headbanging is a secondary accompaniment to the musical performance, rather than the other way around. In traditional rituals, such as the Sufi or Berber practice of "headbanging" mentioned earlier, the music is typically subservient to a larger spiritual or communal purpose, such as transcendence, purification, etc. Headbanging to heavy metal, by contrast, is *subordinate* to the music. To put it slightly differently, unlike ritualistic practices, in headbanging the music remains primary; the bodily movement is a *response*—a direct, visceral, and, most importantly, aesthetically engaged response to the musical performance.

Similarly, it is tempting to theorize headbanging as a form of *catharsis*—a practice that releases or even transforms specific emotions. In response to the question of *why* heavy metal fans engage in headbanging, Paul Henry and Marylouise Caldwell maintain that one explanation is that headbanging offers "catharsis via collective ritual" (Henry and Caldwell 2007, p. 164).

There are at least three reasons to be skeptical of characterizing headbanging primarily as a cathartic practice, however. First, this explanatory framework risks instrumentalizing both the music and the experience, reducing headbanging to a tool for emotional hygiene. The idea that heavy metal fans engage in headbanging in pursuit of emotional clarification or purification detracts from the significance of headbanging as responsive to the music (as noted earlier), and also misconstrues the sense in which headbanging is primarily a physical rather than emotional response.

Moreover, even if the physicality of headbanging has a significant emotional impact, it's not clear what kinds of emotions are involved. One of the interesting features of heavy metal music is the complex relation it enables between aesthetic pleasure and the darker range of emotions it traffics in. As Ted Gracyk points out, heavy metal "offers us a complex variant of the problem of why listeners find value in music that is so emotionally negative" (Gracyk 2016, p. 775). Such emotions—anger, frustration, aggression—may or may not be evoked by the music. But more importantly, heavy metal is not emotionally monolithic: it can be mournful, celebratory, fantastical, or even joyful. The kinds of emotions featured in heavy metal songs, which might evoke headbanging, can range from anger to apocalyptic doom, from the thrill of riding lightning to whatever the emotional state is of a wistful journey on a winged dragon through outer space.

Also unclear is what exactly it is that catharsis *does* with such emotions. Does catharsis offer release from specific emotions? Or is it something more like purification or clarification? According to Henry and Caldwell, "headbanging can. . .] not only relieve frustrations and tensions of daily life, but also facilitate enlightenment and moral justification that empower through positive reevaluation of self" (Henry and Caldwell, 2007, p. 159). Though promising and probably to some extent true, such declarations about the benefits of headbanging are empirically squishy, and may even detract from the more salient and interesting features of headbanging, particularly as it relates to the aesthetic experience of music listening. Whatever cathartic value headbanging may have is likely to be a by-product of the much deeper communal, collective experience it affords. As such, the catharsis model oversimplifies the rich variety of affective states headbanging might correspond to, while wrongly subordinating music to mood.

Finally, and more controversially, headbanging is not, strictly speaking, a form of *dance*. Indeed, scholars of heavy metal tend to characterize headbanging this way. "Crucially," writes Stephen Hudson, "headbanging is an improvised dance" (Hudson, 2015). Similarly, Robert Walser claims that the rhythms of heavy metal serve "only to rouse physical energy and cue collective participation in heavy metal's version of dancing, headbanging" (Walser, 1993, p. 49). While it is perfectly reasonable to think of headbanging as dance, there are compelling reasons to resist the temptation to reduce it to this.

Let's dig a bit deeper into this claim. There is a sense in which it is correct to think of headbanging as a form of dance, particularly if theorizing about heavy metal is seen as a natural extension of the aesthetics of rock music. In his seminal essay on rock music aesthetics, Bruce Baugh claims (rightly, I think) that the sine qua non of any philosophical aesthetics of rock is that the music consciously and emphatically resists formalist analysis. The distinctive feature of rock music is that it works on the body, not the mind, and so our qualitative judgments about it are supposed to shift from features like tone and composition to a much simpler matter of whether it makes you want to tap your foot, or bob your head, or dance. "Rock music," he writes:

> from its origins in blues and country and folk traditions, is for dancing. It's got a backbeat, you can't lose it. In dance, the connection between the music in the body of the listener is immediate, felt and enacted rather than thought. The bad rock song is one that tries and fails to inspire the body to dance.
>
> (Baugh, 1993, p. 26)

Given this picture, it's tempting to see headbanging as a similar kind of physical response to the music, a form of dance. However, unlike most forms of dance, headbanging is not choreographed. Nor is headbanging co-performative in the way that dance often is; it is meant not for spectator consumption alongside the music. But more importantly, headbanging is not aesthetically expressive in the way that dance tends to be. Dance typically communicates something through the body—a narrative, an emotion, a cultural identity. Some dance theorists talk about dance as a kind of "kinesthetic communication," as a way of communicating in and through the motions of the body. For example, Carol and Seeley describe a model "of the processes by which we recognize the kinesthetic and expressive qualities of choreographed movements in dance" (Carroll and Seeley, 2013, p. 179). But headbanging does not express in this way. In dance, movements are communicated *to us*, the audience, and invite our aesthetic appreciation, whereas the movements involved in headbanging are an aesthetic response, albeit a specific kind of aesthetic response to a specific kind of music.

So, headbanging is aesthetically receptive rather than expressive. But why does this matter? Because, as I'll explain more fully below, headbanging is in essence a form of aesthetic judgment. What it communicates, more precisely, is a value judgment about the music to which it is responding. The aim of the next section is to gain a better understanding of what specific kind of judgment headbanging is.

The Kinaesthetics of Heaviness

So far, we've seen that headbanging is conceptually distinct from similar practices, particularly insofar as it communicates a specific kind of aesthetic judgment. Here we can begin to qualify this conception a bit further. The first and most obvious thing to note is that headbanging indicates a *positive* aesthetic judgment. It is a gesture of approval, a response that communicates, more precisely, aesthetic *appreciation* of the music. It is, of course, possible to imagine a person making headbanging movements without music, or even along with music they find distasteful or lame. But I think we'd be right in thinking that such cases are not, strictly speaking, instances of headbanging. There may be some alternative explanation for the headbanging-like movement (e.g. a tic, water in the ear, trying to impress a friend, etc.). But headbanging, properly understood, is a gesture of approval, a positive, distinctly aesthetic response to the music.

More significantly, however, headbanging is an *embodied* form of aesthetic judgment. Headbanging literalizes the positive aesthetic response to the music experience in and through bodily movement. As Hudson describes, it "creates heaviness by adding an additional layer of physical impact to whatever is heard. . . the beat occurs at the nadir of the head's downward thrust, where the brain itself is pressed against the skull" (Hudson, 2021, p. 123). The judgment is not formed cognitively and then expressed in physical movement. In other words, it is formed through the body—that is, it is *kinaesthetic* in nature. By headbanging, one *feels* the quality of the music in the body. The ontology of headbanging resides in this kinaesthetic movement, creating an embodied form of aesthetic judgment I call "kinaesthetic judgment." As a kind of aesthetic equivalent to voting with your feet, the bodily movement of headbanging can be understood as communicating a positive form of kinaesthetic judgment about a music listening experience.

The Social Ontology of Headbanging: Controlled Chaos and Collective Individualism

To summarize, headbanging is an embodied form of positive aesthetic judgment. But there is a significant social dimension to headbanging as well, and a deeper understanding of this will further clarify the account of headbanging developed thus far.

The first thing to make clear is that, although headbanging may appear a frantic and chaotic activity (particularly to the outside spectator), it is in fact a deeply *controlled* activity. Its motions follow and reflect the musical structure, particularly the rhythm. With headbanging, timing and precision matter. To headbang off-beat is not only awkward and socially out of sync; it is also aesthetically incoherent, an indication that the movement is not in fact *responding* to the listening experience. The rhythmic control of headbanging indicates a baseline aesthetic appreciation. But typically, the physical rigor of the movement corresponds to the degree of positive judgment: the more intense the headbanging, the more emphatic the approval.

Further, as discussed earlier, headbanging is a social phenomenon insofar as it typically takes place in shared company, at a concert or live performance, for example. It is in this sense a collective activity. Interestingly, however, headbanging is performed in the presence of others, but not necessarily *with* others. That is to say, with headbanging, everyone is, for the most part, doing their own thing. There are no expectations of synchronization or responsiveness in either movement or intensity. Weinstein calls this "togetherness without the expectation of reciprocity." Each headbanger follows their own impulse, their own style, etc. And yet, at the same time, this mostly solitary movement only makes sense within the mass. Said differently, headbanging happens in close proximity to others, but not necessarily in relation to another. In this respect, we might say that headbanging is *collectively individualistic*—an oxymoronic but apt term for the social ontology of metal fandom. Headbangers do their own thing, but they do it together.

One important caveat: headbanging is a sufficient but not necessary condition of aesthetic approval. Headbanging is a specific kind of aesthetic response, but there are, of course, other ways to communicate aesthetic judgment. In fact, one need not actually practice headbanging to be a headbanger. In the case of a positive aesthetic response to the music, one might appreciate the music silently, or it can be signified through other bodily gestures indicating approval (e.g. air guitaring, devil horns). And in the case of aesthetic disapproval (i.e. the music sucks), the heavy metal fan is likely to withhold headbanging until the music delivers what the fan is looking for. In any event, the key takeaway is that headbanging is not merely a physical response but an embodied *judgment*.

So, again, headbanging is *an embodied form of positive* aesthetic judgment. But what specifically is being judged? What aesthetic feature is the aesthetic judgment about? Put simply, heaviness. In metal scholarship, "heaviness" refers to an aesthetic characterized by rhythmic intensity, sonic density, and timbral weight—double bass drums, distorted power chords, growled or screamed vocals, and crashing cymbals. Hudson notes that "metal music is about these physical experiences of rhythmic intensity and change," which is key to its appeal. But as I've argued elsewhere (Miller, 2022), the heaviness of heavy metal music is much more than any specific set of sonic attributes. Even if heaviness cannot be fully articulated conceptually, however, heaviness is nevertheless the aesthetic quality to which headbanging is responsive. Put slightly differently, it is the heaviness of heavy metal that invites listeners to make a judgment about whether the music merits bodily engagement in the form of headbanging.

Tying the different elements together, then, headbanging can be understood more precisely as *the kinaesthetic appreciation of heaviness experienced in the live performance of heavy metal music.*

Conclusion: Headbanging as Embodied Aesthetic Judgment

Headbanging is part ritual, part dance, part cathartic practice, not to mention a particularly fun and invigorating way of engaging with music. But to reduce headbanging to any one of these would miss what is philosophically interesting about it. Headbanging is a form of *kinaesthetic judgment*, an embodied response to the aesthetic experience of heaviness in live heavy metal music. It is not a performance, not an expression, not even a release. It is a way of knowing through the body, a gesture of felt aesthetic affirmation.

In this, headbanging reminds us that aesthetic judgment need not be verbal, nor even cognitive in the traditional sense. Sometimes, to know that something is good, we must feel it in our bones—or, more precisely, in the beat at the base of our skull, where the body meets the music in a shared, rhythmic affirmation of what is heavy.

References

Baugh, B. (1993). Prolegomena to any aesthetics of rock music. *The Journal of Aesthetics and Art Criticism* 51 (1): 23–29.

Carroll, N. and Seeley, W. (2013). Kinesthetic understanding and appreciation in dance. *Journal of Aesthetics and Art Criticism* 71 (2): 177–186.

Gracyk, T. (1996). *Rhythm and Noise: An Aesthetics of Rock*. Duke University Press.

Gracyk, T. (2016). Heavy metal: genre? Style? Subculture? *Philosophy Compass* 11: 775–785.

Henry, P. and Caldwell, M. (2007). Headbanging as resistance or refuge: a Cathartic account. *Consumption Markets & Culture* 10 (2): 159–174.

Hudson, S. (2015). Metal movements: headbanging as a legacy of African American Dance. *Modern Heavy Metal: Markets, Practices and Cultures International Academic Research Conference*, Helsinki, Finland.

Hudson, S. (2022). Bang your head: construing beat through familiar drum patterns in metal music. *Music Theory Spectrum* 44 (1): 221–240.

Islamian, A., Polemikos, M., and Krauss, J.K. (2014). Chronic subdural haematoma secondary to headbanging. *The Lancet* 384 (9937): 102.

Mackenzie, J.M. (1991). Headbanging and fatal subdural haemorrhage. *The Lancet* 338 (8780): 1457–1458.

Miller, J.M. (2022). What makes heavy metal 'heavy'? *The Journal of Aesthetics and Art Criticism* 80 (1): 70–82.

Walser, R. (1993). *Running with the Devil: Power, Gender, and Madness in Heavy Metal Music*. Wesleyan University Press.

Weinstein, D. (2000). *Heavy Metal: The Music and Its Culture*. Da Capo Press.

Chapter 12
Heavy Timbres: What Makes Heavy Music *Heavy*?

James Dow
Philosophy Department, Hendrix College, Conway, AR, USA

What makes heavy music *heavy*? Low-end stringed instruments can be heavier when you tune them down a few steps. If you downtune a guitar from E to C or a five-string bass from a B to an A, and you add distortion and saturation, this provides an aggressively dense low-end sound. You can EQ a bass synth so that sub-bass lower-end frequencies that are closer to 20 Hz can be stacked with the bass tones. That adds an inaudible vibration to the lows that can be felt below the audible 20 Hz. This leads to both a felt heaviness and a heard heaviness in tandem. Kick drums and floor toms can be downtuned as well. With equalizing and muffling, you can make the sound of a kick drum "phat" and "boomy," which most experience as heaviness. These low-end tones can also be compressed so that the low-end tones are felt with constancy across different contacts. Apart from these sonic qualities, aspects of rhythm and structure might be experienced as heavy. Slow dragging tempos without any swing can be experienced as depth of the earth heaviness. Palm muting a guitar so that less treble tone comes through, and the attack of the rhythm of the guitar is experienced as blows to our viscera. Playing in minor keys, especially harmonic minor, or employing the "devil's interval" or tritones, or downward chromatic movement in a scale can produce experiences of heaviness. When lyrics focus on death, dread, nihilism, or darkness, the experience of the abyss can be felt as a type of heaviness.

Notice that I have attempted here to describe heaviness directly as a tone quality without relying on talking about either heavy metal or particular examples of heaviness.[1] Of course, fans of heavy metal, especially of doom metal like Sleep's "Dopesmoker,"[2] might register the description above as what makes such music heavy metal heavy. However, there are metal-adjacent, post-metal, and even nonmetal songs that are experienced as being heavy. For example, the Melvins' song "Boris"[3] can be described as heavy in these ways even if it's questionable whether the Melvins play heavy metal strictly speaking. (And the band named Boris also makes heavy music that's categorized as droney noisey shoegaze.) In addition, post-metal bands like Russian Circles's song "Calla"[4] fit the descriptions of heaviness above, but as post-metal Russian Circles and other bands are moving beyond the traditional expectations of most metal genres. Chelsea Wolfe's song "Spun"[5] is without a doubt heavy, though metal fans might hear Wolfe's music as mixing gothic rock and folk. Jesu's track "Conquerer"[6] doesn't start out heavy, but when the initial progression drops, it's experienced as heavy. But most people locate Jesu's music in the shoegaze genre even if Justin Broadrick was the lead singer of the metal band Godflesh. Maybe departing even further from metal, Parliament's tune "Flash Light"[7] can be experienced as heavy because of the equalizing of the low-end razor bass tone. Even apart from popular music, Chopin's "Piano Sonata No. 2 in Bb Minor, Op. 35 'Funeral

[1] For a playlist of Heavy Examples, please listen to this https://open.spotify.com/playlist/796YOT7GelYc0dRwvAtnbm?si=862c6474a8fa4612.

[2] Sleep Dopesmoker 2022 Remastered Version Third Man Records 2022.

[3] Melvins Bullhead Boner 1991.

[4] Russian Circles Guidance Sargent House 2016.

[5] Chelsea Wolfe Hiss Spun Sargent House 2017.

[6] Jesu Conquerer Avalanche Recordings 2007.

[7] Parliament Funkentelechy vs. The Placebo Syndrome Mercury Records 1977.

March': III. Marche Funèbre: Lento"[8] has a heaviness in the use of the low end of the piano, in the sludgy rhythm, and in the theme of death throughout. Rap can also be heavy like Rico Nasty's song "Rage"[9] with its use of sub-bass in the kick drum, the doubling of the bass line, and the EQ filtering dropping into the low end when the beat drops. Some songs take a little more auditory squinting, but with some openness, even the Eurythmics "Sweet Dreams"[10] can be experienced as being heavy because of the bass synth and the hitting of the kick drum and echoing low tom punches every other measure. And, listening to Nukariik's "The River,"[11] a wonderful example of Inuit throat singing, involves a depth that most voices cannot achieve, a cavernous resonance in the low end of the vocal chords. One point I want to make with these examples is that heaviness can be considered to be a timbre of musical sounds that is not limited to the various heavy metal genres, even if these descriptions do admittedly highlight the tone qualities of doom metal, sludge metal, or drone metal. Another point I want to make is that if we accept the first point, then we need to inquire about what makes heavy music heavy, distinct from heavy metal.

A recent paper, however, by Jay Miller "What Makes Heavy Metal Heavy?" takes up the question of heaviness in ways that will be helpful to make our way to the account of heaviness discussed in this paper. Miller uses as his central example Sleep's *Dopesmoker* because Miller suggests that *Dopesmoker* is the heaviest album of all time. There's no question that *Dopesmoker* is #heavyAF. However, with any superlative claims such as these, we can usually come up with a counterexample. For example, Miller never mentions Meshuggah's album *Nothing*.[12] Even though he mentions Sunn O))) as a band, Miller never discusses *Monoliths and Dimensions*, which many would argue is even heavier than *Dopesmoker*. "Aghartha" on *Monoliths and Dimensions*[13] has a sub-bass drone that swallows your viscera, tempos that crawl through the mud, themes that are emotionally deep, and a monolithic low end that brings you below an

[8] Chopin Piano Sonatas Nos. 1–3, Mazurkas, Op. 17 and Etudes Leif Ove Andsnes Parlophone Records 1992.

[9] Rico Nasty Sugar Trap 2018.

[10] Eurythmics Sweet Dreams (Are Made of This) SONY BMG Music Entertainment 1983.

[11] Nukariik Inuit Throat Songs and Drumming Nukarik 2008.

[12] Meshuggah Nothing Reigning Phoenix Music 2002.

[13] Sunn O))) Monoliths and Dimensions.

abyss you didn't know was there. *Dopesmoker* is a meditation on heaviness, while *Monoliths and Dimensions* engulfs you with heaviness.

Apart from the question of what album is heaviest of all time, we also need to consider, as we did above with genre, whether thinking about the heaviest album of all time is a good guide to understanding the nonaesthetic and aesthetic properties of heaviness. Any particular example would be unlikely to capture all of the nonaesthetic and aesthetic properties of heaviness. The reason is that albums are expressions of a band at a particular moment in their development, with a particular set of intentions, and sets of constraints that confine the album's process (some intentional and some unintentional). Even if a band set out to make the heaviest album of all time, they may not be able to achieve it for a variety of reasons.

Jay Miller's position in "What Makes Heavy Metal 'Heavy'?" is that the concept of "heaviness" is inarticulable, irreducible, and impossible to define. We will call this "Heaviness Mysterianism" and the basic claim of heaviness mysterianism is that "you know heaviness when you hear it" is the best you can do. Just like other examples of mystery, we have an experience of something beyond us that seems ineffable, we cannot put into words, or seems transcendental, it's beyond being, or seems unknowable, it's beyond our cognitive ken. It may be that heaviness is a type of aesthetic experience that presents itself as *you understand it when you experience it,* but any attempt to capture that experience with any representations falls short. The best you can do is, like the Grim Reaper, point from out of the darkness to the darkness that envelops you.

In this essay, I will argue against Heaviness Mysterianism by suggesting that Miller's arguments do not adequately support Heaviness Mysterianism. And, beyond the analysis of the arguments, Miller hasn't considered ways to positively articulate "heaviness" as a timbral concept. In the introduction above, I gestured at ways that heaviness might be understood that at least gets such a timbral description going. Fans may not be headbanging to the description, but at least they will be nodding, and that's enough to disperse some of the mystery. What are Miller's arguments for Heaviness Mysterianism? I will provide an analysis of the arguments that Miller implicitly relies upon in "What Makes Heavy Metal 'Heavy'?"

The first argument's conclusion is that heaviness is inarticulable, irreducible, and impossible to define. The general motivation for this conclusion seems to be that some aesthetic properties can be experienced by subjects, but that, nevertheless, such aesthetic properties are in principle inarticulable. Heaviness is inarticulable in the sense that whatever language we use to describe it, such language comes up short. The conditions for applying the concept of heaviness cannot be made transparent. Miller suggests that if an aesthetic concept does not have necessary and sufficient conditions for application, then that concept is inarticulable, irreducible, and impossible to define (Miller 2022, p. 71). If we cannot answer what's required to make a song heavy, then we cannot define heaviness. If we cannot answer what's enough to make a song heavy, then we cannot define heaviness. One question that arises immediately here is whether the general principle would have the consequence that most aesthetic concepts would be surrounded by an *in principle* air of mystery that Miller suggests surrounds heaviness. That may be an implication we would not welcome.

When we pick up a large porcelain vessel that's about the size of a basketball, we can say that the vessel is heavy. There may be a heaviest vessel ever made, and it would be easily determined by weighing it against other vessels. Some porcelain vessels *seem* lighter in the sense that the white color, the soft texture, and porcelain itself is associated with airier pieces. But, of all the materials, if we made a larger vessel of porcelain, it would be experienced as heavy. It isn't required, however, to make a heavy vessel for it to be made out of porcelain because it could be made of earthenware. And it's not enough for something to be made of porcelain for it to be heavy, because a light, fragile teacup could be made of porcelain. But, we don't conclude from the idea that porcelain isn't necessary or sufficient for heaviness in vessels that heaviness is *in principle*, inarticulable.

But maybe heaviness in music is sufficiently different. What's Miller's argument that heaviness doesn't have necessary and sufficient conditions in heavy metal? The major claim is that heaviness does not have necessary and sufficient conditions for application, but instead has incompatible properties in the context of heavy metal. Heaviness might be understood in terms of being loud, distorted, and powerful, according to Miller (2022, pp. 75–78). Miller suggests there's some metal that's heavy but not loud, not distorted, and not powerful, and there's some metal that's loud, distorted, and powerful but isn't experienced as heavy. But that particular argument isn't presented in the paper. The putative incompatible properties that are mentioned have to do with whether the metal is fast or slow, high-pitched or low-pitched vocals, or have themes of death or not. Instead, it is suggested that if we increased the loudness, distortion, and powerfulness of a song, we wouldn't necessarily be making it more heavy (Miller 2022, p. 77). But just because there's an upper limit to the effectiveness of loudness, distortion, and power, doesn't mean that loudness, distortion, and power aren't core to the concept of heaviness. As we will see below, distortion itself as a timbral concept does embed in it sensitivity to ambiguously playing with sound being deformed.

The argument that Miller wants to present is that heaviness is inarticulable, irreducible, and impossible to define, and therefore mysterious as an aesthetic concept. He does so by relying upon two major accounts of aesthetic concepts to make the point. Miller discusses Frank Sibley's (1959) ideas that aesthetic concepts do not have necessary and sufficient conditions for application, and also discusses Kendall Walton's (1970) ideas that aesthetic judgments employing concepts are based on understanding the categories of art, which are grounded in art history and the art world's uses of such concepts. However, Sibley's and Walton's ideas don't support heaviness mysterianism.

Sibley does argue that there aren't necessary and sufficient conditions for a sculpture being fragile. There are no definitive rules of application for the concept of fragility. However, Sibley doesn't suggest that this means that aesthetic concepts are mysterious. Sibley's view leaves room for the idea that there's a relationship between nonaesthetic properties of the work and aesthetic properties of the work. With the appropriately cultivated sensibility, a person could articulate the aesthetic concept and say more than that there's a "distinctive know-it-when-I-hear-it character of heaviness" (Miller 2022, p. 71). On Sibley's account of aesthetic concepts, cultivating the sensibility with the concept of heaviness would involve tracking the emergent relationships between at least the nonaesthetic properties I mentioned above, loudness of amps in live performances; overdrive, distortion, and fuzz guitar timbres; downtuning and low-end resonance of guitars; power and constancy in kick drum pattern; and low-end equalizing of kick drum, floor toms, and bass layers, and the aesthetic properties of heaviness as the tone quality of the experience. Of course, listeners would not need to have a complete understanding of the nonaesthetic properties in order to experience music as being heavy, but listeners who cultivated their sensibility by listening for the emergent relationships between the nonaesthetic and aesthetic properties would be more sensitive to the variation in the heaviness.

According to Walton's category theory, aesthetic judgments like "*Monoliths and Dimensions* is the heaviest album of all time," and

"*Monoliths and Dimensions* is heavier than *Dopesmoker*" are judgments that are category relative. The benefit of Walton's category theory is that there are correctness conditions for judgments about both aesthetic properties and aesthetic value of works of art. Aesthetic judgments are guided by categories of art history, art theory, and art criticism, which are proposed as being in opposition to Sibley's noncognitive perceptual account of aesthetic concepts. A work's aesthetic properties depend not only on its nonaesthetic ones, but also on which of its nonaesthetic properties are "standard," which "variable," and which "contra-standard." Nonaesthetic properties are *standard* when they are a determinate feature of category membership, *variable* when the feature is irrelevant to category membership, and *contra-standard* when features tend to rule out category membership.

The standard features of heavy metal as a genre category of music would be loudness, distortion, and use of power chords, and grasping the gestalt of the category is central to grasping the standard features of that category. The variable properties are whether there are vocals or not, for instance, in instrumental post-metal like Russian Circles, the music is heavy, but there are no vocals. Or whether the tempo is slow, for example sludge metal like Crowbar, or fast, for example speed metal like Exciter. Both band's music is still categorized as metal and still experienced as being heavy even if they use vastly different tempos.

Miller asks the general question "What is the Gestalt property of heavy metal?" as a way to articulate the aesthetic property of heaviness in the context of Walton's category theory. He suggests "the Gestalt of heavy metal is treated as a kind of Lockean abstract idea, a common denominator of the heavy metal sound consisting of stylistic features broadly shared among a diverse set of musical exemplars" (Miller 2022, p. 73). Miller suggests that there is no standard features of the heavy metal genre because there are so many differences among different subgenres. However, I would argue that heaviness as an aesthetic property can be realized differently in different subgenres without thereby threatening to make heaviness something that is inarticulable. Grasping the gestalt of a general category of "heavy metal" is much more difficult than grasping the gestalt of a particular category of "funeral doom metal." Walton's own account can make sense of how heaviness might be a standard, variable, or contra-standard aesthetic property within specific genre categories. Walton suggests that perceivers successfully recognize aesthetic features of a category because of familiarity with members of that category, what others have said regarding works they have experienced, or how perceivers are introduced to a given work. The standard properties within the category of funeral doom metal are slow tempos, low-tuned guitars, vocals, and lyrics expressing doom and despair associated specifically with mourning practices, progressions that draw on funeral dirges, guttural vocals that are cathedral reverbed, hauntingly atmospheric synths, and key sounds. Sure, there are disagreements about how we should characterize funeral doom metal, but disagreements don't amount to *in principle* mystery.

The first mystery argument that Miller presents is that heaviness is inarticulable, irreducible, and impossible to define, because in order to define heaviness, we would need to outline necessary and sufficient conditions for the application of heaviness, but there aren't such conditions for heaviness. However, as we have seen, we can articulate and define heaviness without accounting for the necessary and sufficient conditions, on both Sibley's and Walton's accounts of aesthetic concepts.[14] Therefore, the first mystery argument doesn't support the idea that heaviness is as much of a mystery as Miller suggests.

The second mystery argument is related to the first but is more explicit about how we understand music genres. Miller argues that if heavy metal can't be defined as a genre, then heaviness can't be defined. The idea is that aesthetic properties track the genre categories they are associated with. If such categories are not well-behaved as categories, then neither are the features that are associated with those categories. Given that heavy metal can be broken down into speed metal, thrash metal, death metal, black metal, doom metal, sludge metal, and post-metal, heavy metal can't be defined as a genre. Miller suggests this is because of Gracyk's (2016) dilemma: if we define heavy metal generally, then it's not a meaningful category; if we define it more particularly, in terms of subgenres, then it's not a meaningful category, but gets replaced. Miller suggests that this implies that given that heavy metal cannot be defined, it follows that we cannot grasp the genre category-relative concept of heaviness that is standard for heavy metal.

---

[14] I haven't said much about the claim of irreducibility of the aesthetic property of heaviness, because I would argue that many aesthetic properties are emergent properties and as such resist reduction to a set of non-aesthetic properties. Both Sibley and Walton, in different ways, suggest that aesthetic properties are emergent properties, but would both resist the idea that it follows that we cannot articulate such concepts.

A worry about this argument is that we don't need to articulate heaviness in the context of the general genre category of heavy metal. Even if we focus on Miller's question "What makes heavy metal heavy?" It's conceivable that our priorities in questioning *could* begin with "What makes heavy music heavy?" and only after assessing how heaviness manifested in the variety of genres and subgenres of heavy metal as they developed. Most metal fans would accept that the various subgenres of metal would manifest different types of heaviness in different ways.[15] So there would be no assumption that if we did investigate the aesthetic property of heaviness as a category-relative property, we would need to do so within the general category.

For speed metal and thrash metal, heaviness is aggressive, persistent, and powerful. For sludge metal and doom metal, heaviness is low, dark, and despairing. The idea here is that heaviness can manifest in different subgenres and in different bands of subgenres. Black metal surfaces in several different subgenres with different types of heaviness. Bathory's *Blood Fire Death* is a huge inspiration to black metal bands. Agalloch's album *The Mantle* brings black metal to an atmospheric folk heaviness. Alcest's *Spiritual Instinct* brings black metal into contact with the types of heaviness we find in shoegaze. Discussing post-metal heaviness would be a helpful way to make sense of this phenomenon. Post-metal bands like Red Sparowes, Russian Circles, Pelican, and Caspian play heavy music, but with a more instrumental, atmospheric, post-apocalyptic soundtrack style. What makes them post-metal is that they seem to shed the associations with other genres of heavy metal while maintaining the core of the heaviness aesthetic.

My point is that when we notice that with the development of subgenres within heavy metal, while this may make the genre category of heavy metal either no longer helpful (or may require using the category "traditional heavy metal"), that's no reason for pessimism about articulating heaviness as an aesthetic property within each of these subgenres of heavy metal. Focusing on the variations in timbral style of different bands, albums, songs in different genres helps us to clarify the phenomenon of heaviness, it doesn't make it more mysterious.

This brings us to the third argument that Miller presents for his Heaviness Mysterianism. Miller argues for the view that a timbral account

---

[15] One place to do quick comparisons of different genres is to browse the various metal genres at https://everynoise.com/.

of heaviness is not sufficient to capture what makes heavy music heavy. I will discuss timbre in more detail below; however, a theory of timbre is a theory of the tone quality of music. It accounts for what makes for the distinctive "what it's like" qualitative feel of a voice or an instrument that makes it stand out apart from the contribution of pitch, intensity, and loudness. An oboe and a piano could play the same pitch, a middle C, with the same intensity, the same loudness, but be perceived as being different because of their distinctive timbres of the instruments. Miller doesn't go into this level of detail about what timbre is, but instead aligns it with the surplus noise account of rock and suggests that the surplus noise account could describe the heaviness of heavy metal. However, this doesn't show an appreciation for the complexities of what an account of timbre could do for our aesthetic appreciation of heaviness.

According to Miller, the major question is whether we can make judgments like "X is heavier than Y" (comparative judgments) and "x is the heaviest" (superlative judgments), focusing on timbre. Miller suggests that if we cannot make comparative judgments like "Diocletian's song 'Wretched Sons'[16] is heavier than Aosoth's song 'An Arrow in Heart'"[17] and superlative judgments like "*Monoliths and Dimensions* is the heaviest drone metal album of all time" by focusing on the tone quality of heaviness, then a timbral account of heaviness is not sufficient. He argues that we can't make such judgments focusing on timbre. Therefore, a timbral account of heaviness is not sufficient.

Miller makes this argument in his conclusion to the paper:

> the more nuanced judgments of heaviness familiar to metalheads go well beyond the features of loudness, distortion, and the expression of power. And yet, analysis of further conditions of heaviness, such as lyrical content or compositional elements, only confirms that "heaviness" resists exhaustive conceptual articulation. Nor does this seem to be a matter of just refining definitions and qualifying necessary and sufficient conditions more precisely. Rather, the difficulty seems to stem from there being different conceptions of heaviness, comprised of radically different, sometimes incompatible, properties. Sometimes heaviness sounds like heavy metal music, sometimes it does not. Sometimes heaviness is expressed as power, sometimes it is not. Heaviness is, in

[16] Diocletian Gusundrian Osmose Productions 2014.
[17] Aosoth An Arrow in Heart Agonia Records 2013.

> some cases, the surplus "noise" of rock, in other cases it is much more than this. It is both extremely fast and yet extremely slow; both simple and complex; both frantic and restrained. It is manifested in the raucous stirrings of a mosh pit, but also in contemplative meditation. And even if it cannot be wholly understood through all these diverse and contrasting forms, the heaviness of heavy metal can certainly be heard in any and all of them.
>
> (Miller 2022, pp. 80–81)

This quote expresses the pessimism implicit in Miller's heaviness mysterianism. As I have discussed above, I agree with Miller that we should do our best to capture the phenomenon of heaviness without attempting to provide necessary and sufficient conditions for the concept. We should not attempt to reduce heaviness to properties that rule out differences across subgenres, bands, albums, and songs. We should not align heaviness with one particular nonaesthetic or aesthetic property.

Is there any hope for an account of heaviness that doesn't attempt to achieve that type of absolute articulation, while still describing the phenomenon of heaviness as an aesthetic property? Even if doom metal albums like Electric Wizard's *Dopethrone* are personally and subjectively experienced from my point of view as heavier than Sleep's *Dopesmoker*, and even if Sunn O)))'s *Monoliths and Dimensions* is personally and subjectively experienced from my perspective as the heaviest metal album of all time, I think it's important that the conversation not stop with a few counterexamples. A healthy back and forth about differences in genre expectations is important here. Most importantly, a discussion of the timbre of the various types of heaviness that emerge in these albums is important. We shouldn't let our pessimism about reaching an intersubjective agreement stop us from having a conversation about the complexities of what we hear and listen to.

I think what we learn from engaging with Miller's arguments is not that we should accept Heaviness Mysterianism. I think we learn that aesthetic concepts like "heaviness" need not be defined with necessary and sufficient conditions in order to be articulable. If you squint, this is exactly Frank Sibley's point he's making about aesthetic concepts. Part of cultivating a sensibility with aesthetic concepts is working up the skill of making your way from the nonaesthetic properties of heaviness, the perceived differences between the different examples of what allows heaviness to emerge, and the phenomenological differences between the way that heaviness is experienced by different subjects. To adopt a non-cognitivist account of aesthetic concepts involves committing to the view that knowledge, belief, and thought about concepts or categories aren't always necessary to our aesthetic appreciation. In this particular context, one could cultivate the skill of aesthetically appreciating the heaviness of Deafheaven's *Sunbather* even without knowing that Deafheaven is one of the bands responsible for bringing about blackgaze, a mix of black metal and shoegaze styles, as a genre. But we don't need to assume that if we were to provide an account of heaviness, it would have to be a cognitivist account of "heaviness" to describe what makes heavy music heavy, pace Walton's approach to aesthetic judgments.

Also, even if we accept that Walton's category theory helps us to understand the development of genre categories, we need to recognize that simply because a genre has variable properties (even incompatible variable properties) does not mean the genre does not have standard properties or contra-standard properties that can help us to construct a category. Miller's quote above misses this insight from Walton's category theory. High tempo might be a standard property for speed metal, but vocals are sometimes throat-ripping shrieking and sometimes guttural monotonic moaning, and thus might be a variable property for speed metal. But, low tempo might be a standard property for drone metal. For some instrumental doom metal projects like Bongripper's *Terminal*, vocals are variable because they aren't involved at all. This doesn't mean that we cannot still articulate the particular timbres of heaviness found in these bands and albums. It just means we need to approach the question with a more fine-grained sensibility. A general point as well that follows from this is that we don't need to articulate "heaviness" in the context of the genre of heavy metal at all. It might be that a category-independent exploration of heaviness as a timbre of heavy music would be more instructive for an exploration of how each of the subgenres that developed in the history—speed metal, thrash metal, doom metal, sludge metal, death metal, black metal, nu metal, and post-metal. It's likely that the diverse timbres of heaviness developed in these different subcultures, each in their own way. Rather than being pessimistic and mysterian about heaviness, I would suggest that the love of heavy metal involves the exploration and discovery of how heaviness emerged with many different timbres in different contexts. But that might require admitting that heaviness can be found in classical music, in the blues, in rock, in punk, in Americana, and even in jazz. I am willing to accept that as a positive feature of the movement toward describing what it's like to experience heavy timbres.

My suggestion is therefore that we need to investigate the key features of heavy timbre optimistically. So the question will become "What makes heavy music heavy" or more particularly, "What is it like to experience heavy timbre in music?" I would suggest that rather than thinking of aesthetic concepts as definitions involving necessary and sufficient conditions, we can think of aesthetic concepts as *proxytypes*. Proxytypes are complex collective representations stored in our collective memory that are abstracted from associated perceptions.[18] The first thing to notice about proxytypes is that they begin with perception as the basis of the concept: concepts as proxytypes are empirical representations grounded in sensation and perception. Aesthetic proxytypes, as I understand them, are more than sensations and perceptions related to forms or structures, however. Aesthetic proxytypes also include elaborations of those perceptions into aesthetic experiences. A part of this view is that anything that can be perceived can be perceived aesthetically[19] by elaborating a proxytype with various aesthetic types that abstract from the experience.

When we perceive the kick drum, the bass guitar, and the rhythm guitar dropping in unison in Bongripper's song "Doom" at 10.30, fans collectively abstract from that perception using it as a *stand in* or *a typical example* of a solid "drop." As the riff gets more solid in the last third of the song, emerging through a wall of noise, all instruments come down on the one, then there's silence for three beats of the measure, and then the riff that's been developing throughout the epic song comes in without the noise. Of course, there's not only that example but there are several examples of heavy drops that make the complex web of what it means to be a solid drop in a song. In addition, there are different forms of heaviness that emerge from those drops, given the various ways that the collective memory of fans represents such drops. (Think about how metal bands often hold the silence for longer than one measure when playing live to increase the anticipation.) Such aesthetic concepts as proxytypes

[18] I recognize that proxytype theory (especially Prinz's (2002)) usually approaches the definition of proxytypes through an individualist lens by focusing on mental representations that are stored in long term memory, and I agree with that way of explaining and predicting individual psychology, but for the purpose of this paper, I want to pitch the account of proxytype as a socially external concept. To put it bluntly, I think that our questions are best pursued through music sociology rather than solely music psychology.

[19] Cf. Ziff (1979).

wouldn't have necessary and sufficient conditions for application because they are bottom-up representations rather than top-down representations. We can even leave room for there being nonlinguistic and nonconceptual representations on this view, namely collective representations of the experience of the body-crushing sound of witnessing Sunn O))) play *Monoliths and Dimensions* in a live performance. We will return to this later when we discuss the error theory that explains why it *seems* like heaviness is ineffable.

Another feature of the view that I am recommending is that we need to think about the aesthetics of music as involving an individual and collective cultivation of sensibility. Rather than conceiving of the aesthetics of music in terms of a cognitivist account, we can focus on skills of our perceptual sensibility, which involves tracing relationships between nonaesthetic properties and aesthetic properties. We have sensations and perceptions of the nonaesthetic properties of a bass guitar downtuned to C, low EQed so that the frequencies at 80 Hz are increased, and with fuzz, delay, and reverb added. We trace these nonaesthetic properties through abstraction to the aesthetic properties of an experience of heaviness that is felt as nothingness emerging from the abyss and swallowing us with its depth.

It's important for the cultivation of that sensibility to be able to witness different of these abstraction paths from the nonaesthetic to the aesthetic emerging in different contexts: recorded and live; in a bar, at a festival or even in The Caverns in Tennessee; within different subgenres of metal; with different tempos; with riffs in unison and riffs that are harmonically stacked; with or without vocals; vocals that sound like shrieking and vocals that sound like droning, etc. The import of an account of aesthetic concepts that is based on a type of perceptual sensibility is that we can *know how* to recognize heaviness even without *knowing what* heaviness is formally or structurally. Part of the issue with Miller's approach to heaviness is that he assumes that if heaviness were articulable, then it would have to be through a cognitive account of heaviness grounded in heavy metal categories, but the benefit of focusing on our perceptual sensibility as the basis for heaviness makes this assumption seem unreasonable. Daft Punk's bass synth line in "Voyager"[20] is deep and heavy even if it's not at all metal.

[20] Daft Punk Discovery Warner Music France/ADA France 2001.

Another feature of the view that I am presenting is that we can shift away from framing the question of the aesthetics of heaviness in terms of a dilemma between the subjectivity of heaviness (I know it when I hear it) and the objectivity of heaviness—the need to provide an absolute Platonic form of heaviness that enables us to answer our ultimate questions like "What's the heaviest metal song of all time?" I think that the oscillation between the subjective and the objective that guides this type of question should be replaced with an intersubjective phenomenological approach which privileges subjective experiences of heaviness, what it's like to experience heaviness in music, but also frames the concept of heaviness as based in collective experiences that are part of a collective memory. That type of intersubjective web of abstractions is as objective a picture as we need to articulate heaviness.

So what is the heavy timbre proxytype then? As I mentioned above, music theory doesn't really have an adequate theory of timbre. Timbre, or tone quality, is the perceived quality of a note, sound, or tone, e.g. take two notes that are identical in pitch, intensity, and loudness but differ in tone quality, and the perceived difference between the two tone qualities is the timbre. The Acoustical Society of America definition is "That multidimensional attribute of auditory sensation which enables a listener to judge that two non-identical sounds, similarly presented and having the same loudness, pitch, spatial location, and duration, are dissimilar. Timbre is related to sound quality, often specified by qualitative adjectives (e.g., bright or dull)."[21] Timbre is central to understanding musical experience, especially since most contemporary music is created with pedals and effects. Of course, heaviness can be found in the voices of the Inuit throat singers, in the tones of an octobass, in the drones of the tanpura, or the airy heaviness of the shruti box. But, for the most part, heaviness is experienced in the context of electric instruments connected to amps with heads and cabinets, run through analog and digital pedals and effects, and then miked and then run through a mixer with equalizers and more effects before being sent through PA speakers to the audience.

I would suggest that to describe heavy timbres, we should employ an enactivist approach to the aesthetics of music. An enactivist approach to aesthetics argues that perception in aesthetic appreciation is not merely passive but, instead, that aesthetic appreciation is action-oriented. In particular, listening for heaviness in music is more than merely hearing

[21] https://asastandards.org/terms/timbre/.

heaviness, because we are doing something to bring out the experience for ourselves. When we listen to music, timbre can be understood in terms of the agent bonding with the source, which supports what's called a "source-bonding" account of timbre (Clarke 2005, p. 93). A tendency in music theory is to attempt to account for all aspects of musical appreciation within musical parameters such as form, harmony, and meter, but timbre is the aspect of music that is intuitively more accessible to the average listener. When we listen to a sound, we track what the cause or origin of the sound is. When we hear thunder, we look into the distance to see the patterns in the clouds. When we hear a tree branch crack while on a hike, we look above in the canopy to see the exposed wood that shows us the crack. Similarly, when we hear a low drone tone, we listen for the cause or the source of the sound.

Another important phenomenon that is relevant is "source-deformation" which is the perceptual experience of sounds that resists source-bonding between subject and object. For instance, when effects transform the sound from what's recognized as a guitar into noise that is experienced not as a guitar but as an unfathomable growl of heaviness. Some types of heaviness are experienced differently because the source, either the kick, the bass, the guitar, the synth or the vocals have been transformed in the signal chain. Source deformation makes the listener engage in activities of imagining what the source or origin of the sound is in ways that encourage active listening. But, also, that imagining is developed over time through repeated listening, through watching live performances, through talking about how different heavy sounds are made with fans, and, sometimes, by being a musician with similar equipment to develop simulations of the sound on the album. That type of collective imagining of the path from the stage at which the instrument is struck to the listener's constructions of the source and origin of the sound is pivotal to the enactive appreciation of the sound. What is the tone quality of heaviness that listeners collectively focus on?

Now that we have articulated the proxytype account of aesthetic concepts and outlined what an enactivist approach to listening would involve, we can approach the different features of heaviness that listeners are collectively listening for. Not enough consideration has been given in the aesthetics of heaviness to the following: loudness of amps in live performances; differences between overdrive, distortion, and fuzz guitar timbres; downtuning and low-end resonance of guitars; power and constancy in kick drum pattern; and low-end equalizing of kick drum, floor toms, and bass layers. Listening to a live performance of heavy music is vastly different from listening to a recorded album of heavy music. The combination of high-watt amps and PA systems can create decibel levels reaching around 130 dB, on some occasions, the ceilings and walls fall apart. Such loudness cannot be achieved in an average home. But, more importantly, the live performance is an experience of access to the source of the sound to which one is listening. Guitarists occasionally use bass amps, like Josh Homme of Queens of the Stone Age, with higher wattage to be able to reach low frequencies that other guitar amps do not capture.

Something else that's important to the tone quality of guitars is the differences between overdrive, distortion, and fuzz. Overdrive pedals add warmth, sustain, and grit to a guitar tone. When a guitarist plays heavier, the sound is more present. When the guitarist plays lighter, the distortion is less pronounced. Overdrive is usually associated with proto-metal or traditional metal guitar tones, like AC/DC Angus Young's guitar tone. Distortion is heavier than overdrive, because distortion involves a clipping of the sound, which causes the sound to break up. Such clipping introduces harmonics and depth to the sound that is experienced as aggressive, saturated, and "chuggy." Distortion is usually associated with thrash metal guitar tones in Metallica, Slayer, Megadeth, and Anthrax. Fuzz goes beyond distortion in its tone because it breaks up the signal in ways that corrupt the pitch, introduce additional noise, add a buzzing sound, and often involves square wave leaps up and down in tone that create a hollow, raspy, tearing sound. All of these effects are differently important to the tone quality of heaviness.

Downtuning also adds to the tone quality of heaviness. A traditional six-string electric guitar standard tuning is EADGBE, but guitarists wanting to achieve a heavier sound downtune to drop C tuning CGCFAD. Downtuning makes the strings able to reach lower pitches, which gives a fuller, more deep sound. When strings are tuned lower, the strings produce different overtones than standard tuning, which produces a heavier sound. Downtuning can make strings more pliable, so often guitarists who want a heavier tone will increase the gauge on the strings as well as downtune, which makes the guitar tone heavier. A drop C tuning also allows power chords to be formed with a single finger across the bottom three strings. This enables the guitarists to create a solid vibration, which is often mixed with palm muting to make the friction of the strings being struck central to the tone. Attack, which is the build-up from silence to peak volume, can be rapid which adds to the heaviness of the tone. The more defined the transient peaks of the sound are, the more powerful and aggressive the sound will be.

Low EQ also adds to the tone quality of heaviness. For any instrument, but used mostly to make bass guitars sound heavy, is scooping the mids, cutting around 500–800 Hz. If sound engineers want to make a bass guitar sound heavier, they can boost the low frequencies from 80 to 250 Hz and cut the mid frequencies from 250 to 500 Hz. This makes the low end come out without muddiness and allows the high frequencies to contrast with the low end. However, there are heavy sounds that arise, for example in dark ambient music that are achieved through selective EQing of the lower frequency lows below 80 Hz. By filtering out high frequencies and selectively deepening low frequencies, musicians like Lustmord can highlight the heaviness of cave sounds, for example in his album *Alter*. Also, most effects like compression, fuzz, modulators, delay, and reverb also have selective EQ so that you can make the effect itself as its own EQ that can change how the heaviness within that effect is experienced. Of course, none of these tone qualities are either necessary or sufficient for heaviness, but instead are the types of listening that might be involved in source-bonding or in source deformation that enables listeners to hear heavy timbres, thereby adding to the proxytype of heaviness.

So, I have provided a description of what makes heavy music heavy in terms of heavy timbres that listeners can become sensitive to. But, I haven't addressed why it *seems* that heaviness is mysterious. Any attempt to argue for a less pessimistic account of the emergence of heavy timbres needs to say why heaviness seems mysterious to us. An error theory of the mystery of heaviness would say why, though it seems like heaviness is mysterious, there are reasons why it's seeming that way can be accounted for without accepting heaviness as mysterious.

First, because the account that's presented here is a noncognitivist account that focuses on perceptual sensibility to heaviness, the lack of a cognitive and/or conceptual account can offer us a reason why it seems like heaviness is mysterious. Heaviness is felt in our bodies, in our viscera, resonates with our nonconscious experience, engages with our perceptions in ways that tap into the complex relations between perception, feelings, emotions, sentiments, memories, and imagination. Just because such experiences are ineffable, or not available to conscious report, or seem to outstrip our concepts, that doesn't mean we cannot express both the aesthetic experiences of heaviness and our appreciation of how the sources of the sound contribute to our perceptions.

Lastly, it is part and parcel of a source-deformation account of timbre that heaviness is experienced as coming from a seemingly unknown source or origin. It's no surprise, according to a source-deformation account, that the lack of bonding with the source of the sound would also add the sentiment of mystery to our experience. Of course, that's one of the wonderful features of the way that art moves us: it creates a type of wonder about how the artwork has managed to affect us in the way it has. Given that heaviness as an aesthetic experience is created through patterns of nonaesthetic properties that themselves have been deformed through downtuning guitars, various pedals and effects, amps, and equalizers at multiple stages, it isn't surprising that heavy timbres leave us wondering. So, while it appears that heaviness is something that is inarticulable, irreducible, and impossible to define, if we approach the phenomenon of heaviness through an enactivist account of the proxytypes of the various heavy timbres, the mystery can be dissolved.

References

Clarke, E. (2005). *Ways of Listening: An Ecological Approach to Musical Perception*. Oxford: Oxford University Press.

Gracyk, T. (2016). Heavy metal: genre? Style? Subculture? *Philosophy Compass* 11: 775–785.

Miller, J. (2022). What makes heavy metal heavy? *The Journal of Aesthetics and Art Criticism* 80: 70–82.

Prinz, J. (2002). *Furnishing the Mind: Concepts and Their Perceptual Basis*. Boston, MA: MIT Press.

Sibley, F. (1959). Aesthetic concepts. *Philosophical Review* 68: 421–450.

Walton, K.L. (1970). Categories of art. *Philosophical Review* 79: 334–367.

Ziff, P. (1979). Anything viewed. In: *Essays in Honor of Jaakko Hintikka on the Occasion of His Fiftieth Birthday* (ed. E. Saarinen, R. Hilpinen, I. Niiniluoto, and M.P. Hintikka), 285–293. Dordrecht: Reidel.

Part IV

Violent Sleep of Reason: On Epistemology

Chapter 13
Anti-social Black Metal Epistemology: Forming Beliefs Without Trust in an Evil Environment

Mikael Janvid
Department of Philosophy, Stockholm University, Stockholm, Sweden

No pouting for glory - No small-minded sheep
No media whores - No dishonest wimps
No life made of comfort - No ...
No talking for money - No radio waves
No forces of lies - No need to speak

No swelling their egos - Just satanic greed
From the track "Rebirth" from Gorogoroth's album
Quantos Possunt Ad Satanitatem Trahunt from 2009[1]

Introduction

Trust plays an important role in human life and society. Trusting each other, as well as various authorities, enables human society to prosper. The higher the amount of trust is in a society, the easier it flourishes. Trust and prosperity thus seem to go hand in hand. The Nordic countries provide a fitting illustration. They score high on levels of trust and are also among the wealthiest countries in the world.[2] Moreover, as an important element of such trust, citizens of their society specifically need to trust exchanges of information between one another as well as various authorities, both of which they do to a large extent in these countries.

In contrast to traditional individualist epistemology dominating the subject all the way back to Antiquity, *social* epistemology investigates the epistemic aspects of various social interactions—how subjects pursue epistemic goals "*with the help* of, or *in the face of*, others" (Goldman and O'Connor 2021, p. 2). One central topic within this recent branch of epistemology is *testimony*: when subjects convey information to one another and, more precisely, what epistemic standings the recipient thereby acquires.[3] It is accordingly testimony that shall be my main focus in this paper. Its epistemic importance is evident since, as Laurence Bonjour notes:

> I receive information via testimony on a very wide range of subjects: it would be practically impossible for me to check firsthand about very many of these, and quite a few involve matters that I am unable to check on my own even in principle.
>
> (BonJour 2010, p. 158)

---

[1] Word of caution: the band apparently ordered the removal of the official lyrics in 2004, so there is no authorized rendering, and I have not found any attempt to spell out the third line in its entirety. The Latin title can charitably be translated as "They draw as many as they can toward Satanism."

[2] According to the website *Our World in Data*, Norway, the home country of Gorgoroth, is among the top countries in the world. For instance, in 2020, 93.1% of Norwegians agreed that they trust people in their neighborhood and 94.3% that they trust their national government(!), the highest score in both cases among the countries participating in the survey. For the general importance of trust for society, see Faulkner (2018).

[3] See, for instance, Gelfert (2014) and Lackey (2008).

Several influential views within this relatively new field of research have picked up on the central role of trust in testimonial exchange specifically. A trustworthy informant needs to be both *sincere* and *competent* regarding the information they convey, but doesn't the recipient also need, in turn, to trust them in both these respects? It is naturally unlikely that the recipient will take on board the information unless they trust the informant to be both sincere and competent on the topic at hand. As the stats show, citizens in the Nordic countries do so to a large extent.

And yet in one of these countries at the top of the list, a surge of black metal swept across the land in the nineties, the so-called second wave of black metal bringing chaos (as well as excellent music!) in its wake. How to precisely distinguish black metal from other branches of metal is a delicate question, but aside from typical musical differences, the genre differentiates itself very consciously from its closest kin, death metal, by its sincerity in embracing Satanism.[4] While death metal bands, as well as the first wave of black metal, by the way, employed Satanist themes and props in lyrics and shows as well as on albums and merchandise, they were charged by the second-wave black metal bands for merely regarding them as provocative ploys. According to the second wave bands, Satanism should be sincerely embraced!

One of the most controversial bands in this wave, which is to say a lot(!), is Gorgoroth founded in 1992.[5] Their albums contain highly provocative lyrics praising Satan, blasphemy, and the imminent end of the world (and so on indefinitely). From their perspective, the close-knit Norwegian community is in the grip of lies spread and maintained by religious and political authorities; a conspiracy if one so wishes. Neither reality nor humankind are in fact good. Those who spread religious teachings and political ideologies stating the opposite are hypocrites. These lines from the song "Prayer" from the album *Quantos Possunt Ad Satanitatem Trahunt* reveal the hypocrisy of their main target Christianity:

> Silence of apostles, the atheism of confessors
> The filth of holy virgins and blasphemy of the righteous man.[6]

[4] For musical differences, see Khan-Harris (2007, pp. 31–33) and Thompson (2018, pp. 37–39). For sincerity, see Thompson (2018, pp. 36–37) and Håkansson (2023, pp. 228–230).

[5] The name of the band is taken from Tolkien's fantasy world Middle-earth (a common source of inspiration for names for extreme metal bands). Gorgoroth is the name of a plateau in Mordor, the land of evil.

[6] Track "Prayer" from the album *Quantos Possunt Ad Satanitatem Trahunt*. Regain Records (2009).

I will address whether these preachers are held to be insincere or instead "merely" unable to live up to the standards they preach later in this chapter, but in any case, they are *not* to be trusted.

As suggestive as the noted correlation between trust and various beneficial consequences may seem, we shall put trust under scrutiny below. As already indicated, my focus will be on the epistemic aspect of trust. The structure of this chapter is more precisely as follows. After this introduction, the following section investigates the role of trust in the epistemology of testimony. Then, I will present the anti-social epistemology of black metal, mainly based on my interpretation of the lyrics from songs by Gorgoroth and another Norwegian black metal band from the same wave. The final section briefly brings these topics together in the form of a challenge. Ultimately, I will argue that a follower of this epistemological outlook can, if not thrive, then at least cope successfully without trust and thus that trust is not of such vital importance in the epistemic domain as the theories I investigate below claim.

The Role of Trust in Testimony

What, then, is trust, and, more precisely, what does its epistemic significance consist in? As indicated in the previous section, trust seems relevant for the recipient actually coming to believe in the testimony of informants. However, nothing has so far been said about whether the belief the recipient thereby forms is *justified* or not.[7] As we shall investigate below, too many people may, as a matter of fact, trust untrustworthy informants, in which case trust makes them form *unjustified* beliefs instead. Maybe people simply are too gullible and/or the informants are skilled in deception. In this section, we shall look at a couple of suggestions on how trust can possess epistemic significance.

Starting with some conceptual analysis, several philosophers classify trust as a kind of *reliance*. Humans rely on each other, as well as various

---

[7] See Faulkner (2020, p. 329). In this chapter, I will exclusively be concerned with *epistemic* justification unless otherwise stated. What does the distinguishing attribute "epistemic" signify here? Here, I happily align myself with William Alston: the epistemic "point of view is defined by the aim at maximizing truth and minimizing falsity" (Alston 1989, p. 83).

objects, in a number of ways.[8] More narrowly, trust proper, or trust in the rich sense, is often taken to be restricted to *persons*. Trust necessarily possesses an *interpersonal* aspect—a relation between (at least) two persons. Objects cannot fulfill this condition.

Unlike mere reliance, trust is often thereby claimed to evoke certain reactive attitudes—typically when trust is violated. When this happens, the subject feels betrayed. Attaching such reactive attitudes excludes objects as targets of trust, but also a number of cases of mere reliance on humans. The citizens of Königsberg relied on Immanuel Kant's extremely regular walking habits to set their clocks,[9] but it would be misplaced of them to feel betrayed if he did not show up on time on some occasion.[10] It is in virtue of these characteristic reactive attitudes that trust takes on a salient moral aspect.

Venturing now into the social epistemology of testimony and leaving out the trust component from reliance for the moment, reliance is itself importantly understood differently depending on what general epistemological views one takes, more precisely, internalist reductionist versus externalist nonreductionist views, respectively. They will thereby differ in their views of how the reliance is more precisely taken up by the subject. Allowing myself to simplify in what follows, from an externalist perspective, the recipient need not have access to the reliance itself, nor its justification. The subject need not be aware that they rely on the informant nor that they are justified in doing so. It suffices that they do and that the informant *is* reliable in the case at hand.[11] From an internalist perspective, however, that mere fact of reliable reliance is insufficient for bestowing justification on the testimony. The recipient *also* needs to have access to reliable reliance. Otherwise, the beliefs they form would be unjustified even if the informant is reliable. Mere brute reliable reliance is not enough.

Next, externalism naturally aligns with an anti-reductionist stance according to which testimony constitutes a *sui generis* source of

---

[8] This classification is made both in and outside of epistemology. Aside from this subdiscipline in focus here, trust is investigated in disciplines like philosophy of language, normative ethics, and political philosophy.

[9] Example taken from Hawley (2019, p. 3) and Goldberg (2020, p. 97). A further difference will be presented below.

[10] As reportedly happened once when he became engrossed in Rousseau's *Émile* for several days.

[11] See Goldberg (2010, p. 92). In this book, Goldberg provides an excellent investigation of the role of reliance in social epistemology from an externalist perspective.

justification independent of other sources. Testimony stands on its own feet epistemically. By contrast, the requirement of accessibility pushes internalism toward a reductionist view where testimony is in need of further justification from some other source—typically experience in the form of inductive track records of the reliability of the informant in question.[12] Only after a reliable track record of the informant has been duly noted by the subject will they, the recipient, be justified in believing their testimony.

Both views face objections. Nonreductionism seems to allow for gullibility—noncritical acceptance of hearsay and propaganda. How could the subject differentiate between good and bad testimony without access to the reliability of the sources of information? Reductionism, on the other hand, is vulnerable to the point made in the quotation from BonJour in the Introduction: it is simply not possible for us to justify most of our testimonial beliefs in some other way. The result thus seems to amount to skepticism. My impression is that trust is often added from an internalist perspective, partly to avoid reductionism without being charged for gullibility, thus steering a middle way between these undesirable outcomes.

Let us next step back and ask why we should distinguish between trust and mere reliance from an epistemic perspective. Is there any epistemic difference between the two? Why is not "mere" reliance enough? Here, adherents of the so-called assurance theory pride themselves that they alone provide trust with such a role. Let us therefore investigate this theory more carefully.

According to one of its main proponents, Paul Faulkner, "acts of trusting crucially differ from acts of reliance in that trusting is necessarily willing" (Faulkner 2020, p. 332).[13] Willing acts of trust can therefore not entirely consist of beliefs since they are not under our direct control. A subject cannot choose to believe what the capital of France is or what is in front of them at the moment. Thus, while reliance is stored in the subject as a (typically implicit) belief, trust is internalized in some other way. According to Faulkner, more precisely, it is internalized as an *attitude* toward the reliance of the informant. Trust being an attitude also explains why feelings of betrayal occur when trust is betrayed.

[12] See, for instance, Gelfert (2014).

[13] Assurance theorists differ among themselves on whether trust itself constitutes a belief or not where Faulkner thus favors a variety where it is not.

Applied to testimony, then, when the recipient comes to trust the informant to tell the truth by the testimony, they "will *see* [the informant]'s telling *as* the assumption of responsibility it purports to be and for this reason believe" the testimony (Faulkner 2020, p. 332; italics in original).[14] By this assurance, the informant presents themselves as a guarantor for the truth of the testimony. Now, according to Faulkner, the assurance given by the informant provides an epistemic reason. By trusting, the recipient thereby receives a justified belief in the testimony. Trust thus manifests a "second-personal participatory" (another phrase for stressing the interpersonal character of the trusting relation) stance that shores up the interpersonal reliability. To show trust is to invest a hopeful attitude in the informant, thereby creating a "bootstrapped" epistemic reason to believe in the testimony (Faulkner 2011).[15]

Understood in this way, we can note a further difference between trust and mere reliance in line with the emphasized interpersonal aspect of the former: when they give their assurance, the informant is *aware* of being trusted on, unlike cases of reliance where this need not be the case, irrespective of whether an object or a person is being relied on. Moreover, as already mentioned, a person can in turn sometimes rely on somebody or something without being aware that this is the case. Their behavior displays their reliance without any accompanying conscious thought.[16]

As a further illustration of the bootstrapped character from the perspective of the informant, Karen Jones employs the following thought experiment to highlight the distinctive value trust adds to mere reliance. Imagine a world where perfect reliance rules in interpersonal relations. Jones claims that,

> When we add trustworthiness to this world we introduce sensitivity to the reason, 'she's counting on me' and with it, the possibility of giving

[14] Trust is thus a three-place relation, in the case of testimony between a recipient, an informant, and the testimony. It is in virtue of the first two *relata* that the relation is interpersonal (see above).

[15] In epistemology, the term bootstrapping "to pull yourself up by your bootstraps" is used to characterize circular justification. Such justification is usually considered vicious, but in this particular case is claimed to be beneficial. The informant assures the informant of their own trustworthiness. This is what the instrumental (epistemic) value consists of. Trust also generates final value, typically moral value, when such a relationship is established, or so its adherents claim.

[16] A yet further difference between trust and reliance is that in virtue of this interpersonal character, the addressed recipient is justified in believing the testimony in a way no one else is. An eavesdropper would thus be less justified in their belief in the same testimony. This purported difference is rightly criticized by Lackey in Lackey (2008, pp. 233–240), but is not so relevant for my concerns in this paper.

> the one who is being counted on a direct reason to act as they are being counted on to act that did not exist prior to that very counting.
>
> (Jones 2017, pp. 100–101)[17]

However, since perfect reliance already rules in this world, one may wonder whether this further reason merely adds superfluous justification.

I remain unconvinced that the assurance theory succeeds in providing trust with epistemic significance,[18] but I am here less interested in whether this account captures what the essence of trust really is or the distinctive epistemic role it plays in testimonial exchange, as I am about the purpose of this account as well as other such accounts. I am not sure why they put so much effort into finding a role for trust in general and in testimony in particular. Why this attempt to bridge the gap between ethics and epistemology? It seems obvious that epistemic and moral standings easily come apart. To reiterate the point made at the beginning of this section, with the terms we have now inquired into, we only reach our epistemic goals to a higher extent with trust compared to mere reliance *if* the informant is worthy of such trust and is responsive to such virtuous circles as described by the assurance theorist. Any further epistemic boost trust will provide depends on the underlying reliability of the informant (including to what extent they care about being trustworthy).[19] Only then will interpersonal relationships and society in general flourish epistemically. It is an empirical question to what extent these conditions obtain and thus to what extent such hope and optimism are justified.

For the purposes of this chapter, I can thus grant that the assurance theory has succeeded in developing a coherent account of trust in testimony, but still wonder whether the class of such cases remains empty in the actual world. In other words, there *could* be positive epistemic standings generated by trustworthy testimony, but in fact, there are not any.

---

[17] This passage is also quoted in Fricker (2023, p. 735). Of course, as we shall see below, the enlightened metalhead believes themselves to live in the opposite world. By the way, this is what I shall call the targeted subject for the remainder of this paper. For want of a better term, I shall employ the Platonic term "enlightened" even though it is not apt here since this subject believes that we, by contrast, live under the dark sun. "The *gnosis* of Satan" bestows darkness rather than light.

[18] Aside from being a metalhead myself (albeit perhaps not sufficiently enlightened), I also subscribe to an epistemically externalist narrow view according to which justification consists in truth conduciveness. I thus agree with the verdict that the assurance theory provides a failed attempt to "create justification or warrant epistemologically ex nihilio" (Lackey 2008, pp. 239–240).

[19] See Lackey (2008, pp. 244–248). See Kappel (2014) for a contrasting reliabilist account of epistemic trust.

The latter issue is what is at stake here. As far as I can see, the same distinction can be drawn for any other account of trust in testimony. As we shall see in the next section, the enlightened metalhead regard themselves as one of the few who have seen through the false hope, the assurance theory, and other accounts of trust promise.

Likewise, as a further example outside of the assurance theory specifically, John Greco (2019) has recently argued for a vital role for trust in what he calls testimonial knowledge *transmission*. He distinguishes between such transmission and knowledge *generation*. Testimonial knowledge generation takes place when a designated subject acquires information from a source or informant external to the *epistemic community* they belong to. Such acquisition can be understood along the lines of reductionism: the recipient is tasked with assessing the sincerity and competence of the informant. Testimonial knowledge transmission can then take place *within* the epistemic community after the designated member has acquired that knowledge. This transmission involves trust as an essential part of joint agency between that member and the other members of their community. They need to understand each other's intentions and cooperate to reach the intended result—distribution of knowledge within the community. Trust here plays the essential role of freeing the other members from undertaking the same careful assessment that the first member provided on their behalf. Testimonial exchange thus takes place in a different way with an outsider compared to other members of the community, according to Greco. Nonetheless, I take it that Greco does not think that the designated subject as a representative of the community must distrust external sources. Mere lack of trust is sufficient for such an assessment to be called for. I shall return to this distinction below.

I have doubts here as well concerning, for instance, analyzing knowledge in terms of success from ability, as successful agency or achievement, as Greco does, but once again I can grant the possibility of the phenomenon of testimonial knowledge transmission, but then, on behalf of the enlightened metalhead, deny the existence of beneficial epistemic communities in the relevant sense on empirical grounds. Recall that such transmission never occurs outside of them. As a radical individualist, especially[20] the enlightened metalhead will not belong to any. For better

[20] See Kahn-Harris (2007, p. 42); even "elitist misanthropy" in the case of black metal specifically (see also p. 128).

or worse, they have to do without such transmission. As we shall see in the next section, they claim to be better off.

It is thus primarily these two accounts of trust that the enlightened metalhead will provide a test case for in the next section.

Finally, according to Katherine Hawley and others, it is also important to pay attention to *distrust* as well (Hawley 2019, pp. 4–7; D'Cruz 2020).[21] Distrust does not form the mere complement to trust but constitutes something over and above mere lack of trust. Since one can neither trust nor distrust someone, trust and distrust form a contrary, rather than a contradictory, pair. Hawley suggests we distinguish distrust from non-reliance in a similar way which we distinguish between trust and mere reliance in virtue of the reactive attitudes we display. As we have seen, in the case of distrust, those would be feelings of betrayal or the like. She claims that "[t]o distrust someone to do something is to believe that she has a commitment to doing it, and yet not rely upon her to meet that commitment" (Hawley 2019, p. 9). When we now, in the next section, turn to explore the perspective of the enlightened metalhead, we shall unsurprisingly see that distrust is precisely the attitude they take toward (almost all) authorities.

Treating People like Thermometers

It should be clear from the discussion of trust and the two provided examples, in particular, that the enlightened metalhead does not trust anyone in the senses presented in the previous section, and thus that the assurance view picks out the empty set from their perspective. The reason is simply that they do not think anyone is worthy of such trust. As far as they can see, religious and political authorities show a dismal track record. Moreover, humankind itself does not possess the good-natured character to deserve such trust.[22] It is therefore wasteful to invest hope in humankind. According to Trudy Govier, distrust is warranted when people

> lie or deliberately deceive, break promises, are hypocritical or insincere, seek to manipulate us, are corrupt or dishonest, cannot be counted on to

[21] It should be noted that Hawley's focus is primarily on the moral aspect of trust. Thanks to Natalia Nealon for prompting this clarification.

[22] I leave out the complexity added by original sin for our discussion here.

> follow moral norms, are incompetent, have no concern for us or deliberately try to harm us.
>
> (Govier 1992, p. 53)[23]

Both authorities as well as most people fulfill all of the above sufficient conditions! As a result, the enlightened metalhead thus lacks "faith in humanity."[24]

In addition, as already been pointed out, the enlightened metalhead will refrain from becoming a member of any epistemic community, so they will decline to take part in any testimonial knowledge transmission. Unlike the aforementioned representative of an epistemic community, the enlightened metalhead not only lacks trust but precisely distrusts all sources of information for the reasons the quote above lists.

But what about the metal community itself? Here, the quote from the preamble is helpful: fellow metalheads are as driven by selfish desires ("satanic greed") as everyone else. They differ from most other people in being honest about their true motives unlike the hypocritical followers of the false doctrines the authorities indoctrinate unenlightened people in. I discern a common strand among philosophers who argue for an important role of trust in epistemology, a strong desire for epistemic and moral reasons to go hand in hand, an aim which the enlightened metalhead, then, dismisses as grandstanding or wishful thinking.

Having discarded trust, what then about reliance? Here, the answer is less clear-cut. The previous negative verdict remains the same for all those aforementioned authorities whose untrustworthiness partly precisely resides in their unreliability. They are insincere or incompetent. (Note that the disjunction is inclusive!) However, their lack still leaves open the possibility that there are other reliable sources uncontaminated by them that the enlightened metalhead may profit from. They can selectively and tentatively rely on such sources when they need to,[25] as in the

[23] Passage also quoted in D'Cruz (2020, p. 46). As D'Cruz points out, the list is not exhaustive.

[24] To cite the title of Preston-Roedder (2013), where he claims such faith "is a centrally moral virtue," employing Gandhi as well as the fictious character Alyosha from Dostoyevsky's novel *The Brothers Karamazov* as examples. A virtue, then, which the enlightened metalhead deliberately lacks. Did they start out with such faith originally and then lost it or did they lack it from the start? Both options are possible I suppose, but often I believe the former alternative to be the case: "Asking for guidance. Begging in vain" track "Building a Man," from Gorgoroth's album *Quantos Possunt Ad Satanitatem Trahunt*.

[25] Recall the quoted line "No forces of lies – No need to speak" from the track "Rebirth" in the preamble above thus implying this will not occur often.

aforementioned example with Kant. Here, the enlightened metalhead treats Kant and other reliable people like thermometers.

It is an interesting question what the enlightened metalhead should think about science. They will not initially trust scientists *per se* any more than they trust anyone else, but can they still rely on scientific findings? Well, enlightened metalheads will disregard those scientists trapped in the current trend of activism, so they go by the board along with politicians and priests. That said, the enlightened metalhead can rely on such findings based on the impressive track record of many scientific disciplines. The enlightened metalhead is not averse to knowledge as such: on the contrary, they think that they alone have become enlightened! Just as in the case of Augustine, there is a close relation between faith and understanding, "unless you believe you will not understand."[26] In their view, however, some scientific results provide a mixed blessing: the efforts of medicine to save and prolong life, for instance, are questionable in an evil world.

Does this systematic suspicion toward testimony amount to a form of reductionism? Not necessarily. Anti-reductionism may still be able to account for this predicament since in the wake of their enlightenment, the metalhead becomes alerted to *defeaters*. Defeaters form the counterpart to justification. Instead of bestowing positive epistemic status on beliefs, such as knowledge or justification, defeaters deprive them of such status. Defeaters come in two kinds: while a *rebutting* defeater to the belief that p provides justification for non-p, an *undercutting* defeater to p undercuts the justification for p. The enlightened metalhead is faced with both kinds of defeaters: the aforementioned authorities' poor testimonial track record thereby displays their unreliability and thus constitutes an undercutting defeater. The particular instances of testimony are also gainsaid by other more reliable sources, like their own experience, thereby providing rebutting defeaters. Now, from an externalist anti-reductionist perspective, once the subject has been alerted to the presence of defeaters, then unreflective reliance no longer bestows justification by default.

---

[26] The metalhead seeks and finds enlightenment by embracing Satanism:
No single book was beholden by me
Oh, no question I cannot do answer
Only one single lamp does show me the way
And this is the eye of Satan
From the Norwegian black metal band Darkthrone's track "Quintessence" from the album *Panzerfaust*. Peaceville Records (1995).

Given that the enlightened metalhead can rely on some informants about certain topics in certain contexts, what is really wrong with settling for mere reliance from an epistemic point of view? Assuming for the sake of argument that trust provides an epistemic boost as the assurance theorists claim, in the good scenario where the informant really is trustworthy (i.e. sincere and competent) one may miss out epistemically, as well as morally and socially by treating people like thermometers, but in the bad scenario, the evil environment the metalhead thinks they inhabit, where most informants in fact are untrustworthy, you are safeguarded from a massive load of misinformation. In such a context, the subject would hardly receive any true information anyway, but will avoid forming many false beliefs based on all these untrustworthy sources.

Faulkner addresses the problem that the good scenario and the bad scenario may be subjectively indistinguishable to the recipient. What help and role can trust then play? In response, he acknowledges that the belief the subject forms in the bad scenario will be unjustified, but claims that the belief nonetheless will be "epistemically reasonable" in virtue of the constitutive relation between trust and truth of the belief in the good scenario (Faulkner 2020).[27] A point which, even if true, provides small comfort to the recipient indeed!

I, then, picture the enlightened metalhead as endorsing the traditional epistemic goals of maximizing truths and avoiding falsehoods, but surmise that in their impoverished environment, they would prioritize avoiding falsehoods over maximizing truths. Because of the high risk of deceit, the enlightened metalhead thus take themselves to be in an epistemically high-stake scenario where most of the information they receive is very likely false and where they also face grave consequences were they to believe in it.[28] That the deceitful information is important explains the efforts the deceitful authorities put in presenting the good scenario, at least *prima facie*, as indistinguishable from the real one, a topic which will be explored further in the final section. According to the enlightened metalhead, these considerations show why distrust rather than mere lack of trust is called for.

---

[27] The problem is presented on p. 333 and the solution is provided on p. 338. Faulkner (2011, pp. 153–159) suggests trust raises the probability of the testimony. This claim is, however, dependent on empirical assumptions precisely disputed by the enlightened metalhead in the main text.

[28] Such high-stake scenarios figure extensively in the discussion surrounding epistemic contextualism, the view that the epistemic standing of a subject changes in contexts when high stakes are introduced.

The enlightened metalhead can lend support for the pessimistic, albeit realistic, outlook from the externalist objection to internalism as presenting a hyper-idealized picture of humans as epistemic and moral agents.[29] Humans are simply not as intellectually and morally advanced as internalists and trust theorists require them to be. Various forms of bias as well as the so-called situationist challenge can be invoked to argue this point further.[30]

But can the enlightened metalhead really succeed in detaching themselves from all bonds of trust as well as all epistemic communities? In answering this question, it is important distinguish between whether we *could* do without trust in our lives psychologically and socially versus whether we *should* do without this aspect of ordinary human life from an epistemic perspective. The difficulty in thus coping without trust is precisely one reason why our environment is evil! The enlightened metalhead can acknowledge the challenge and, then, without the hope of complete success, strive for self-sufficiency and independence. As Keith Kahn-Harris notes "Black metal emphasizes austerity, self-control and solipsism" (Kahn-Harris 2007, p. 105).[31] The enlightened metalhead thus aspires for total epistemic (as well as moral) autonomy.

The enlightened metalhead will therefore refuse to take on any of the commitments characteristic of Hawley's aforementioned account of trust.[32] They reject any normative expectations on them and refrain from imposing them on anyone else. No bonds of loyalty are formed with any other person. No human being deserves any goodwill (themselves included). An enlightened metalhead can only be relied upon when they themselves stand to gain something from the reliance and *vice versa*, and they will in turn only rely on someone else when both will benefit from it. You are on your own and cannot count on anyone unless there is something in it for them as well! Those who do not realize that cooperation in

---

[29] Strictly speaking, the externalist charge concerns hyper-intellectualization, see Burge (2013, pp. 26–27), but I use idealization as a generalization to also include the moral aspect.

[30] The latter challenge is usually raised against various ethical theories, but Alfano (2012) extends this challenge to so-called responsibilist virtue epistemology. The challenge consists in the fact that numerous studies show that instead of the evidence the subject is willing to cite, the holding of their belief is in fact due to various accidental factors of the situation such as their mood or the mere presence of bystanders, etc.

[31] See also Thompson (2018).

[32] Hawley analyzes trust in terms of taking on certain commitments rather than motives. The enlightened metalhead will, of course, lack any such motives as well.

effect amounts to mutual exploitation only have themselves to blame. An enlightened metalhead will never lower their guard.[33]

The systematic indoctrination the aforementioned authorities undertake can be characterized as a conspiracy in that at least some representatives deliberatively deceive people for their own gain. As already mentioned, other representatives may, however, honestly believe in their teachings and thus be incompetent (and thus themselves deceived) rather than insincere. By becoming enlightened, the metalhead is able to see through their deception. Conversely, the beliefs of the enlightened metalhead are in turn regarded as forming a conspiracy by the unenlightened. As is not uncommon in these cases, we thus face a symmetry and a polarized standoff here.

As with many other conspiracies, the beliefs of the enlightened metalhead seem *prima* facie internally coherent as well as responsive to new relevant information. So far, we have explored the option of doing without trust from within the perspective of the enlightened metalhead. I suspect the reader has not found this perspective particularly appealing. In the next and final section, I briefly raise the question, what can be said in their favor from an outside perspective.

The Predicament of the Enlightened Metalhead

In this brief final section by playing the Devil's advocate (sic!), I simply want to raise the question whether you, dear reader, know that you are not in the predicament Gorgoroth describes? How do you know whether you find yourself in the good or bad scenario Faulkner struggled with in the previous section? While the good scenario appears as indistinguishable from the bad one to a trustful subject, black metal epistemology shows the subject a way out. Upon further reflection, how trustworthy are your priests and politicians? How pious was the last priest you met? How honest was the last politician you came across? How accurate is the grandstanding, as well as profit seeking media, you follow? Moving on, are you not fooled, manipulated, and exploited by fellow humans on a daily basis? Do you really experience the world being run by the goodwill of Providence? If your answers to these rhetorical questions are not the intended ones, do you really have good reasons to back them up? Are you

[33] To use an expression, Faulkner employs to characterize trust in Faulkner (2011, p. 153).

not, then, rather the product of indoctrination? Maybe it is time to listen to *Quantos Possunt Ad Satanitatem Trahunt* with an open mind and bind yourself to the powers of hell?[34] And thus finally "to be free"?[35,36]

References

Alfano, M. (2012). Expanding the Situationist challenge to Responsibilist Virtue Epistemology. *The Philosophical Quarterly* 62: 223–249.

Alston, William 1989 "Concepts of epistemic justification" in his *Epistemic Justification. Essays in the Theory of Knowledge*. Ithaca: Cornell University Press, 81–114.

BonJour, L. (2010). *Epistemology: Classic Problems and Contemporary Responses*, Second Edition. Lanham: Rowman & Littlefield.

Burge, T. (2013). *Cognition Through Understanding*. Oxford: Oxford University Press.

Darkthrone 1995 *Panzerfaust*. Peaceville Records.

D'Cruz, J. (2020). Trust and distrust. In: *The Routledge Handbook of Trust and Philosophy* (ed. J. Simon), 41–51. New York: Routledge.

Faulkner, P. (2011). *Knowledge on Trust*. Oxford: Oxford University Press.

Faulkner, P. (2018). Finding trust in government. *Journal of Social Philosophy* 49 (4): 626–644.

Faulkner, P. (2020). Trust and testimony. In: *The Routledge Handbook of Trust and Philosophy* (ed. J. Simon), 329–340. New York: Routledge.

Fricker, M. (2023). Diagnosing institutionalized 'distrustworthiness'. *The Philosophical Quarterly* 73 (3): 722–742.

Gelfert, A. (2014). *A Critical Introduction to Testimony*. London: Bloomsbury.

Goldman, A. and O'Connor, C. (2021). Social epistemology. In: *The Stanford Encyclopedia of Philosophy* (ed. E.N. Zalta) https://plato.stanford.edu/archives/win2021/entries/epistemology-social/, 1–29. Stanford Encyclopedia of Philosophy (Winter 2021e).

Goldberg, S. (2010). *Relying on Others*. Oxford: Oxford University Press.

Goldberg, S. (2020). Trust and reliance. In: *The Routledge Handbook of Trust and Philosophy* (ed. J. Simon), 97–108. New York: Routledge.

[34] To paraphrase from the track "Prayer" from the album *Quantos Possunt Ad Satanitatem Trahunt*.

[35] From the track "Building a Man" from the album *Quantos Possunt Ad Satanitatem Trahunt*.

[36] I am grateful to the editors Ben McCraw and Aaron Simmons for inviting me to contribute to this book and to Natalia Nealon and James Nguyen for helpful comments on an earlier version of this chapter.

Gorgoroth 2009 *Quantos Possunt Ad Satanitatem Trahunt*. Regain Records.
Govier, T. (1992). Distrust as a practical problem. *Journal of Social Philosophy* 23 (1): 52–63.
Greco, J. (2019). The role of trust in testimonial knowledge. In: *Trust in Epistemology* (ed. K. Dormandy), 91–113. New York: Routledge.
Hawley, K. (2019). *How to be Trustworthy*. Oxford: Oxford University Press.
Håkansson, N. (2023). *Tung Metall*. Nirstedt.
Jones, K. (2017). But i was counting on you. In: *The Philosophy of Trust* (ed. P. Faulkner and T. Simpson). Oxford: Oxford University Press.
Kahn-Harris, K. (2007). *Extreme Metal. Music and Culture on the Edge*. Oxford and New York: Berg.
Kappel, K. (2014). Believing on trust. *Synthese* 191: 2009–2028.
Lackey, J. (2008). *Learning from Words. Testimony as a Source of Knowledge*. Oxford: Oxford University Press.
Preston-Roedder, R. (2013). Faith in humanity. *Philosophy and Phenomenological Research* 87 (3): 664–687.
Thompson, C. (2018). *Norges Våpen. Cultural Memory and Uses of History in Norwegian Black Metal*. Uppsala: Acta Universitatis Upsaliensis.

Chapter 14
Talk Shit, Get Kissed: Death Metal, Misogyny, and Epistemic Resistance

Benjamin W. McCraw[1,2]

[1]Department of History, Political Science, Philosophy, and American Studies, University of South Carolina Upstate, Spartanburg, SC, USA

[2]African Centre for Epistemology and Philosophy of Science, University of Johannesburg, Johannesburg, Gauteng, South Africa

Content warning: expletives, mentions of sexual violence, and general misogynistic awfulness

A few years ago, in the middle of a Cannibal Corpse show I attended, the vocalist—George "Corpsegrinder" Fisher—introduced a song by dedicating it to all of the women in the audience. I immediately cringed. Anyone with even a passing familiarity with Cannibal Corpse would immediately understand that was not going to be a love song. However, once Corpsegrinder's dedication growled out, a huge wave of very feminine-sounding screams of endorsement followed from all corners of the venue. Cannibal Corpse then played "Stripped, Raped, and Strangled."[1] Notoriously, the genre of death metal bathes in blood, violence, and gore—and this song definitely reflects those traits. Importantly, though, death metal doesn't revel in violence done *to* just anyone (and *by* just anyone), or gore exacted from any kind of flesh. Instead, much of both traditional and also contemporary death metal tends to revel in violence done to *female or feminine* flesh, and such violence is largely perpetuated by men. Death metal reeks of the putrefaction of feminine bodies, autonomy, and their very existence.

But, as I shall argue in this chapter, there are important stirrings *within* death metal *against* such violence. More exactly, I shall use José Medina's (2012) epistemology of resistance to uncover a small, but hopefully grow(l)ing, group of death metal musicians who push back, in varying ways, against death metal misogyny. I will deploy Medina's concept of a "hermeneutical hero" to conceptualize these death metal resisters (death metal *hero(in)es*?) undermining misogyny. The misogynist paradigm(s) that tend to typify death metal evince a deeply resistant lack of comprehension into the seriousness of its misogyny, and it takes heroic efforts working to dislodge it. Interestingly, and perhaps ironically, in a genre where transgression is so central to its core aim, such death metal heroes offer a transgression of death metal's transgressive norms themselves.

Death Metal: The Aestheticization of Transgression

To begin, we must locate our target: death metal (hereafter DM). Though the term may be familiar, it's not immediately clear just what the genre is (if anything) or what inscribes its boundaries (if there are any). To ask

[1] From *The Bleeding* (1994, Metal Blade Records).

what DM is or how to characterize it immediately presents us with at least two deep worries. First, there are philosophical worries about just how to go about the project of defining or settling the boundaries of a genre in general. Second, there are more fine-grained worries about how to do that specifically with DM, given the three decades of diverse music that comprise it.

I simply note these worries as legitimate but want to move forward without fully addressing them. We must begin somewhere if we are to focus on DM at all, so let me simply offer some corresponding provisos: I don't have or assume any particular philosophical stance on the nature and process of defining genres, and I will not "get into the weeds" regarding just who is or isn't DM (especially into the tall, forest-like weeds regarding the various subgenres of DM that now abound). With these provisos in place, let's try to start some coherent discussion of DM's characteristics. Natalie J. Purcell's (2003) discussion is a good place to start.

> Death metal music is usually fast, low, powerful, intense, and played very loudly. The guitars are often tuned down. A great deal of Death Metal consists of speedy, chaotic guitar riffs...In Death Metal, drums are often very dominant and very fast. Hyper double-bass blast beats...are common and utilized frequently. [...] The lyrics and vocals, which would strike the casual listener before anything else, only augment the extremity of the music...[are] very low, beast-like, almost indiscernible growls as vocals....
>
> (Purcell 2003, pp. 10–11)

Despite such a careful account, very quickly Purcell goes on to note that some DM fails to satisfy these central sonic characterizations. For example, death-doom is quite slow and melodic DM (melodeath) features guitar work typical of *traditional*—not *death*—metal. Is there any helpful way to pick out DM? Purcell's last line gives us hope: it's the vocals.[2]

[2] Of the nine quotations from those in the DM scene Purcell (2003, pp. 11–12) cites, six of them explicitly note growled vocals as essential to the genre.

Can extreme growled vocals give us a good way to pick out DM (from whatever other things it may *not* be)? Zachary Wallmark (2018) claims that "[in] death metal, the vocals, more than everything else, serve as shibboleth to demarcate the borders of a noise-identified community" (72). In Michelle Phillipov's (2012) analysis of DM and music criticism, the vocals take up the first and most extended part of the discussion. Finally, for Matthew Unger (2016), "[p]eople outside of the metal community generally recognize extreme metal by [its] gruff, low, aggressive, growled, and often indecipherable vocalizations" (18).

So, growling vocals offer us the best way to locate DM. Other sonic properties fail to demarcate the genre as consistently as the vocals. What else can such vocals tell us about DM? They give us insight into one of the central aims or functions of DM: transgression.[3] Academics examining DM will, almost universally, prize transgression in their analysis.[4] As I have examined at length elsewhere (see McCraw 2024, pp. 7–11), the same sort of growled vocals by which we are most likely to pick out DM also constitute one of its central ways of performing a transgressive aim or function relative to the standard melodious singing of other genres. Accordingly, Unger presents extreme metal as "a certain kind of aestheticization of transgression" (2016, p. 40). However, we'll soon see that (too often) DM doesn't value *generic* systemic execution, but, more specifically, as an incarnation of lust for *misogynistic* horror and gore. However, before we can make good on this claim of misogyny in DM, no matter how obvious it may be to any who are or aren't familiar with it, we must be clearer on misogyny itself. Getting more precise on misogyny will help us better diagnose its role in DM and, later, will ground our discussion of the hero(in)es who attempt to resist it.

[3] I don't claim that *only* DM has such an aim or function. I only want to accent the connection between DM vocals and transgression but without implying that no other musical features also have a transgressive function.

[4] See just a few significant examples: Allett (2012), Kirner-Ludwig and Wohlfarth (2018), Scott (2016), Unger (2016), Phillipov (2012), and others.

Misogyny

Important to Kate Manne's (2017) conception of misogyny (and my use of it in this chapter) is what misogyny is *not*. For Manne, the "naïve conception" sees misogyny "primarily [as] a property of individual agents (typically, although not necessarily, men) who are prone to feel hatred, hostility, or other similar emotions toward any and every woman, or at least women generally, *simply because they are women*" (2017, p. 32; emphasis original). The naïve conception follows the term's etymology by construing misogynistic attitudes as "unified by their psychological nature and basis"—specifically the hatred of women (2017, p. 33).

For Manne, the naïve conception faces at least two serious problems. First, it predicts that "...misogyny would be rare within a patriarchal setting..." (2017, p. 47). Why? It would require that misogynists hate women, even when women help them under patriarchy.

> [W]e would expect even the last enlightened man to be well-pleased with some women, that is, those who amicably serve his interests. It is not just that being hostile toward these women would be doubly problematic, in being both interpersonally churlish and morally objectionable. It is that it would be highly *peculiar*, as a matter of basic moral psychology. To put the problem bluntly: when it comes to the women who are not only dutifully but lovingly catering to his desires, what's to hate, exactly?
>
> (Manne 2017, pp. 47–48; emphasis in original)

The naïve conception would have men hating those who help them by "performing certain forms of emotional, social, domestic, sexual, and reproductive labor...in a loving and caring manner or enthusiastic spirit" when women follow patriarchal norms (2017, p. 46). Second, the naïve conception faces an epistemological problem: "[f]or what lies behind an individual agent's attitudes, as a matter of deep or ultimate psychological explanation, is frequently inscrutable. So the naïve conception would threaten to make misogyny very difficult to diagnose, short of being the agent's therapist (and sometimes not even that would be sufficient)" (2017, p. 44). Better, then, to pull the plug, so to speak on the naïve conception.

Manne's assessment of the naïve conception's failure opens the path toward a better account.

> By the lights of the naïve conception, misogyny essentially becomes too psychologistic a notion, on the model of a phobia or a deep-seated aversion. It becomes a matter of psychological ill health, or perhaps irrationality, rather than a systematic facet of social power relations and a predictable manifestation of the ideology that governs them: patriarchy.
>
> (Manne 2017, p. 49)

Misogyny should be understood as a structural or social phenomenon rather than a description of individuals' psychology. More specifically,

> *Constitutively speaking*, misogyny in a social environment comprises the hostile social forces that
>
> **(a)** will tend to be faced by a (wider or narrower) class of girls and women because they are girls and women in that (more or less fully specified) social position; and
>
> **(b)** serve to police and enforce a patriarchal order, instantiated in relation to other intersecting systems of domination and disadvantage that apply to the relevant class of girls and women (e.g., various forms of racism, xenophobia, classism, ageism, transphobia, homophobia, ableism, and so on). [...] (Manne 2017, p. 63; emphases in original)

Manne's conception of misogyny provides the following corollary for analyzing "misogyn*ist*": "individual agents count as misogynists if and only if their misogynistic attitudes and/or actions are significantly (a) more extreme, and (b) more consistent than most other people in the relevant comparison class (e.g., other people of the same gender, and perhaps race, class, age, etc., in similar social environments)" (2017, p. 66). Thus, Manne's account won't require that a misogynist must hate women or make them suffer, but rather excessively and consistently put pressure on them to accept a patriarchal grip on their actions, attitudes, relations, etc.

Before we see that much of DM embodies Manne's conception of misogyny, let us note a few implications. First, insofar as misogyny is a property of social institutions or structural features of our communities, it need not require any particular psychological attitude in the misogynist—much less one so strong as hatred or hostility. Thus, Manne's first problem with the psychological basis of the naïve conception will not apply here. Second, to know if someone counts as genuinely misogynist, we don't need to know inscrutable facts about their motives. All we need is evidence that they reinforce patriarchal norms. Thus, Manne's conception has no problem addressing the epistemological concerns for the naïve conception. Let's note a clear implication of these two points: *someone* with *any or no* psychological basis can be a misogynist or enact misogyny so long as they consistently and excessively police and reinforce patriarchal norms. There's no mental decay or hideous (psychological) infirmity constitutive of the misogynist. Nothing, on Manne's account, prevents a woman promoting misogyny just as often or strongly as a man,[5] and nothing prevents a person with no particular intention in their own mind to do the same. We must look beyond the individual, much less any particular individual psychological characteristics, to determine their misogyny.[6] Finally, we can note that Manne's conception can be applied to things that are neither social structures nor individuals:

> ...*derivatively*, an individual agent's attitudes or behavior counts as misogynistic within a social context insofar as it reflects, or perpetuates, misogyny therein. We can give analogous definitions of misogyny as a property of practices, institutions, artworks, other artifacts, and so on.
>
> (Manne 2017, p. 66)

[5] See Manne's comment:there's no mystery (and little doubt) about the fact that women police other women, and engage in gendered norm enforcement behavior. On the view of misogyny I've developed in this book, we would expect women who channel misogynistic forces against other women to be excessively moralistic toward—for example, prone to blame and punish—those who do not adhere to gendered norms and expectations.(2017, p. 256)

If a woman, thus, "channels misogynistic forces" in a more extreme/consistent manner than others in a particular context, then that women will satisfy Manne's characterization of a misogynist from above.

[6] Manne is clear about the anti-individualism implication of the account (2017, p. 60).

An artwork—like a piece of music, album cover, etc.—can thus count as misogynist when it reinforces the same patriarchal norms constitutive of misogyny. With Manne's conception in hand, we can see how (too) often DM satisfies it.

Death Metal Villains: (Too Much) Death Metal as Misogynistic

Up to this point, I have set up the first main claim: much of DM is misogynistic. To be brutally honest, I think that many people with even a limited grasp of the genre might find this claim so obvious as to undermine any need for a whole section on it. However, as we'll see quite soon, this claim might be harder to demonstrate decisively than it may seem. Nonetheless, let's try to see why the misogyny of DM is so clear to some (many).[7] Let's call this the DM Allegation of Misogyny (DAM): according to DAM, much of DM legitimately counts as misogynistic.

As my first step in showing the plausibility of DAM, I'm simply going to rattle off a quick list of song titles for those who may be oblivious to the misogynist evil DAM alleges. The *titles* will be sufficient—I won't even dig into the lyrics themselves. Then, for a more comprehensive look at the genre, I'll suggest that aspects of the genre beyond the lyrics are natural resources for substantiating DAM. The following is a short and curated, but not atypical, list of song titles.[8] We begin with one of the original, core DM bands, Cannibal Corpse:

- "Orgasm through torture"[9]
- "Dismembered and molested"[10]
- "She was asking for it"[11]
- "Meathook sodomy"[12]

---

[7] Purcell (2003) comes to the discussion of DM's misogyny very soon in the chapter on lyrics, for instance.

[8] I should also point out that my curation of the list is not just to pick only *some* of the offending (and offensive) titles: I also leave out some of the titles that I find to be the worst offenders. The fact that the list below excludes things that, to me at least, are *worse* may be the most DAM-ing move of all.

[9] *Vile* (1996, Metal Blade Records).

[10] *Gallery of Suicide* (1998, Metal Blade Records).

[11] *The Bleeding* (1994, Metal Blade Records).

[12] *Butchered at Birth* (1991, Metal Blade Records).

Next are some representative, and by no means underground, groups.

Devourment:
- "Molesting the decapitated"[13]
- "Babykiller"[14]
- "Carved into ecstasy"[15]
- "Over her dead body"[16]

Avulsed
- "Sick sick sex"[22]
- "She's hot tonight (in my oven)"[23]

Putrid Pile
- "My semen rots in you"[27]
- "Whore annihilation"[27]
- "You dead = me satisfied"[27]
- "Human stress reliever"[27]

Prostitute Disfigurement[17]
- "Dead before she hits the ground"[18]
- "Postmortal devirginized"[19]
- "She's not coming home tonight"[20]
- "Fatal fornication"[21]

Gorgasm
- "Destined to violate"[24]
- "Carnivwhore"[25]
- "Erotic dislimbing"[26]

Torsofuck
- "Amputated tits"[28]
- "Necropervert"[28]
- "Vaginal disembowelment"[29]
- "Mutilated for sexual purposes"[30]

A quick point is worth noting here: these songs aren't simply about the most horrific chaos one can cause or the most creative ways one can send a woman to the grave, they target "whores" or women viewed as promiscuous. Thus, it's not just valorizing the destruction of women *in general* but an annihilation of the "wicked" women who use their own bodies (for sex). Now, in these songs, their bodies are *being used by another*—a clear attempt to deny them autonomy and remove their agency.

However obvious these titles may make DAM seem compelling, I think it is worth discussing misogyny beyond the semantic content of

[13] *Molesting the Decapitated* (1999, United Guttural Records).
[14] *Butcher the Weak* (2005, Corpse Gristle Records/In-Cess Underground).
[15] *Conceived in Sewage* (2013, Relapse Records).
[16] *Unleash the Carnivore* (2017, Unique Leader Records).
[17] The band name alone should be more than sufficient to lead credence to DAM.
[18] *Prostitute Disfigurement* (2019, Rising Nemesis Records).
[19] *Deeds of Derangement* (2003, self-released).
[20] *Deeds of Derangement* (2003, Morbid Records).
[21] *Descendants of Depravity* (2008, Willowtip).
[22] *Yearning for the Grotesque* (2003, Avantgarde Music).
[23] *Nullo (The Pleasure of Self-Mutilation)* (2009, Ibex Moon Records).
[24] *Destined to Violate* (2014, New Standard Elite).
[25] *Destined to Violate* (2014, New Standard Elite).
[26] *Orgy of Murder* (2011, Brutal Bands).
[27] *Paraphiliac Perversions* (2016, Severed Records).
[28] *Postpartum Exstasy* (2023, Morbid Generation Records).
[29] *Disgusting Gore and Pathology* (2020, In Case You Missed It).
[30] *Erotic Diarrhea Fantasy* (2004, Goregiastic Records).

the music. Note that the lyrics and titles are only part of the package which a DM band provides on an album. There is the album artwork. These covers, just like the titles above, convey exactly the same misogynistic worries as the blood-soaked symphonies above. For just a few examples of how DM imagery can support DAM, let me describe just some of the albums from which the songs listed above come. There is a Jack the Ripper sort of figure stabbing a woman who's been chopped in half (Prostitute Disfigurement's eponymous album), a woman's body that has been split open and carved into (Avulsed's *Nullo: the Pleasure of Self-Mutilation*), a man masturbating to a naked woman's bloody corpse (Gorgasm's *Masticate to Dominate*), lingerie-clad woman bound by chains whose genitalia is being mutilated (Gorgasm's *Stabwound Intercourse*), a mound of various bloody female body parts (Putrid Pile's *Paraphiliac Perversions*), and two Asian women in school uniforms kissing each other covered in what looks like diarrhea (Torsofuck's *Erotic Diarrhea Fantasy*). It should be clear from these descriptions, just as it is from listing the titles above, that the images from the albums strongly suggest DAM obtains.

But there is an immediate response from the defensive DM fan. Interviews from Purcell's (2003) sociological investigation of DM provide it:

> One of the youngest pre-teenage survey participants took a moment to write this in defense of his favorite music: "Death Metal just talks about crazy slaughter that you know never happens,[31] but [it] is just making fun of it all...Death Metal fans don't go out and slaughter people and eat them because Death Metal lyrics shouldn't be taken seriously. They should be laughed at." Nearly every interviewee agreed with this fan on the topic of Death Metal's gore lyrics.
>
> (2003, p. 46)

According to this defense, the misogynist lyrics and imagery don't really mean anything—much less that women (or anyone) should be treated as they seem to suggest. The hammer smashed faces conjured by these words and images are meant for nonserious, nonliteral entertainment. It's all just harmless "fun."

What this "defense" assumes is something like Manne's naïve conception of misogyny: these songs/albums aren't misogynistic because there is no hatred of or hostility to women in their musicians or fans.

[31] One is tempted to push back against this point—and I suspect vigorously....

Again, it's all just irreverent "comedy." Though the factual accuracy of this can (and *should*) be contested, let's grant the point for the sake of argument. These aren't apostles of evil, but rather purveyors of transgressive, rule-breaking dark comedy.[32]

With this line of defense in tow, we can offer a more sophisticated defense of DAM without assuming the naïve conception. Of course, we already have in place Manne's conception of misogyny as policing patriarchal norms. But, here, it will help to provide more detail about those norms to see how DM can violate them. A bit more from Manne helps clear things up: "if patriarchy is anything here and now [...] I believe it consists largely (though by no means exclusively) in [an] uneven, gendered economy of *giving and taking* moral-cum-social goods and services" (2017, p. 107; emphasis original). What are such gender coded goods? Here is Manne:

> *Hers to give (feminine- coded goods and services)*: attention, affection, admiration, sympathy, sex, and children (i.e. social, domestic, reproductive, and emotional labor); also mixed goods, such as safe haven, nurture, security, soothing, and comfort; versus
>
> *His for the taking (masculine- coded perks and privileges)*: power, prestige, public recognition, rank, reputation, honor, "face," respect, money and other forms of wealth, hierarchical status, upward mobility, and the status conferred by having a high- ranking woman's loyalty, love, devotion, etc.
>
> (2017, p. 130; emphases in original)

The feminine goods generate norms regarding what women are *obligated* to provide via the patriarchal demands that misogyny (re)enforces, and the masculine goods produce patriarchal norms implying what a "good" woman is *prohibited* from possessing.[33]

To vindicate DAM under Manne's conception, we should see DM reinforcing norms that women either: (1) must give these feminine-coded goods or (2) give up or refrain from having/taking masculine-coded goods. We see plenty of examples of both (1) and (2) in DM. However, vindicating (1) without defaulting to the naïve conception's hatred or hostility

[32] Purcell (2003, p. 46) cites Matthew Harvey (guitarist for Gruesome and Exhumed) as endorsing this interpretation of DM's misogynistic-appearing content.

[33] Manne uses language describing a "good" woman as one who is good by patriarchy's lights by falling in line with these norms and a "bad" woman as violating them.

directed to women is a bit tricky: most of the DM songs about women giving feminine goods tend to frame their treatment violently. But, such ways of vindicating (1) will be susceptible to the "it's all fun" attempted defense. What's needed to condemn DAM on *Manne's* conception of misogyny are instances where women are expected to provide feminine-coded goods without the aggression we already considered: songs where women must provide these goods but *not* through their deaths.

A few examples come to mind. Consider Black Breath's *Heavy Breathing* LP, which features the song "Eat the Witch."[34] Given the twisted minds described by so many DM songs, this could be mistaken for just another tune about eating people, but let's just say that the witch survives the ordeal. We have a DM song fantasizing about a woman because "inside her the devil has lived."[35] But, note that her role is simply to provide sex (for the narrator and Satan, presumably). Also consider Black Dahlia Murder's "Deathmask Divine."[36] Inspired by the story of Carl Tanzler's obsession with Elena Milagro de Hoyos, the song describes a man who taxidermies the woman he loves. (Important for the story: he didn't kill her, de Hoyos died of tuberculosis and Tanzler, a medical doctor, did what he could to save her life.) Though the song is *very* gory, since taxidermy requires extensive working on a dead body, the narrator doesn't desire sex with a corpse: he frames his (thoroughly icky) actions as motivated by the desire to be with his beloved forever in a kind of symbolic immortality. However, this is not really a love song—his beloved quite literally cannot consent. She, or rather her venerated corpse, is there to satisfy the longing, desperation, and pain of the man who "loves" her. Again, though she is not merely a site upon which to visit violence, she remains only a resource for affection by a man. In these cases, though a man does no real violence on a (living) woman and attests genuine concern for her, she is still seen as a source for his own satisfaction. Patriarchal norms are, thus, enforced, even without the overt hatred/hostility so often countenanced in DM.

Next, let's examine (2). Reading (2) in DAM requires examples of DM that reinforce patriarchal norms by discouraging women to have masculine-coded goods. The best way to see this would be instances where men and only men possess and traffic in masculine-coded goods. Such examples

[34] (2010, Southern Lord Recordings).

[35] Is she desired because she's had sex with Satan, carried Satan's child, is uniquely in tune with Satan, or some/all of the above? I'm not sure, but I don't think it matters: she is desired for her Satan connection and the evil spells that her sexuality affords.

[36] *Nocturnal* (2007, Metal Blade Records).

are easy to see. Melodeath stalwarts, Amon Amarth, have made a career out of leaning into the frozen winds of all things characteristically Viking. From honor fights against one's closest friends ("The Way of Vikings"[37]), steely resolve to conquer ("Find a Way of Make One"[20]), hedonistic memorials to comrades slain in battle ("Raise Your Horns"[38]), praising glorious death in battle ("Runes to My Memory"[39]), and war in general (*so* many songs—too many to list), much of Amon Amarth's discography relies on the hypermasculinist tropes of warfare, glory, honor, and the prizing of extreme violence. One song in particular deserves attention. "Valkyria"[40] appeals, naturally enough, to the famed Valkyries who transport those fallen in war to Valhalla, but also Vár and Eir, the Norse goddesses of oaths and healing, respectively. Their role in the song, though, always centers on how they can help the narrator: either survive the battle (keeping his oath) or to bring him to the glorious afterlife to the battle slain. This is precisely what Manne's conception of misogyny envisions—women (goddesses!) are expected to provide important services for men, and the services themselves are feminine-coded (with respect to this cultural context). One need not go quite so specifically Viking. Much of, for instance, Dying Fetus' output emphasizes the masculine desire for power, vengeance, and outright aggression, even if the violence lauded isn't always (or even often) unleashed upon women. Just a few characteristic songs from their oeuvre will do: "Subjected to a Beating,"[41] "Unbridled Fury,"[42] "Wrong One to Fuck With,"[43] "Pissing in the Mainstream,"[44] "Die With Integrity,"[43] and so on. DM, thus, has no shortage of masculine-coded content to help reinforce the patriarchal norms that Manne's conception locates as essential to the structure of misogyny.

One last point before we end our defense of DAM. Recall that anyone—even a woman—may enact misogyny on Manne's view, so long as they consistently and extremely reinforce patriarchal norms. In the last few paragraphs, we've developed in a bit more depth just what those norms can look like in DM. What we should also see, I'm highlighting

[37] *Jomsviking* (2016, Metal Blade Records).
[38] *The Great Heathen Army* (2022, Metal Blade Records).
[39] *With Oden On Our Side* (2006, Metal Blade Records).
[40] *Berserker* (2019, Metal Blade Records).
[41] *Reign Supreme* (2012, Relapse Records).
[42] *Make Them Beg For Death* (2023, Relapse Records).
[43] *Wrong One to Fuck With* (2017, Relapse Records).
[44] *Destroy the Opposition* (2000, Relapse Records).

here, is that even female DM musicians can contribute to both (1) and (2). Women in DM sing (growl) lyrics that glorify exactly the same kind of violent, brutal treatment of women seen widely in DM.[45] I take it that we have successfully defended DAM: on either the naïve conception or the more sophisticated from Manne, one finds significant misogyny in DM.[46] In the next section, I will examine José Medina's epistemology of resistance as a resource to understand how to work against such harmful hegemonic structures. I will use Medina's concept of hermeneutic or epistemic "heroes" to uncover ways that musicians from with DM puts pressure against the DM "villains."

In Praise of Epistemic Friction: Medina's Epistemology of Resistance

José Medina (2012) offers a rich and developed account of epistemic resistance and how it might be brought to bear against oppressive, unjust, and dominant perspectives/structures. Such perspectives may be racial, gendered, heteronormative, etc. and so Medina's work can be generalized to any such structure. Misogyny, of either the naïve or Manne's conception, will certainly form a target for such resistance.[47] Attempting to lay out Medina's whole account in a short section is foolish, and so I won't attempt it. Instead, the goal is to isolate some key threads that we may draw together, in the next section, to show how some DM musicians work toward the kind of resistance that Medina discusses.

For Medina, "epistemic injustices...call for epistemic resistance, that is, for the use of our epistemic resources and abilities to undermine and change oppressive normative structures and the complacent cognitive-affective functioning that sustains those structures" (2012, p. 3). Since problematic cognition sustains such structures, we need more than just

[45] See Cerebral Bore's "Epileptic Strobe Entrapment," "The Bald Cadaver," "Open Casket Priapism," and "24 Year Party Dungeon" (*Maniacal Miscreation* (2011, Earache Records)) and Once Human's "You Cunt" (*The Life I Remember* (2015, earMUSIC)) for a few examples.

[46] Obviously, #notalldeathmetal, but enough from influential bands to make it a noteworthy problem for the genre taken as a whole.

[47] Medina's language calls out "sexism" rather than "misogyny." They seem to be identified for Medina even if Manne distinguishes them. Our purposes here, though, don't require any stance on this issue. So long as Manne's conception of misogyny counts as an oppressive, dominant perspective for Medina (and it does), we don't need to worry about whether it is more aptly termed "sexism" or "misogyny." Either way: it is to be resisted.

social or political resistance to dismantle them. We need *epistemic* resistance aimed at the cognitive roots feeding them. With the epistemology of resistance thereby motivated, we must examine what characterizes the cognition to be resisted. Here is Medina:

> I will argue that in contexts of sexual and racial oppression there are cognitive-affective deficits that amount to specific forms of epistemic *insensitivity*: the inability to listen and to learn from others, the inability to call into question one's perspective and to process ... significantly different perspectives.
>
> (Medina 2012, pp. 17–18; emphasis in original)

By being blind, so to speak, to others, one might think the central problem is a straightforward blindness to the truth about them, their experiences, etc. Yet, the insensitivity in question goes beyond mere first-order blindness. Medina calls the real source a kind of "meta-blindness": one is blind to one's own blindness to differently situated others (2012, p. 75). This sort of second-order ignorance ("active ignorance") actively militates against any attempt to neutralize it. Epistemic resistance moves forward only to the extent that it can push against the second-ordered-ness of the meta-blindness/ignorance which sustains oppressive structures. Medina's main "antidote" to meta-blindness is "epistemic friction" (2012, p. 78).

Medina exploits the metaphorical idea of epistemic friction as a path of fierce resistance.[48] Medina describes it as "a friction that enables us to acknowledge and engage alternative viewpoints and to reach epistemic equilibrium among alternative perspectives on a problem or phenomena" (2012, p. 176), which naturally works against meta-blindness/ignorance insofar as such friction produces engagement with other perspectives. These "epistemic counterpoints," thereby, offer a way to resist the second-order ignorance that produces and is produced by the insensitivity which sustains oppressive perspectives. Such friction, via such counterpoints, leads to the opposite of meta-blindness: meta-lucidity (212, 186).[49]

Yet, we don't know how such friction may be produced. How can epistemic counterpoints be brought to light and, perhaps, even forced on

[48] Literally, friction is a kind of resistance between two surfaces, after all.

[49] Much like Socrates' description of "human wisdom" in the *Apology*, Medina's meta-lucidity consists precisely in recognizing that one has blind spots or bodies of ignorance (2012, p. 196). The meta-lucid and meta-blind have blind spots, to be sure, but the former and not the latter is aware of *that* fact about their own ignorance.

those who may be otherwise (meta-)blind to them? Here, Medina's concept of a hermeneutical "hero" becomes relevant.

> It may appear that we will need *hermeneutical heroes* to [bring about more hermeneutical openness to other perspectives]—that is, that we will need extremely courageous speakers and listeners who defy well-entrenched communicative expectations and dominant hermeneutical perspectives, and against all odds are lucky enough to change (or at least disrupt) hermeneutical trends so as to make room for new meanings and interpretative perspectives.
>
> (Medina 2012, p. 111)

Such heroes will defy the dominant perspective *for the sake of making others' perspective(s) appreciated*—especially those who aren't heard, understood, or given any prior credibility. Such "rebellion," via hermeneutical heroes, aims to force upon the dominant perspective openness to and consideration of unheard/unappreciated standpoints and, thereby, the friction needed to dislodge meta-ignorance (2012, p. 115). Crucially, such friction can be "internal" to a perspective: those from within it can, somehow, defy its own norms thereby opening it to other perspectives to which it has been blind. Hermeneutical heroes, especially the most defiant ones, exist inside the dominant perspective that's pierced from within by their own epistemic friction (2012, p. 232).

We can draw many threads together running throughout Medina's epistemology of resistance. Hermeneutical heroes bring about epistemic friction via defying norms, sometimes from within the dominant perspective itself, and the resulting openness to other views helps undercut the meta-blindness/ignorance which sustains and is sustained by such oppressive structures. Thus, such heroes epistemically resist these structures—in which some of them currently dwell. In the next section, we'll complete our discussion of DM heroes by seeing instances of DM hermeneutical heroism and, thereby, the resistance against the misogyny their own genre promotes.

Death Metal Hero(in)es: Anti-misogynist Death Metal Resistance

Recall that Medina understands a hermeneutical hero as a person who will have "well-entrenched communicative expectations and dominant hermeneutical perspectives" (2012, p. 111). However, given Medina's aim doesn't specify what kind of expectations/perspectives will be transgressed, we can return to Manne's conception of misogyny to provide more particular content that *anti-misogynistic* hermeneutical heroes will defy.

We've seen earlier that Manne's conception provides us with two patriarchal norms that misogyny enforces for a woman to be a "good girl." Women either: (1) must give the feminine-coded goods which patriarchy takes as obligated or (2) give up or refrain from having/taking masculine-coded goods. In many of the examples I will discuss, violating (1) and (2) are co-implicated: often a woman fails to give feminine-coded goods *by* possessing or taking masculine-coded goods. However, before we examine these DM hermeneutical heroines, I shall argue that there's another way that DM musicians can resist and defy the patriarchal norms which constitute misogyny.

We might ask, at this point, what a man might be able to do to resist misogyny? Obviously, a male DM musician could write a song about a woman violating (1) or (2). But are there no ways that a man can resist misogyny without, in effect, doing so by proxy? I think so. If patriarchal norms enact misogyny by enforcing them, then one can resist such patriarchal norms by men violating the *inverse* of (1) and (2). If patriarchal norms *require women* to give feminine-coded goods, for instance, then the same norm will *prohibit men* from giving the same.[50] As Briana Toole (2019) notes,

> the cultural work of misogyny is not just, as Manne argues, to confine women to those roles associated with femininity, but also to *enforce the expectations of masculinity*. These expectations are such that men are punished when they show compassion for others, especially as this is taken to be a feminine trait. [...] Misogyny works, then, I suggest, not merely by policing women so as to ensure that they adhere to certain social norms, but by *policing men as well*. When men effectively live up to the patriarchal norms to which they are held and successfully perform masculinity, they participate in and perpetuate the false belief that men are inherently stoic[51] creatures...
>
> (Toole 2019, p. 12; emphases added)

[50] See Digby (2003) for a discussion of how sexism (or misogyny, for Manne) enacts patriarchal norms for men.

[51] "Stoic" being the patriarchal norm for masculinity.

Thus, if a man either: (3) gives feminine-coded goods or (4) gives up or refuses to possess masculine-coded goods, then these actions will defy the same patriarchal norms foisted on women but from the opposite position. As such, men in DM who may work toward (3) or (4) will produce misogyny-resistant DM in a similar, but inverse, way that women work against (1) or (2). Thus, we should cast our hermeneutical hero net wider than simply women who may violate (1)/(2) but to also look for men who satisfy (3)/(4). Accordingly, I suggest that we have two categories of DM "heroes": women who violate the feminine-coded norms by engaging in masculine-coded goods and men who violate the masculine-coded norms by engaging in feminine-coded goods. Examples of both kinds of heroism will be instances of misogyny-resistant DM.

Let's first examine how DM heroines defy misogynistic norms by taking masculine-coded goods. One thing we can quickly note in the norms Manne associates with patriarchy's "good girl" is a loss or diminishment of one's agency or autonomy. Since women are conceived, by misogynist lights, as mere providers of feminine-coded goods like emotional support, sex, etc., a central way to violate such norms would be for women to enact and embody a more fully agential stance. We have examples of this. Venom Prison's "Slayer of Holofernes,"[52] for instance, retells the traditional tale of Judith from the titular apocryphal text. In this story, a woman is *literally* the heroine; saving her nation using extreme violence to behead the general of the oppressing army. We'll see more examples of violent women below, but the agency Judith displays in this story/song is what needs emphasis. Another Venom Prison song, "Pain of Oizys"[53] (named after the Greek goddess of anxiety) is about dealing with trauma and the various emotional bricolage with which it often comes. But, it is the speaker's response to trauma that bears emphasis: she will bow to no one and get off of her knees, even amidst life crushing pain, to find peace in the "roughest seas." For I Am King's[54] "Pariah,"[55] similarly, tells a story of struggling with some kind of "darkness" that the speaker ultimately has the strength to overcome, even to the point of telling others that *they* will drown in *her* misery. Finally, Monochromatic Black's "Hail to the

[52] *Primeval* (2020 Prosthetic Records).
[53] *Erebos* (2022, Century Media Records).
[54] Note the gendered language. Though the vocalist is a woman, the use of "king" suggests an autonomy, agency, and power that patriarchal norms would deny women.
[55] *Crown* (2023, Prime Collective).

Queen (The Hive)"[56] is ostensibly about a beehive—the "queen" being literally a queen bee. But, the imagery of a powerful female with male drones simply there to serve isn't lost within a genre where women are too often beings that are merely soon to be dead. In fact, the dominance of the queen, according to the song, is why bees are greater and humanity is envious. Songs like these describe autonomous, powerful women who exercise their agency from within a genre where women are mere objects hacked up for barbeque.

Second, and relatedly, we see examples of women enacting extreme violence themselves—following the *masculine* role of the traditional DM songs like those from the list earlier. What we see, I suggest, is precisely the same kind of extreme, gory violence typical of DM, but committed (and enjoyed) by women. But, we can note two different ways, or better, targets, of female extreme violence. They can be violent *in general* or *to men specifically*. For a band consistently providing the former, Stabbing has a range of songs that depict DM's standard brutal violence but without any gendering of the victims.[57] These lyrics come from the mouth of a woman, Bridget Lynch. Next, we see a few examples of violence done intentionally on men by women. Recall Venom Prison's "Slayer of Holofernes": the speaker doesn't just focus on violence to Holofernes, but that "no man is safe" and that it's kill or be killed. Similarly, their "Desecration of Human Privilege" deploys extreme violence on a (male) murderer.[58]

More specifically, one finds a range of examples of DM songs—by female and male vocalists alike—specifically about killing rapists: Castator's "The Emasculator" and "No Victim,"[59] Abnormality's "Curb Stomp,"[60] Venom Prison's "Perpetrator Emasculation,"[61] Sanguisugabogg's "Dick Filet,"[62] and Devourment's "Truculent Antipathy,"[63] just to name a few. The last song deserves a bit more discussion. The attentive reader will note Devourment on the earlier list of DM "villains." The long-running group act has been among the poster bands for extraordinarily

[56] *Predacious* (2024, self-released).
[57] See, e.g. the following songs: "Razor Wire Strangulation," "Southern Hacksaw Execution," "Final Flesh Feast," and "Pulsing Wound."
[58] Also, note the language—it's (male) *privilege* that's *desecrated*.
[59] Both from *No Victim* (2015, Horror Pain Gore Death Productions).
[60] *Sociopathic Constructs* (2019, Metal Blade Records).
[61] *Animus* (2016, Prosthetic Records).
[62] *Tortured Whole* (2021, Century Media Records).
[63] *Obscene Majesty* (2019, Relapse Records).

misogynistic songs. In fact, Devourment was named as one of the worst offenders in a widely-read VICE article on misogyny in extreme metal.[64] However, getting called out seems to have opened their eyes (co-opting Medina's blindness/sight metaphor) to their misogyny. In a moment of clarity, Chris Andrews, their guitarist, reflects that the VICE article "did kind of hold up a magnifying glass to [their misogynistic content] ... If you're getting called out for it, you're obviously not writing a shocking horror movie here, you're just pushing this misogyny button over and over again. Why are you doing that?"[65] Their last record, *Obscene Majesty*, features the same violence Devourment has described for nearly 30 years, yet only one song has gendered violence in it. "Truculent Antipathy" describes the infernal end of a serial rapist who is captured, tortured, and murdered by a potential victim. The song describes his maze of torment, at her hands, in *first-person* terms. The man has become the site for violence, and we see the violence from the "victim's" perspective (rather than the victimizer), further turning the genre standard rape story on its head. Perhaps, Devourment's case is evidence that some anti-misogynistic epistemic resistance might be successful, even if to a limited extent.[66]

Finally, one band mentioned above deserves special discussion. Castrator, an international group of female DM musicians, which their vocalist describes as composed of "unapologetically strong, independent, and pissed-off females."[67] A song like "Honor Killing" wears its concern on its face, and "Brood" describes the patriarchal view of a woman as, effectively, a machine to produce children. Additionally, "Tormented by Atrocities" describes a murderer languishing in a cell. Further, "Forsaken and Deprived" seethes at the number of unsolved and un-/under-investigated instances of rape and murder. Most of Castrator's lyrical content, as well as the name of the band (obviously enough), is about describing and calling out misogyny.

So, we have a range of examples of DM where women violate patriarchal norms by taking on the extreme violence which traditional DM

---

[64] Mikkelson (2024).

[65] Quoted in Zorgdrager (2019).

[66] Recall that Medina construes hermeneutical heroes as those that don't just *contribute resistant language* but also those that *hear* the resistant language—i.e. those on whom the friction has started to get a grip. Devourment might be evidence for those who have *heard and responded* to epistemically resistant overtures. This helps us see the other side of Medina's conception of hermeneutical heroes *as listeners*.

[67] Quoted in Kelly (2024).

tends to deploy on women by men and reverses it. Accordingly, they take on the masculine-coded norms that the tradition has reserved for men. In taking this perspective, they serve as hermeneutical heroines defying the entrenched communication/perspective of DM seeing women as the passive victims of violence rather than the agents of violence. Now, women can perform the murderous rampage, not just men, and very often *on* men. Next, let us see if there is a DM that defies and resists the inverse: men who take up the feminine-coded goods/roles.

First, let's consider the band responsible for this chapter's title: Brojob.[68] The leader in hyper nonheteronormativity (homonormativity?) for DM, Brojob's songs take the sexualized aggression typical of DM but upend traditional expectations in various ways. Most obviously, many of their songs laud, in caricatured and exaggerated detail, homoerotic acts. For the sake of space, I'll provide only titles again: "Bottom Feeders,"[69] "We Are the Boyfriend Stealers,"[70] "Pen Island,"[71] "Tickle War,"[70] and "Be My Valentine."[72] So many of the DAM-able lyrics in the songs listed earlier explicitly focus on male/female "sex" acts. Brojob's homoerotic lyrics are, as one would expect in DM, aggressive and cartoonish, but the sexualized violence is always male/male. Brojob goes beyond this, however. One could use homosexual actions but, by taking the dominant/aggressor role, reinforce the hypermasculinist perspective anti-misogynist heroes need to defy.[72] But, the Brojob speaker will often take the recipient role: "If there's one thing in life I've learned/It's how to take a load" ("Talk Shit, Get Kissed").[70] Brojob takes the aggression typical of DM and applies it to very un-DM glorification of homosexuality.

But, a similar response can push against my reading of Brojob as hermeneutical heroes that we see above in raising DAM. Brojob's homosexuality is *so* extreme, cartoonish, and outlandish that it might appear to be just a joke. The thought is that they aren't *really* pushing against heteronormativity but, perhaps the reverse, doubling down on hypermasculinity by making fun of homoeroticism. Interestingly, Brojob seems aware of

[68] "Talk Shit, Get Kissed" (*Talk Shit Get Kissed* (2018, Hollowed Records)) clearly plays with Body Count's "Talk Shit, Get Shot" (*Manslaughter* (2014, Sumerian Records)).
[69] The Heaviest Album of All Time (2021, Hollowed Records).
[70] *Talk Shit Get Kissed* (2018, Hollowed Records).
[71] Which, I assume, is a play on "penis land." *Talk Shit Get Kissed* (2018, Hollowed Records).
[72] Here, I'm thinking of Catullus 16. Though the speaker aggressively describes homosexual actions, they are always the agent enforcing their will in the passive recipient of whatever action is being described, or better, *threatened*.

the charge in "Erection Injection"[52]: "Like, what the fuck man/Chill out/It's just a joke." But, the next line is telling: "But seriously I really do want to/suck your dick so bad/So fucking deal with it bitch." And Brojob does more than simply write hyperhomoerotically aggressive songs. "Teenie Weenie" is about just that—having a small penis.[70] "Temper Tantrum,"[69] "Keyboard Warriors,"[69] and "The Incel Anthem"[73] explicitly (and hilariously) troll hypermasculine dudes on the internet. "Extra Thicc"[69] turns DM songs describing misogynist cannibalism on their heads by violently describing eating normal food.

Finally, "Tuff Love"[69] plays with the misogynistic violence of DM in ways that explicitly undermine it. For instance, when the chainsaw is introduced, it's to make a statute to the beloved rather than a morbid way to die. Every act of standard DM violence becomes an act of love. And the chorus makes it explicit: "Tuff love bitch/Is another word for a female dog/And should never be used to/Degrade women." In various ways, Brojob takes the expectations marshaled in DAM and defies them. Here, then, we have Medina's hermeneutical heroism for DM.

Another band that pushes against dominant misogynist perspectives is Sanguisugabogg. With less caricature-y humor and much more serious violence, they often push against the masculine-coded goods/roles typical of much DM. A first example is "Menstrual Envy."[62] Here, the male speaker violently mutilates his genitalia and encourages a parasite in the penis so that it will continually bleed, all with the attempt to feel what it's like to menstruate and thereby empathize (not merely sympathize) with the female beloved. Next, "Felching Filth"[62] takes the homoerotic overtones of Brojob but without the humor. This song describes *homosexual* sex with a dead body, overturning the standard heterosexual necrophilia of DM, but retaining DM's core disgusting imagery. When the DM speaks of robbing the grave, the usual target is a female. Thus, Sanguisugabogg works within the confines of DM *while* defying it. Similarly, many of Sanguisugabogg's songs (e.g. "Dead as Shit,"[62] "Black Market Vasectomy,"[74]

---

[73] "The Incel Anthem" (*The Heaviest Album of All Time* (2021, Hollowed Records)) is a good example for us. Manne's (2017) account of misogyny often uses incels and incel violence as evidence for and ways to help conceptualize misogyny.

[74] *Homicidal Ecstacy* (2023, Century Media). Note, too, that the botched vasectomy described ends up deforming the speaker's genitalia. It's hard not to see this as a way to confront gender nonconformity in a DM context, especially given that Sanguisugabogg's former guitarist and bandleader Cameron Boggs is a self-described "queer nonbinary homie" (Staff, Revolver. "Sanguisugabogg: Meet Inclusive Ohio Death-Metal Crew Born from Acid Trip." Revolver, January 26, 2021. https://www.revolvermag.com/music/sanguisugabogg-meet-inclusive-ohio-death-metal-crew-born-acid-trip.).

"Dragged by a Truck,"[68] and "Gored in the Chest,"[62]) describe extreme violence but *done on the males—often the narrator*. Again, the echoes of DM tropes remain in the extreme violence and gore presented in these songs, but the masculine viewpoint becomes that of the victim rather than the aggressor.[75]

Finally, some bands throw off even the gore, violence, and aggression. My analysis of DM has generally focused on the vocals, so we are free to look at bands who may reject even more of the lyrical and stylistic tropes, so long as growled vocals remain. I will specifically consider the band Aether Realm.[76] In what may be a rare DM ballad, the speaker of "Guardian" takes on the role of the emotional care-giver that Manne sees as feminine-coded.

> I will be your guardian from loneliness
> Feel my love surround you
> Share your burden
> I will carry it
> A refuge all around you
> When sorrow overtakes you
> You can call on me
> Lay your troubles on me friend
> I'll be with you 'til the end
> I'll be your guardian[77]

This kind of positive, uplifting, and caring attitude is *far* from the DM songs listed above in our examination of DAM. "Guardian" *protects* despondent souls rather than brutally violating them. And this is anti-misogynistic by virtue of taking on the feminine-coded role that patriarchy prohibits for men. "Cycle"[78] describes, in emotional honesty, a cyclic pattern of trying to improve one's (emotional) life, failing in some regard, and attempting again. Even in a song that's not really emotionally loaded, "Redneck Vikings from Hell," we see a call to inclusivity in metal. The title itself conjures up the masculinist tropes we see paradigmatically in

---

[75] Here, we recall Bloodbath's infamous "Eaten" (*Nightmares Made Flesh* (2004, Century Media Records)), written about German cannibal, Armin Meiwes, and his consensual victim, Bernd Brandes. The song, though, is from the perspective of the one who is and desires to be eaten: not the one who *does* the eating.

[76] Aether Realm is composed entirely of men.

[77] "Guardian" *Redneck Vikings from Hell* (2020, Napalm Records).

[78] Redneck Vikings from Hell (2020, Napalm Records).

the Viking-themed metal of Amon Amarth. However, when one asks how a person might be both a redneck and a Viking, the speaker answers:

> See, some folks would say
> That you had to be born down south
> And still others would say the frozen north
> But I reckon that ain't it
> See, when it comes down to it, it ain't about
> Where you were born or how you were raised
> Being a redneck viking is about one thing;
> Whether you know how to fuckin' party[79]

Being a Viking, even a redneck one, isn't about being a male or even masculine. It's about having a good time, and that's open to all persons of all (or no) genders (or races and creeds).

In various ways, these bands defy the expectations DAM-guilty bands set up and push against the perspectives which have often organized and constrained much DM. Sexual roles are defied, emotional roles are overturned, and the active/passive distinction is reversed. All of these ways of defying, or better transgressing, the received DM traditions and codes provides us with bands that serve as Medina-n hermeneutical heroes to the kind of misogyny Manne describes.

Conclusion: Meta-transgression

So much of DM sounds like fury's manifesto on the world, and, notably, such fury is too often brought to bear against women. Thus, we have seen how DAM seems entirely appropriate as a challenge to DM, informed by Manne's conception of misogyny. With Medina's hermeneutical heroism in hand, I examined various examples of DM in that push against misogyny. There, we find heroic women who take masculine-coded goods and explicitly call out misogynistic norms and men who overturn patriarchal standards by occupying feminine- (or at least non masculine-) coded roles. By defying these expectations, norms, and perspectives these DM musicians will, thereby, count as hermeneutical hero(in)es.

[79] "Redneck Vikings from Hell" *Redneck Vikings from Hell* (2020, Napalm Records).

In conclusion, then, I want to point out the transgressive function of such heroes and how such transgression fits into a genre that makes it central. By prizing and centering transgression, DM becomes unstable. How can *transgression* be a *norm*? Transgression, by definition, violates norms, so DM seems to set up a self-targeted tension: a norm that must undermine itself. However, by vindicating DAM and recognizing DM hermeneutical heroism, I suggest that DM might gain a kind of stability through meta-transgression.

Lest we forget, one reason why DM wallows in violence, gore, and horror is transgression itself. The extremity of the lyrics matches the extremity of the sound, which underpins the transgressive function of DM. So, by defying *misogynistic* violence, while often maintaining violence *simipliciter*, hermeneutical heroes in DM can transgress the genre's core transgressive function *from within*. Their heroism can satisfy DM's definitive transgressive function by transgressing one of the key ways that the genre itself enacts that transgression (=misogyny). Such heroism not only capitalizes on the function of the transgressive practices themselves (=misogynist violence) but, in making them now the transgress*ed* practices, fulfills a higher order transgression: when a genre seems to put everything under a transgressive lens, the only thing left to transgress will be the genre itself. When it comes to misogynist violence in music, there may be none so vile as DM; however, if we look in the right places, we can find heroic efforts to pull it from the depths of its own depravity.[80]

References

Allett, N. (2012). The extreme metal 'connoisseur'. *Popular Music History* 6: 166–181.

Digby, T. and Department of Philosophy, Florida State University (2003). Male trouble: are men victims of sexism? *Social Theory and Practice* 29 (2): 247–273.

Kelly, K. (2024). Castrator's brutal 'no victim' EP is a perfect feminist death metal revenge fantasy. VICE, July 28, 2024. `https://www.vice.com/en/article/rgpqjx/castrator-interview-stream` (accessed 13 May 2025).

[80] For anyone interested in a playlist of the death metal hero(in)es here, you can hear them on my Spotify "Death Metal Heroes" playlist (https://open.spotify.com/playlist/2pPfB8oC80nTkZP9OX7eOm?si=f5cf68b298c44204&pt=7479b6994891d5847d9085ea5b855598). There are also some "Easter Eggs" scattered throughout this chapter. For anyone interested in them, check out my "Death Metal and Misogyny Easter Eggs" (https://open.spotify.com/playlist/2pPfB8oC80nTkZP9OX7eOm?si=f5cf68b298c44204&pt=7479b6994891d5847d9085ea5b855598).

Kirner-Ludwig, M. and Wohlfarth, F. (2018). METALinguistics: face-threatening taboos, conceptual offensiveness and discursive transgression in extreme metal. *Metal Music Studies* 4 (3): 403–432.

Manne, K. (2017). *Down Girl: The Logic of Misogyny*. Oxford: Oxford University Press.

McCraw, B.W. (2024). Brutal truth: modern(ist) aesthetics and death metal. *Journal of Aesthetics & Culture* 16 (1): 1–13.

Medina, J. (2012). *The Epistemology of Resistance: Gender and Racial Oppression, Epistemic Injustice, and Resistant Imaginations*. Oxford: Oxford University Press.

Mikkelson, J. (2024). It's time to stop making excuses for extreme metal's violent misogynist fantasies. VICE, August 4, 2024. https://www.vice.com/en/article/rb8bnd/death-metal-misogyny (accessed 13 May 2025).

Phillipov, M. (2012). *Death Metal and Music Criticism: Analysis at the Limits*. Lanham: Lexington Books.

Purcell, N.J. (2003). *Death Metal Music: The Passion and Politics of a Subculture*. Jefferson, NC: McFarland & Company, Inc. Publishers.

Scott, N. (2016). Heavy metal as resistance. In: *Heavy Metal Music Studies and Popular Culture* (ed. B.G. Walter, G. Riches, D. Snell, and B. Bardine), 19–35. Basingstoke: Palgrave Macmillan.

Toole, B. (2019). Masculine foes, feminist woes: a response to down Girl. *APA Newlsetter* 18 (2): 10–14.

Unger, M.P. (2016). *Sound, Symbol, and Sociality: The Aesthetic Experience of Extreme Metal Music*. Palgrave Macmillan.

Wallmark, Z. (2018). The sound of evil. In: *The Relentless Pursuit of Tone: Timbre in Popular Music* (ed. R. Fink, M. Latour, and Z. Wallmark), 65–87. Oxford: Oxford University Press.

Zorgdrager, B. (2019). How brutal death metal is confronting its misogyny problem. Kerrang!, August 29, 2019. https://www.kerrang.com/how-brutal-death-metal-is-confronting-its-misogyny-problem (accessed 13 May 2025).

Chapter 15
The Heaviness of Play in Heavy Metal

Shelby Moser
Division of Games, University of Utah, Salt Lake City, UT, USA

Introduction

Two distinct experiences come to mind. One is from a Nekrogoblikon (Death Metal) show, where the band's iconic goblin-masked, suit-wearing mascot ran around on stage—a sight hard to forget. But even more memorable was the big, sweaty guy in the pit wearing an inner tube, bouncing people off him as he wildly moshed. This was unexpected and, from my vantage point, everyone was having a great time. The other memory is from a HEALTH (Industrial Metal) show, where a mosher emerged from a particularly chaotic pit with a bloody nose, a huge smile, and a question: "What happened to my shoe?"

Despite their differences, what strikes me about both experiences is the sense of togetherness, enjoyment, and trust they embodied. Within the chaos of heavy metal shows, there are moments of shared playful experiences, much like what scholars of games explain happens in "the magic circle." Within this magic circle, attitudes and activities take on a slightly different form than in ordinary life. While this phrase is somewhat mysterious, we can imagine a space where we experience a state of flow or an immersive, ideal environment. This should not suggest a complete separation between ordinary life and the magic circle—the two realms can be quite porous. Still, however else we can characterize it, a magic circle can be understood as a special space or play community with its own play governance and boundaries for those who opt in.[1]

The fact that these spaces are voluntary is important and partially explains why the two experiences mentioned above were perceived as enjoyable. As I will show here, opting in is more than mere consent. After all, we can consent to something without knowing much about it, and then later change our minds. Rather, certain norms are governed by implicit rules which help build a sense of willingness and trust.

What I've described so far are concepts relating to play and playfulness, but the question—do these concepts adequately capture the heavy metal culture—probably remains. A quick Google search reveals several defining characteristics of heavy metal music—loud, powerful, distorted, and aggressive. For some, these traits also extend to metal enthusiasts, or "metalheads," who are often perceived as intense, unrestrained, and heavy as the music they embrace and the concerts they attend. How can we reconcile such disparate concepts such as playfulness and heaviness? Here, I propose that play fits under a "gestalt of heaviness," that play helps explain some normative attitudes and behaviors of metalheads, and that play is an undersold value of heavy metal.

The Heaviness of Heavy Metal

Heavy metal is a broad genre with numerous subgenres, each with its own distinctive sounds, characteristics, and structures. That heavy metal has such disparate characteristics raises a fundamental question: how do we aesthetically appreciate such varied styles as part of the same musical category? Consider the following examples. Classic heavy metal bands such as Judas Priest and Iron Maiden emerged in the 1970s and 1980s and are characterized by their powerful vocals and clean production sounds. These formative bands laid the foundation for subsequent

---

[1] For more on The Magic Circle, see Huizinga (1949); Tekinbas and Zimmerman (2003) especially pp. 93–99). For more on play communities, see De Koven (2013); Pearce (2011).

subgenres, of which there are *many*. While there are countless subgenres, here are just a few. Doom metal is characterized by slow tempos, low-tuned guitars (giving it an especially heavy sound), and extremely loud amplifiers—exemplified by bands like Pentagram and Black Sabbath. In contrast, Death Metal features fast tempos, complex drum patterns, and deep, guttural vocals, as heard in bands like Blood Incantation, Cannibal Corpse, and Dying Fetus. Bands like Lamb of God and Pantera belong under Groove Metal, a subgenre that focuses on rhythmic or "groovy" sounds often with down-tuned sludgy guitar sounds. Black Metal, different still, is known for its fast tempos, lo-fi production, tremolo-picked guitar riffs, and lyrics often exploring Satanism or anti-Christian themes, with bands such as Darkthrone and Zeal & Ardor.

Beyond these examples, heavy metal branches into even more subgenres, including Industrial Metal, Prog, Nu, Sludge, and Thrash. There are also "sub-sub-genres" that emerge from the fusion of characteristics from larger subgenres. For example, Doom Metal splits into Stoner Doom (e.g. Green Lung, Sleep, and Electric Wizard), which incorporates occult themes, and Funeral Doom (e.g. Bell Witch and Warning), which leans toward melancholic and somber sounds. Blackened Doom, such as Ragana and Mizmor, integrates features from both the Black and Doom subgenres. Similarly, Deathcore bands like Lorna Shore blend elements of Death, Metalcore, and Hardcore Metal. Will Ramos' pig squeals—heard in "To the Hellfire" (On *...And I Return to Nothingness* [EP]. Century Media Records, Shore (2021), especially around minute 5: 45), clearly showcase Death Metal's influence on Lorna Shore's vocals, while the tremolo-picked guitars reflect Black Metal's influence.

This vast network of subgenres and their hybrids illustrates strong diversity within heavy metal, challenging our perceptions and belief that the many disparate sounds might fit under a single genre (Gracyk 2016). Is there a distinctive, unifying aesthetic feature? Regardless of their distinct differences–and apropos of its genre name–we're told there might be a unifying aesthetic of "heaviness" (Miller 2022). While some consider heaviness an inaccessible aspect of heavy metal music, metalheads view it as a defining and desirable trait. If this is the case, it suggests that heaviness holds significant aesthetic value, as Jason Miller believes (Miller 2022). But such a term is not so easy to define and, according to his article on the subject, Miller acknowledges that an aesthetics of heavy metal resists articulation. Fully articulating an aesthetic of heaviness is complex, as the term has been used to describe both the aesthetics and ontology of rock music—a broader category with a longer history and a larger body of research than heavy metal. Additionally, various methods have been employed to study heaviness, ranging from philosophical and sociological approaches to empirical analysis (Miller 2022).

According to Miller, "'Heavy' is every bit as common as terms such as 'beautiful', 'graceful', 'delicate', 'dainty', 'garish', and so on (if not more so), yet there seems relatively little controversy concerning the correctness of its application" (Miller 2022). Drawing on Kendall Walton's perceptual account of aesthetic appreciation and standard features (Walton 1990), Miller argues that this is a helpful way forward. Standard features guide us in perceiving the "gestalt of a category," a particularly useful concept when certain categories resist strict necessary and sufficient conditions (Walton 1990: 340). In the context of heavy metal, elements such as loudness, distortion, and dissonance contribute to a "gestalt of heavy," broadly unifying the aesthetics across its many diverse subgenres (Miller 2022).

And it's not just the sounds that are heavy—certain behaviors and appearances of metalheads also embody heaviness, sometimes aggressively so. Moshing, headbanging, crowd surfing, and "raising the horns"—a hand gesture formed by extending the pointer and pinky fingers while tucking in the middle and ring fingers—are commonplace, especially at heavy metal concerts. Depending on the subgenre, it's not unusual to see someone emerge from the pit with injuries or a rogue shoe separated from its owner. Metalheads also tend to favor dark clothing, often paired with Doc Martens, Converse, piercings, tattoos, and other stylistic choices that reinforce the heavy aesthetic. While each subgenre has its own distinctive features, they all contribute to the broader *gestalt* of heaviness.

Yet despite its heaviness, metal has a distinct sense of playfulness—especially when metalheads gather at concerts.

Characterizing Play

"Play" and "playfulness" are likely the terms least associated with the heavy metal scene—a culture typically linked to dark symbols, aggressive behavior, and heavy sounds, themes, and appearances. While these elements may seem at odds with play, I argue that play can also fit within the gestalt of heaviness, revealing something distinctive about heavy metal.

Before returning to our discussion of heavy metal, we must briefly examine the concept of play. Playfulness is typically understood as an attitude toward an object or activity. It is often characterized as a disposition that is lighthearted, cheerful, and open-minded—an attitude that embraces enjoyment, spontaneity, fun, and creativity. A playful attitude invites engagement in play, humor, and exploration, often facilitating positive interactions with others. This attitude often leads to play—the activity that arises from it. With that said, there is some debate about the sequence of play. Contemporary literature generally suggests that play is an action that brings enjoyment (or other feelings), such as unwinding with a game of basketball, joining friends for Dungeons & Dragons, or casually gaming on your phone. In contrast, some classical scholarship proposes that play begins as an emotion, which then motivates a physical manifestation, such as jumping for joy after a sports win or swaying to music. Despite these differing views, there is broad agreement on certain features of play: it is voluntary, distinct from ordinary life, and typically improves our emotional state. Some scholars have likened these experiences to being in a "magic circle," where, once engaged in play, ordinary responsibilities become less salient.

While I have just mentioned games in my discussion of play above, the concept of play—as I intend it here—is distinct from gameplay. In other words, I do not propose that metalheads play games when engaging with heavy metal music. Although play can have game-like qualities, play is more free form and open-ended.[2] While games ranging from chess, and basketball, to Baldur's Gate 3 have formal rulesets and goals, the rules of play are more implicit and are more loosely coordinated. For example, when children pretend a tree stump is a bear, they imply certain implicit rules, such as the simple rule that "this tree stump is a bear at this moment." However, this does not mean that all children will pretend all tree stumps are bears. In other instances, a tree stump might be a time machine, a fun platform to jump from, or simply a tree stump.

Just as I have distinguished between play and games, I also want to emphasize that play isn't always about pretending or make-believing something exists. My examples of children pretending a tree stump is a bear or a time machine serve to highlight the open-ended, engaging nature of play, and to differentiate it from highly structured rule-bound games. Similarly, a playful attitude doesn't always require imagination or pretense. For example, I might follow a recipe very precisely when making dinner, or I might be more spontaneous, playing with the process

[2] Micheal Ridge would call "pure play" unscripted activities to distinguish them from the scripted activities of games that prescribe us to follow formal rules (Ridge 2022).

by using the recipe more as a guideline. What this illustrates is that play doesn't always involve a game, and—like the tree stump—props can be used to facilitate and guide play in loosely coordinated ways.[3]

Before returning to heavy metal, I want to raise one more caveat. Terms like playfulness, fun, and spontaneity are often regarded as secondary when it comes to aesthetic appreciation. These kinds of pejorative notions are nothing new. For example, E. H. Gombrich recognizes that "[t]he idea of fun is even more unpopular among us than the notion of beauty" (Gombrich 1984, found in Sharp and Thomas 2019: ix). John Sharp and David Thomas highlight the marginalization of the concept of "fun" in broader game scholarship, arguing that it has been overlooked in favor of less ambiguous and contentious terms (Sharp and Thomas 2019). There is also doubt about whether play itself can be a serious endeavor—something worthy of our time—or if it's better left understood as childish and frivolous entertainment. As you might imagine, much work has been done to defend the value of play. For example, Plato defends that play leads to "the good life" (*eudaimonia*), Bernard Suits says that [game]play gives humans opportunities and capacities that other activities cannot, and Thomas Hurka defends that play helps us to achieve things like a skill, better health, and other outcomes. Like the concepts of fun and play, heavy metal has often been dismissed within the music hierarchy, so these kinds of dismissive concerns will be familiar to metalheads. Therefore, for the sake of space, I trust that the reader will accept *prima facie* that play has intrinsic value, even if this point remains debatable.[4] That said, I still need to draw clearer connections between play and heavy metal and demonstrate that the "heaviness" of play is another important value of the genre.

The Heaviness of Play

As it stands, play may not seem at all heavy, especially in the way it is characterized above. But we can engage in play quite seriously and for serious reasons. Perhaps the aims of play are taken seriously when we

[3] For more on make-believe, props, and play, see Walton (1990). For make-believe props and video games, see Bateman (2011).

[4] For more on the value of play, see: Suits (2014), Salen and Zimmerman (2004), Hurka (2019), Hurka and Tasioulas (2006), Kidd (2019), Ridge (2022), Nguyen (2020), and Patridge (2021).

play earnestly, or maybe the outcome of play is serious (e.g. meaningful friendships that are formed, a joke with a more serious meaning). Play does not have to be serious, but it can be.[5]

For our purposes, we can substitute "serious" with "heavy" to convey a similar idea. So, how do metalheads express this "heavy" form of play? There are both broad and niche examples we can point to. Each subgenre of heavy metal has its own implicit rules of play. In other words, the rules that loosely govern each subgenre are context-dependent. Take the sign of the horns, for example. This is a common symbol at just about any heavy metal concert. Although the horns may serve as a symbol of the intensity of the music, they also double as a playful prop for both musicians and fans. These hand gestures function as a means of expressing identity and fostering a sense of community among both performers and concert goers because they encourage active participation; when someone raises the horns, it's tacitly understood as an invitation for others to reciprocate the gesture. In this regard, the horns operate as a social agreement among community members, representing a form of expression that conveys willingness, commitment, and (at least a growing) trust (more on trust in a moment). This is not much different than children making an informal pact or understanding when playing games like Ring-Around-the-Rosie, or siblings chasing each other in the yard, or colleagues engaging in office pranks.[6]

So, the horns not only act as a prop for play but also extend an invitation to engage in play. They also act as a playful form of gatekeeping. As Deena Weinstein notes, this gesture serves as a "visual signature" that allows metalheads to identify each other and connect in a shared celebration of the music (Weinstein 2000). On that note, the horns represent a form of play that communicates a sense of belonging and camaraderie among fans. Someone who doesn't reciprocate the horns gesture can be seen as either a spoilsport or perhaps someone who has not fully gained enough trust to engage, essentially standing outside the community "playground" by declining to participate in the social commitment.

Moshing, the high-energy dance style that often accompanies heavy metal concerts, is another expression of the playfulness within the

[5] Huizinga suggested this line of thought that the "play concept as such is of a higher order than is seriousness. For seriousness seeks to exclude play, whereas play can very well include seriousness" (Huizinga1949, p. 45).

[6] I'd like to think that we were all moshers-in-practice when playing Ring-Around-the-Rosie as kids.

culture. Mosh pits are like a designated magic circle or what we can think of as a community of play. Characterized by frenzied dancing, bumping, and pushing, the space may seem chaotic and even aggressive to outsiders. However, within the context of a metal concert, this physical expression is loosely governed by certain norms of the subgenre. For example, fans of Windrose (dwarf metal) may simulate movements of digging holes in the pit while Viking metal fans sit and simulate a rowing motion. Notice how these two examples in particular complement Walton's concept of imagination, props, and play. On a different note, moshing at a thrash concert, for example, will appear significantly chaotic and aggressive with more vigorous pushing. Even heavier, hardcore moshing or "slam dancing" often entails windmill arm gestures, kicking, and body slams, presenting a stronger perception of violence than some other subgenres. Although it can be violent, the goal is not to inflict violence but, like the other subgenres, to express the heaviness of the music. By contrast, Doom audiences may not mosh at all.[7] Despite their differences, these implicit rules remain—don't pull people into the pit, obey the boundaries, and immediately pick up the person who falls.

That moshing has implicit rules suggests that it is distinctively social in how the music is experienced and appreciation is expressed. In other musical genres—such as classical, jazz, and rock—individuals may gather to listen to the music, but it remains largely an individual experience. In contrast, metalheads often listen, mosh, headbang, and engage *together* in more collective and expressive ways.[8]

That is not to suggest that interpersonal sociality is required to fully enjoy the music or feel a sense of togetherness. Hume has something to say about this with his premise regarding art appreciation:

> A man, who enters the theatre, is immediately struck with the view of so great a multitude, participating of one common amusement; and experiences, from their very aspect, a superior sensibility or disposition of being affected with every sentiment, which he shares with his fellow-creatures.

---

[7] Anecdotally, I went to a three-day Prepare the Ground Doom festival in Canada in 2024 and I witnessed little to no moshing the entire time. Whether that was more to do with the location or the subgenre, I'm not sure.

[8] Here is where I could further a discussion on heavy metal shows and shared and collective agency. But both are more nuanced than I have space to fully do them justice.

> He observes the actors to be animated by the appearance of a full audience, and raised to a degree of enthusiasm, which they cannot command in any solitary or calm moment.
>
> (Hume, Treatise, Book II, Part 2, section 5, pp. 234–235. Found in Guyer 2014, p. 137)

Similarly, the playfulness of heavy metal isn't exclusively experienced when one physically participates in moshing, headbanging, and the like. As Paul Guyer explains, it's in the sharing of our canon of taste that our pleasure can be intensified (Guyer 2014: 137). Spectators then can also be great appreciators. The metalhead listening on their own to Lorna Shore's "To The Hellfire" participates in the gestalt of heaviness, including the heaviness of play—maybe to some degree—within the confines of their own space. Also, the playfulness and heaviness of metal is no less understood or enjoyed when standing at the side of the mosh pit from a safe(er) distance. What is more, the metalhead-spectator loosely coordinates with the implicit rules of moshing by remaining outside the boundaries of the pit, and they trust that the moshers will abide by the same implicit rules by not pulling them in, for example, just as much as the moshers trust the relevant behaviors of those who do mosh.

In all of this, play seems to require an element of trust. But what is trust? Literature on the subject often refers to concepts like goodwill or reliability, typically attributing trust to independent agents such as people or institutions. When trust is broken, we feel betrayed. A more recent attitudinal account of trust suggests that "trust involves something more than mere reliance, and betrayal involves something more than mere disappointment" (Nguyen 2022, p. 7). This account emphasizes that trust often involves an "unquestioning attitude" rather than relying strictly on agent-directed explanations, where the trustor attributes a specific agential state to the trusted party (Nguyen 2022, p. 14). When trust is broken, we experience betrayal not just as disappointment, but as a deeper sense of intimacy being violated, especially when we've approached someone or something with that unquestioning attitude (Nguyen 2022, p. 38). For example, if your car breaks down, you might feel frustrated and disappointed because you trusted it would function properly, but you will not likely experience a sense of betrayal in the same way you could if, say, you were unwillingly dragged into the mosh pit.

In the same way that playing formalized games requires trust in other players to adopt the appropriate rules, goals, and behaviors, a similar trust is needed for engaging with heavy metal. Those unfamiliar with the scene may lack trust or, as Nguyen suggests, may still be in the process of developing it. To an outsider, for example, heavy metal can seem unsettling or even frightening. Similarly, a Doom enthusiast might feel apprehensive about attending a hardcore concert if they are unfamiliar with that subculture. In both cases, they may not have the necessary trust to engage in play, or at least, according to Nguyen's model, their trust has not yet reached the level of "unquestioning acceptance." Of course, trust can be lost.

However, one does not need to be fully acquainted with the specific implicit rules of each subgenre to develop trust. Understanding such rules exist within a subgenre might be enough—trusting that moshers and headbangers will behave appropriately in the given context. In this sense, the context(s) of heavy metal itself provides the foundation for trust. So even the Doom enthusiast can—with an unquestioning attitude—trust that "X will P" at a hardcore show, even if the particulars of X and P are unknown. Thus, the more familiar we are with the implicit rules and the more likely we are to adopt an attitude of unquestioning trust, the more inclined we become to engage fully in the heaviness of play.

Because the gestalt of heaviness governs both the sounds and behaviors of heavy metal the play community helps form strong connections among its fans. These connections reveal something intimate about its appreciators in ways that more mainstream genres may not. This idea is drawn from Ted Cohen's concept of low art versus high art (Cohen 1993). According to Cohen, low art is niche and therefore more personal and intimate, while high art tends to be more universal and therefore reveals less about an individual.[9]

For example, imagine striking up a conversation with a stranger and asking about their music preferences. If they tell you they enjoy mainstream rock or pop, all you've discovered is that they like music most people find agreeable (even if it's not your personal taste). But what specifically have you learned about them? If instead they reveal a preference for something more niche—such as Egg Punk, Mumble Rap, or music featuring the hurdy-gurdy—you've learned something more unique about them, which could lead to a greater sense of understanding and connection. Under Cohen's framework, I suggest that heavy metal functions similarly, particularly due to the idiosyncrasies of its various subgenres. Such intimate connections help metalheads to adopt an unquestioning attitude of trust.

[9] Cohen's conception differs from the more standard low art–high art distinction stating that low art is utilitarian and popular in nature, while high art is more aesthetically valuable.

The Upshot of "The Heaviness of Play"

An aesthetic of heaviness encompasses different sounds, textures, recording styles, lyrics, themes, and other characteristics of heavy metal and its subgenres. In other words, heaviness pervades the many diverse features of the genre. Play, I argue, is another defining characteristic that has been neglected under the umbrella of heaviness. However, play—broadly conceived as described here—helps explain certain attitudes, behaviors, and communities within the heavy metal scene, particularly at concerts. The "heaviness" of play sheds light on a distinct kind of play community and another reason we might value heavy metal.

Bernard De Koven recognizes the value of play communities when he says, "The need for this community holds true whether we are players or spectators" (De Koven 2013, p. 11). And we, he argues, establish different play communities in a variety of ways. For example,

> When a mother and child play together, regardless of what they are playing, they are establishing a play community in which both people operate under the convention that they take precedence over the game. When the child cries, the mother stops playing.
>
> When children play together, in the street or in the back lot, they too establish a play community. When someone gets hurt, the game stops.
>
> (De Koven 2013, p. 11)

In contrast, De Koven suggests that adults playing games often prioritize the game itself over the play community or winning over the trust that binds the players together (De Koven 2013, p. 12). That's why I have argued that heavy metal communities are more closely related to play communities rather than suggest metalheads play games. That is not to say that the community is more important to us than the music. Rather, it is to say that the heaviness of play is another characteristic of heavy metal that we value, and the heaviness of the sounds and other standards of the subgenre often motivate and designate different kinds of play communities.

Communities are often built on trust and certain conventions of heavy metal help shape the community. My goal here is to propose that an attitudinal account of heavy play helps explain why the inner-tuber (and fellow moshers) and the shoeless, bloodied mosher—both mentioned at the start of this chapter—were both perceivably having fun (or whatever word we want to ascribe). This sort of play, I claim, can extend to spectators or solo-listeners as well. While heavy play is not unique to heavy metal—punk and heavy rock certainly share similar characteristics—it is a distinctive value that heavy metal can claim.

Acknowledgments

I would like to thank the editors for inviting me to contribute to this volume. I am also grateful to the audience and fellow panelists on the topic of heavy metal music at the American Society for Aesthetics Annual Meeting (2023) for their helpful comments on an earlier draft of this essay.

References

Bateman, C. (2011). *Imaginary Games*. New York: John Hunt Publishing.

Cohen, T. (1993). High and low thinking about high and low art. *The Journal of Aesthetics and Art Criticism* 51 (2): 151–156. https://doi.org/10.2307/431380.

De Koven, B. (2013). *The Well-Played Game: A Player's Philosophy*. Cambridge, MA: MIT Press.

Gombrich, E.H. (1984). *Tributes: Interpreters of Our Cultural Tradition*, 139–163. Oxford: Phaidon Press.

Gracyk, T. (2016). Heavy metal: genre? style? subculture? *Philosophy Compass* 12: 775–785.

Guyer, P. (2014). *A History of Modern Aesthetics*, vol. 1. Paperback e. Cambridge: Cambridge University Press.

Huizinga, J. (1949). *Homo Ludens: A Study of the Play Element in Culture*. London: Routledge.

Hurka, T. (2019). Slightly revised, slightly restricted. In: *Games, Sports, and Play: Philosophical Essays* (ed. T. Hurka).

Hurka, T. and Tasioulas, J. (2006). Games and the good. *Proceedings of the Aristotelian Society, Supplementary Volumes* 80: 217–264.

Kidd, S.E. (2019). *Play and Aesthetics in Ancient Greece*. Cambridge: Cambridge University Press.

Miller, J. (2022). What makes heavy metal 'heavy'? *The Journal of Aesthetics and Art Criticism* 80 (1): 70–82. doi: 10.1093/jaac/kpab065.

Nguyen, C.T. (2020). *Games: Agency as Art*. Oxford: Oxford University Press.

Nguyen, C.T. (2022). Trust as an unquestioning attitude. In: *Oxford Studies in Epistemology*, vol. 7 (ed. T.S. Gendler, J. Hawthorne, and J. Chung), 214–244. Oxford University Press.

Patridge, S. (2021). Games, motives, and virtue. *Journal of the Philosophy of Sport* 48 (3): 369–379.

Pearce, C. (2011). *Communities of Play: Emergent cultures in Multiplayer Games and Virtual Worlds*. MIT Press.

Ridge, M. (2022). Why so serious? The nature and value of play. *Philosophy and Phenomenological Research* 105 (2): 406–434.

Salen, K. and Zimmerman, E. (2004). Game design and meaningful play. In: *Handbook of Computer Game Studies* (ed. J. Raessens and J. Goldstein), 50–79. Cambridge, MA: MIT Press.

Sharp, J. and Thomas, D. (2019). *Fun, Taste, & Games: An Aesthetics of the Idle, Unproductive, and Otherwise Playful*. Cambridge, MA: MIT Press.

Shore, L. (2021). *To the Hellfire* [Song]. On *...And I Return to Nothingness* [EP]. Century Media Records.

Suits, B. (2014). *The Grasshopper: Games, Life, and Utopia*. Peterborough, ON: Broadview Press.

Tekinbas, K.S. and Zimmerman, E. (2003). *Rules of Play: Game Design Fundamentals*. Cambridge, MA: MIT Press.

Walton, K.L. (1990). *Mimesis as Make-Believe: On the Foundations of the Representational Arts*. Cambridge, MA: Harvard University Press.

Weinstein, D. (2000). *Heavy Metal: The Music and Its Culture*. Cambridge, MA: Da Capo Press.

Index